Shelley
and the
Romantic Imagination

Shelley
and the
Romantic Imagination

A Psychological Study

Thomas R. Frosch

DELAWARE

Newark: University of Delaware Press

Associated University Presses
2010 Eastpark Boulevard
Cranbury, NJ 08512

The paper used in this publication meets the requirements of the American National Standard for Permanence of Paper for Printed Library Materials Z39.48–1984.

Library of Congress Cataloging-in-Publication Data

Frosch, Thomas R.
  Shelley and the Romantic imagination : a psychological study / Thomas R. Frosch.
    p. cm.
  Includes bibliographical references (p.) and index.
  ISBN-13: 978-0-87413-978-5 (alk. paper)
  ISBN-10: 0-87413-978-3 (alk. paper)
1. Shelley, Percy Bysshe, 1792–1822—Criticism and interpretation. 2. Shelley, Percy Bysshe, 1792–1822—Psychology. 3. Shelley, Percy Bysshe, 1792–1822. Alastor. 4. Shelley, Percy Bysshe, 1792–1822. Prometheus unbound. 5. Shelley, Percy Bysshe, 1792–1822. Triumph of life. 6. Poetry—Authorship—Psychological aspects. 7. Romanticism—England. I. Title.
  PR5442.P74.F76 2007
  821'.7—dc22

                                        2006034690

For Mary
and for Daniel and Jonathan

Contents

Acknowledgments

THIS WORK WAS SUPPORTED IN PART BY A FELLOWSHIP FROM THE American Council of Learned Societies and a grant from The City University of New York PSC-CUNY Research Award Program.
For help of various kinds I would like to thank John Beer, Nancy Comley, Morris Dickstein, Tamara Evans, James Frosch, Marilyn Gaull, Geoffrey Hartman, Jerrold Hogle, and Charles Molesworth. I would also like to thank Charles Carter and Laura O'Keefe of the Carl H. Pforzheimer Collection of Shelley and his Circle. I was fortunate to have Christine Retz to oversee the editing and Laura Rogers to prepare the index. For encouragement and inspiration over many years, I am grateful to Harold Bloom. My mother, Annette Frosch, introduced me to poetry before I could read, and my father, John Frosch, gave me my interest in psychoanalysis; this book, bringing together my interests in poetry and psychoanalysis, ultimately owes its existence to their combined intellectual influences. As for my introduction to Shelley, I would like to thank George Creeger, who many years ago in an undergraduate Romantics seminar asked if there were any future Shelleyans in the class; his comments on Shelley piqued my curiosity, and I raised my hand, with no idea that within a few years a love of Shelley would become a major theme in my teaching and writing. My sons, Daniel and Jonathan, were very young when I started out on this project, but by the time the book was in press they were both professional writers, and it was gratifying to be able to share the ins and outs of the writing process with them. Of the help given by my wife, Mary Frosch, I can only say that she contributed and shared and put up with so much that I think of her as my virtual co-author.

Texts and Quotations

IN THE ABSENCE AT THIS WRITING OF AN AUTHORITATIVE COMPLETE text of Shelley's poetry and prose, I quote from several Shelley sources. For quotations of the poetry I use, unless I indicate otherwise, the second edition of the Norton Critical Edition of *Shelley's Poetry and Prose*, edited by Donald H. Reiman and Neil Fraistat. For poems not in that edition I use, wherever possible, the Longman Poets Edition of *The Poems of Shelley*, volumes 1 and 2, edited by Kelvin Everest and Geoffrey Matthews. For poems in neither the Norton or the Longman, I use the Oxford Standard Authors Edition of *Shelley: Poetical Works*, edited by Thomas Hutchinson, corrected by Matthews. For the prose, I use the Norton where possible; the Longman for Shelley's notes to *Queen Mab*; E. B. Murray's edition of the early prose, *The Prose Work of Percy Bysshe Shelley*, volume 1; and, otherwise, *Shelley's Prose, or The Trumpet of a Prophecy*, edited by David Lee Clark. In the case of the older Hutchinson and Clark editions, I have checked quoted passages against manuscript facsimiles and Murray's "Annotated Manuscript Corrections of Shelley's Prose Essays," but kept the Hutchinson and Clark punctuation and capitalization, while noting any other significant discrepancies. For discussions of the history of Shelley editions, see Reiman and Fraistat, *The Complete Poetry of Percy Bysshe Shelley*, 1:xxii–xxix, and Murray, *The Prose Work*, 1:xxvii–xxx.

Parenthetical numbers after quotations of poetry are line numbers. Numbers after the following abbreviations in parentheses are page numbers:

C   Clark

E   Everest and Matthews

H   Hutchinson

L   *The Letters of Percy Bysshe Shelley*, 2 volumes, edited by Frederick L. Jones

M   Murray

R   Reiman and Fraistat (Norton)

SE   *The Standard Edition of the Complete Psychological Works of Sigmund Freud*

Citations of other authors are accompanied in the text by parenthetical page or, in the case of poetry, line numbers unless further information about the source is necessary, in which case a note is used.

In citing the Garland facsimiles of Shelley manuscripts in the Bodleian Library, I abbreviate Bodleian MS. Shelley adds . . ., in *The Bodleian Shelley Manuscripts* . . . as Bod. MS . . ., in *Bod. Shelley* . . .

Emphases in quotations are those of the original author.

Lines from Milton, *Methought I Saw My Late Espoused Saint,* are reprinted from *John Milton: Complete Poems and Major Prose*, ed. Merritt Y. Hughes. Copyright © 1957 by The Odyssey Press. By permission of Hackett Publishing. All rights reserved.

Passages from *The Letters of Percy Bysshe Shelley*, 2 vols., edited by Frederick L. Jones (1964), are reprinted by permission of Oxford University Press.

Passages from *The Prose Works of Percy Bysshe Shelley*, vol. 1, edited by E. B. Murray (1993), are reprinted by permission of Oxford University Press.

Passages from *The Bodleian Shelley Manuscripts*, 23 vols., gen. ed. Donald H. Reiman, are reproduced by permission of Routledge/Taylor & Francis Group, LLC. Copyright © 1986–2001.

Passages from *The Manuscripts of the Younger Romantics: Shelley*, 9 vols., gen. ed. Donald H. Reiman, are reproduced by permission of Routledge/Taylor & Francis Group, LLC. Copyright © 1985–96.

Passages from W. B. Yeats, *Essays and Introductions*, are reprinted with the permission of Scribner, an imprint of Simon & Schuster Adult Publishing Group, from *Essays and Introductions*, by W. B. Yeats. Copyright © 1961 by Mrs. W. B. Yeats. Also with the permission of A. P. Watt Ltd., on behalf of Michael B. Yeats.

Preface

It was Keats, not Shelley, who compared the imagination to Adam's dream of Eve in *Paradise Lost*—"he awoke and found it truth"[1] —but the situation of Adam's dream is recurrent and central in Shelley's poetry. This study focuses primarily on three works—one early, *Alastor*; one middle, *Prometheus Unbound*; and one late, *The Triumph of Life*—that concern the imagining of an ideal woman and, more generally, the prime Romantic idea of the realization of the imagined, the idea, as Blake put it, that "What is now proved was once, only imagin'd."[2]

This study seeks to bring together such Romantic dreams with modern dream-interpretation, as offered by psychoanalysis. Can psychoanalysis have anything other than a de-idealizing impact on Romantic visions? In a psychoanalytic perspective, can the typical Romantic hero, yearning for the absolute satisfaction of desire in secular terms, be anything more than an epitome of the neurotic? Can the Romantic myth of the imagination as a source not only of art but also of great changes in reality be anything more than a Freudian illusion, an idealized refusal to give up childhood dreams of magic and omnipotence? I once heard someone say that Spenser, a great precursor of the Romantics, ultimately did not have an adult mind. Is an adult mind for us one in which idealization and regression have no major roles to play?

Barbara Schapiro has used psychoanalysis to update Matthew Arnold's view of Shelley as an escapist, whose poetry was "not entirely sane."[3] Despite the valuable efforts of modern Shelleyans to stress Shelley's skepticism and urbanity, his irony and tough-mindedness, even, in Frederick Pottle's case, his "manly" quality, Arnold's famous picture of "a beautiful *and ineffectual* angel, beating in the void his lu-

minous wings in vain" still persists.[4] This study takes another look at
the Shelley that Arnold was talking about: Shelley at his most "ro-
mantic," in the casual, pejorative sense of the word; at his most ide-
alizing and mythologizing; even, to bring up another of Arnold's
charges against him, at his most self-deceiving. After we have studied
the political Shelley, the philosophical Shelley, Shelley the craftsman,
and Shelley the proto-deconstructor, that Shelley still remains for us
to face. We like Romantic poetry once again, but sometimes it seems
that we like it in spite of its romanticism.

The goal of this work is to use psychoanalysis to understand Shel-
ley's poems and even to underscore the power of their idealizations,
to set his poetic myths in a human complexity of ambivalence and
conflict, to study how, as Erik Erikson showed of Martin Luther, "any
greatness also harbors massive conflict" (245). My goal is to show
how Shelley's poetic formulations are grounded in the patterns of
early impulses and archaic struggles and gain strength and reso-
nance from that grounding.[5]

I am particularly interested in four impulses and struggles in Shel-
ley's poetry. First, while he celebrates eros and indeed wished to be a
spokesman for love, he is also one of the great poets on the theme of
aggression; but aggressive elements in his work are attended by dis-
turbance and ambivalence. As Steven Jones writes, his "stated antipa-
thy toward violence is better known than his propensity for it" (16).
Second, his poetry plainly expresses regressive impulses, and Stuart
Sperry comments that "Much of the violent modern antipathy to
Shelley springs from the recognition of the regressive character of
his genius, which stands in sharp contrast to the governing ideals of
our own society and culture";[6] but Shelley himself is ambivalent
about regression. The terms aggression and regression generally
have negative connotations, but throughout this study I use them
neutrally. By aggression I mean attitudes and acts not only of anger
and destructiveness but also of protest, ambition, mastery, and de-
tachment; aggressive energy plays a role in any assertion of the self to
change things. By regression I mean ultimately an inner return to the
mother and to what Romain Rolland, writing to Freud, called the
"oceanic feeling" and what psychoanalysis has discussed as a sense of
oneness associated with the infant at the breast and, even more
strongly, with the fetus in the womb; regressive energy, as I treat it,
plays a role in feelings of elation and transcendence and in any sense
of connection or union.[7] For Freud, "regression" carried its familiar

negative connotations, although the psychoanalyst Géza Róheim later found it so central to the psyche that he referred to "the regressive or human trend."[8] Rolland spoke of the "rich and beneficent power" of the oceanic feeling.[9] In Shelley, unconscious fantasies of a return to the mother are associated with both "beneficent power" and anxiety. My concern is to examine how he seeks to transform both aggressive and regressive energy for constructive purposes. The other two struggles in Shelley concern the parents. Shelley's poetry dramatically emphasizes positive feelings toward woman and negative feelings toward male authority; however, his poetry also reveals less open but influential negative feelings toward the mother and positive feelings toward the father. We do not have to go as far as Freud, who thought that "the need for a father's protection" was even greater than the need for the connection with the mother, to appreciate that the former is one of the primary needs of childhood and survives, unconsciously in its full power, into later life.[10] That survival is one of the deep currents of Shelley's poetic imagination, where it is particularly intriguing, entangled as it is with strong feelings of rebellion.[11]

Several other psychoanalytic concepts and issues are important in my approach to Shelley. Although some psychoanalytic literary criticism stresses the oedipal themes of incest and castration and some stresses the preoedipal themes of narcissism and the breast, I think that a reasonably full and flexible commentary must attend to both preoedipal relations with the mother and oedipal relations with both parents. This is an issue in Shelley criticism in that we have had excellent work on oedipal relations with the father, from Leon Waldoff, and excellent work on preoedipal relations with the mother, from Schapiro, Christine Gallant, and Barbara Gelpi, but no commentary, at least full-length, that attends extensively to both. Finally, in my use of psychoanalysis I have been eclectic but emphasize other psychoanalytic writers than Lacan and the French theorists. Indeed, this study is shaped by a conviction that there are additional psychoanalytic writers worth paying attention to. At various points I draw on Róheim, Sandor Ferenczi, Melanie Klein, Heinz Kohut, Margaret Mahler, Janine Chasseguet-Smirgel, Anton Ehrenzweig, Heinz Hartmann, and Ernst Kris. In general approach, I draw particularly on the ego psychologists, whose contributions have been occulted, even dismissed, in academic criticism but who I believe continue to have much to offer students of literature. I have found five specific post-Freudian

concepts especially responsive to the workings of Shelley's poetry:
Kris's concept of regression in the service of the ego; Róheim's con-
cept of a normative conflict in the id between regressive and progres-
sive, or uterine and genital, impulses; Mahler's concept of rap-
prochement, the conflict in the small child between impulses toward
autonomy and dependence; Chasseguet-Smirgel's concept of the
child's wish to break away from the omnipotent primal mother; and
Hartmann's concept of the sublimation of aggression.[12]

But most basically, I have sought a way of speaking about Shelley
that respects his idealizing sensibility and the integrity of his poetic
myths and that also is open to the insights of Freudian analysis, a way
of reading that looks toward both unconscious fantasies and imagi-
native visions. A similar doubleness appears in the material, for Shel-
ley was a student of introspection and, in his own way, of the uncon-
scious mind, as well as a maker of exuberant Romantic fictions. One
of his intriguing characteristics is that while the oceanic feeling is
strong in him, so is a rational, self-analytical tendency. He called him-
self a "strict anatomist of his own" heart (*L*, 2:324), and in *Peter Bell
the Third* he attacked Coleridge as "a mighty poet—and / A subtle-
souled Psychologist," who understood all things "But his own mind"
(378–82). The idea of charting the workings of his own mind is a re-
current concern for Shelley, one that he approaches in a proto-
Freudian spirit: "Let us reflect on our infancy, and give as faithfully as
possible a relation of the events of sleep" (*C*, 193).[13] In the following
passage from the fragmentary *Speculations on Morals and Metaphysics*,
the quest for self-knowledge leads to a confrontation with the limits
of consciousness and a world beyond it:

> If it were possible that a person should give a faithful history of his
> being from the earliest epochs of his recollection, a picture would be
> presented such as the world has never contemplated before. A mir-
> ror would be held up to all men in which they might behold their
> own recollections and, in dim perspective, their shadowy hopes and
> fears—all that they dare not, or that daring and desiring, they could
> not expose to the open [light] of day. But thought can with difficulty
> visit the intricate and winding chambers which it inhabits.[14]

In Blake, who is in many ways as close to Shelley as any writer, self-re-
flectiveness often seems the negation of true vision, and it is disturb-
ing to think that Blake might have assigned such a passage to his de-
luded rationalist Urizen, who loses himself in the exploration of his

own "dens."[15] In Shelley, however, the mind commits itself to both self-knowledge and the visionary or mythmaking imagination. What is the Shelleyan relation between self-knowledge and imagination?

As for the elusive concept "imagination" itself, in this study it appears in three general senses. First, imagination, as a poetic theme of the period, appears as a myth of power. This is the dread magic of Coleridge's *Kubla Khan* poet, building pleasure domes with his music; and it is Blake's inner divinity, "The Real Man The Imagination which Liveth for Ever" (p. 783). Second, it appears as fantasy, which includes illusion but, more neutrally, any representation in image, narrative, or abstract idea of wishes fulfilled or anxieties realized. Finally, it appears as the poetic shaping of fantasy, the molding of common psychic material into individualized literary structures. That the three senses impinge on each other is the reason for following common practice and using the same word for all.

I have been stressing that psychoanalysis opposes, or exposes, Romanticism, but Freudian thought also mirrors, like a doppelgänger, the Romantic fascination with subjectivity, memory, dream, the unconscious, desire and anxiety, melancholy and elation. Psychoanalysis includes the sense of imagination as fantasy. As in Heine's line, admiringly quoted by Freud, "By creating, I became healthy,"[16] it also includes the sense of imagination as creative shaping. This sense appears as well in various formulations of ego psychology, such as the idea that the ego synthesizes our internal functions or the idea that regression can appear in the service of the ego. But when Wordsworth says in the *Prospectus to The Recluse* that his poetry is the spousal verse for a marriage of nature and the human mind that will give birth to paradise for all people, or when Blake says, "The Nature of my Work is Visionary or Imaginative it is an Endeavour to Restore <what the Ancients calld> the Golden Age,"[17] when, that is, they say, "By creating, I can make the world healthy and even ideal," the psychoanalytic and the Romantic concepts of imagination part company. I tell my students that the most difficult experience they will have as skeptical modern readers in studying the Romantics is understanding that these poets and many of their readers really did believe in the possibility of paradise.

But if the most controversial sense of imagination is as a myth of power and paradise, its most complex sense is as an organizing or synthesizing force. I do not mean only conscious shaping. A key concept of ego psychology is that the ego is not wholly conscious but that much of its most crucial work, defense and resistance, is carried on unconsciously. That is, some imaginings defend against other imaginings. Accordingly, the commentaries that follow are interested in the interplay in poems between fantasies and anxieties both with other fantasies and anxieties and with more conscious themes. Few once-respectable concepts have lower prestige in literary and theoretical studies nowadays than the psychological ego and the subject in general. For Lacan, "The essential function of the ego is very nearly [a] systematic refusal to acknowledge reality" (12). For Foucault, "The subject (and its substitutes) must be stripped of its creative role and analysed as a complex and variable function of discourse" (138). For Bakhtin, the self is "a function of the social,"[18] and we must study the polyphony, the multiple voices, that make up seemingly individual utterances. Extending Bakhtin's work on the novel to Shelley's poetry, Jerrold Hogle has written compellingly of Shelley's refusal of identity and selfhood and his striving for multiplicity and "an interplay of changing voices" (viii); and Shelley critics often cite the passage in the essay *On Life* in which the personal pronouns are said to be "merely marks employed to denote the different modifications of the one mind" (*R*, 508). I hope to show, however, that for Shelley both the oceanic feeling and a coherent, organizing ego are important. Both Dionysos and Apollo play roles in his poetry. In this study, I am interested in the variety of unconscious fantasies within Shelley's poetic imaginings and, within them as well, the workings of what W. W. Meissner has called the psyche's "problem-solving agent."[19] I am interested in following the adventures of an ego—that part of the psyche that experiences anxiety and deploys defenses but that also learns, masters, chooses, loves, and creates—as it negotiates its way among competing impulses and ambivalent tendencies, somewhat like Adam and Eve setting out at the end of *Paradise Lost* into a world of choices and decisions, dangers and possibilities, that lies before them.

ᢊᡓ ᢊᡓ ᢊᡓ

In addition to bringing particular psychological concepts and questions to the study of Shelley, I approach him with a particular sense of his historical and literary context, best defined by Meyer Abrams and Harold Bloom. Shelley wrote within the idealizing, visionary tradition of Spenser, Milton, and Wordsworth, and he wrote, further, in a time of extreme imaginings: Southey said, "Few persons but those who have lived in it can conceive or comprehend what the memory of the French Revolution was, nor what a visionary world seemed to open upon those who were just entering it. Old things seemed passing away, and nothing was dreamt of but the regeneration of the human race."[20] What Hazlitt said of Wordsworth, that "the political changes of the day were the model on which he formed and conducted his poetical experiments,"[21] was certainly true of Shelley, who called the French Revolution "the master theme of the epoch in which we live" (*L*, 1:504). In the affectionate satire of Shelley's friend Thomas Love Peacock, the Romantics were "a confederation of regenerators" intent on the "thorough repair of the crazy fabric of human nature."[22] Their "poetical experiments" were experiments in the creation of paradise. The Romantic mythology of imagination finds its typical plot in the quest for a communal or personal ideal, its typical hero in the poet or seer, the one who envisions and creates, and its typical literary mode in romance, or some renovated form of it, the mode in which anything, especially the marvelous, is possible, the mode, as Northrop Frye writes, of the pure imagination.[23] Central to that mythology as well is a fascination with origins and a quest for originality. Keats's comparison of the imagination to Adam's dream distills that mythology into a single rich figure, which, as William Ulmer writes, is "virtually paradigmatic for the visionary romances of Shelley's era" (27).

René Girard's distinction between romantic, in the general sense, and novelistic works, which are, respectively, unaware and aware of their own illusions (14–17), is characteristic of our most common reaction to those visionary romances. Modernism and postmodernism, New Criticism and critical theory agree in their skeptical view of the Romantic mythology. Especially interesting critiques have come from within Romantic studies. Anne Mellor has pointed to the "self-absorbed, often abstracted meditations" of "masculine English Romanticism" and its usurpation of traditionally female qualities like emotion and imagination (11, 13, 29). Jerome McGann has insisted that we should detach ourselves from the bourgeois Romantic ideology of a transcendent Imagination and "the centrality of the Self" and that the greatness of Romantic works lies in their exposure of such "cultural illusions" that dominated the age.[24] Yeats characterized Shelley's poetry as "the poetry of desire,"[25] but Romantic desire is not what we tend to admire in Romantic poems. What stands out in Ulmer's study of Shelley is his analysis of the limitations, contradictions, and final tragedy of "idealizing desire" (177), and Barbara Gelpi unfavorably contrasts Shelley's exaltation of desire with his adumbrations of an ethos of relationship (272–73). Mellor, McGann, Ulmer, and Gelpi treat their Romantic subject matter with sensitivity and insight, but despite the value of such perspectives, I think that the work of Abrams, Bloom, and Frye, as well as Geoffrey Hartman's work on the apocalyptic and visionary currents in Wordsworth's sensibility and on the Romantic struggle with romance, is fundamental for an understanding of Romanticism. I think too that Romantic poems celebrate Romantic desire even when they present it negatively or tragically and that that celebration is an essential part of what draws readers to Romantic poems. At a time when our reflex is to demystify and demythologize and when even Romanticists bend over backward not to be too romantic, the goal of this study is to bring back into view— even into a view influenced by Freudian psychoanalysis—the beauty, depth, and exhilaration of the Romantic myth of imagination in its Shelleyan inflection.

I turn to a discussion of Adam's dream and its echoes in Romantic tradition to introduce further the poetic and psychological issues I will be exploring in the details of Shelley's poetry.

Introduction:
Adam's Dream, or the
Romantic Imagination

In comparing the imagination to Adam's dream, Keats is alluding to *Paradise Lost*, book 8, in which Adam actually has two dreams that become realities. In the first, the newly created Adam, having fallen asleep after searching for his unknown "great Maker," dreams of a "Guide," who leads him into the Garden of Eden (278, 298). There he wakes to find "Before mine Eyes all real, as the dream / Had lively shadow'd" (310–11). The mystery of his origins is then clarified as the Guide introduces himself as the "Author" Adam has sought and answers the questions that had bothered him, "who I was, or where, or from what cause" (317, 270)—questions that haunt Shelley's last poem, *The Triumph of Life*.

A short while later, Adam complains of his solitude. He can find no companionship among the animals, nor is he self-sufficient like God, and God promises him "Thy likeness, thy fit help, thy other self, / Thy wish, exactly to thy heart's desire" (450–51). Adam's second dream follows. With "Fancy my internal sight," he sees God open his left side, take a rib from the bleeding wound, and fashion a creature, "so lovely fair, / That what seem'd fair in all the World, seem'd now / Mean, or in her summ'd up" (461, 471–73). "Shee disappear'd, and left me dark," but he wakes to find her, and he prophesies that he will unite with her as "one Flesh, one Heart, one Soul" (478, 499).

Adam's dream of Eve looks back in turn to Prince Arthur's dream of Gloriana in *The Faerie Queene*. Arthur has grown up scorning love "As losse of time, and vertues enimy" (1.9.10.2). But Cupid takes revenge; Arthur falls asleep in the forest to dream of a "royall mayd," who lies beside him all night long: "But whether dreams delude, or true it were, / Was never hart so ravisht with delight" (13.7, 14.5–6). He wakes to discover "her place devoyd, / And nought but pressed gras, where she had lyen" (15.1–2), and he sets off in search of her, a wound still bleeding in his "riven brest" (7.4).

For the Romantics, the imagination could be a vision of truth even in a world far from Eden or Faerieland. So Wordsworth asks us to believe that "Paradise, and groves / Elysian, Fortunate Fields" are not "A history only of departed things, / Or a mere fiction of what never was."[1] Adam's dream brings together the theme of imagination with another central Romantic theme, ideal eros. But the engagement of Romantic eros and Romantic imagination has complex and often negative results. In Blake's final epic, *Jerusalem*, the dreams of the sleeping Albion are dominated by two visionary loves, the illusion-mongering Vala, veil of nature, and Jerusalem, or liberty, the true spouse of the Poetic Genius in all human beings. In Coleridge's *Christabel*, the heroine dreams of her betrothed knight, then goes out to the midnight woods to find the serpent-lady, Geraldine. In Byron's *Manfred*, the relationship between Adam's dream and waking reality is reversed, as the hero has his vision of his mistress after their love and her destruction, and the vision torments him. Keats rings many changes on Adam's dream. In *The Eve of St. Agnes*, Madeline dreams of Porphyro and wakes to find him but is disappointed that he doesn't match her dream of him; however, he is transfigured, and "Into her dream he melted" (320). In *La Belle Dame Sans Merci*, the knight, like Manfred, has his dream vision after he has embraced his fairy mistress; it is a vision that reveals that he is now enthralled, and he wakes to solitude and barrenness. In *Lamia*, the dreams of gods are real, and Hermes is able to enter his vision of his beloved nymph; but Lycius, who comes upon Lamia when "His phantasy was lost, where reason fades, / In the calm'd twilight of Platonic shades" (1.235–36), loses her when he takes her back to the waking world. As for Wordsworth, most of his great visions concern nature or himself as a child, but he too has a number of variations on Adam's dream. The most powerful involve death, like the premonitory daydream of Lucy's death in *Strange fits of passion have I known*. In *The Ruined Cottage*, Margaret's Penelope-like conviction that her husband will return is so strong that the storyteller, Armytage, is drawn into her imagination; even after her death he has momentary trances in which he sees her reawaken to human life "when he shall come again / For whom she suffered."[2] Even more poignant is a sonnet, *I saw the figure of a lovely Maid,* in which Wordsworth presents his daughter's death in terms of a vision—"no Spirit," however, but a "bright corporeal presence"—that slowly dissolves into air.[3]

ఴ ఴ ఴ

In *Paradise Lost* Adam's dream is anticipated by a dark parody. In book 2 Satan, envious at the elevation of the Son, gives birth to Sin, who springs armed out of his head: his idea of disobedience, his dream of usurpation. Now he beholds his own "perfect image" (764), and from his narcissistic and incestuous delight in her comes their child, Death, a "Son and foe" (804), who rapes his mother; the resulting monsters return to Sin's womb to feed on her entrails.

Adam in his two dreams discovers forms of otherness—divine and human, parental and sexual—that are essential to him, and that need for otherness is always his chief motivation. In Romantic terms his dreams embody the sympathetic imagination, and their quest is for continuity. Satan's dream, on the other hand, seeking discontinuity and self-elevation, embodies a solipsistic imagination. While the Adamic sensibility emerges from the intolerability of solitude, the Satanic emerges from the intolerability of competition and limitation, the impinging of otherness on the self. While Adam embodies a psychic movement outward, Satan suggests a return to narcissism from rejection.

A struggle between Adamic and Satanic tendencies appears in Eve, who when first created has to be drawn out of the mode of Satanic vision. Her narcissism, however, has a tone not of frustration and rage but of regressive longing. She falls in love with her own image in the water, and "there I had fixt / Mine eyes till now, and pin'd with vain desire" (4.465–66). But God's warning voice calls her away from herself and to Adam, "Whose image thou art" and to whom she will bear, in a sublimated narcissism, "Multitudes like thyself" (472, 474). At her first sight of Adam she is disappointed, as Madeline will be by Porphyro, and turns back to "that smooth wat'ry image" (480), but she finally yields to his pursuit. Yet her instincts remain narcissistic, and so her fall comes as a consequence of her openness to self-elevation. Adam, on the contrary, falls because of his desire for otherness: he eats the apple, "Against his better knowledge"

(9.998), to share Eve's destiny, for "Our State cannot be sever'd, we are one, / One Flesh; to lose thee were to lose myself" (958–59).

For Eve the passage from primal narcissism to object love involves a loss in rapture for the sake of a feasible reality and its ultimate higher rewards, and so Freud tells us that in order to love we must yield up some of our ego libido; what we give up will be returned to us in the other's love.[4] Adam makes no emotional sacrifice in the creation of Eve, but he does make a physical sacrifice. In one of Blake's variations on Adam's dream, in *The Book of Urizen*, Enitharmon is torn out of the body of Los as an incarnation of the divisive pity, or softness, he feels at the spectacle of the Fall: "All Eternity shudderd at sight / Of the first female now separate" (pl. 18, lines 9–10). In the stunning illustration that accompanies the text, the tortured Los is doubled over "a round globe of blood / Trembling upon the Void" (pl. 13, lines 58–59) and still attached to him by fibers. This is a picture of a man giving birth, a man functioning as a woman. It is also a picture of castration.

We can understand the wound of Adam in a similar sense. Through the Oedipus complex the male child loses his sense of wholeness, both in that he suffers castration anxiety and in that the mother as she once was and as he would like her to be is torn away from him. This is the wound to his self-esteem that forces his love outward. There he can eventually find what he has lost, both in a new love object and in the experience of coitus, a new form of his pre-oedipal sense of connectedness, elation, and power. This is a return of the lost that is a similitude of the original but permissible because it is outside, that is, outside the confines of, to use Wordsworth's phrase in the *Ode: Intimations of Immortality*, "those first affections" (152).

In *Paradise Lost*, the mother appears symbolically in the nourishing Garden of Eden itself and in the forbidden tree, the father's fruit, that part of the relation to the mother that must be renounced. But Milton seems less interested in any renunciation of the mother than in sheer obedience to the father. Indeed, God's three figurative sons embody three stages in the son's oedipal relation to the father. Satan is the son as rebel, the destroyer who in his regressive anticulture of vengeance, narcissism, incest, and cannibalism would undo the father's world. Adam is the son as returned prodigal; he has come through the Oedipus complex and set out on his journey into culture and history. Messiah is the son identified with the father, able to take on his tremendous power. At the same time, Adam, Satan, and God, who has "begot" the Son, are all connected by a myth of male parturition (5.603).[5] In Hesiod, before Zeus gives birth to Athene from his head, he swallows his pregnant consort, Metis, or Wisdom. Jane Harrison describes the story as a patriarchal attempt "to rid [Athene] of her matriarchal ancestry."[6] God, Satan, and Adam give birth in different ways, but in none of these cases is there even an anterior female principle to introject. Man is the creator of woman, not the reverse, as it may appear in nature. Of Milton's primal beings, the only one with a mother is Death. In *Paradise Lost* Milton elaborates a fantasy of usurping the creative power of woman that he seems to have had outside the poem: according to the anonymous contemporary biography known as *The Earliest Life of Milton*, when he had composed poetry in his head and wished to give dictation, he said that "*he wanted to be milked.*"[7]

Like Adam, Arthur too has a wound in his breast, one that will not be fully healed until he finds the fairy queen. But, if we may entertain a literalistic question, why is this such a problem for him when everybody else seems to know exactly where she is?

Behind Arthur's dream is a rich tradition of fairy mistresses in medieval literature and especially in Celtic folklore; the motif is among the staples of the romance mode.[8] Chaucer uses it in a spirit of burlesque in the tale of Sir Thopas. Heretofore a scorner of love, Sir Thopas dreams that "an elf-queene shal my lemman be" and sets out to find any elf queen he can; indeed, "Alle othere wommen I forsake, / And to an elf-queene I me take" (788, 794–95). Arthur too forsakes all other women in his quest for his supernatural lover. The fairy mistress thus has the effect of keeping her devotee from mortal lovers—somewhat like Rousseau's Madame de Warens, whom he calls *Maman* and who sleeps with him to protect him from other women. Typically, in fairy mistress episodes, it is the elf queen who takes the initiative. This is a story of seduction from a more powerful state of being, a story suggesting seduction of a child by an adult—that is, the primal scene of hysteria. In his detailed discussion of the motif, Tom Pete Cross observes that "some form of tabu is almost universally characteristic of stories in which supernatural beings enter into relations with mortals" (628). Often the fairy forbids the mortal to speak of their love. This too suggests child-adult liaisons. That the ultimate taboo, the incest prohibition, lies behind the motif is suggested by tales that Cross analyzes in which the knight who is seduced by the elf queen also holds out against the attempts of a human queen—that is, in common Freudian symbolism, the mother—to seduce him.

The quests of Spenser's knights in *The Faerie Queene* originate at the court of Gloriana; so Arthur, whose own origins are a mystery, is trying to get back to where everybody else begins. Furthermore, his quest is for the female authority figure of the world of the poem, a figure who, associated in the proem to book 1 with Venus and the Muse, is its principle of fertility and inspiration. If the Faerie Queene, who is literally the object of a young man's sexual quest, is also symbolically a maternal origin, then we can understand why the quest is so difficult to complete. In Milton, glory belongs to the father, in Spenser to the mother. Milton dreams of a world in which nothing is owed to a woman and in which a man might have all the creative power of the mother—a suggestive situation in a poem in which envy and usurpation appear in Satan and Eve as the heart of evil. Spenser, in contrast, dreams of a maternal world, in which everything is given by a woman; but to take all that is offered has unconscious intimations of danger.

In Milton, God is the validator of Adam's visions. In Spenser, God does not make an appearance to validate the reality of Arthur's fairy mistress, but we have independent confirmation in the poem of her existence and goodness. Unlike Spenser and Milton, the Romantics characteristically accepted nothing external to tell them if the vision was phantasmal or potential, creative or destructive. Even as they sought the sympathetic imagination, they also sought a mode of imagining that was self-begotten, not God-begotten. In giving birth to Sin and indeed in his entire rebellion, the envious and voyeuristic Satan, who repeatedly spies on Adam and Eve, attempts to occupy the primal scene; he presumes to create, to take over God's work. Adam's two dreams, in which he receives a creator, a paradise, and a woman, all ideal, express what a deconstructive critic might call "our desire for plenitude and authority."[9] Satan wishes to be the origin of plenitude and authority; he tries to appropriate the infinite self-sufficiency that Adam sees in God; to conceive of himself as not the originator of his own being would be intolerable: "We know no time when we were not as now; / Know none before us, self-begot, self-rais'd / By our own quick'ning power" (5.859–61). For Milton, Satan can only destructively parody divine creation. But for the Romantics, especially for Blake, Byron, and Shelley, imagination has rebellious associations, and for Harold Bloom, Satan, with such claims of self-authorization and self-authorship, becomes the archetype of the modern poet with his anxiety of being influenced by the great authors of the past. Adam in his first dream accepts the need for a father, and the spirit of that dream does make itself powerfully felt in Mary Shelley's *Frankenstein* when the monster pleads to his maker: "Remember that I am thy creature; I ought to be thy Adam, but I am rather the fallen angel, whom thou drivest from joy for no misdeed" (95). But more characteristic in Romanticism, at least at the manifest level, is Wordsworth's description of imagination as "an unfathered vapour."[10]

One of Milton's closest approaches to Romanticism occurs in still another version of Adam's dream, his Sonnet 23:

> Methought I saw my late espoused Saint
>> Brought to me like Alcestis from the grave,
>> Whom Jove's great Son to her glad Husband gave,
>> Rescu'd from death by force though pale and faint.

She comes to him now as he will someday see her in heaven, "vested all in white, pure as her mind":

>> Her face was veil'd, yet to my fancied sight,
>> Love, sweetness, goodness, in her person shin'd
> So clear, as in no face with more delight.
>> But O, as to embrace me she inclin'd,
>> I wak'd, she fled, and day brought back my night.

The Romantics rewrote this poem many times. Although Milton speaks of Hercules, "Jove's great Son," the force he uses in the attempt to bring his wife back from the dead is not physical but the power of his fancied sight, or imagination. God is not present to realize the vision, and so it fails. Milton still has his trust that the realization will come in heaven. If we eliminate that faith, we have a sense of, say, Keats in *The Fall of Hyperion*, standing before his visions "Without stay or prop, / But my own weak mortality" (388–89). That self-reliance was not only imposed on the Romantics; it was also sought. Seeking both otherness and freedom, the Romantic imagination, as we find it in Shelley, involves a varying interplay of the Adamic and the Satanic—and an interplay too of a Spenserian tendency toward the mother and a Miltonic tendency toward autonomy and mastery.

As we study Shelley, we will find different versions of Adam's vision of ideal completion and Satan's vision of aggression. We will find, as well, Eve's vision of regression. And we will find intimations of Adam's first vision of a fatherly author and guide. All these visions have for Shelley disturbing as well as compelling qualities. We will find him not only expressing them but also struggling with them, trying to contain them, play them off against each other, purify them, integrate them.

As in *Paradise Lost*, such visions occur in Shelley within an overarching drama of loss and gain, of paradise, fall, and adaptation. In a psychoanalytic perspective, we can never realize the fullness of our imaginings or recover all we have lost, but we can find a realistic measure of satisfaction in permissible similitudes or substitutes. In Milton, we are given a series of substitutes—a various world of freedom and experience, a paradise within, and a future redemption— through which we can actually attain a greater state than the original one. Blake, however, believed in "the return of Adam into Paradise."[11] For Shelley too at his most extreme no fall can be fortunate. Freud in "Mourning and Melancholia" wrote that "people never willingly abandon a libidinal position, not even, indeed, when a substitute is already beckoning to them" (*SE*, 14:154); we often find Shelley speaking for that resistance within us. Wordsworth follows Milton in presenting our original state of splendor as permanently lost to us. In the *Immortality Ode*, we fall from divine glory to the world of nature, our "Foster"-mother, and eventually, through the substitute satisfactions of earthly life, to the "prison-house" of maturity (82, 67). The *Ode* itself begins in that adult dimension and struggles toward a new kind of visionary consciousness, which compensates for the loss of the kind we once knew. What Wordsworth does, after recognizing that he has fallen, is accept a further fall, which takes him into the depths of memory and what we would call the unconscious, and that journey, the poem promises, can carry us beyond the melancholy of mourning: "To me the meanest flower that blows can give / Thoughts that do often lie too deep for tears" (206–7). But in the strictest Shelleyan view, Wordsworth still accepts an absolute passage from paradise to a fallen world of substitutes, where we must make the best of it. In Shelley, we fall not, like Adam, into history and common nature but, like Satan, straight into Hell. We have the choice either of soaring back to recapture what Wordsworth mourns for or of grieving without compensation or consolation. Central to Shelley's entire career is a manifold attempt to reverse the poetic myth of the *Immortality Ode.*

For Wordsworth, as for Freud, being able to let go of paradise is itself an ideal, difficult of attainment; in the *Ode* he spends more poetic energy on the idealization of the primal affections than on the imaginative need to relinquish them. The Wordsworthian sensibility at its most powerful is a state of mind in which the attempt to let go and the attempt to maintain our first affections are both present in a creative clash of contraries. Shelley does not idealize letting go. However, his ambition to recapture the lost glory is engaged with other forces, conscious and unconscious, in the total structure of his sensibility. Among them are his humanism, his Enlightenment skepticism, his proclivity to despair and an overwhelming sense of failure, and his realism: "Nothing is more idle," he writes in *A Philosophical View of Reform,* "than to reject a limited benefit because we cannot without great sacrifices obtain an unlimited one" (*C,* 256). In addition, as much as he idealizes a recovery of primal bliss he also idealizes the advance of civilization and its arts and sciences. "The whole of human science is comprised in one question," he writes in *Queen Mab:* "How can the advantages of intellect and civilization be reconciled with the liberty and pure pleasures of natural life?" (*E,* 1:411). How can we have the advantages of both progression and regression, otherness and primal narcissism, civilization and contentment, sublimation and oedipal or preoedipal bliss?

It should also be noted that for Shelley, unlike Satan, belatedness involved an awareness not only of prior greatness but also of prior failure. Blake, Wordsworth, and Coleridge lived through the dawning of the Age of Revolution with its millenial imaginings; they also had to live through the shock of revolutionary failure and find new ways of continuing the spirit of renovation. Shelley grew up in the aftermath of these events, and they threw a shadow over his own hopes and projects. In *The Two Spirits—An Allegory,* a Second Spirit, who "plumed with strong desire / Would float above the Earth" (1–2), is preceded by a First Spirit, who foretells his failure. It was Shelley's historical place to be a Second Spirit, always to follow a prophecy of doom. But within this haunted condition he carried on the Romantic quest to undo the apparent disadvantage of belatedness. Blake believed in an ideal of perpetual imaginative progress. Wordsworth created myths of compensation, in which the gains of time might balance or even outweigh the losses, in which, for example, experience does not bring its full wealth to us until, as in *I wandered lonely as a cloud*, it has undergone the gestation of memory. Shelley tried repeatedly to create in his writings a revised revolution, in which the mistakes of the original French Revolution would be undone. In Shelley we have an opportunity for correction and remaking. In the poetic myth of the second chance, belatedness is converted into a blessing.

The Two Spirits illustrates the way in which the Shelleyan quest to realize the imagined is characteristically set in a matrix of questions, perspectives, and competing forces. In this poem a sense of extraordinary possibility is qualified by skepticism and complicated by anxiety but still persists. The Second Spirit, carrying "the lamp of love," seeks the "deathless stars" beyond "the shade of night" (11, 9–10). The quest itself provokes a tempest that pursues him, and the cautionary, realistic First Spirit urges the abandonment of his efforts. The poem ends with a double conclusion. In the first, romance collapses into irony as the goal vanishes completely, and the quester and the tempest pursue each other eternally around a ruined, frozen evergreen. In the second conclusion, Shelley gives us his most concise version of Adam's dream and one of his most beautiful:

> Some say when the nights are dry [and] clear
> And the death dews sleep on the morass,
> Sweet whispers are heard by the traveller
>   Which make night day—
> And a shape like his early love doth pass
> Upborne by her wild and glittering hair,
> And when he awakes on the fragrant grass
>   He finds night day.
>
>   (41–48)

I
THE MISSING FIRE

1
Magician of the Enlightenment

AT THE AGE OF TWENTY, SHELLEY WROTE TO GODWIN THAT UNTIL HE read Godwin's *Political Justice* he had been but a "votary of Romance"; now, however, he had turned from an "ideal" world to the real one and learned of his "duties to perform" (*L*, 1:227–28). By "Romance" Shelley meant, above all, Gothic romance. In early letters to Godwin and others, his immersion in Gothic is equated with "intellectual sickliness and lethargy"; characterizing himself as "an undivided votary" of reason, he wrote, "I have rejected all fancy, all imagination."[1] Gothic, made to bear the burden of his entire fascination with the "ideal," becomes the symbol of his innocence; and with its sacrifice he tries to found his mature literary identity.

Shelley called his youthful romances *Zastrozzi* and *St. Irvyne* "the distempered altho unoriginal visions" that epitomized his adolescent sensibility (*L*, 1:266). They do, however, reveal motifs that recur in his later work. *Zastrozzi* features the passive Verezzi, who, unable to choose between a pure love and a sensual one, commits suicide, and the atheistic and diabolical Zastrozzi, who plots to avenge the seduction and betrayal of his mother by the man who is both his and Verezzi's father.[2] A prime source of evil in this work is aggressive male sexuality, both in the father and, in Verezzi's case, in the self. *St. Irvyne* is a story of demonic curiosity, filled with secrets and mysteries as well as hints of sibling incest. It features the suicidally depressed Wolfstein, who is tortured by "the wild retrospection of ideal horror," haunted by a nameless "event almost too dreadful for narration," and the antinomian Ginotti, who makes a pact with the devil in his "desire of unveiling the latent mysteries of nature."[3]

At the end Wolfstein witnesses the spectacle of Ginotti's seizure by the devil, an explosive disaster that destroys the voyeur as well as the participant.

The world of Gothic romance was one in which it was easy to be "very far gone," as Shelley noted; in his adolescence he would "read Novels & Romances all day, till in the Evening I fancy myself a Character" (*L*, 1:11, 2). In the following, to Godwin, the taste for Gothic is an irresistible impulse: "I was haunted with a passion for the wildest and most extravagant romances: ancient books of Chemistry and Magic were perused with an enthusiasm of wonder almost amounting to belief. My sentiments were unrestrained by anything within me: external impediments were numerous, and strongly applied— their effects were merely temporary" (1:227). The world of Gothic was one ruled by the attractions of rage and violence. It was one in which sexuality appeared in the form of incestuous guilt or thrilling fear or a "poniard" penetrating an "alabaster bosom."[4] And in contrast to its aura of instinctual release, it was one in which the self was both possessed by inner forces and controlled by other people. With its medievalism, its revenge plots, and its hauntings and horrifying "retrospections," Gothic was for Shelley a world dominated by the alluring, inescapable, and ruinous power of the past. It was a world of "unoriginal visions" in which influence became persecution and in which the self was compelled into uncanny and destructive repetitions.

In the romances Shelley used light for special effects of mystery and horror, as in the moonlight that accompanies Verezzi almost like a second self, the lightning in which Ginotti is seized to hell, or the fiery eyes that remain in his skeleton. *Queen Mab*, his epic version of the Enlightenment and his personal encyclopedia of eighteenth-century radical thought, celebrates instead "the steady ray of reason and common sense" (*E*, 1:403).[5] *Queen Mab* opens with an epigraph from Lucretius, which concludes, "I untie men's minds from the tight knots of religion,"[6] and in the poem the fables and miracles of religion are coolly disposed of: "But even supposing that a man should raise a dead body to life before our eyes, and on this fact rest his claim to being considered the son of God;—the Humane Society restores drowned persons, and because it makes no mystery of the method it employs, its members are not mistaken for the sons of God" (*E*, 1:401). Like Lucretius, Shelley hopes to free people from the darkness of belief by giving them an understanding of nature, a word that experiences its finest Shelleyan hour in this work. Closely related to nature in *Queen Mab* is Necessity, an eighteenth-century concept with scientific and antisupernatural connotations.[7] Insofar as we can distinguish them, nature is the "unvarying harmony" (6.203) of the universe, and Necessity is the power that compels the elements of the universe into the form of that harmony. Alexander Pope, with his faith in an ordered nature, regarded Borgias as the earthquakes or hurricanes that had to be accepted as part of the human world,[8] but for Shelley tyrants offend nature, and Necessity will sweep them off their thrones.

In its imagery *Queen Mab* depicts a struggle between the light of reason and truth that prevails in nature and a phantasmagoric human night of greed, war, famine, corruption, and slavery. Godwin had complained about Shelley's love of "a perpetual sparkle and glittering,"[9] but even after that criticism Shelley in *Queen Mab* carries the light imagery much further than his symbolism requires. Fireworks like the following are common: "The atmosphere in flaming sparkles flew," and a chariot with "burning wheels" cuts a "fiery track" through a heaven "Radiant with million constellations" and "Flashing incessant meteors" (1.214–15, 227, 233, 236). The glitter of Southey's romance *Thalaba* is an immediate source of passages like this one. But the major point to recognize about the poem's light imagery is that ultimately Shelley is not writing about the light of Godwin, Paine, and Holbach, the light of reason; he is writing about the glory and the radiance that in the *Immortality Ode* we have lost forever; he is transforming the light of reason into a more primal splendor: the heavenly radiance that Milton prays might illuminate his dark world, or the light of a beatific state of preexistence that Plato writes of in the *Phaedrus*.[10] *Queen Mab* is not simply a versification of Enlightenment doctrines but a converse of the *Ode*, and in this sense the sparkle and glittering are of the poem's essence. Outglowing all else in the poem's blazing universe is the temple of *Queen Mab* herself, an "etherial palace" with "floors of flashing light," a "vast and azure dome," and "fertile golden islands / Floating on a silver sea" (2.29, 32–35). The Fairy's Fane is an analogue of Wordsworth's "imperial palace," our ultimate home.[11]

The poem is accompanied by long ideological essays disguised as notes. Originally, Shelley intended the poetry to be a smokescreen for the dangerous ideology.[12] The notes, however, are not always the most frankly radical part of the poem. The line "There is no God"

(7.13), for example, is accompanied by an essay that is merely agnostic. Today the poem's considerable romance apparatus—with its magic, its ecstatic imagery, its space odyssey to the Fairy's Fane, its supernatural characters, its elaborate description of the mechanics of a dream vision—is often taken as mere sugarcoating.[13] But we need to understand the entire romance apparatus, as in the case of its important component, the imagery of light, as integral to the poem's deep purposes. In that apparatus, the superstition and enthusiasm that are attacked by the ideology make their reappearance—almost like a return of the repressed.[14] Shelley changes cool rationality into a kind of magic and writes a romance of Reason. While it would be too much to say that the ideology of *Queen Mab* is a sugarcoating for its romance apparatus, that would be at least as close to the truth as the opposite position.

I do not mean, however, that the romance apparatus undermines the ideology—except that part of the ideology that can be taken to denigrate fancy. Shelley grew up intellectually in the Enlightenment and sought grounding there. Furthermore, the use of a romance framework for a work of radical ideology is not original with him; he found models for such a format in the influential *Ruins* of Count Volney and other works of the period.[15] But we need to see Shelley's use of romance in the context of his rejection of it and the ambivalence toward it that Geoffrey Hartman and Patricia Parker view as a central theme in Romanticism in general.[16] Since the seventeenth century, romance has been the id of modern literature, a primary poetic magic repressed in the search for realism, experience, freedom from illusion, and high seriousness. But for the Romantics what Keats called "old romance" is, as Hartman has shown, resisted in the process of creating a new romance, one that is both "enchanting and rational,"[17] as well as, in Shelley's case, political.

Indeed, *Queen Mab* tells the story of the politicization of the romance imagination. The poem is cast as a nonsexual version of Adam's dream, in which the Fairy Queen grants a dream vision to a sleeping maiden named Ianthe. In that dream, Ianthe is taken up to Mab's temple, where she is given a sense of the ideal. She is then given an awareness of how far humanity has fallen from that ideal and how its misery, corruption, and false conceptions contrast with the principles of the universe. Then with the entrance of a new character, Ahasuerus, the Wandering Jew, her developing sensibility is given an element of prophetic wrath. This is a key point in *Queen*

Mab. Ahasuerus by himself is a hopeless, tormented creature, almost a Zastrozzi, consumed by anger and alienation. But to be able to integrate that explosive anger into a more comprehensive consciousness and thus make it creative instead of self-consuming is one of the goals of *Queen Mab*. After Ahasuerus reveals the roots of falsehood in the Judeo-Christian concept of God, he himself returns to the shades from which he will never escape; but the education of Ianthe is completed as she is given an Edenic vision of a renovated future. She is then sent back to the waking present with a sense of mission.[18]

At the center of Shelley's new romance are three poetic conceptions: Ianthe, representing the Human Spirit; the Spirit of Nature, or Necessity; and Queen Mab. What is the relationship among them? Strictly speaking, Mab is an intermediary, or daemon, between the Spirit of Nature and the Human Spirit. But both the Spirit of Nature and Queen Mab have temples, and Shelley does not draw his lines of distinction very sharply. In effect, Shelley develops a double female deity. Toward the male deity of Judeo-Christian tradition the poem tries out three attitudes. Sometimes it is atheistic, and sometimes it is agnostic, arguing that humanity invents divine names to cover its ignorance of causes. The most forcefully argued position is that of Ahasuerus, who, like Satan, believes in God but hates him. In any case, the father god is torn down and replaced by a mother: "Spirit of Nature! all-sufficing Power, / Necessity! thou mother of the world!" (6.197–98).

And just as mothers replace fathers as authority figures, so daughters replace sons as potential redeemers. Ahasuerus, the sonlike rebel against authority, is a partly positive character, but he is finally too enmeshed with authority in a web of mutual aggression to be a redeemer. The poem begins and ends with Ianthe's lover, Henry, devotedly watching over her in sleep. David Duff suggests that *Queen Mab* is a romance without a hero (112); indeed, Henry—the young male who would typically be the hero of a romance and the figure as well with whom Shelley might identify—is so minor and seemingly gratuitous a figure that one might wonder why he is in the poem at all. But he is there precisely to display the inconsequentiality of the young male. Oedipal combativeness is projected into the scapegoat-figure of Ahasuerus, leaving Henry free of male aggression to serve as a blameless, pure self-image for the author. In *Queen Mab*, the role of the sons is to watch admiringly as the mothers and daughters get rid of the fathers.

Ianthe, however, may seem a skimpy vehicle for such a redemptive mission. But her passivity too is exactly the point. It is, in Wordsworthian terms, a "wise passiveness."[19] Redemption in *Queen Mab* is identification with Necessity; Shelley writes that humanity must become one with nature and her "blindly-working will" (9.5) to "undertake regeneration's work" (6.43). In gradually perfecting itself, the Human Spirit may become like the Spirit of Nature and achieve with its new "omnipotence of mind" (8.236) a similar power within its own realm. The poem's deeper ideal, however, is not to become an active, parentlike power but to cleave to the mother like an infant. *Queen Mab* offers a preoedipal vision of renovation. Its great hope is that the regressive dream of rejoining the mother, of regaining attachment to that archaic source of power, may prove the origin of actual progress.

Necessity in *Queen Mab* is thus not a harsh *Ananke* as in Greek tragedy or in Freud but a kind mother. The ocean shrinks, to be canopied by green woods; the animals stop devouring each other; the world recovers the Eden of the early mother: "The fertile bosom of the earth gives suck / To myriads" (8.109–10). Queen Mab and Necessity are two faces of the mother. In the infant's perspective, the former is the mother who gives, and the latter is the mother who, literally, is a necessity to us, the mother as an absolute power upon whom we are completely dependent. In *Queen Mab* that seemingly impassive, impersonal, blind will has paradisal ends in store for us.

The poem's myth of benevolence is extended to the individual's inner world. In the new state of being, reason and passion will cease their combat, each realizing new dimensions of potentiality. In *The Greeks and the Irrational*, E. R. Dodds writes that the Greeks called daemons what we would think of as interventions from within the psyche (11–14). Mab—the Daemon of the World, as Shelley called her in a revision of the poem—is the poem's prototype of what such an intervention might ideally be, not disturbing but inspiring. And so our impulses and passions in the renovated world become "bland" and "kindly" (8.200, 202); the fierce aggression of Ahasuerus, while not dispelled because it is felt to have a specific value, is contained, an isolated storm within a vast serenity; the inner world, just like the outer, becomes a "wilderness of harmony" (2.79). Benevolence, although a prime Enlightenment principle, takes its special impetus in Shelley both from its association with the mother and from its association with the ideal of organizing an unruly psyche, one that, unlike

Gothic, is not reflective of intellectual sickliness. The Shelleyan Enlightenment does not, however, abandon or cure the Gothic fascination with incest and violence; rather, it seeks to transform it creatively. Incest is sublimated into the ideal of a return to the universal mother; violence is harnessed as the wrath that, safely distanced and contained, helps drive the process of reform.

One further transformation is important in the poem. "Imagination delights in personification," Shelley wrote to Elizabeth Hitchener; "were it not for this embodying quality of eccentric fancy we should be to this day without a God" (*L*, 1:101). The inner quest of *Queen Mab* is to redeem imagination. Shelley seeks a model of imagination that is progressive, enlightened, radical, and benevolent; the mischievous elf queen is made acceptable by being turned into a revolutionary. Nor are her visions airy illusions, for it is her special power "fancy's thin creations to endow / With manner, being, and reality" (7.62-63).

"How wonderful is Death, / Death and his brother Sleep," the poem opens, continuing for forty-four lines to describe the sleeping form of Ianthe and to wonder whether she will wake again. In the dream theory of Géza Róheim, sleep is a return to the self-enclosure of the uterine state, while the dream embodies a contrary libidinal impulse, a phallic flight toward life in the face of apparent dissolution. And just as sleep, the most extreme form of regression, contains the progressive movement of the dream, so the culminating expression of libido, coitus, contains the fantasy of a return to the womb. Similarly, in *Queen Mab* the sleep of Ianthe contains a progressive dream-flight, which in turn contains a fantasy of regression. Róheim's theory illuminates the interplay of fantasies within the apparatus of the poem, an interplay between Shelley's fear that the romance imagination is a kind of death and his hope that it is an awakening, full of wonders.

In the soaring of Ianthe's dream from her sleeping body, Shelley gives us one portrayal of the birth of imagination. He gives us another in a portrayal of the sun sinking into the ocean:

> And yet there is a moment,
> When the sun's highest point
> Peeps like a star o'er ocean's western edge,
> When those far clouds of feathery gold,
> Shaded with deepest purple, gleam
> Like islands on a dark blue sea;

> Then has thy fancy soared above the earth,
> And furled its wearied wing
> Within the Fairy's fane.
>
> (2.13–21)

This is a moment in which things assume figurative appearance ("like a star," "like islands"). But figuration is only a preliminary stage of imagination. We actually enter the fairy's temple, or achieve the fullness of the visionary imagination, by a defensive movement upward, against the direction of the sun as it is about to be extinguished. Imagination is an escape from drowning. Even the sky has become a dark blue sea. The imperial palace of Mab is a substitute, sublime womb in place of the extinguishing womb of darkness and the sea; it is also an inextinguishable source of light in place of the seemingly extinguishable sun. Imagination here is not as accepting of nature and Necessity as Shelley elsewhere in the poem wishes it to be. Romain Rolland characterized the oceanic feeling as the essence of religion.[20] In Shelley's imagery of the setting sun, we see what we have seen in the inner drama of the poem as a whole with its romance-charged attack on religion: an oceanic resistance to the oceanic feeling.

2

Proteus and Mutability:
The *Alastor* Volume

J UST AS S HELLEY CONSIDERED *Q UEEN M AB* A NEW BEGINNING AFTER
his repudiation of the Gothic juvenilia, so he wrote that *Alastor* was
"my first serious attempt to interest the best feelings of the human
heart" (*L*, 1:462). This implies a rejection of *Queen Mab*; yet the 1816
Alastor volume included the revision of *Queen Mab*, *The Daemon of the
World*. This abridgement, primarily covering Ianthe's chariot ride to
the Fairy's Fane, gives us the romance apparatus without the ideol-
ogy. In a new passage, the Daemon tells Ianthe:

> For thou hast earned a mighty boon,
>   The truths which wisest poets see
> Dimly, thy mind may make its own,
>   Rewarding its own majesty,
>   Entranced in some diviner mood
>   Of self-oblivious solitude.
>   (1.84–89, *E*, 1:494)

The major subject of the revision is not the content of the vision but
the personal, solitary experience of the visionary, which is also the
subject of *Alastor*. In both poems, a dreamer is visited by a female fig-
ure and given a sense of lifelong mission. One poem ends with the
promise of success, the other with failure and desolation. A debate is
thus built into the volume, one that will continue throughout Shel-
ley's career.[1]

The volume also includes several shorter poems, chiefly concerned
with mutability. In *Stanzas—April, 1814,* a love affair comes to an end
as "duty and dereliction" call the poet back to the solitude of his "sad

and silent home" (8–9). The poem was occasioned by Shelley's happy visit to Cornelia Boinville Turner and her mother shortly before the breakup of his marriage to Harriet Westbrook. In *Mutability*, human beings are "clouds that veil the midnight moon," momentarily radiant but soon lost forever in darkness (1). *O! there are spirits of the air* addresses one—Coleridge, according to Mary Shelley[2]—who failed to find his ideal in either "the false earth's inconstancy" or the "faithless smiles" of lovers (20, 25, *E*, 1:449). In *To Wordsworth*, Shelley laments Wordsworth's desertion of his own ideals, and in *Feelings of a Republican on the Fall of Bonaparte*, he mourns the betrayal of the French Revolution through the failure of its makers to root out the deep causes of oppression. At this time Shelley translated a sonnet by Guido Cavalcanti, pertinent to the volume although not included in it, in which Guido accuses his once-loved Dante of apostasy: "In vain / I seek what once thou wert" (10–11, *E*, 1:454). Together these poems describe a world in which promising beginnings are subverted and potential lost. In their spectrum of mutability, they point to the falseness of both earth and spirits, the failure of ideals, and the betrayal of others. Perhaps the most subversive mutability of all is an inconstancy within the self. In *Mutability*, we are like Aeolian harps, with "dissonant strings" under the "varying" wind, never knowing "One mood or modulation like the last" (5, 6, 8). In the *Alastor* volume, Mutability replaces Necessity as the mother of the world; in Shelley's vision of faithless smiles and unending change we can discern a sense of the inconstancy of the primal object.

The image of the father has also changed from *Queen Mab*, for the chief paternal image in these poems is not the tyrant but the failed hero. Shelley would later scribble in his notebook,

> Proteus Wordsworth who shall bind thee
> Pro[th]eus Coleridge who shall find thee
> Hyperprotean Proteus, Southey,
> Who shall catch thee, who shall know thee[3]

The changeful visionary of the volume represents the best of the previous generation, the heroic fathers who failed, in Shelley's eyes, to sustain a revolution and a moral and poetic vision.[4] The volume reveals the complexity of Shelley's attitude toward the father. On the one hand, he rebelled vehemently against his own father, identifying him with Christianity and everything oppressive in society. He was also defensively sensitive to any appearance of unoriginality. No writer is "a fit model for any succeeding writer," he wrote. "True genius vindicates to itself an exemption from all regard to whatever has gone before" (*L*, 2:290). On the other hand, he was extraordinarily open to literary influence. As Carlos Baker says, he "displayed a singular capacity for projecting himself imaginatively into the literature he admired" (27). He actively sought literary guides and fathers, discipling himself with particular intensity to Plato in the past and Godwin in the present. In Godwin, Shelley appoints a new father for his rebirth into the Enlightenment, a father to save him from the old magic of romance and guide him in the great duty of ameliorating reality. Plato, Richard Holmes reminds us, was not an academically respectable writer in Shelley's time (26). He made a radical and subversive literary father. At the same time, championing a writer who is out of favor, translating him and propagating his ideas, is an aggressive form of discipleship. To a certain extent, Plato is for Shelley a father to be saved; the rescue of a parental figure is one of the two types of family romance identified by Freud and Otto Rank, the other being the invention of glorious origins.[5] Plato and Godwin were only two of the literary and cultural fathers Shelley adopted, among many others, such as Calderón, William Drummond, and John Frank Newton, advocate of "naturism," or vegetarianism and nudism. Indeed, Shelley created fathers as actively in his literary life as he tore them down in his familial life and political ideology. Even as he attacked authority, literary precedence, and what he called in *Queen Mab* "The merciful, and the avenging God" (6.104), Adam's first dream of a worthy and reliable fatherly guide—a dream of the "longing" for "a father's protection" that Freud saw at the origin of the "the religious attitude" (*SE*, 21:72)—was psychologically alive for him.

In the Proteus lines, Shelley goes on to refer to "Aristeus, Menelaus"; Aristeus and Menelaus both came to Proteus for help in solving desperate problems, but unlike the original Old Man of the Sea, the current authorities, Shelley implies, have no help to give; they have the changeableness of Proteus without his vision. The apostasy of others—both friends and idols, both men and women, parent-figures, peers, and disciples—was a major theme in Shelley's life. All around him greatness was falling "into the gulph of error," he complained to Elizabeth Hitchener (*L*, 1:208); she herself was soon to go the same way in his opinion. Shelley was attracted to figures—Godwin, Byron, and his friend Hogg are examples—who kept disillusioning him and whom he kept cultivating or valuing. Wordsworth was a prime example. A short time after criticizing him in *To Wordsworth*, Shelley was so enthusiastic that he would "dose" Byron with his poetry, as Byron put it.[6] Later in Shelley's career, he cried out in anger over Wordsworth's treachery, "That such a man should be such a poet!" (*L*, 2:26). Even after that, Shelley called his lyric *An Exhortation* (*H*, 579), in which poets, compared to chameleons, change their color only because they cannot find love and recognition, "kind of an excuse for Wordsworth."[7] For Shelley, Wordsworth was always an icon of failing greatness.[8]

But if the father and the mother were mutable, in at least one respect Shelley himself was notably mutable in this period, and that was in his love relationships. Caught between the Boinvilles, mother and daughter, and Harriet, whom he had once idealized but to whom he now felt tied only by duty, he wrote to Hogg, "I am a feeble, wavering, feverish being" (*L*, 1:383). In the *Alastor* volume the inner self is as inconstant as the object, or mother, and the ego-ideal, or father. In the letter in which Shelley applies *An Exhortation* to Wordsworth, he first applies it to himself and Mary; indeed, the poem is more readily applicable to Shelley than to Wordsworth in its complaint that poets have difficulty in finding fame, hardly a problem for Wordsworth. In the poem *Alastor*, which deals with a young man who goes off to seek his destiny, Shelley turns to the problem of founding his mature career, of imagining what kind of poet and visionary he might be, of conceiving a self separate from and superior to the fallible parents, of seeking a steadfastness within the soul. As it turns out, he is unable to detach himself from the failed parents enough to imagine a successful hero. He can, however, promise a more meaningful and glorious failure than theirs, a failure not of mutability or self-betrayal but of tragedy.

3

The Quest for
the Veiled Maid

ACCORDING TO IMLAC'S FAMOUS TREATISE ON "THE DANGEROUS prevalence of imagination" in Samuel Johnson's *Rasselas*, "No man will be found, in whose mind airy notions do not sometimes tyrannise, and force him to hope or fear beyond the limits of sober probability. All power of fancy over reason, is a degree of insanity" (150). Imlac attributes this malady to solitude: "He who has nothing external that can divert him, must find pleasure in his own thoughts, and must conceive himself what he is not; for who is pleased with what he is? He then expatiates in boundless futurity, and culls from all imaginable conditions that which for the present moment he should most desire" (151–52). At last "fictions begin to operate as realities" and "life passes in dreams of rapture or of anguish" (152). Imlac's listeners immediately resolve to banish their imaginations, and even the melancholy astronomer, in whom the "disease of the imagination" is most severe (162), emerges from his solitude to enjoy sublunary pleasures, although he suffers relapses whenever he is alone again.

A "morbid ascendancy of the imagination" is the theme of *Alastor, or The Spirit of Solitude*, according to a contemporaneous reviewer, who went on to say that the whole poem was as guilty of the charge as its hero.[1] *Alastor* is, in part, a romantic, nonsatirical confirmation of *Rasselas*, whose hero set out from his "Happy Valley," saying, "I fancy that I should be happy if I had something to persue" (16). In fact, the melancholy, Johnsonian sense of imagination persists in Shelley's contemporaries alongside a more prominent exaltation of the faculty. Byron, for example, in *Childe Harold's Pilgrimage*, gives us a version of Adam's dream in which the love we seek is a mere creation of our own "desiring phantasy": "Of its own beauty is the mind diseased, / And fevers into false creation" (4.121.7, 122.1–2). The Romantics even went beyond Johnson to invent new anxieties of the imagination. In *Kubla Khan*, the poet is filled with a power that could recreate paradise but could also burst fearsomely out of control: the poet's listeners must "Weave a circle round him thrice," magically containing his magic (51). And Keats, in the poem to John Hamilton Reynolds, laments that "our dreamings" sometimes take us "into the core / Of an eternal fierce destruction."[2]

Current readers do not seem to share the contemporaneous reviewer's rejection of *Alastor*; it is now one of Shelley's most studied poems. But the *Alastor* Poet himself must still be one of the most disapproved of characters in literature who is not a criminal or someone directly hurtful to others. He is commonly criticized for his commitment to fantasy and isolation, his autoerotism, his rejection of people in general and women in particular; he is regarded as narcissistic, suicidal, insane.[3] Stuart Sperry is about as positive as recent criticism gets when he writes that we must admire "the limitlessness of his ambition and insatiability of his desire," while adding, "However, his failure drives the world only deeper into desolation."[4]

The poem's own treatment of its hero is far more positive than any of these assessments but is itself filled with conflict because Shelley partly shares his readers' misgivings. The two paragraphs of the preface plunge us immediately into that conflict. In the first paragraph, the young Poet, like Adam, yearns for a companion of his own nature and embodies all his imaginings of perfection in a "single image." When the world proves not to contain "a prototype of his conception," he is destroyed by disappointment and dies young (*R*, 73). The second paragraph opens with a sudden shift in moral perspective, as Shelley claims that his hero is destroyed in revenge for his "self-centred seclusion." But just as suddenly Shelley shifts back to a sympathetic perspective: the hero's doom is brought about by his sensitivity to a "Power" that kills quickly those who give themselves to it and slowly and ignobly those who ignore it. Those "meaner spirits" are "deluded by no generous error, instigated by no sacred thirst of doubtful knowledge, duped by no illustrious superstition." He briefly invokes a third class of people, who follow a life of sympathy and social usefulness, but quickly returns to the two classes of the alienated, those who perish from the intensity of their quest for sympathy and those who, "selfish, blind, and torpid," make up "the lasting misery and loneliness of the world" (*R*, 73). In the course of the paragraph the charge of self-absorption is thus shifted from the hero to those who might condemn him. The preface displays a proleptic rhetoric in which Shelley defends the Poet against the expected objections of the reader and against his own criticism. That defense culminates in a quotation of Wordsworth's terrifying lines on Margaret from *The Excursion*: "The good die first, / And those whose hearts are dry as summer dust, / Burn to the socket!"[5] Allying the Poet with Margaret —who sacrificed her well-being, her children, and finally her life to her imaginings of her husband's return and her "spot" of land[6]— makes the Poet a subversive Romantic saint, subversive not only to common humanity and common sense but also to Shelley's own ideals of sympathy, commitment to social progress, and faith in Enlightenment principles.

Alastor carries a second epigraph, from St. Augustine's *Confessions:* "Nondum amabam, et amare amabam, quaerebam quid amarem, amans amare"—"I did not yet love, and I wanted to love; I sought something to love, being in love with love." For Augustine, the only love object that could satisfy our longings for both infinity and sympathy was God. Shelley, after destroying Christianity in *Queen Mab* and after cleansing the mind of magic, Gothic, and superstition, now wonders how the oceanic feeling might be satisfied. Earl Wasserman writes that the epigraph points to the Romantic theme of *Sehnsucht*, "love-without-an-object, or infinite subject with only finite immediate objects" (27). *Alastor* is perhaps as close as English Romanticism comes to the world of Novalis's blue cornflower and to the erotic yearning of Rousseau and Chateaubriand. In its second epigraph, *Alastor* asks, in effect, how an Adam without God can realize his imaginings of perfection.

The poem itself begins with an invocation in which the Narrator prays to "Earth, ocean, air, beloved brotherhood!" What of the fourth member of that brotherhood? Fire makes its delayed entrance in line 64 as the Narrator tells us that the fire of the Poet's now-dead eyes "has ceased to burn." But a central point of the invocation, as well as of the entire poem, is that fire is missing. The world of *Alastor*, as described in the poem's imagery, is made of earth, wind, and water. It is, additionally, a world of nature, and civilization with its arts of fire plays little part in it. The most important function of fire in *Alastor* is to be conspicuously absent or to appear briefly and then vanish.[7]

The invocation continues with a prayer to the "Mother of this un-fathomable world" (18). The Narrator's devotion to nature and his claims of "natural piety" (3), as well as other Wordsworthian quotations and echoes, have led Wasserman to describe the poem as an account of a visionary as told by a Wordsworthian naturalist.[8] Some commentators since then, however, have argued that in certain respects the Narrator is highly un-Wordsworthian.[9] As Mary Frosch points out, he is a seeker after daemons and dark knowledge (118). He tells his "Great Parent" that he has watched "Thy shadows and the darkness of thy steps, / And my heart ever gazes on the depth / Of thy deep mysteries" (45, 21–23). He portrays himself as a Faustian magician, an alchemist, a figure from Gothic romance; he has haunted charnel heaps and sought ghosts at midnight, but none of his spells has succeeded in lifting the veil of the Parent Nature's "inmost sanctuary" (38) and in bringing back the secrets of death—or bringing back the dead. The invocation does conclude, however, in a Wordsworthian strain, as the Narrator hopes that his song will harmonize with all the other sounds of nature and the "deep heart of man" (49). The Narrator is thus a strange combination of natural piety and natural impiety. Both the Narrator and the Poet are lovers of nature but are dissatisfied with its laws and seek beyond them; both, unlike Wordsworth, refuse to make peace with loss. The Narrator does in his mind or in his magical art what the hero does in his actual wanderings.

The Poet is one to whom, as Rousseau said of himself, Providence offered what he needed for happiness and he refused.[10] In his youth nature, imagination ("solemn vision, and bright silver dream" [67]), and culture join in giving him an ideal education, but he leaves "His cold fireside and alienated home" in quest of "strange truths in undiscovered lands" (76–77). Like the Narrator, he pursues "Nature's most secret steps" (81), and he gazes on ancient ruins, "memorials / Of the world's youth" (121–22), "till meaning on his vacant mind / Flashed like strong inspiration" (126–27). That inner vacancy, his Adamic need for completeness, is the characteristic that determines his destiny.

While he is absorbed in his spectacular visions, an Arab maiden falls in love with him, but like the typical hero of the fairy mistress tale, he does not respond to human love. Then in a lonely dell in the Vale of Cashmir, he dreams that a veiled maid speaks to him with a voice that is "like the voice of his own soul" (153). A poet like himself, she sings of his own favorite topic, knowledge. Her music grows wilder, her veiled limbs glow, he reaches out to meet her, she embraces him "in her dissolving arms," and suddenly she is "swallowed up" by night and sleep—or, since he immediately wakes up, "Roused by the shock," we can say that she vanishes into his orgasm (187, 189, 192).

In this dream, the missing fire appears as a "permeating fire" that is "kindled through all her frame" (163, 162). In her radiance Shelley sexualizes the "visionary gleam" of the *Immortality Ode* (56). Wordsworth's radiance fades gradually, but for the Poet glory has all at once been changed to "The cold white light of morning" (193). The Narrator echoes Wordsworth's lament for the lost splendor: "Whither have fled / The hues of heaven?" (196–97).[11] In the preface the vision was described as an attempt to fill an emptiness, but it leaves the Poet with an intensified sense of emptiness: his brain is "vacant" (191); he wakes in the "vacant" woods (195); his eyes "Gaze on the empty scene as vacantly / As ocean's moon looks on the moon in heaven" (201–2).

Without Adam's God to verify and realize this dream, how does the Poet try to recover and possess his Eve? As Luther Scales notes, this Adam becomes Satanic (136), for just as Satan in *Paradise Lost* "overleap'd all bound" into Eden (4.181), so the Poet "pursues / Beyond the realms of dream that fleeting shade; / He overleaps the bounds" (205–7). He transgresses in giving complete faith to his own inner world and in refusing to give up on something that has vanished. He also tries to realize his vision through solitude. The people the Poet meets on his travels treat him with kindness and awe, and young maidens, in particular, are drawn to him, but he seems enchanted by solitude itself. Another means to realization is the feverish wandering that occupies him for the rest of his life. Before his dream, his voyaging was a deliberate investigation of the world's mysteries, but his traveling now—an extreme form of Romantic, Childe-Harold wandering—is an expression of his discontent and his endless yearning,[12] as well as of his passivity: "driven" by "the light / That shone within his soul," he follows wherever nature takes him (232, 492–93).

Above all, the Poet thinks of death as the way to find the Veiled Maid. The Narrator himself wonders whether death may "Conduct to thy mysterious paradise, / O Sleep" (212–13). But the thought of death also expresses the Poet's despair of success. Seeing a swan fly-

ing home to its mate, he wonders why, with his greater spirit, he
should live with no mate or home of his own, "wasting these surpass-
ing powers / In the deaf air" (288–89). But with the general uncer-
tainty between inner and outer that is characteristic of him, he reacts
to the thought of suicide as if it were suggested by some "fair fiend
near him," not by "his own deep mind" (297–98). He continues to
live but with the idea of meeting "lone Death on the drear ocean's
waste" (305). As a fierce tempest drives his boat across the sea and
into a cavern, he tries, as Shelley was to put it later in *Adonais*, to "Fol-
low where all is fled" (466):

> "Vision and Love!
> . . . I have beheld
> The path of thy departure. Sleep and death
> Shall not divide us long!"
>
> (366–69)

The cavern is cleft in the side of a mountain in the Caucasus. With
icy summits "Among the stars like sunlight" (354), cliffs in the moon-
light, and waves at its base, this mountain links high stars and low
water, moon and sun, darkness and radiance, sea, land, and sky. It is
what Mircea Eliade has called the cosmic mountain, common mythic
symbol of the center of the world, the omphalos or navel, nexus with
another mode of being.[13] Within the cavern a whirlpool hurls the
boat inward toward a "treacherous" pool "Reflecting, yet distorting
every cloud" (386, 385); but just before it is about to plunge into the
emptiness beneath the distorted images, in another deferral of de-
struction the wind deflects it into a peaceful cove bordered by yellow
narcissi gazing "on their own drooping eyes, / Reflected in the crys-
tal calm" (407–8). Here the Poet symbolically comes into contact
with the precursor to whom he is often compared, Ovid's Narcissus.[14]
Shelley establishes the kinship between the two figures when the
Poet longs to adorn himself with the flowers. But Shelley is primarily
concerned to distinguish his hero from Narcissus and from the nar-
cissi. These flowers gaze "For ever" (407) in a contemplation beyond
desire; they possess a perfect, serene self-containment. The Poet, on
the other hand, while he cannot find the swan's natural rapport with
otherness, is also cut off from the completeness of a natural self-en-
closure. In fact, his presence disrupts that perfection, as the waves of
his boat mar the images of the flowers. That the Poet's journey does
not end here suggests a divergence from the human narcissism of

Narcissus as well as the natural narcissism of the flowers. While nar-
cissism is idealized in the passage, Shelley is telling us that the Poet is
finally different from and greater than his Ovidian precursor. His
voyage goes farther; he seeks something other than himself. He is
also a more glorious figure, a genius and a tragic hero, not, we might
say, a beautiful youth who was victimized by a curse. In the episode of
the narcissi Shelley as a poet asserts that he is going beyond both
Ovid and common narcissism. His Poet is a greater narcissist than
Narcissus.

But soon he too comes to his own reflection in the water. In a thick
forest, he studies his own image in a well, "as the human heart, / Gaz-
ing in dreams over the gloomy grave, / Sees its own treacherous like-
ness there" (472–74); the delusive reflection in the mirror of death is
immortality. Again, the thought of suicide seems to come from with-
out: beside the well stands a Spirit, with whom the Poet communes
"as if he and it / Were all that was" (487–88). But he also becomes
aware of another phantom or projection, "Two starry eyes . . . in the
gloom of thought," beckoning him with "serene and azure smiles"
(490–91), and those eyes lure him away from the destructive charms
of the well. Thus, instead of dying immediately, the Poet continues
his previous course of following nature out of nature. Here is a dark,
Shelleyan version of what Hartman has called Wordsworth's myth of
the *via naturaliter negativa*, nature's way of gently leading the soul be-
yond nature, as opposed to any sudden and violent transcendence.[15]
The Poet is an ideal Shelleyan Wordsworth in that he remains true to
his vision and in that his vision concerns an absolute ecstasy. But he is
also a Wordsworthian Shelley in that he never completely gives up his
faith that nature can lead him to his goal.

Since entering the cavern, the Poet has been following a rivulet, to
which, in another mingling of inner and outer, he compares himself:

> Thy darksome stillness,
> Thy dazzling waves, thy loud and hollow gulphs,
> Thy searchless fountain, and invisible course
> Have each their type in me . . .
>
> (505–8)

Obsessed with reflections, he turns the world into an image of him-
self, and he now emerges from the luxuriant forest into a wasteland
of ancient, gnarled roots that reflects his own premature physical
withering. The rivulet takes him up the cosmic mountain, which sud-

denly breaks off in a precipice that overlooks a twilight panorama of seas, rivers, and mountains, of sunset, moon, and stars, a panorama not of abundance, however, but of emptiness. At the edge, a pine stretches its boughs "athwart the vacancy" (562), and the stream "Fell into that immeasurable void / Scattering its waters to the passing winds" (569–70). The plenitude of nature has no meaning to the Poet; it does not include the Vision and Love he seeks.

Instead of following the stream over the precipice, the Poet, in one last deferral, diverges into a tranquil nook that seems "to smile / Even in the lap of horror" (577–78). The last of the poem's many bowers, it is both a place of eternal fertility, clasped by Bacchic ivy "for ever green" (580), and a brilliantly colored burial ground where the "autumnal whirlwind" brings its leaves (583).[16] Here the Poet undergoes his equivalent of a *Liebestod*, or *Dichtungstod*. In the end-game, the moon that has presided over his nocturnal voyage is a crescent lying on its back; as it sinks, so too does the Poet, whose blood "ever beat in mystic sympathy / With nature's ebb and flow" (652–53). At last "two lessening points of light alone / Gleamed through the darkness" (654–55), a spectacular last appearance of those two alluring eyes that hung in the gloom of thought. Then the "minutest ray" (657) is quenched, and the Poet dies. There is no flight upward into an imperial palace as there was at the quenching of the light in *Queen Mab*. Pursuer of a dream, he himself becomes "a dream / Of youth, which night and time have quenched for ever" (669–70). But if there is nothing in the poem to suggest that he has found the transcendent ecstasy he sought, he has at least in his last moments found tranquillity—freedom from "Hope and Despair, / The torturers" (639–40)—a state of mind much missed and valued in Shelley's poems and letters. He has pursued desire if not to its fulfillment, then to its end. Perhaps what is most subversive about the poem is that its antisocial and self-destructive hero seems to die contented. Perhaps too we can see in the repetitive character of his journey, from enclosure to enclosure, Freud's death drive propelling him "*to restore an earlier state of things*" through repetition itself until at last he finds what every organism seeks, "to die only in its own fashion" (*SE*, 18:36, 39).

Just as night originally "involved" the Veiled Maid, so too "the murky shades involved" the Poet (660), and indeed the Narrator is to the Poet as the Poet is to the Veiled Maid: the one left behind. The Narrator, however, does not wish to follow the Poet; he wishes to bring him back. He futilely invokes the old powers of dark magicians and of Medea, who knew the secret of rejuvenation, and he laments that God, "Profuse of poisons" (676), granted immortality only to one man, the Wandering Jew—Shelley's Ahasuerus—and then only as a torment. The Narrator's poetic magic is as powerless as his necromancy, for, unlike, say, Milton, mourning his dead poet Lycidas, he is unable to imagine any afterlife or godlike role for his hero. At this point in the poem, all ambivalence of judgment is gone, and we are lamenting not a generous failure but a "child of grace and genius" (690). The Narrator can only foresee the time when the corpse will be completely obliterated and the Poet will "live alone / In the frail pauses of this simple strain" (705–6); that is, he will "live" only as a conspicuous absence.

At the end of the *Immortality Ode*, Wordsworth says that even though he has lost the glory of a child's special sensibility, he has gained a new power, a mature and humanized mind capable of seeing in "the meanest flower that blows . . . / Thoughts that do often lie too deep for tears" (206–7). Shelley integrates Wordsworth's great phrase in a conclusion that reverses its meaning and denies Wordsworth's claims of compensation in a nearly apocalyptic evocation of a world gone dark:

> It is a woe too "deep for tears," when all
> Is reft at once, when some surpassing Spirit,
> Whose light adorned the world around it, leaves
> Those who remain behind, not sobs or groans,
> The passionate tumult of a clinging hope;
> But pale despair and cold tranquillity,
> Nature's vast frame, the web of human things,
> Birth and the grave, that are not as they were.
>
> (713–20)

We have come far from the benevolent and sympathetic world of the invocation, where Nature was a Great Parent. But in one respect the ending was foreshadowed in that opening: there the fire was absent; now it has vanished permanently.

જ્ઞ જ્ઞ જ્ઞ

Wordsworth's martyr Margaret sacrifices everything to her indefatigible vision of her husband's return and her virtually rooted connection to her "peculiar nook of earth," and her story gives the narrator in *The Ruined Cottage* a new sense of spiritual repose, as well as paying tribute to both imagination and nature.[17] Shelley's martyr is defended and celebrated, but the Narrator of *Alastor* is left in unrest and despair, and both imagination and nature are severely interrogated in the poem. In *Queen Mab* we can achieve great ends by allying ourselves to nature. In *Alastor*, we are inspired by nature, carried along by nature, our blood beating in mystic sympathy with it, and finally buried by nature, but we cannot be fully satisfied by it. Nature even betrays us: the breath of the Great Parent becomes the "unfeeling storm" on which the Poet's music is scattered and the "senseless wind" that wears down his "divinest lineaments" (597, 705, 704). But the imagination too betrays us. Once it erupts into our lives, it will never again leave us content. While in *Queen Mab* human sympathy and imagination draw us in the same direction, *Alastor* expresses the fear that the visionary imagination and social redemption may simply be incompatible. The imagination first grew out of a need for communion, but referring to nothing in common humanity or nature, it leads us from solitude to solitude.[18] *Alastor* also, in effect, fails to confirm another poetic myth of both *The Ruined Cottage* and *Queen Mab*. Margaret finds peace in death, joining nature, and *Queen Mab* tries to take away our fear of death, making it a gateway to "azure isles" (9.162), but the Narrator of *Alastor* rages against death, calling it "king of this frail world" (614).

At one point in his voyage the Poet is said to be "led / By love, or dream, or god, or mightier Death" (427–28). The farther he goes, the less certain become the exact source and goal of his quest. The Veiled Maid is a "fleeting shade" (206); the two starry eyes beckon the Poet away from the "dark shades" in the forest (486), and finally he is engulfed by "murky shades" (660). So too in the forest, nature, imagination, and death are linked by a single word: the natural scene is one of "evening gloom" (485), the starry eyes hang in "the gloom of thought" (490), and the grave with its immortal image is "gloomy" (473). Nature, imagination, eros, and death are all entangled together. The poem is filled not only with puzzling conflations but with secrets and questions; it echoes Adam's first dream as well as his second. The hero asks questions about sleep, death, vision, and the afterlife; he asks, "And what am I that I should linger here?" (285); the Narrator seeks some "ghost" "to render up the tale / Of what we are"

(27–29). The poem itself is riddling in the sheer number of possible causes that Shelley assigns for the doom of his hero. He might have suffered his fate because he turned from human sympathy, because he sought too passionately for human sympathy, because he was destroyed by a Power that kills us whether we follow or repudiate it, because he tried to capture the infinite in a single, idolatrous image, because he fell into delusion, because the good die first. He might have failed because the insufficient world does not contain the prototype of our imaginings or because our imaginings alienate us from the world. He might have failed because Ruin prepared for "His brother Death [a] rare and regal prey" (619), because "Silence, too enamoured of that voice, / Locks its mute music in her rugged cell" (65–66), or because "The spirit of sweet human love has sent / A vision to the sleep of him who spurned / Her choicest gifts" (203–5). In *Alastor* overdetermination reaches a point at which it becomes a new way of asking a question.

Norman Thurston puts the case well for a programmatic skepticism in *Alastor*, describing the poem as "a controlled investigation," in which Shelley explores the limits and possibilities of two "opposing (and related) points of view," the Narrator's Wordsworthian naturalism and the hero's idealism (129, 128). But how deliberate and controlled can the questioning and ambivalence be when Shelley didn't even know what to call the poem? Peacock, in supplying the poem's title, had to tell him what, in Peacock's opinion, he had been writing about.[19] *Queen Mab* was a poem of answers, but *Alastor* is a poem of anxiety and doubt. In its "unfathomable world" and its "obstinate questionings" (18, 26),[20] *Alastor* is suggestive of such greater works of the interrogative mood as the book of Job, *Oedipus Rex*, and *Hamlet*. But *Alastor* has no God to answer the questions; nor is there any sense in the poem of manipulating the reflections, as Hamlet does in his play within a play to find the answers to at least some of his questions; and while the Poet early in his career stands before a "mutilated sphinx" (114), he is no sphinx-killer, and the poem as a whole finally stands silent before its own profusion of questions about human destiny.

Alastor is both a convincing romance and a metaromance that thinks about and questions the idea of the romantic quest. The Poet is called an "elemental god" (351), and he is an elemental god of literature, a virtual personification of the spirit of romance. In the

Poet's quest for the Veiled Maid we can see the literary quest of a pure votary of romance, who makes no concession in his pursuit of that particular poetic magic, and the poem thus seems an elegy for a once-radiant mode that is no longer within the grasp of a serious, enlightened, political, contemporary literature. But the poem's attitude toward romance is exactly as complicated as its attitude toward the hero. Shelley does far more to defend and glorify the Poet against anticipated criticism and his own misgivings than to discredit him, and to the same extent, he smuggles a defense of the romance mode under the implied criticism of its antisocial, superstitious, futile, and self-destructive character. It is the criticism that makes the idealization of romance acceptable to the modern reader within Shelley and within us. That modern reader can accept romances, at least sublime romances, only in negative form, only when they appear to say that the romantic sensibility needs to be repudiated. Antithetical in other respects, *Queen Mab* and *Alastor* are thus both founded in the same type of negative gesture—although the rejection of romance in *Alastor* is both more massive and more openly ambivalent because illustrious superstitions, rather than purely fraudulent ones, are at issue.

Alastor is a romance that questions the romance mode in the deep interest of renewing and expanding it. Shelley does create a new and strong romance for his age, a romance that, in Hartman's formulation of the Romantic revival of the mode, struggles with romance, and that in Bloom's formulation of the same phenomenon, is internalized, an adventure within the psyche, centering on the imagination.[21] But this was not enough for Shelley. *Alastor* defends the Poet as a saint and martyr of the imagination but still ultimately presents him as a failure. He tries to achieve his vision through nature, dream, solitude, self-communing, wandering, internalization, fantasy, and death; but neither the Narrator nor the preface-writer shares in whatever satisfaction he may find through these means. In the Narrator's lamenting the inadequacy of "Art and eloquence" to mourn the Poet's death (710), Shelley also laments the limitations of his own art and eloquence in *Alastor*, for he sought a poetry that would help realize the vision. Shelley both defends certain poetic and personal impulses and shows that by themselves they are not sufficient. In a way we can say of *Alastor* and its hero what Milton said of the devils in *Paradise Lost*: their song was beautiful but "partial" (2.552)—here, not so much "biased," as in Milton, as incomplete.

To study further that part of a yet-unachieved fuller music, I turn now to explore some additional elements of what we might call the *Alastor* complex in Shelley's poetry.

4

Doubles and Similitudes

THE *ALASTOR* POET AWAKENS FROM HIS VISION INTO A WORLD AGONIZ-ingly divided into realms of dream and waking reality. He is also divided within himself, as hopes and fears about death contend within him. Another solitary visionary in Shelley, the hero of *Athanase,* has "an adamantine veil / Between his heart and mind." In addition, each of these faculties is divided by "separate strife" (87–89, *E,* 2:318). Shelley frequently imagines ideal conditions of unity, as in *To Jane: The keen stars were twinkling:* "some world far from ours / Where music and moonlight and feeling / Are one" (22–24). Yet doubleness in Shelley appears in several modes besides dualism or conflict and is not always something to escape or overcome.

A pervasive form of doubleness in *Alastor* is its imagery of images, its shadows and reflections. Shelley often uses shades and shadows in a predictably negative sense, as when in *A Defence of Poetry* he compares Roman culture to Greek as shadow to substance (*R,* 523). But he also uses them to depict the effect of a glorious presence on the world, as in the "awful shadow of some unseen Power" in the *Hymn to Intellectual Beauty* (1). Reflections can be alluring delusions, as in *Love, Hope, Desire, and Fear,* in which the Lady Desire has a "magic mirror" that tempts us to embrace a "bright error" (18–19, *H,* 648).[1] But they can also be superior to nature: "Why is the reflection in that canal more beautiful than the objects it reflects?" he writes in a fragment; "The colors are more vivid and yet blended with more harmony," and the details "surpass and misrepresent truth" (*C,* 337). In the *Defence of Poetry,* poetry itself is a sublime reflection: "The story of particular facts is as a mirror which obscures and distorts that which should be beautiful: Poetry is a mirror which makes beautiful that which is distorted" (*R,* 515).

Another form of Shelleyan doubleness appears in his fondness for prefaces that discuss in a clinical tone a poetic protagonist who is clearly a self-representation and may even, as in *Julian and Maddalo* and *Epipsychidion*, be the "I" of the poem. Here, as in the *Alastor* preface, the self that watches the self is not narcissistically self-absorbed but self-analyzing, as well as self-judging and self-protecting. Above, I referred to Shelley's idea of writing a complete record of one's life to provide a mirror in which all people could see their own recollections, hopes, and fears, but he saw an obstacle in the way of this epic project, what he called the "dizzying" and "tumultuous" "passage from sensation to reflection" (*C*, 186). The *Alastor* preface begins in the vein of this analytical self-consciousness—"The poem entitled 'ALASTOR,' may be considered as allegorical of one of the most interesting situations of the human mind" (*R*, 72)—and through its use of Poet and Narrator, the poem attempts to be in the two places of experience and reflection at once. And if self-consciousness is one double of the experiencing, conscious subject, the unconscious is another, and Shelley's sense of its presence was strong. In *An Allegory*, we pass a cavern of shadows on the highway of life; the "curious" "Pause to examine," but "they learn little there, except to know / That shadows follow them where'er they go" (12–15, *H*, 624). At a certain point we gain such a shadow; even the curious don't know much about it; chiefly, to put it in Shelleyan terms, we feel that it is there.

Another manifestation of doubleness appears in the entangling of ideals with their opposites. The cleft mountain that rises from the water in *Alastor* "Exposed those black depths to the azure sky" (375). In this poem we are not permitted to see the visionary azure without being reminded of the black depths. So in *Adonais* Shelley describes himself as "a Power / Girt round with weakness" (281–82). In the *Essay on the Punishment of Death*, to die is to be stripped of "all that intertexture of good and evil with which Nature seems to have clothed every form of individual existence" (*C*, 156).

But good also has a disturbing way of slipping into evil. In the *Defence*, Shelley says that the poet, more ardent than other men in his pursuit of pleasure and avoidance of pain, "both his own and that of others," may fall into error when in his passion "he neglects to observe the circumstances under which these objects of universal pursuit and flight have disguised themselves in one another's garments" (*R*, 534). Above, I noted Shelley's feeling that his personal heroes

were always falling into a "gulph of error";[2] the *Alastor* Poet is only
one of a number of his poetic heroes of whom this is also true. He
writes, for example, of Margaret Nicholson, the failed assassin of
Louis XV, "Much as we may deplore the fatal and enthusiastic ten-
dency which the ideas of this poor female had acquired, we cannot
fail to pay the tribute of unequivocal regret to the departed memory
of genius, which, had it been rightly organized, would have made
that intellect, which had since become the victim of frenzy and de-
spair, a most brilliant ornament to society" (*E*, 1:114). Genius in Shel-
ley is hard to keep on its course to radiance. The hero of his satire on
Wordsworth, *Peter Bell the Third*, is a poet who once brought a "diviner
flame" to the Earth (436) but then became "dull; then prosy and
dull; and now dull—o so dull! it is an ultra-legitimate dulness" (*R*,
340). In the same poem, he writes of Coleridge,

> This was a man who might have turned
>   Hell into Heaven—and so in gladness
> A Heaven unto himself have earned;
> But he in shadows undiscerned
>   Trusted,—and damned himself to madness.
>   (383–87)

Shelley's failed geniuses are, in part, projected elements of himself
that he feels ambivalent about. Even Peter Bell has Shelleyan ele-
ments: the reviewers of Peter's work, savaging his moral character, ac-
cusing him of incest and adultery, sound like the reviewers of Shel-
ley's work; Peter's mind, "At once circumference and centre / Of all
he might or feel or know" (294–95), sounds like the *Alastor* Poet's.
The Coleridge character too sounds like Shelley when he speaks of
the divinity of poetry, "a light—a love," "A power which comes and
goes like dream" (389, 393). "So near grows Death to Life," says Mil-
ton's Adam of the two great trees in the Garden (4.425). Sometimes
in Shelley the distinction between the ideal and its double vanishes
completely. In *Athanase*, the narrator says of the hero's mysterious
melancholy, "And so his grief remained—let it remain—untold"
(124, *E*, 2:319). To this line Shelley appends a remarkable note: "The
Author was pursuing a fuller development of the ideal character of
Athanase, when it struck him that in an attempt at extreme refine-
ment and analysis, his conceptions might be betrayed into the as-
suming a morbid character." It is as if Spenser suddenly told us that
Una and Duessa might turn out to be the same person.

The most famous mode of doubleness is that of the second self. Shelley is fond of splitting his heroes: Verezzi-Zastrozzi, Wolfstein-Ginotti, Julian-Maddalo.[3] The *Alastor* Poet has numerous second selves. The Veiled Maid is a desired, completing double, a "spirit's mate," in the words of the early *The Retrospect* (60), as well as an idealized female embodiment of his own inner being. The illusory "fair fiend" (297) and the Spirit by the well are evil counselors embodying the ego-dystonic, while Ruin and Death are pursuers embodying the anticipation of punishment. The Narrator and Poet are alter egos, each a separate and real individual, and that type of doubling has a complex function in the poem. In "Mourning and Melancholia" Freud said that the ego must be able to regard itself as a detached object before it can unleash the aggression necessary to destroy itself (*SE*, 14:252). A person cannot kill himself unless he feels as if he is killing someone else, unless he feels, paradoxically, as if he is going to survive. Studying the double in more normative terms, Otto Rank saw in self-division a wish for immortality; if we have two selves, we may triumph over death.[4] The Natural Man dies, said Blake, but "The Real Man The Imagination . . . Liveth for Ever."[5] In a way, *Alastor* reverses Blake's formula, for one difference between the Narrator and the Poet is that the Poet dies. The Narrator takes it upon himself to mourn the death and create the poetic survival of the Poet. Despite his solicitude and advocacy, however, we can see him as presiding over a sacrifice of the hero so that he, who is much like him, can survive. But the Narrator's advocacy is not a false mask. The sacrifice and the celebration of the hero are traditional complements. In this case, the sacrifice of the scapegoat has a dual purpose. Shelley divides himself first in the hope of preserving himself from the consequences of imagination and desire at their most perilous and absolutist, and second in the hope of seeing those valued elements survive despite social disapproval and his own fear of them.

Another type of Shelleyan doubleness is duality of viewpoint, what Judith Chernaik has called Shelley's "double perception," both "mystic or visionary" and worldly or "rational" (29–30) and what Wasserman has called his "characteristic skeptical tendency to conceive of everything as open to ambivalent perspectives" (85). Although I have argued against a programmatic skepticism in *Alastor*, Wasserman's idea of doubleness works extremely well in the debate of *Julian and Maddalo*. Julian, representing Shelley himself, believes in the power of man over his own mind and his conditions, while Maddalo, representing Byron, considers man helplessly enchained and has "an intense apprehension of the nothingness of human life" (preface, *R*, 120). The speakers, Wasserman writes, are equally forceful, and the surrounding description supports the ambivalence: the day is "cheerful but cold" (34), the conversation "forlorn / Yet pleasing" (39–40). In visiting the Maniac, Julian and Maddalo are posing the question of which of them "is on the path to madness," and the ease with which commentators have been able to use the Maniac to support either vision, Wasserman continues, suggests that the ambivalence is final (73–75). The poem closes with a report of the Maniac's death and with Julian's refusal to tell the "cold world" the exact circumstances of the melancholy case (617), but also with the promising presence of Maddalo's young daughter, "a wonder of this earth," "Like one of Shakespeare's women" (590, 592).

While accepting Wasserman's philosophical description of doubleness in the poem, I would add a psychological description. If, as Wasserman argues, the Maniac's soliloquy confirms the visions of both Julian and Maddalo, that is, if both paths lead to madness, we can say that in the structure of their debate, each vision serves as a defense against the other's dangerous tendencies. Neither opponent wins the debate, and both survive, while the Maniac, the scapegoat who embodies the consequences of both their visions, is lost to insanity and death. Doubleness is here creative, preservative, dialectical; it serves to contain impulses that by themselves are troubling. The Maniac's speech, by contrast, is shot through with a tormenting doubleness: he is shadowed by "pale Pain" (324), mocked by ghastly presences, and forced to wear a "mask of falsehood" (308), and he has a "spirit's mate" (337) who personifies inconstancy. In this doubleness there is no dialectic of defense, only a haunted singleness. We see in this poem what a structure of reciprocal defense ultimately means to Shelley; in its absence, the mind collapses into madness.

In *Julian and Maddalo* we can observe too how skepticism and the mode of romance work together in a similar dialectic of defense. Skepticism is a negative mode; it destroys superstitions and discredits our ability to reach answers.[6] Romance, on the other hand, provokes in us a suspension of disbelief before its prolific spectacle of dreams, fantasies, and ideals. If romance in *Alastor* leads to death, skepticism saves us from that death. But skepticism itself is killing in its negations. Romance leads to oblivion but fills the emptiness of skepticism;

skepticism opens voids but saves us from falling into the abyss of romance. Each in relation to the other is a surge toward life; each carried to its own conclusion is a form of death. Julian says of the Lido,

> I love all waste
> And solitary places; where we taste
> The pleasure of believing what we see
> Is boundless, as we wish our souls to be.
> (14–17)

Romance turns the waste place into oceanic boundlessness, while skepticism reminds him that this is his own fiction; even so, he can love such fictions.[7] Skepticism and romance answer each other like infinite reflections in opposed mirrors. At the conclusion of the poem, Maddalo's Miranda-like daughter out of Shakespearean romance, on the one hand, and the vacancy of unanswered questions and failed human efforts and ideals, on the other, also defend against each other—although in this case the latter leaves the stronger impression. The dialectic of defense is not necessarily a match of equals. In *Julian and Maddalo* as a whole the skeptical tendency outweighs the romance, but the romance is present to exert a saving resistance.

In *The Witch of Atlas*, by contrast, the dialectic is weighted in favor of romance. The poem gives us a tour of a world of wonders before

> Error and Truth, had hunted from the earth
>   All those bright natures which adorned its prime,
> And left us nothing to believe in, worth
>   The pains of putting into learned rhyme.
> (51–54)

The Witch herself embodies the romance imagination with her magic powers, her marvelous deeds, and the visions she gives to humans. At her birth the mythic beings of nature come to pay their respects. In contrast to Milton's *Nativity Ode*, in which the birth of Jesus banishes the old daemons of pagan romance, this great birth is a culmination of romance. At the same time, the poem begins with an apology to Mary Shelley, who complained that it lacked human interest, and Shelley lightly defends it as a pure fiction, neither false nor true, a playful kitten without claws, a "visionary rhyme" (8). The poem ends with the poet promising to continue his heroine's adventures some other time,

> for it is
> A tale more fit for the weird winter nights
> Than for these garish summer days, when we
> Scarcely believe much more than we can see.
> (669–72)

This poem leaves us, above all, with a sense of wonders and marvels, while the skeptical detachment provides the resistance and the prolepsis.

Richard Harter Fogle writes that Shelley "is continually putting together Time and Eternity, Relative and Absolute, Fluctuating and Fixed, Seen and Unseen, to determine how they will relate and interact. The stress thus set up is the essential condition of his poetry, the climate in which it exists" (229–30). So in Plato Shelley admired "the rare union of close and subtle logic, with the Pythian enthusiasm of poetry" (preface to *The Banquet of Plato* [*The Symposium*], *C*, 336). In his attraction to opposites, we can see the largeness of his sympathies; we can also see a motive of healing and unifying; but we can additionally see another manifestation of defensive doubling. The dialectician can see the one and the many, says Socrates in the *Phaedrus*;[8] in Shelley such mobility saves us from a dangerous absorption in either pole of the antinomy. In *Nightmare Abbey*, Peacock portrayed his satirical Shelleyan hero, Scythrop, passing back and forth between his two ladies, Marionetta and Celinda, "like a shuttlecock" (62). In effect, Peacock was lampooning Shelley's way of thinking as well as his love life. Fogle writes that Shelley himself never quite succeeds in his own attempts at union (229). This may be because it is certain forms of doubleness that he is seeking, after all.[9]

Let us return to the reflections in the water. Often they suggest a second world, as in *Evening: Ponte al Mare, Pisa*:

> Within the surface of the fleeting river
> The wrinkled image of the city lay,
> Immovably unquiet, and forever
> It trembles, but it never fades away.
> (13–16, *H*, 654)

A favorite Shelleyan motif is the peacefulness and perfection of the world in the water. The reflection in the water is the object transformed by a sense of oceanic oneness with the mother. To see oneself in such a mirror is to experience oneself as a double entity, as an infant does in the mother-child dyad; it is also, in effect, to see oneself in the womb. In the *Defence*, poetry itself, as a purifying mirror, becomes a medium for recreating the world in the water.

The *Alastor* Poet tries patently to recreate that world by seeing his life reflected in the rivulet. But *Alastor* specializes in dissonant similes that make us aware of the gap between the compared terms. For example, the Poet's boat journey is described as follows:

> As one that in a silver vision floats
> Obedient to the sweep of odorous winds
> Upon resplendent clouds, so rapidly
> Along the dark and ruffled waters fled
> The straining boat.—A whirlwind swept it on.
> (316–20)

The simile expresses the wrenching conflict in a poem in which it is difficult to tell the difference between silver visions and self-destructive inner storms. Later in the Poet's voyage, another figure of dissonance appears as flowering parasites around the trees of the forest are compared first to "restless serpents" (438) and then to innocent infants. And just after the Poet's dream, Shelley gives us a wishful and self-questioning simile in which the relationship between the beautiful reflection in a lake and the black depths beneath is used to wonder whether, by inverse analogy, the loathsome face of death holds beyond it the paradise of vision (211–19). At the same time as sought likenesses are unfound, unsought ones are plentiful. Hope is like despair, flight is like pursuit, communion is like solitude. So Ovid's Narcissus asks, "Am I the lover / Or beloved? . . . Since I / Am what I long for, then my riches are / So great they make me poor" (book 3; 99).

Indeed, reflections in the poem, such as the one that is likened to man's immortal self, can be explicitly dangerous; and the idea of a world in the water in Shelley is not always idyllic, as, for example, in the instance of Venice sinking into the sea in *Lines written among the Euganean Hills* (115–20). Margaret Mahler has studied the crisis of rapprochement, a transitional stage between dependence and autonomy in which the child, in conflict between contradictory impulses, resists its growing separateness.[10] In this context the child's reflection would pleasurably reawaken its sense of the old dual unity. But the same reflection might also be treacherous in two ways. First, in reawakening the dyad, it might threaten to undo progress, and second, it might renew the feeling of the mutability of the mother, who originally fell away from the dyad to become a mere separate person and even, as it might seem, a rejecting one.[11] Heinz Kohut discusses the "mirroring" relationship of mother and child, the child's need to be reflected or acknowledged by its first love object.[12] In the dissonant similes of *Alastor,* a mirroring that should take place does not.

At least when the child deals with the other in the literal mirror he or she can control its movements and its comings and goings, and the pleasurable exercise of such control is a progressive tendency opposing the desire to enter the mirror of the dyad. Shelley brings both desires together in *Alastor* in a poetic world that with its blurred boundaries, its questioning similes, its sought and feared doubles, and its separations and convergences, including those of the Narrator and the hero, recalls those points in early development that, like rapprochement, are crises of transition. The world of the poem is reminiscent of a time of life when the relationship between one and two is tenuous, a time when the child can yearn both to move away from the mother and to go back to her, can feel both rejected by her and impeded or overwhelmed by her. In the poem, as in rapprochement, the emotional stress falls on the return to the dyad.

The conventionality of binary thinking does not by itself account for the sheer profusion and multivalence of doubling in Shelley. One great impulse within his poetic urge to create doubles is a desire to reproduce the dyad, even if he must find a shadow for every brightness. Even self-consciousness can take on the aura of the dyad: one becomes a mother to oneself. A second force driving Shelleyan doubleness is the need to create defensive structures. Ultimately, the defensive force defends specifically against the intense fascination with the dyad. The doubling of Poet and Narrator thus maintains a sense of differentiation that reacts against the self-destructive impulse toward merger and dissolution embodied by the Poet's quest.[13]

One final form of doubleness remains to be considered here. Narcissus lived on Helicon, mountain of the Muses, and we have seen that Shelley can think of poetry as a dyadic double, a purifying mirror or perfected uterine world. But poetry or art may also appear in Romanticism as another type of double, which we can call recreative, after the recreative, or active, repetition compulsion, in which the subject reproduces a disturbing event or pattern in order to master it.[14] An example in Blake is Golgonooza, the city of art and civilization, in which Los reclaims from nonentity the "spectres" fallen from eternity by giving them "semblances," or earthly forms, a first stage toward bringing them back to Eternal Life.[15] In Wordsworth, recreative doubling appears in the reflections of memory. Only in this doubling of experience is the full potentiality of the original realized: "I gazed—and gazed—but little thought / What wealth the show to me had brought."[16] In *The Prelude* such reflection is carried to a logical poetic conclusion as Wordsworth recreates his entire life. In Coleridge, the Primary Imagination is our repetition in the act of perception of God's creation of the world, while the Secondary Imagination, "re-create[s]" the world, giving life to its "fixed and dead" objects.[17] In all these cases, to reflect the reflections is not, as in Plato's vision of art, to compound our limitations but to progress to a higher state.

In *Alastor*, recreative doubling appears only implicitly in the act of Shelley's writing about a part of himself. In the relationship of the preface writer to the hero recreative doubling is hard to distinguish from defensive doubling. Unlike Blake, Wordsworth, and Coleridge, Shelley does not in *Alastor* exhibit an explicit, full-scale concept of recreative doubling. His urge to seize the original in unmediated form is too strong to allow for that.

5

The Sole Self

IN KEATS'S *ODE TO A NIGHTINGALE*, "THE FANCY CANNOT CHEAT SO WELL
/ As she is fam'd to do, deceiving elf" (73–74); she is a failed Queen
Mab, and the poet is tolled back from union with the nightingale in
the world of romance to his "sole self" (72). In Shelley too the sole
self is like the child exiled from the dyad. It can also be a source of
evil. Shelley's early letters are filled with diatribes against the sole self:
"I cannot endure the horror the evil which comes to self in solitude"
(1:77). Repeatedly he accuses himself of "egotising folly" (1:29),
apologizes for his "delirious Egotism," bids "adieu to egotism": "I am
sick to Death at the name of self" (1:34). He rails against not only
self-aggrandizement and morbid self-absorption but ordinary self-
gratification and self-expression as well. In Mary Shelley's journal he
notes, "The most exalted philosophy . . . consists in an habitual con-
tempt of self: a subduing of all angry feelings: a sacrifice of pride &
selfishness" (36). He writes to Hogg, "I am afraid there is selfishness
in the passion of Love . . . but I will feel no more! it is selfish—I would
feel for others" (1:36). Elsewhere he claims that by rejecting all fancy
and imagination, he has destroyed "all pleasure resulting to self"
(1:101). Enlightenment ideals of benevolence and disinterestedness
are at work in his wish "wholly to abstract our views from self"
(1:277), but so are peculiarly strong feelings of inner isolation and
self-revulsion. He writes that on a pleasurable visit to friends he has
"escaped . . . from the dismaying solitude of myself" (1:383).

According to the narrative fragment *The Coliseum*, we are all such
dismaying sole selves: "The internal nature of each being is sur-
rounded by a circle, not to be surmounted by his fellows; and it is this
repulsion which constitutes the misfortune of the condition of life"
(*C*, 227).[1] Trying to surmount that circle is one of Shelley's most per-

sistent concerns. In Godwin's utopia in *Political Justice*, "Every man will seek, with ineffable ardour, the good of all," and men "will know that they are members of the chain, that each has his several utility" (777). Shelley's version of the theme is still more extreme, as he envisions a new revolutionary spirit that "reconciles all private feelings to public utility" (*L*, 1:352).

But if Shelley dreams of totally reconciling the self with society, he dreams simultaneously of reconciling the self to itself. In the following, solitude is a confrontation both compelling and dreadful: "what [a] strange being I am, how inconsistent, in spite of all my bo[a]sted hatred of self—this moment thinking I could so far overcome Natures law as to exist in complete seclusion, the next shrinking from a moment of solitude, starting from my own company as it were that of a fiend, seeking any thing rather than a continued communion with *self*" (*L*, 1:77–78). We can understand why one of his most cherished ideals is self-esteem.

The protagonist of the early *The Solitary* is "an isolated thing" who "cannot love" and both longs and fears to end his miserable life (2, 10, *E*, 1:144). In later poems, however, the solitary receives a more complex treatment that includes idealization. It is the *Alastor* Poet's solitude that enables him to discover unknown beauties of nature, such as the final nook on the precipice: "One human step alone, has ever broken / The stillness of its solitude" (589-90). In *Laon and Cythna* solitude is a "wizard wild" of benevolent enchantments (2539, *E*, 2:167).

The solitary in *The Sensitive-Plant* embodies the poetical and the romantic as the *Alastor* Poet does but is also completely blameless. Isolated in a paradise of reciprocity, the Sensitive-Plant receives "more than all," but, with "small fruit" and no flower or smell, it cannot make any return (1.72, 70). As is often noted, the actual Sensitive-Plant, or mimosa, shrinks from the touch and is hermaphroditic. Shelley's Sensitive-Plant, however, is far from self-contained. Not only does it receive in abundance, but it "desires what it has not—the beautiful!" (1.77). Its love and its nature are intractably opposed. It alone has imagination, which sends its yearnings outward, but it alone has no creative capacity, which keeps it locked within itself.

In *Mazenghi* (*E*, 2:354), the solitary is unambiguously heroic, even a misunderstood savior. Mazenghi is a Florentine exile who finds refuge in a pestilential seaside marsh, which his resourcefulness turns into an Eden. He tames the animals and learns the secrets of

nature; he also communes "with the immeasurable world," and his
mind develops new "powers and thoughts" (142, 151, *E*, 2:360). Here
imagination is not a curse but a salvation. Nor does it stand in oppo-
sition to relationship with "his own kind" (168, *E*, 2:360): the poem is
incomplete, but in the original story Albert Mazenghi sees an invad-
ing ship and warns the city that has cast him out.

Like *Alastor, One word is too often profaned* shows a disturbing con-
nection between a passionate sensitivity to ideal love and an inability
to love in a common way:

> I can give not what men call love,—
>   But wilt thou accept not
> The worship the heart lifts above
>   And the Heavens reject not,
> The desire of the moth for the star,
>   Of the night for the morrow,
> The devotion to something afar
>   From the sphere of our sorrow.
>   (9–16)

In *The Aziola,* too (*H,* 642), we find at the origin of the sublime a
movement away from relationship. In the poem Mary asks the poet if
he hears the Aziola cry; the poet assumes the Aziola is "some tedious
woman" (6), but when he learns it is an owl, he is elated "to know
that it was nothing human, / No mockery of myself to fear or hate"
(8–9). He has heard that cry before, but it takes, as it were, a sudden
moment of unrecognition to bring home to him the sublime poten-
tialities of the Aziola's unlikeness to himself or to anybody else: "Sad
Aziola! from that moment I / Loved thee and thy sad cry" (20–21).

In "On Narcissism" and "Mourning and Melancholia," Freud de-
scribed two related types of solitude; he sought the workings of nar-
cissism in, among other phenomena, the egoism and self-observing
character of dreams and the workings of melancholy in grief. In *Alas-
tor* Shelley portrays a solitude of dreamlike vision; in *Athanase* he de-
picts a solitude of sadness. Like Mazenghi, the noble-spirited Athan-
ase loves and works for humanity; in addition, he has many friends
who try to analyze his problems, with more sympathy than Job's
Comforters but with no better results, and he also has a deep friend-
ship with an old philosopher, Zonoras. Even so, he is isolated by a
"grief, which ne'er in other minds / A mirror found" (75–76, *E*,
2:317), and which he himself cannot fathom. Freud's melancholy of

grief for a lost object is evident in the poem. In a fragment of the un-
finished piece Zonoras suggests that the sorrow may be rooted in un-
returned love, and another fragment describes a woman whose eyes
are like the moon, or mutability (19–24, 1–3, *E*, 2:325, 328).

But solitude in *Athanase* is not purely associated with grief. Cele-
brating the springtime intoxications of eros, the narrator asks, "How
many a one, though none be near to love, / Loves then the shade of
his own soul half seen / In any mirror" (12–14, *E*, 2:326). Narcissism
here is not a distortion of eros but one expression among others of
its irresistible and universal joy. In Shelley's ambivalence over his soli-
tary heroes, we can see a conflict over narcissism itself.

Although narcissism—the libidinal investment of the self, in
Heinz Hartmann's definition[2]—is often regarded as a regressive re-
placement of object relations brought on by danger, frustration, or
loss, Heinz Kohut proposes that many culturally valuable attitudes
and forms of behavior represent not conversions of narcissistic libido
into object libido but transformations of narcissism in its own sepa-
rate current of development. Kohut calls artistic creation, for exam-
ple, the attempt of artists "to re-create a perfection which formerly
was directly an attribute of their own; during the act of creation . . .
they do not relate to their work in the give-and-take mutuality which
characterizes object love."[3] Even empathy is a development of narcis-
sism, founded on the "primary empathy with the mother."[4] For
Kohut, the sense of identity depends on narcissism; Irvine Schiffer
describes the self in Kohut as a continuous "structure in the mind
cathected with instinctual energy" (64). Further, our achievement of
a "cosmic narcissism," an identification with eternity, in which we
recreate our "primordial experience of the mother," enables us to
come to some acceptance of transience and death and attain a wise
steadfastness.[5] Kohut writes that a transformed narcissism even en-
hances object libido, since a person with a firm and cohesive self is
"better able to offer his love . . . without undue fear of rejection."[6]

Shelley, however, has great difficulty in accepting any narcissism
within himself. Spenser's Britomart first sees her future love in a
glassy globe, and Keats's Endymion sees in a pool not his own face
but the face of the actual goddess he will finally join. These cases ex-
press a faith that love, even at its most visionary, passes outward from
its self-centered beginnings to others. But *Alastor* expresses a fear
that a certain destructive narcissism may be inevitable within eros, at
least at its most extreme, as well as within the poetic vocation. No

such fear appears in Blake with his exultant desire to make his own poetic world replace common nature: "If the Spectator could Enter into these Images in his Imagination . . . then would he arise from his Grave then would he meet the Lord in the Air & then he would be happy."[7] And Wordsworth finds a powerful way of safely expressing a poetic narcissism, or "egotistical sublime,"[8] large enough to drive the first epic-length verse autobiography in history: he encloses that narcissism within a frame of reverence for nature, and he recurrently exhibits the sole self being lovingly chastened, subdued, corrected by nature. But in Shelley a powerful tendency toward narcissism—both the oceanic feeling of primal narcissism and the self-absorption of secondary narcissism—is so hard to admit that it sometimes provokes, by reaction, a condemnation of any self-investment at all: "I will feel no more! it is selfish." In *Alastor* Shelley makes an ambivalent attempt to sacrifice the compelling narcissism that he senses within both art and love. That the self-centered conditions of Athanase and the Maniac in *Julian and Maddalo* are treated with less ambivalent sympathy suggests that the introversion of grief is less morally provocative to him than the introversion of ecstasy.

The Shelleyan solitary is not only superior to others; he is also beyond their influence. The *Alastor* Poet is uninterested in the help and love offered by others; Athanase is far above others, willing to take seriously only the words of his teacher, Zonoras; the Maniac is oblivious even to the presence of others. In Freud, narcissism limits "susceptibility to influence" (*SE*, 14:73); in narcissism, libidinal interest is withdrawn from objects, as in the normative and pathological cases, respectively, of sleep and psychosis. Within Shelley's own receptiveness to influence we can sense a distinct vulnerability. He wrote, for example, of his discontent in the company of Byron and his circle; he himself "belonging to the order of mimosa thrives ill in so large a society" (*L*, 2:368). The self-enclosed solitary, however, may seem secure from destructive external influences of any kind; Athanase's name means "deathless." But "the most touchy point in the narcissistic system," Freud writes, is its illusion of immortality (14:91).

Shelley's solitaries stand out from their surroundings not only in their isolation but also in their extreme or obsessive characteristics. They are not like anyone else. In *On Christianity*, he writes, "Every human mind has, what Lord Bacon calls its *idola specus*, peculiar images which reside in the inner cave of thought. These constitute the essential and distinctive character of every human being" (*M*, 261). This is not quite what Bacon meant. In Bacon, such idols—individual predilections—are obstructions in the search for truth, but Shelley is not using the concept censoriously. In *Alastor*, the Poet's essential and distinctive character consists in his idolatry or obsession. In studying doubleness we observed Shelley's attraction to the dyad and his less evident need to create structures—defensive doubles—that guard against that attraction. Here, studying singleness, we observe Shelley's attack on the sole self and at the same time an attraction to it that he often finds difficult to accept. The impulses toward singleness and doubleness can also function in concert. Although the separate self is opposed to the dyad, the solitary is what a Shelleyan character becomes in pursuing the dyad. The figure of the sole self can be the vehicle of two contrary wishes: the wish to differentiate oneself or guard one's individuality and the wish to regain oceanic union.

The Shelleyan solitary is often the possessor of a secret. Athanase has his secret grief; the Maniac has his unknown, traumatic past. The *Alastor* Poet pursues the secrets of nature and civilization until he discovers a secret part of himself; the dream is the birth of his inner world in its full being, and for the rest of his life he tries to find his way into that unknown inwardness, Sleep's Paradise. When the protagonist of *The Solitary* speaks, "the cold words flow not from his soul" (14, *E*, 1:144); his inwardness is beyond the reach of his words. Athanase's grief is "untold" (124, *E*, 2:319); not only the hero but also the text has a secret, unspoken part. The Maniac speaks a great deal, but he too, not daring "To give a human voice to my despair" and frustrated by "How vain" words are, is gripped by an "incommunicable woe" (305, 472, 343). Like *Athanase, Julian and Maddalo* is also a secretive text about a secretive character; at its close, Maddalo's daughter "told me how / All happened—but the cold world shall not know" (616–17). *Julian and Maddalo* moves from a dialogue of friends to a monologue of a solitary to silence. As for the *Alastor* Poet, although he enchants those who hear "his passionate notes" (61), he at the same time is said to sing "in solitude" (60) and his final fate is to be "unremembered" (671); his is a great poetry that we will never know.

Shelley was personally gregarious and voluble, but in his poetry the difficulty of expression and communication and the reservation of speech are recurrent motifs. Frequently the unspoken is the elusive or the inexpressibly beautiful, as in the following fragment:

My thoughts arise and fade in solitude—
The verse that would invest them melts away
Like moonlight in the beam of spreading day—
How beautiful they were—how firm they stood
Freckling the starry sky like woven pearl!—

(*E*, 1:550)

In *Alastor*, the Veiled Maid's own poetry builds toward a rapture beyond words: "The eloquent blood told an ineffable tale" (168). But in *Julian and Maddalo* the unspoken is the unspeakable: the Maniac offers himself and his lady as models for those "Who intend deeds too dreadful for a name" (456). Another sense of the unspoken appears in *Alastor* when the Poet, moved by his sight of the swan, speaks of its "dying notes" (286). The legend that the mute swan sings only at its death is provocative in the context of Shelleyan silence, suggesting that there is something dangerous in verbalization; to speak is to die. Indeed, all three of the Poet's speeches concern his own imminent death.

Margaret Mahler stresses that the acquisition of speech is a major step from symbiotic unity with the mother toward autonomy.[9] If that unity is figured as a lost glory, then we can understand one sense in which to speak is to die; and so in the *Immortality Ode* our continuing allegiance to our pre-earthly existence can make "Our noisy years seem moments in the being / Of the eternal Silence" (159–60). Shelley darkens the theme; in *The Cenci*, in which nearly all the characters lie, the passage into language is associated with moral violation; Beatrice Cenci is said to be "pure as speechless infancy" (5.2.69).

Keats in the Cave of Quietude in *Endymion* imagines a "Dark paradise" within the "native hell" of our inner being, where a sleep both desolate and pleasurable may be found (4.538, 523). This Keatsian unconscious has benevolent possibilities, as do sleep and unconsciousness generally in this poem. But Shelley, as eager as he was to make the voyage of descent into his own mind, had no faith that he might find there even a dark paradise. When he set out in the *Catalogue of the Phenomena of Dreams* to describe his dreams, before long he broke off in "thrilling horror."[10] *Alastor* shows us the Spirit of Solitude in ambivalent form. Elsewhere that spirit was associated with a dreadful self-confrontation, and to be alone was specifically to be alone with a secret too elusive or too terrible to verbalize.

6

The Voyage
to the Source

. . . Could the morning shafts of purest light
Again into the quivers of the Sun
Be gathered—could one thought from its wild flight
Return into the temple of the brain
   Without a change, without a stain,—
   Could aught that is, ever again
   Be what it once has ceased to be:
      Greece might again be free!
      —from Fragments written for *Hellas* (*H*, 648)[1]

THE THEME OF A RETURN TO THE SOURCE HAUNTS SHELLEY'S POETRY.
He even raises the question of survival apart from the source: he
writes of Athanase that his life "Was failing like an unreplenished
stream" (59, *E*, 2:316). A particularly fierce and pessimistic recasting
of the *Immortality Ode* puts it more dramatically: "When the lamp is
shattered / The light in the dust lies dead" (*H*, 667).

In his search for a lost glory, the *Alastor* Poet journeys eastward to
the Indian Caucasus, traditional birthplace of humanity, and his last
moments are taken up with "images of the majestic past" (629). But
even before the dream of the Veiled Maid the Poet has been travel-
ing into the past toward "The thrilling secrets of the birth of time"
(128). From the start his journey takes him from vale to dell to bower
to nook; he goes from one womb to another. Seeking nature's "cra-
dle, and his sepulchre" (430), he enters a cleft mountain and travels,
as it were, inside the body of the Great Parent until he finds her final
bower.[2] The dream intensifies and sexualizes a regressive quest that
has preoccupied him from the very beginning, a quest in which the

Poet leaves his "alienated home" (76) to find home, in which he seeks an exoticness that is, as in Freud's Uncanny, a return of the familiar. He does at the very end come to a uterine place of repose, although one that is provocatively located beside a precipice over which "homeless" waters plunge into the void (566).

Doubleness is thus only one expression of Shelley's fascination with the dyad; the motif of the voyage to the source can lead us deeper into the meaning and power of regression in his work. We can see, for example, an oral need in the Poet's quest. He is recurrently described in images of thirst: "The fountains of divine philosophy / Fled not his thirsting lips" (71–72); "He drinks deep of the fountains of knowledge, and is still insatiate," and his mind "thirsts for intercourse with an intelligence similar to itself" (R, 72–73). Thomas Weiskel sees in him an "anxiety of deprivation" (144). The Poet's death scene, by contrast, is characterized by an imagery of liquid abundance and replenishment; the moon "poured / A sea of lustre" that "overflowed [the] mountains": "Yellow mist / Filled the unbounded atmosphere, and drank / Wan moonlight even to fulness" (602–6). The relationship between the sinking Poet and the sinking moon, with its drinkable moonlight, is like that between a nursing infant and its mother;[3] indeed, the horizontal crescent is reduced to "two lessening points of light" (654), like nipples. We can thus understand the tranquillity of the Poet in his final bower. At last the moonlight is completely "quenched" (658), and so, in two ways, is the Poet: his thirst is slaked, and he dies. His death is, paradoxically, both a final separation from and a final merger with the Great Parent. In death he is described as empty and desiccated, no longer nourished by a source: a cloud at night once "fed" with sunbeams, "a dream / Of youth" now "Still, dark, and dry" (663, 669–71).

Complementary to the imagery of thirst and quenching is a persistent imagery of waste and scattering. The hero wanders in "Many a wide waste" (78) and on the "ocean's mountainous waste" (342), and he himself is "wasting these surpassing powers / In the deaf air" (288–89). "The desolated tombs / Of Parthian kings scatter to every wind / Their wasting dust" (242–44); the Poet "Scatter[s his] music on the unfeeling storm" (597); the stream plunges over the last precipice, "Scattering its waters to the passing winds" (570).[4] Anterior to the anxiety of deprivation in the poem is an anxiety of expense. It is as if psychic supplies, or a sense of internal sufficiency and power, were bodily fluids and these supplies were felt to be fi-

nite. Nor does the subject feel that he can regenerate his own sup-
plies. Through the poem runs a fantasy of redressing expenditures
of energy at the original source of nourishment, the breast. This psy-
chic economy, in which we are in danger of running out of limited
or ephemeral reserves, may seem idiosyncratic, but it is related to a
typical Romantic concern, the search for, in Wordsworth's terms,
"something evermore about to be," or, in Blake's terms, the "Pro-
lific,"[5] the search, that is, for some plenitude or some sustaining prin-
ciple of being. The search is particularly intense in Shelley, who was
as lavish in his poetic expenditures of imagery and emotion as he was
in his personal expenditures of energy and commitment in his fran-
tic, supercharged life.

The problem of how, given such expenditures, to conserve or re-
plenish supplies is an issue throughout his poetry, and we can ob-
serve him trying out many answers. One such answer is a fantasied re-
gression to the source of supplies. In his translation of a passage
from Virgil's Fourth *Georgic,* this takes the form of an actual descent
into the water:

> And the cloven waters like a chasm of mountains
> Stood, and received him in its mighty portal
> And led him through the deep's untrampled
>   fountains.
>
> He went in wonder through the halls immortal
> Of his great Mother and her humid reign . . .
>   (1–5, *E,* 2:363)

Another answer is the pursuit of the infinite. "So long as it is possible
for his desires to point towards objects thus infinite and unmea-
sured, he is joyous, and tranquil and self-possessed," the preface says
of the Poet (*R,* 73). Another is the guardedness of some Shelley
poems, the sense, implicit or, as in *Julian and Maddalo* and *Athanase,*
explicit, that they are withholding something from us. A secret or the
missing answer of a riddle is something not yet spent, something ev-
ermore about to be.

Still another response to the anxiety of expense is the fascination
with narcissism. In narcissism, Freud writes, a depleted ego is re-en-
riched by the "withdrawal of libido from its objects." Freud writes fur-
ther that "another person's narcissism has a great attraction for those
who have renounced part of their own narcissism and are in search

of object-love"[6]—and perhaps particularly for those others who ex-
perience an anxiety of deprivation or expense. The unfinished *Yet
look on me* is Shelley's rendition of the same theme:

> Yet look on me—take not thine eyes away
> Which feed upon the love within mine own
> Although it be but the reflected ray
> Of thy sweet beauty from my spirit thrown.
> Yet speak to me! thy voice is as the tone
> Of my heart's echo, and I think I hear
> That thou yet lovest me—yet thou alone
> Like one before a mirror, [? take no] care
> Of aught but thine own [? form] imaged too truly there.
> And yet I wear out life in watching thee,
> A toil so sweet at times, and thou indeed
> Art kind when I am sick, and pity me . . .
>
> (1–12, *E*, 2:652)

In this connection of narcissism and supplies we may recall that Nar-
cissus fell in love with his reflection when he bent down to the water
to quench his thirst. We may further recall that this was a return to
the origin for him, for his mother had been raped in the water by a
river-god.

The voyage to the source is also in Shelley an intellectual quest for
an answer or secret. The *Alastor* Poet is typical of Shelleyan heroes in
being, in the words of *An Allegory*, "by more curious humour led"
than most human beings (12, *H*, 624). In a notebook *Note on Shake-
speare*, Shelley meditates on a line from *Oedipus Rex*, which he trans-
lates as "Coming to many [paths] in the wanderings of careful
thought."[7] Oedipus has been thinking specifically about what he can
do to save his city, but Shelley seems to have more in mind the later
Oedipus, who "was destined to wander, blind & askin[g] Charity."[8]
He writes that in Sophocles' image the mind is "a wilderness of intri-
cate paths . . . which he, who seeks some . . . knowledge with respect
to what he ought to do, searches throughout, as he would search the
external universe for some valued thing which was hidden from him
upon its surface." There follows a reference to "the dim ghost of an
imagination which now is dead for want of breathing the native air in
which it was con[ceived & born]."[9] The search for knowledge is for
Shelley, as for the investigator Oedipus, a search for a remedy. It is
also a search for home; to know the secret is to return to the secret

place, the native place. Oedipus, Géza Róheim observes, does finally return to his mother since he is both born and dies in places sacred to the earth goddess.[10]

As a quest for a secret, the voyage to the source appears in Shelley's fascination with science, the problem of causality, and such figures as Bacon and Lucretius. Virgil called Lucretius "happy in having understood the causes of things."[11] Bacon sought "a way at length into [the] inner chambers" of nature, and the foundation of his New Atlantis was "the knowledge of Causes, and secret motions of things."[12] In *Queen Mab* Shelley pays tribute to a coming "omnipotence of mind, / Which from its dark mine drags the gem of truth" (8.236–37); a regressive voyage into a concave darkness is the way to cultural progress.

Curiosity leads Shelley forward to the end as well as back to the beginning. It even tempts the protagonist of *Ye hasten to the grave* to suicide: "Thou vainly curious mind which wouldest guess / Whence thou didst come, and whither thou must go" (6–7, *H*, 625).[13] In *A Summer Evening Churchyard*, Shelley compares himself to an "enquiring child" as he wonders about the "secrets" of the "wormy beds" below (27, 29, 22, *E*, 1:453). In *Alastor* before the dream the work of the inquiring mind is divided between the Narrator, who is interested in the secrets of death, and the Poet, who is interested in the secrets of origin; but as the Poet pursues his quest, birth and death increasingly merge for him, as he seeks his sepulchre and nature's cradle. As Shelley puts it in a later fragment, "The babe is at peace within the womb / The corpse is at rest within the tomb / We begin in what we end" (*E*, 2:711).

Often in Shelley the search for answers is impeded, as, for example, by the limits of language: "How vain is it to think that words can penetrate the mystery of our being!" (*On Life, R*, 506). Often we find Shelley attacking precisely that search for the deep cause that elsewhere fascinates him: "There is a disposition in the human mind to seek the cause of whatever it contemplates. What cause is, no philosopher has succeeded in explaining, and the triumph of the acutest metaphysician has been confined to demonstrating it to be inexplicable" (*On Polytheism, C*, 337). And often the pursuit of curiosity is attended by retributive danger. In the *Speculations on Morals and Metaphysics*, thought "is like a river whose rapid and perpetual stream flows outwards—like one in dread who speeds through the recesses of some haunted pile and dares not look behind" (*C*, 186).

In a notebook fragment about a writer named Lionel, or Shelley himself, an imaginary critic complains of the difficulty of extracting any central meaning from Lionel's mad, mazelike subtlety: "If we could for the sake of some truth [as] fair as Ariadne vanquish the monster of his thought, I fear lest we should find no thread to guide us back thro the labyrinths which led us to its den."[14] To enter his own mind, Shelley suggests, would be to discover a monster.

One may think of this monster of thought when one reads Shelley on the question of remembrance. Unlike Wordsworth, Shelley does not typically idealize memory, which may seem strange in one enchanted by returns. Indeed, he tends to represent it as a pain-giving faculty. In *Home*, memory embitters our "earliest hopes and joys" (1, *H*, 535); in *Wilt thou forget the happy hours*, memories "make the heart a tomb" (9, *E*, 2:710);[15] a lyric of abandonment and desolation is called *Remembrance* (*H*, 643). In Wordsworth, memory can transport the mind to a time before loss, but in Shelley it does not go back that far. The case against memory is even stronger in *An Ode: Written October, 1819, Before the Spaniards Had Recovered Their Liberty*, in which Shelley writes, "Ye were injured, and that means memory" (35, *H*, 576). At times Shelley gives the impression that to return to the source would be to find something unbearable.

The Poet's regressive journey is similarly attended by the threat of destruction. We have seen that while the stream that the Poet follows plunges into nothingness, his own path diverges into a "green recess," which is as much a place of death as the precipice: as soon as he enters, "he knew that death / Was on him" (625–27). Here is a serene womb-death rather than a violent and meaningless scattering, but here also are a few more moments of life. Indeed, the Poet has repeatedly escaped or rejected immediate death, as if not only to find the one right form of death but also to keep living. Twice he is "Suspended" (362) at the top of a wave that pauses before crashing down, and each time he avoids destruction in the "bursting mass" (348). In the dream he is embraced by the Veiled Maid's "dissolving arms" (187), and then sleep, "Like a dark flood suspended in its course, / Rolled back its impulse" (190–91). Later a "strong impulse" (274) urges him to the seashore, a "restless impulse" (304) drives him onto the sea, and a "strong impulse" (415) will not let him rest among the narcissi. His voyage after the dream seems like a journey from an impulse to its discharge. The impulse is associated with ecstasy, dissolution, sleep, and death, and the discharge is recurrently postponed. We can see in the Poet's journey both a quest for more life and a quest for perfect repose, and we can also see in it the resistance of an ego for which more life means not magical supplies but self-preservation.

The Poet's voyage of curiosity and regression is, again, partly successful; he does reach places heretofore hidden from humanity, and he finds a serenity not unlike that of Oedipus in the grove of the Earth Mother at Colonus. As one who discovers and violates secret places and who acts out repressed regressive wishes, he must be sacrificed. Ultimately, however, Shelley wanted more than a scapegoat hero. He was, as Daniel Hughes puts it, concerned with "a cleansing, a redeeming" of the origin.[16] The Poet returns to the source, but he does not make it his own; he does not change it in any way. At his greatest, the hero, as Joseph Campbell has studied his archetypal career, returns from his great voyage with a boon for his society (246). But the Poet reaches the origin and dies, both as a man and as a poet. He seeks to return to the source with full consciousness; he begins his quest wishing for the Veiled Maid "beyond the realms of dream" (206), or in waking experience. But instead of raising the unconscious to consciousness or even further to the poetic imagination, he is submerged into unconsciousness; he too becomes hidden from us. The bower in which he concludes his search looks out over a panorama of the world in what is figuratively a neonate's prospect from the body of the mother; but this inhabitant of the womb does not seem about to go anywhere else. Whatever Nirvana belongs to his destiny, he has already reached it in the bower. In *Alastor* the origin is found, but there is no rebirth.

As a complete poem, *Alastor* is born in reaction to a sense of the deathwardness of regression. Regression in the poem is not in the service of the ego, nor is there any sense that it might be. At the same time regression provides the poem with its basic energy; more precisely, a deep conflict over regression is at the poem's emotional origin. Shelley's own later comment about *Alastor* can be disputed aesthetically, but its psychological accuracy is poignant: "What has become of my poem?" he wrote Peacock from Geneva. "I hope it has already sheltered itself in the bosom of its mother, Oblivion, from whose embraces no one could have been so barbarous as to tear it except me" (*L*, 1:490).

7

Psychosexual Patterns
in *Alastor*

Some of us have in a prior existence been in love with
an Antigone, & that makes us find no full content in
any mortal tie.

—Letter to John Gisborne, 2:668

ONE MAJOR DIFFERENCE BETWEEN THE DAEMONIC VISITATION IN *QUEEN
Mab* and that in *Alastor* is that the latter is an erotic experience. Inso-
far as the dream of seduction leads to the Poet's death—indeed, im-
mediately makes him think of death—it would be difficult not to at-
tribute much of the poem's complexity and melancholy to its
sexualization of the theme of imagination.

Shelley typically portrays sex in exalted terms. In *Rosalind and
Helen*, for example, lovers become "One soul of interwoven flame, /
A life in life, a second birth / In worlds diviner far than earth" (979–
81, *E*, 2:296). Sex has an opposite effect, however, in *The Sunset* (*E*,
1:509), which ends with a woman waking after a night of love to find
her lover dead. Here, even more directly than in *Alastor*, sexual rap-
ture is fatal.

In *Rosalind and Helen* sex is perilous as well as sublime. The title
characters meet in a dell, compared to a primitive fane and once
haunted by a child, a lady-fiend, and "The ghost of a youth with
hoary hair" (151, *E*, 2:274), an old young man, a version of the *puer
senex* archetype, like the Poet, Athanase, Ahasuerus, and Ginotti.[1] In
life, the youth and the lady had been incestuous siblings who used
the dell for their trysts; it was there that a mob seized them, together
with their child, to be killed.

In this spot Rosalind and Helen exchange stories. Rosalind was engaged to marry a young man when she discovered that he was her brother; the shock of the revelation killed him. Helen loved a revolutionary, whom she cared for in his mother's home after an imprisonment, playing his mother's harp to soothe him, but he died in her embrace. Their son survived, however, and meets Rosalind's daughter by the man, a tyrant and miser, whom she married after her brother's death. The son and daughter grow up as companions, and in their eventual union "their parents saw / The shadow of the peace denied to them" (1290–91, *E*, 2:305).

As we pass from one couple to the next—the legendary brother and sister, Rosalind and her brother-lover, Helen and the lover to whom she is a substitute mother, and the two children—we witness a progressive sublimation from outright incest to desired but avoided incest to unwedded love with incestuous overtones to the idealized love of two similar though unrelated children who are brought up together. The fanelike dell is consecrated by incest and its punishment. There stories of forbidden love may be revealed, and within it resides a power both terrible and healing.

An idealization of forbidden love also appears in the unfinished *The Zucca*, in which the poet is filled with *Sehnsucht*: "I loved, I know not what—but this low sphere / And all that it contains, contains not thee, / Thou, whom, seen nowhere, I feel everywhere" (20–22, *H*, 665).[2] In his wanderings he sees a dying plant, "Like one who loved beyond his nature's law, / And in despair had cast him down to die" (43–44). Contrary to *Rosalind and Helen*, the poem moves from sublimated eros, obscure and transcendent, to tabooed sexuality. *The Zucca* breaks off with the poet taking the plant home to nurse it back to health. This development suggests not a sacrifice of the forbidden impulse but an effort to keep it alive and untransformed.

The Veiled Maid in *Alastor* is a succubus, and Ernest Jones has interpreted the incubus/succubus fantasy as the "imaginary fulfilment of certain repressed wishes for sexual intercourse, with the parents."[3] Leslie Brisman writes that the Poet, who "has been preoccupied with the search for origin, 'poring on memorials / Of the world's youth' " (121–22), turns in his dream "to the origins of sexual love in his own mental memorials of youthful dissolution into a maternal embrace."[4] The dream of the Veiled Maid occurs immediately after the Poet has not responded to the sexual availability of the Arab maiden. As the narrative passes from Arab maiden to Veiled Maid, a sexual object becomes ideal through being made over into a specifically incestuous object.

To the moon and the Great Parent Nature we can add the Veiled Maid as another epiphany of the maternal imago. Herein lies the coherence of a poem in which nature and imagination seem both opposed and confused, for both the Poet's pursuit of his visionary love and the Narrator's pursuit of the mysteries of nature are driven by the same incestuous desire. As Brisman puts it, "The Poet's dream brings to a climax the narrator's own yearning" for a "great Mother."[5] "I have loved / Thee ever, and thee only," the Narrator tells the "Mother of this unfathomable world" (19–20, 18). In his quest for her "inmost sanctuary" (38) he is the antithesis of Shelley's Peter Bell, who "touched the hem of Nature's shift" but "never dared uplift / The closest, all-concealing tunic" (315–17). In destroying the visionary hero and preserving the nature-worshipping Narrator, the poem sacrifices the desire for the mother in one guise so that it may be continued in another.

The theme of incest, frequent in Romanticism, found a particularly strong "correspondent breeze" in Shelley. He calls incest "like many other *incorrect* things a very poetical circumstance. It may be the excess of love or of hate. It may be . . . the highest heroism" or "cynical rage" and "selfishness" (*L*, 2:154). Incest is a paradigm of the kind of situation that typically compels his fascination, one in which the extremes of the ideal and the morbid meet. And yet in the case of *Athanase*, Shelley claims that something beyond incest lies at the root of his hero's melancholy; he speaks of "Tears bitterer than the blood of agony" of "those who love their kind, and therefore die" (303, 305–6, *E*, 2:325). What lies beyond incest in Shelley, so unacceptable to him that, unlike incest, it cannot break through into poetic themes and images, at least idealized ones?

In character the Veiled Maid, a female similitude of the Poet, is much more like a sister than a mother. Explicit parent-child incest appears rarely in Shelley, and when it does it is never "a very poetical circumstance": in *The Witch of Atlas*, "Incestuous Change bore to her father Time" the "cruel Twins," Error and Truth (49–51); Beatrice Cenci is raped by her father, an act presented as the most monstrous of crimes. But sibling incest is frequent and always idealized. In the antinomian paradise described in *The Assassins*, a young brother and sister play with a pet snake, which "leaped into her bosom" and "glided" from one to the other (*M*, 139). In *Misery*, the speaker and

Misery are like a sister and brother, and the speaker proposes a "bridal bed— / Underneath the grave," where no one can forbid their love (41–42, *E*, 2:704). In *Alastor* when the quest for the maternal is explicitly sexualized, the poem's ideal female object is changed from a maternal Nature to a sisterly Veiled Maid; then, with the Poet seeking nature's cradle, the object becomes increasingly maternal again. Quasi-sibling incest seems to screen a more deeply desired and feared parental relationship.[6] It may even serve as an actual defense against parental incest. We can call it a homeopathic defense, a fighting of fire with fire.

Certainly in his life Shelley cultivated friendships with idealized older women, just as he cultivated literary fathers. In a letter to Hogg—in which he also sends his regards to the Boinvilles, "especially" the mother, and calls the statue of Niobe and her children in Florence his favorite of all pieces of sculpture—he writes, "I have been fortunate enough to make acquaintance here with a most interesting woman [Lady Mount Cashell], in whose society we spend a great part of our time. She is married, and has two children; her husband is, what husbands too commonly are, far inferior to her . . . You will have some idea of the sort of person, when I tell you that I am now reading with her the 'Agamemnon' of Aeschylus" (2:186). Hogg did have an idea of the sort of person Shelley was involved with, although not the idea Shelley consciously had in mind: "I am amused by what you say of the fair Grecian with whom you read the 'Agamemnon' of Aeschylus," he wrote back. "When you have finished that Tragedy, read with the lady (whom, as you have not named, I must call Clytemnestra) the 'Electra' of Sophocles, that you may be deterred from following the example of Aegisthus" (2:188).[7]

In *Alastor* the mother is evident not only in the Great Parent, the Veiled Maid, the moon, and the entire natural setting of seas, forests, nooks, and cleft mountains, but also in the wind. The wind appears as the breath of the Great Parent, which the Narrator, like a "long-forgotten lyre," awaits to inspire his song (42); the storms and whirlwinds that drive the voyager, "floating among the winds" (592); the autumn winds that sweep fallen leaves into nature's last bower; and the winds that scatter the Poet's music to oblivion. At the end, the dead Poet is, like the Narrator at the outset, an abandoned lute, on which "The breath of heaven did wander" (668). Both inspiring breath and "unfeeling storm" (597), the wind, like the moon, is an inconstant mother.[8] In "On Narcissism," Freud made a famous distinction between the anaclitic love object, the one who cares for us, and the narcissistic love object, the one who resembles us (*SE*, 14:87–88). A narcissistic object choice is often made after loss or in anticipation of loss; when commitment to an external object seems perilous, it may seem advantageous to restrict libido to the self or what resembles the self. In *Alastor*, when desire for the mother appears, so too does the anxiety of losing her; the anaclitic object is not to be trusted. In moving from the Arab maiden, who tends the Poet, to the Veiled Maid, who resembles him, the poem not only turns the unrelated woman into a kindred one but also, as a further step, makes over an anaclitic object into a narcissistic one. Thus the transference to an object that is, in part, sisterly may be not only a defense against a more fearsome maternal incest but also a criticism of the mother.

֍ ֍ ֍

The day after his dream the Poet "kept mute conference / With his still soul." However,

> At night the passion came,
> Like the fierce fiend of a distempered dream,
> And shook him from his rest, and led him forth
> Into the darkness. . . .
>
> (223–27)

This sounds like a lyrical description of compulsive masturbation— not that the Poet literally tries to recapture the spirit of the wet dream through masturbation but that his cyclical, obsessive behavior has the same emotional quality. It is not surprising that Shelley, who tried to be frank about sexual issues, should, intentionally or not, include symbolic hints of masturbation within a poem about adolescent sexual fantasy. Sexual dream and fantasy is a recurrent topic in his writing.[9] A "distempered dream" is also what he calls an unfinished love poem, its vision vanishing "at the cold clear light of morning. Its surpassing excellence and exquisite perfections have no more reality than the colour of an autumnal sunset" (*L*, 1:384). In the preface to his translation of *The Symposium*, Shelley comments that sexual desire can be consummated without intercourse: "If we consider the facility with which certain phenomena connected with sleep, at the age of puberty, associate themselves with those images which are the objects of our waking desires; and even that in some persons of an exalted state of sensibility that a similar process may take place in reverie, it will not be difficult to conceive the almost involuntary consequences of a state of abandonment in the society of a person of surpassing attractions, when the sexual connection cannot exist" (*C*, 222). Particularly relevant to *Alastor* is the suggestion that the imagination comes to the aid of libido "when the sexual connection cannot exist," as for example, when the object of desire is forbidden.

Rousseau, in his own pursuit of the ideal woman, was less exalted; he devotes many passages of his *Confessions* to sexual reverie and one to autoerotic activity of a more normative kind than Shelley describes: he tells us of "that dangerous means of cheating nature, which leads in young men of my temperament to various kinds of excesses, that eventually imperil their health, their strength, and sometimes their lives. This vice, which shame and timidity find so convenient, has a particular attraction for lively imaginations. It allows them to dispose, so to speak, of the whole female sex at their will, and to make any beauty who tempts them serve their pleasure without the need of first obtaining her consent" (108–9).

Romantic tradition also includes D. H. Lawrence, who speaks of masturbation as an ultimate symbol of "the vicious circle of self-consciousness" (75) and Blake, who in the *Visions of the Daughters of Albion* tells us that "the youth shut up from / The lustful joy. shall forget to generate. & create an amorous image / In the shadows of his curtains and in the folds of his silent pillow" (pl. 7, lines 5–7). Shelley, with his idealizations of sexual fantasy and dream, would seem to be at the opposite pole from Blake and Lawrence. Yet *Alastor* owes its most prominent theme, the deep conflict over imagination, to its troubled association of imagination with "distempered" adolescent autoerotism, as well as with more radical phenomena like narcissism, incest, and regression. Insofar as the image at the end of the voyage of the stream rushing over the precipice, "Scattering its waters to the passing winds" (570), suggests ejaculation, we can even say that the Poet, in almost a literal sense, dies of a wet dream.

Freud said that sex in puberty is taken up where it was left off before latency: masturbation is a revival of childhood genital play, and the sexual fantasies of puberty are often incest-related. Curiosity, or sexual research, and voyeurism are also among the common psychosexual patterns revived in puberty.[10] The Poet's curiosity takes a specifically visual form, as he "ever gazed / And gazed" at "memorials / Of the world's youth" (125–26, 121–22); earlier, the Narrator's heart gazes at Mother Nature's "mysteries" (23); and the gazing culminates in the vision of the Maid's limbs glowing within her "sinuous veil" (176). In the forest the Poet wanders among beautiful parasites that are like "infants' eyes" that "Fold their beams round the hearts of those that love" (441, 443). They are also like "restless serpents" (438); looking at those that love provokes phallic strivings.

Early in his researches the Poet sees a "mutilated sphynx" (114). For Freud, the riddle of the sphinx expresses the question of where children come from,[11] "The thrilling secrets of the birth of time" (128). The sphinx itself is both human and animal, and while it first appeared in Egyptian art and myth as a male, it changed in Greek culture to a female, although sometimes a bearded one.[12] In its very form it expresses the anxiety associated with a violation of boundaries. It is an unnatural or forbidden combination, like incest; the sphinx and Jocasta are the dangerous and desirable aspects of the sexualized mother.[13] The male-female sphinx is also like another shocking and monstrous combination, the mother and father copulating.[14] That the Poet's sphinx is "mutilated" has psychological resonance, for the primal scene is often associated with mutilation, whether the destructiveness that the child sees in copulation, the destructiveness that he feels toward the parents who are excluding him, or the destructiveness that he fears as punishment for his spying and his wishes.

Shelley uses another image in *Alastor* that is sphinxlike in its puzzling, ominous quality and its monstrous, compound form: a bird of prey struggling with a serpent. The figure has an ancestry going back to Homer.[15] In Ovid's *Metamorphoses*, it has dramatic associations with sexual anxiety and the primal scene: the nymph Salmacis tries to rape the youth Hermaphroditus in a pool, wrapping herself around him like "a snake caught by an eagle." She prays that they may remain embraced forever, and they grow together, "nor boy nor girl, / Neither yet both within a single body" (book 3; p. 122). Ever after, men who drink from this pool "Become effeminate or merely zero" (120).

Shelley first uses the image to describe how the Poet is driven by the dream, like an eagle feeling "her breast / Burn with the [serpent's] poison" and "Frantic with dizzying anguish" in "her blind flight" (228–29, 231). The Poet is identified with the female eagle, and the serpent is the aggressor, poisoning the female breast in a violent parody of not only intercourse but also nursing. Shelley then employs the figure to describe the stormy ocean waves: "Higher and higher still / Their fierce necks writhed beneath the tempest's scourge / Like serpents struggling in a vulture's grasp" (323–25). Here Shelley assigns no genders, but now the bird is the aggressor and the serpents are victims. Together, the two passages suggest certain types of infantile sexual confusion: sexual intercourse is conflated with nursing, the infant's paradigm of intimacy; the sense of gender is not yet certain; the subject is also unsure whom to identify with in the primal scene; and the phallus appears both in danger and as a weapon. All these forms of confusion are consistent both with the poem's regressive atmosphere and with its situation of a psyche thrown into turbulence by the sudden onset of sexual maturity.

Structurally, then, the poem shows us three layers of the Poet's sexual character in action simultaneously: an adolescent layer, evident in images suggesting autoerotism; an oedipal layer, evident in images suggesting incest and the primal scene; and an infantile, or narcissistic, layer, evident in images of separation, merger, and mutability. The autoerotism is a vehicle for the oedipal impulses, which in turn are invested with the desire to undo separation. Chronologically, the narrative of the Poet begins in the spirit of an adolescent search for knowledge, a return of infantile curiosity, resulting in the discovery of "awful ruins," "memorials" of youth that include castration ("fallen towers"), the lost breast ("pyramids"), and the primal scene ("mutilated sphynx") (108, 110–11). Coming right after such discoveries, the appearance of the Arab maiden leads to a sexual awakening, which is assimilated to the incestuous wishes and anxieties of the journey's regressive ambiance.

We can see in the poem Jocasta, the desired mother, and the sphinx, the feared mother and the mother in intercourse. We can see the great preoedipal mother Nature, the mother as mutable moon, and the archaic mother of the womb, in whom the Poet disappears. In his final resting place, a "tranquil spot" within a "lap of horror," we can see the ineluctable doubleness of that archaic mother (577–78). Indeed, the avenging *Alastor* is in one sense the other side of the sought mother, just as, according to Jane Harrison, Nemesis, the goddess of vengeance, was hard to distinguish from the maternal Dike, the order of life.[16] "*Alastor*" means not only "the Avenging Deity" but also "one who suffers from divine vengeance," and in *The Eumenides* the mother-killer Orestes, both a vehicle and a victim of divine vengeance on the House of Atreus, calls himself an *alastor*.[17] But in this picture of psychic development and conflict one important element is still missing. Before the meeting with the sphinx and the marriage with Jocasta comes the fight with Laius. Where is the father in *Alastor*? This absence is especially notable in view of the preoccupation with the father in *Queen Mab*, with its attacks on God and king. Coming after the defiant *Queen Mab*, *Alastor* is also notable for its downplaying of aggression. We have seen that signs of struggle and violence do appear in the poem—the shattered mountain, the mutilated sphinx, the warring bird and serpent, the tempest and whirlpool—but they appear around the Poet; he is serene in the midst of the turbulence, as if all the violence had nothing to do with him.

The absence of aggression in the Poet and the absence of the father in the poem return us to the conspicuous absence with which the poem begins: the missing fire in the opening invocation of the elements. When fire does make a delayed entrance in the "permeating fire" "kindled" in the body of the Veiled Maid (163, 162) and in the Poet's burning eyes that behold that fiery vision, it has conventional sexual connotations; mature genitality is also missing in this poem of eros. The poem's invocation informs us of an absence, and the rest of the poem thus enables us to associate that absence with a regression from adult sexuality and a denial of aggression and, further, to associate both these absences with the absence of the father. At the end of the poem, the Narrator, helpless to undo the hero's death, laments that the vision "Of dark magician . . . / Raking the cinders of a crucible / For life and power" has no reality in this world (682–84). Fire is associated here with an ideal magic that we can only wish for. Fire is the sexual and aggressive strength of the father and his marvelous capacity to bring things about.

Alastor presents a family romance, a revision of origins, in which Shelley imagines a mother but is unwilling or unable to imagine a father. But the "father," in Shelley's culture and his own imagination, is also the power by which a desire is realized, and to deny the father is to cut oneself off from that power.[18] The Poet is an Adam not only without an author but also without any authorizing capacity of his own. If a hero doesn't receive power from a friendly father, he might steal it from a hostile one. But here there is no father to steal from; there is no father to struggle with, to test oneself against, to model oneself on, to imitate, to revise, to use in any of the ways a son might use a father. There is no external father, and there is no internalization of the father. Nor is the hero, or the Narrator, conceived of as a father in any sense. The Poet is no fire-bearer, no tamer and giver of fire, no culture-bringer. The missing fire is always something beyond him, something that he pursues, even when it is within him. Avoiding the sun, traveling by night, he voyages in a moon-world, a fatherless, female, maternal landscape. *Alastor* expresses a wish that one might find one's way, like Oedipus, to the sacred bower of the Great Parent without, like Oedipus, first fully confronting the sphinx and the father. At the same time, the conclusion Shelley imagines for his fatherless myth is oblivion. In *Alastor* Shelley can construct a family romance for himself as a poet in which the poet has beauty but not one in which he also has "life and power."

In *Queen Mab* Shelley obliterates the father, and in *Alastor* he explores the consequences of that obliteration. Actually, like aggression and mature sexuality, the father can be detected in the poem as a presence detached from the hero. In the conclusion, we see the father as a murderous God, "Profuse of poisons" (676), who has exempted only one man, Ahasuerus, from his curse of death and then only as a dreadful punishment. The violent enemies of *Queen Mab* find their way into the gentle moon-world of *Alastor*; aggression and the father, submerged throughout the poem, thus make a cameo appearance at the end. William Crisman notes two instances in the poem in which fire and poison are associated: the eagle's breast burns with the serpent's poison (229), and springs of "fire and poison" (89) appear in the Poet's early wanderings (Crisman, 142). If the father's fire is poisonous, if his power is destructive, then it appears that fire is not only something the Poet does not have; it is also something he does not want.

In the course of the Poet's wanderings, fathers are twice mentioned explicitly: the Arab maiden brings the Poet food "from her father's tent" (130), and, later, maidens watch "his departure from their father's door" (271). The Poet acts here in a conspicuously un-Shelleyan way, for we do not often find Shelley rejecting women either in his poetry or in his life. He was entranced with the platonic notion of love as an educational relationship, of molding a lover and disciple into an ideal being, and he applied the idea repeatedly, sometimes sexually and sometimes platonically: Harriet Grove, Harriet Westbrook, Mary, Claire Clairmont, two of his sisters, and Teresa Viviani were such disciples. Indeed, one of his persistent fantasies was to steal a young girl and educate her.[19] Usually, the chosen girl was imprisoned by a heartless and despotic father; in *Alastor* the Arab maiden, just like the Poet himself, has a "cold" home (138). He proposed the plan to his sister Hellen and carried it out with both his wives. Of his courtship of Harriet, he wrote, "Why is it that the moment we are seperated [*sic*], I can scarcely set bounds to my hatred of Xtianity" (*L*, 1:71). He called her father a fiend, and in the early letters his own father and Christianity seem synonymous. In *The Fugitives*, two lovers sail away through a storm while back on land "the gray tyrant father" curses his escaped daughter (53, *H*, 639). Freud interprets the fantasy of rescuing a maiden imprisoned by a monster as embodying the wish to take the mother away from the father.[20]

When he wrote *Alastor*, Shelley had recently stolen two young women, Mary and Claire, from a man whom he respected and even sought out as a substitute father. The *Alastor* Poet, in contrast, leaves daughters to their fathers. In the poem we see a negation of a pattern that was recurrent in the author's life. *O! there are spirits*, in which the quester longs for the "starry eyes" that are "Another's wealth" (13, 15, *E*, 1:449), contains a similar negation in its epigraph from the *Hippolytus* of Euripides; in the full passage from which the epigraph is taken, the chorus says, "Sister Graces, why did you let him go / guiltless, out of his native land, / out of his father's house?"[21] Like Hippolytus, the *Alastor* Poet is really innocent: Hippolytus actually didn't steal his father's "wealth" although he was banished and killed for doing so. *Alastor* is a poem that denies oedipal incursion. We often think of writers as acting out in their art fantasies unfulfilled in their lives. In *Alastor* Shelley represses an urge he repeatedly acted out.

The hero of *Alastor* tries to rejoin the mother without offending the father. In the case of Godwin, Shelley himself apparently wished to keep the father. The idealized Godwin was to betray him by proving just another paternal ogre, but, as I have noted, Shelley, despite explosions of anger, was to continue placating and cultivating him, partly because of Mary, partly because of his tremendous respect for Godwin's work, and partly, perhaps, because of his continued attraction to the old romance situation in which the father is present, necessarily in an adversarial position. But *Alastor* goes further than either placating or keeping the father. At the end the Narrator wishes for "Medea's wondrous alchemy" (672), her power to rejuvenate the aged; Medea even restored Jason's dying father at Jason's request. *Alastor*, in this allusion, expresses a wish to save the father. Róheim writes that "the two fundamental tendencies of the Oedipus situation"—positive, or love of the mother and hatred of the father, and negative, or love of the father and hatred of the mother—"are awakened in the child when he observes the primal scene."[22] In *Athanase*, the hero's real father, a noble warrior, dies when the boy is three, and his teacher, Zonoras, is a wise and gentle substitute father. Idealized sibling incest in *Alastor* screens an incestuous impulse toward the mother, but it also screens the wish for the father's love. These are two impulses that, unlike sibling incest, Shelley cannot idealize or even explicitly write about.

On first impression Zonoras would seem an ideal father figure in that he both is benevolent and can easily be surpassed: the pupil "soon outran / His teacher, and did teach with native skill / Strange truths and new to that experienced man" (14–16, *E*, 2:325). But by virtue of this reversal, Zonoras, although he is a good counselor, is unable to solve the problem of the hero's grief. As attractive as Zonoras may be, the passage from the original father to the substitute represents a decline in strength and greatness. We have seen Shelley's openness to influence; we have seen his wariness of influence; we have seen him challenging and defying the tyrannical father; we have seen him mourning and criticizing the lapsed, Protean father, the good father who betrays the cause. The father Shelley seeks most deeply is more powerful than Zonoras, one more like the protective father of early childhood; yet he seeks an engagement with that authority in which he will not be oppressed or overwhelmed by its greatness; he seeks to be inspired without being destroyed. In *Alastor*, the urge toward a fatherless world comes into conflict with a desire to keep or save the father and with a recognition that to evade the father is to cut oneself off from a necessary source of power. The young poet and revolutionary Laon in *Laon and Cythna* says that he drew "Words which were weapons" from his "glorious intercourse" with the "deathless minds" of the past (842, 840, 838, *E*, 2:101, 100). Shelley cannot fully define himself as a poet without an engagement with both paternal and maternal imagoes. The entire problem never arises in *Queen Mab* because there Shelley is purely tearing down the bad fathers; but in *Alastor* he is tentatively confronting and arguing with authorities he respects, such as Wordsworth and, in the personal background of the poem, Godwin. These are the fathers whom he would like to join and surpass, the fathers who, although great, could not sustain their goodness.

The irresolute handling of the issue of the father appears in the poem's conclusion when the Narrator, more than alluding to Wordsworth, actually quotes the *Immortality Ode* in saying that the Poet's fate is "a woe too 'deep for tears'" (713). In the *Ode* we may, through "recollections of early childhood," the "philosophic mind," and the "human heart," gain thoughts "too deep for tears" that partly compensate for the loss of glory.[23] In one sense, Shelley is rejecting Wordsworth's poetic myth of compensation and growth. But in quoting, rather than revising, correcting, or integrating and thus making his own, he is, in effect, reminding us of the greatness of the *Ode*. He is paying tribute to somebody who said it better. The father was wrong, and he can't help us; but his greatness is still beyond Shelley, and in a way Shelley is still reaching out to him, bringing him into the poem not in a Shelleyan guise but in his own person.

For Shelley, regression is essential to poetry, but it is only part of a complete poetic identity. The Poet is the obverse of Ahasuerus, the eternal *puer senex* of *Queen Mab*. Ahasuerus is the wanderer of wrath and aggression; the Poet is the wanderer of ideal love and dreams. Each alone is a figure of tragedy and frustration. To put these two sides of a heroic image together is the problem posed for Shelley by his own early work. We turn now to follow him beyond the ambivalences of *Alastor* toward his vision of Prometheus, the thief of fire.

II
THE WANTING VOICE

8

Introduction:
The Glory of Passivity
and the Glory of Action

Nietzsche contrasted "the glory of passivity" as it appears in the Oedipus cycle to "the glory of action, as it irradiates the *Prometheus* of Aeschylus" (62). Oedipus passively undergoes misfortunes on his way to "transcendent serenity" (60), while Prometheus embodies "the glorious power to *do*" (63). In these tragedies of knowledge and trespass, Nietzsche finds two primal types of human suffering, that of the saint and that of the artist. Shelley's *Alastor* and *Prometheus Unbound* can be contrasted in similar fashion. The *Alastor* Poet lacked an active power of realizing his vision; he was, in essence, a saint, not an artist, and while we can see in him the glory of a saint, we can also see in him the pathos of a failed creator. But in Shelley's next major narrative, *Laon and Cythna,* and then in *Prometheus* he tries to build a conception of the imagination as a creative, not a tragic, force. In these two works of epic synthesis, he tries, as well, to socialize the imagination and to confront poetically the aggression missing in Alastor.

At the same time he does not repudiate passivity. For Shelley, as for Wordsworth in his "wise passiveness,"[1] passivity remains an important element of creativity, as well as a compelling psychological attraction. He seeks now to integrate it into a comprehensive poetic myth and to imagine forms of passiveness and activeness that do not lead to the alternate failures of the *Alastor* Poet and Ahasuerus. The particular importance of *Laon and Cythna* for this study is that we can see in it the fullness of the resistance Shelley has to face in dealing with activeness. Just as *Alastor* shows an inner conflict with its own source of inspiration, regression, so *Laon and Cythna* shows a similarly troubled and unresolved relation to the aggression that is its particular imaginative and psychological source.

9

The Revolution
of the Golden City

In *Laon and Cythna, or The Revolution of the Golden City*—first published as *The Revolt of Islam*—Shelley attempts to deal fully with both eros and aggression in the same poem; he portrays both a quest for absolute love and an explicit confrontation with authority; he tries to rewrite *Queen Mab* and *Alastor* in a single work of protest and enchantment.[1]

Choosing the stanza of *The Faerie Queene* for this project, Shelley cultivates an encounter with romance in its greatest native form. By virtue of Shelley's prosody, Spenser, who adapted romance to a moral, political, and religious function, is brought into the poem as a benevolent presence to authorize and guide the redemption of the romance imagination from the spirit of solitude. But while Spenser is the good father, Shelley also radicalizes his vision. Spenser enlisted the traditional romance subjects of love and war to advance an embattled although mainstream Protestant vision, but in *Laon and Cythna* love and war become incest and atheistic revolution. *Laon and Cythna* engages not only a father but also an older sibling, for the poem was written in the stanza that Byron had used in *Childe Harold* and on a topic, the French Revolution, that Shelley had first recommended to Byron.[2] In the preface he claims that he does "not presume to enter into competition with our greatest contemporary Poets," but he adds, "I am unwilling to tread in the footsteps of any who have preceded me . . . designing that even if what I have produced be worthless, it should still be properly my own" (*E*, 2:38). The influence of writers of his own time is a sensitive point in the preface. He admits that contemporary writers may involuntarily resemble each other because of their common "subjection" to the spirit of the age (*E*, 2:41). Later he was dismayed that a reviewer had ignored this explanation and attacked him as an "unsparing imitator," especially of Wordsworth.[3]

The issue of originality appears in the preface in another form as well. Shelley writes that the sympathizers of the French Revolution were appalled "by the atrocities of the demogogues and the re-establishment of successive tyrannies in France" and suffered "the melancholy desolation of all their cherished hopes"; as a result, the present age and its literature have been consumed by "gloom and misanthropy" (*E*, 2:36–37), a mood Shelley sets out to correct. Although the previous generation had the advantage of knowing directly "the master theme of the epoch in which we live" (*L*, 1:504), he claims an advantage in being able to understand and overcome the failures of the Revolution. *Laon and Cythna* is a reimagining of the French Revolution with the purpose of liberating a generation from a paralyzing trauma and of saving idealism in an age of disillusionment. This revisionary project is an example of a redemptive, recreative doubleness.[4] Shelley's theme is that there is a second chance. He thus takes an aggressively belated stance, in the hope not of finding satisfaction in some form of sublimation but of recapturing and fulfilling an original impulse.

The introductory canto opens with a "monstrous sight" (191). The narrator, in despair after the French Revolution, sees from a mountaintop overlooking the ocean "An Eagle and a Serpent wreathed in fight" (193). After a daylong battle, the defeated serpent falls into the sea. On the shore, the narrator finds a woman singing in an unearthly language to waves now "Calm as a cradled child" (261), and the serpent swims to shore and coils himself in her unveiled bosom. To the narrator, the woman's singing is reminiscent "of some loved voice heard long ago" (317).[5] In this scene of maternal comfort by the sea, the unintelligible and compelling voice suggests the infant's, or "cradled child's," sense of the mother's voice. But Shelley also wrote in the manuscript at this point the last two words of a line from *Kubla Khan*: "By woman wailing for her demon-lover."[6]

The Eagle and Serpent, the woman explains, are equal powers of evil and good, originally appearing to the first human as "A blood-red Comet and the Morning Star / Mingling their beams in combat" (356–57). When the star sank into the sea, that first man killed his brother. In this poem the first man is not the first lover, Adam, but the first killer, Cain. The Spirit of Evil then changed his "starry" adversary into a snake, which would be shunned by mankind (368). Thenceforth humanity was taught to worship the Fiend as king and God, but now whenever humanity rises against oppression, "The Snake and Eagle meet—the world's foundations tremble!" (423). In the poem's vision, then, the French Revolution and also the Greek revolt against the Ottoman Empire, current in Shelley's time and the inspiration of the poem's plot, are episodes in an ongoing struggle against evil that will not end with any local defeat.

The primal scene of a poem of revolution like *Laon and Cythna* is appropriately a scene of aggression. But what for Shelley in this poem is the primal aggression? In *Alastor* the composite, sphinx-like figure of serpent and eagle suggested both parental intercourse and nursing. But in *Laon and Cythna,* the eagle and serpent are both male. We can see in the figure a fraternal combat, and it is worth noting that, as Charles Robinson reminds us, Shelley portrayed Byron as an eagle in *Julian and Maddalo* and Byron's pet name for Shelley was "the Snake" (4–5). But we can also see in the scene by the ocean another primal combat, with the defeated oedipal hero, both child and demon-lover, returning to the mother. In the pre-Olympian, earth-centered religion of the mother goddess, the male hero—the goddess's consort, the society's king—often appeared as a snake.[7] The serpent is the male in the world of the mother, the phallic power that serves the goddess of fertility. *Laon and Cythna* opens with the mother comforting her champion after a battle with the fatherly sky god. Revolution in Shelley is thus identified with a resurgence of the old order of the mother. We have now seen three fantasies in which that order is reawakened. In *Alastor,* the son rejoins the pregenital dyad. In *Queen Mab,* the father is overthrown by the archaic power of the mother alone as a primal Necessity. In *Laon and Cythna,* the father is challenged by the combined power of the mother and the phallic son.

Shelley takes as an epigraph to the poem lines from Pindar that include the following: "Neither by ships nor by land can you find the wondrous road to the festival place of the Hyperboreans."[8] The Hyperboreans were a happy people who lived a paradisal existence beyond the north wind; Apollo spent his winters with them.[9] The narrator now accompanies the woman and the serpent beyond the polar ocean, "Nature's remotest reign" (553), to a paradisal Temple of the

Spirit. Like the Fairy's Fane in *Queen Mab*, the Temple represents the imagination as a building. But while the imagination in *Queen Mab* is identified with nature and Necessity, the imagination here is associated with human wisdom. The "native home" of genius (570), the Temple holds a "mighty Senate" of the great ones of the past (606). The *Alastor* Poet worried where his thoughts would go when he died (507–14), but in Shelley's Temple the visions of the great survive forever. Its existence assures us that although fighters against evil may be defeated and die, nothing is lost of their ideals.

Inside the Temple, the woman and serpent metamorphose into the Spirit of Good. Described as a winged youth with the morning star on his brow (500–501), the Spirit of Good is a compound of three traditional figures: the rebel Lucifer; Cupid, a version of the son-companion of the fertility goddess; and Venus herself. The Temple, where the ideas of individual genius survive and also where the son and mother are mingled in a dual identity, is a place of both preserving and dissolving. Apollonian and Dionysian, progressive and regressive, the Temple embodies an attempt to hold together two forces that in *Alastor* were at war.

The Spirit introduces two further "mighty Spirits," Laon and Cythna, to tell the narrator "A tale of human power" to raise him out of his despair (645, 648). Laon's story begins with his idyllic childhood "In Argolis, beside the echoing sea" (676). He associates Argolis with "The starlight smile of children, the sweet looks / Of women, the fair breast from which I fed" (667–68). Onto this native world of women and children, tyranny descends, but Laon tries to arouse the people with his poetry. One of the poem's prime themes is the communication and realization of imaginings through words. Unlike the hero of *Alastor*, Laon is a poet who seeks a bond with an audience, and in the response to his words, he feels "that we all were sons of one great mother" (817).

His early experience includes an obscure episode about a special friend who proves treacherous, possibly an allusion to Hogg,[10] and he turns from his disappointment to companionship with his twelve-year-old sister, Cythna. In the dyadic ideal of *Alastor* the hero merges into a maternal figure; in that of *Laon and Cythna* he finds a poetic mate and coworker. The poet, as poet, never marries, Harold Bloom writes, whatever the person may do;[11] but in Cythna, Shelley dreamed that the imagination might find a bride, as Blake did in his myth of Jerusalem, the Emanation. Cythna is a combination of the Wordsworthian seer-child of the *Immortality Ode* and the *Alastor* Poet's Veiled Maid; she is Laon's "second self, far dearer and more fair" (875). Cythna also plays a role in the theme of poetic communication; she is an ideal audience, who—another seaside singer—chants Laon's hymns to "the enchanted waves" (918), and she is his muse: "communion with this purest being / Kindled intenser zeal, and made me wise" (946–47). She, furthermore, proposes to help transform his vision into reality: "from our uniting minds," she tells him, a spark will be ignited to consume "all the kinds / Of evil" (1075–76). She even seems to embody the transcendent and nourishing Spirit of Beauty that Shelley celebrated in the *Hymn to Intellectual Beauty*: she is "Like the bright shade of some immortal dream" (872) and "like some radiant cloud of morning dew" (868) wandering through the air "To nourish some far desert" (870).

Cythna takes as her particular mission the emancipation of women, "the slaves of slaves" (987), for, as Laon tells her, "Never will peace and human nature meet / Till free and equal man and woman greet / Domestic peace" (994–96). Woman has to be liberated especially from the tyranny of male sexuality: under the despotic Sultan Othman "grace and power were thrown as food / To the hyena lust" (988–89), and the sultan is himself represented as an inhuman "Lust" sitting alone "in its palaces" (1607–8). Later it will be Cythna's mission to lead a rebellion of harem women against him, that is, to rescue the father's women from his sexuality. But now she herself is stolen away for his harem in the Golden City. Trying to rescue her, Laon kills three of her captors, and in a Promethean and Christlike punishment he is chained to a mountaintop column and falls into madness.

At last he is released by an old hermit, who cares for him for seven years until his sanity is restored. Punished by the evil father, he is rescued by the good one, specifically a maternal father who saves him from starvation and tends him "even as some sick mother seems / To hang in hope over a dying child" (1402–3).[12] Like Zonoras in *Athanase*, the hermit is a father who is both enlightened and surpassable. Although wise, he always believed that humanity was fated to remain abject, until Laon and his martyrdom inspired him to put his knowledge and ability to revolutionary use as a propagandist. The hermit is a precursor who rescues, nurtures, and then subordinates himself to the son-student: "I have been thy passive instrument," the old man tells the younger man, reversing the filial relationship (1549).

Indeed, during his madness Laon has been, in a fantasy of influence, an unmoved and unmoving source of power, for through the hermit and through the work of a female revolutionary named Laone his inspiration has brought the rebels to the verge of victory. But the poem is concerned not only with the means to triumph but, even more, with the handling of triumph once achieved: the hermit now urges Laon to use his "charmèd voice" to sway the course of the revolt away from violence (1659). Arriving at the rebel camp, Laon finds the lost friend of his youth, and with this shadowy figure, whom we will have to explore, he is, again obscurely, reconciled. He also finds the rebels about to execute a band of assassins and intervenes to save their lives, even incurring a spear-wound from his own people in doing so. This is a key point in the poem psychologically as well as politically. Laon is checking aggression that he himself has inflamed, that is, ultimately, his own aggression. His invocations of brotherhood prove so persuasive that the multitudes within the Golden City welcome the rebels inside their gates. There the sacrifice of aggression is repeated. Laon finds the sultan pitiful and helpless, abandoned by all but a little girl, another mysterious figure, who reminds him of Cythna and to whom he gives a "father's kiss" (1934). Although the crowd wants the tyrant's blood, Laon swerves from the French model of violence: he arranges for Othman an exile in which "Some likeness of his ancient state was lent" (2038).

In France, the revolutionaries held festivals in which new ideals like Reason and Liberty were raised in place of Christianity.[13] Similarly, the people of the Golden City celebrate their liberation with a great festival, at which Laone-Cythna praises "Eldest of things, divine Equality!" (2212), a new parent power. The Shelleyan liberation has an explicit sexual component; in the absence of the old authority, the people are, in essence, given permission to make love: Laone tells them, "man and woman, / Their common bondage burst, may freely borrow / From lawless love a solace for their sorrow" (2229–31). Reason and Liberty appeared in the French festivals as goddesses, and Shelley too elevates a female authority: the end of violence and the dawn of the paradisal age is celebrated by a vegetarian banquet, as the "general mother," Earth, "reconciles / Her warring children," assuring with her own abundant sustenance that they will not have to prey on each other (2299, 2302–3).

The deep fantasies of the poem have not yet been fulfilled, however; nor has the engagement with aggression been played out. That night Othman's foreign allies strike. Laon leads the resistance, but even this defensive violence appalls him: "how ugly and how fell / O Hate! thou art, even when thy life thou shed'st / For love" (2471–73). Laon's friend and the hermit die by his side, and he himself, the last resister, is about to be cut down when Cythna rides in on a giant black horse to carry him away.

Like many horses of fantasy, this stallion of turbulent speed and power has clear phallic implications.[14] "Mount with me, Laon, now," Cythna commands (2514), and their wild gallop anticipates the mounting at the end of the ride. Animals often represent not only the animal portion of the self, the id, but the parents, as in totemism; and what is most important about this particular horse is that it was taken from the enemy army. Sexual power is here stolen from the father.

The father's horse takes them up the "rugged breast" (2531) of another cosmic, maternal mountain overlooking the ocean, and on the summit the brother and sister consummate their love. One of the distinctive characteristics of this love scene—along with *Epipsychidion*, Shelley's greatest piece of erotic writing—is how integral skepticism is to its ecstasy. The scene begins with a statement of agnosticism: "We know not where we go . . . Nor should we seek to know" (2587, 2592). In the absence of any possible knowledge of a transcendent authority we become our own authorities, and "To the pure all things are pure," even incest (2596).[15] Once skepticism has cleared away the conventional morality associated with divine authority, that is, once the father has been disposed of, eros can emerge. Skepticism must also accomplish a related task. We cannot know "what sweet dream / May pilot us through caverns strange and fair / Of far and pathless passion" (2587–89). Skepticism must conceal the longing for the mother that drives the questing of eros; skepticism in this case is a force of mystification, not demystification.

The lovers' passion is the culmination of their common blood, their shared memories of childhood, and their physical resemblance: "those / Who grow together cannot choose but love, / If faith or custom do not interpose" (2686–88). Thus Laon finds what was missing for the *Alastor* Poet: "and then I felt the blood that burned / Within her frame, mingle with mine, and fall / Around my heart like fire" (2634–36). Celebrating sexual passion in general, the sequence stresses in particular the sublimity of incestuous love, developing that theme in a simile drawn from ancient Egypt, land of incestuous rulers: a tree in the sacred grove at the source of the Nile clasps "its own kindred leaves" in the sunlight and keeps clasping them "when darkness may dissever / The close caresses of all duller plants" (2694–96). Further, the incestuous springs of love in childhood are a source of all later love, "feed[ing] human wants, / As the great Nile feeds Egypt" (2701–2).

But a nightmarish scene follows. Descending from the mountain to search for food, Laon comes upon a war-ravaged village filled with corpses. The only living creature he can find is a haggard, fiendish woman who embraces him in a lethal parody of the ideal sex he has just experienced, and tells him, "Now Mortal, thou hast deeply quaffed / The Plague's blue kisses . . . / My name is Pestilence" (2765–67).

A second nightmarish parody of "love's delight" (2876) follows. When he returns, Cythna tells him of her own sufferings, beginning with her rape by the tyrant in his harem, a violation that she compares to copulating with a grimacing skeleton. She is driven mad by this "loathsome agony" (2875), and when the other harem slaves begin to sympathize, Othman has her imprisoned at the base of a funnel-like cave in the sea. Food is brought to her by an eagle, who in her madness appears as "a fiend, who bore / Thy mangled limbs for food" (2961–62).

The poem, in this episode, takes a turn toward regression. In a variation of the traditional romance adventure of submersion, the dangerous, enforced return to the waters of origin that heroes undergo on the way to a second birth, Cythna herself gives birth to a child in her prison in the sea; pregnancy itself is treated as a return to the womb for the mother.[16] Indeed, mother and daughter play together, "Both infants," and at night "We, on the earth, like sister twins lay down / On one fair mother's bosom" (3018, 3021–22). In this blissful time of the dyad, Cythna, in a near-quotation of Wordsworth, "had no mortal fears" (2998);[17] but the intimacy of mother and child is disrupted by the tyrant, who takes the child away.

Another kind of gestation also occurs within the womblike cave, a development in Shelley's dream of language and poetic communication. Cythna tries to make contact with the eagle, "By intercourse of mutual imagery" (3088), to teach it to bring her ropes. When this quest for a natural, universal language, an Adamic verbal power, fails, she turns inward, but unlike the *Alastor* Poet's, her inward turning leads toward others and toward freedom. She finds within herself "One mind, the type of all, the moveless wave / Whose calm reflects all moving things that are" (3104–5). Reminiscent of Freud in his self-analysis, Cythna finds through her exploration of her own mind an understanding of the human mind in general. Unlike Freud, she also finds in herself the oceanic feeling. Her mind becomes not only a mirror of all other minds but also a version of the womblike world in the water, a finer reflection of all things. And this imaginative development, in turn, leads to new powers of writing:

> "And on the sand would I make signs to range
> These woofs, as they were woven, of my thought;
> Clear, elemental shapes, whose smallest change
> A subtler language within language wrought."
>   (3109–12)

We see an impulse in Shelley's secret-haunted mind to create secrets in the midst of the common language. Cythna's subtler language is compared to "The key of truths which once were dimly taught / In old Crotona" (3113–14), an allusion to the mathematical religion of Pythagoras—or, as his followers called him, Apollo Hyperboreas. Jane Harrison notes that Pythagoreanism was a revival of matriarchalism and, in essence, a women's movement.[18] With her subtler language, Cythna makes a secret, subversive place for the wisdom of the mother within the language of the father. Perhaps above all, we see in her new language a dream of being able to know and express everything in the mind, a dream Shelley adumbrated when he wrote elsewhere of the difficulty of thought visiting its own "intricate and winding chambers" (C, 186).

With that new mastery Cythna is ready to fulfill another Shelleyan dream of language and poetry, the dream, as he wrote in the preface, of "awakening in others sensations like those which animate my own bosom" (E, 2:41). After many years, an earthquake liberates Cythna from her cave, and she is reborn as no longer a disciple but a revolutionary leader. Having been rescued from the sea by a ship bringing maidens to the harem, she sets out to reform Othman's mariners. She teaches them that the God they worship is only a human projection and that under such a God all relationships assume a tyrannical structure of ruler and ruled. They are so moved that they rise in oedipal revolt; they release the captive maidens, take them as lovers, and sail back to the Golden City to liberate it.

Now, much later, when the revolt has been crushed, Cythna still envisions a triumphant future. Even now, in "the winter of the world," "The seeds are sleeping in the soil" (3685, 3676). Heroes, poets, and sages may die (3714), but their thoughts and deeds will lead to a rebirth as certain as springtime; in an ecstatic passage, the shade cast by the death of the lovers will become the wings of a renewed world, and "From its dark gulf of chains, Earth like an eagle springs" (3693). Still, Cythna's speech is laced with reminders of individual doom: "we shall be dead and cold," "So be the turf heaped over our remains / Even in our happy youth" (3694, 3721–22). At last the theme of hope is overwhelmed:

> "There is delusion in the world—and woe,
> And fear, and pain—we know not whence we live,
> Or why, or how, or what mute Power may give
> Their being to each plant, and star, and beast,
> Or even these thoughts:—Come near me! I do weave
> A chain I cannot break—I am possessed
> With thoughts too swift and strong for one lone human breast."
>   (3759–65)

The impulse to destroy divine authority and thus enable human beings to be free and equal finds expression in skepticism, but so does a deep melancholy and an overwhelming sense of living among endless enigmas. Cythna's penultimate words are not of a return of spring but of a plunge toward oblivion: "All that we are or know, is darkly driven / Towards one gulf" (3779–80). We get rid of the blocking father but are left with a mother associated with death, an oceanic dissolution; the spirit of *Alastor* has triumphed over the spirit of *Queen Mab*. Even so, Cythna ends with a gesture of determination: "Lo! what a change is come / Since I first spake—but time shall be forgiven, / Though it change all but thee!" (3780–82).

The world outside the lovers' bower is indeed being darkly driven. In the land, devastated by Othman's allies, the plague spreads among the unburied corpses; among those still alive, famine is rampant; people fall victim to madness, seeing "Their own lean image everywhere . . . / A ghastlier self beside them" (3983–84). In the terror of the times, the religions of mankind are trotted out (including the Zoroastrianism commonly judged to be an influence on the poem[19]), as each votary howls, "Our God alone is God!" (4069). Religious warfare is about to break out, when a fanatical "Christian priest" urges that Laon and Laone be found and sacrificed to appease God's anger (4072). He whips up the people to build a great pyre, to which "Men brought their atheist kindred," and some feast "like fiends upon the infidel dead" (4196, 4210). In an attempt to save Cythna, Laon surrenders, but at the last moment Cythna rides in on her great stallion and joins her lover on the pyre. The flames "Burst upwards" in "a blood-red gleam" (4588, 4587), mirror-image of the lovers' fire-like blood that mingled in their consummation.

Suddenly pyre, pestilence, tyrant, and throng disappear, and the lovers find themselves in a garden. A boat arrives piloted by a winged child, Othman's companion, now recognized by Cythna as her own lost daughter. The child tells Laon that she "knew that I was thine" from the moment he kissed her in the tyrant's palace (4660). She herself has died of the plague and become a "wingèd Thought" (4720) in the Temple of the Spirit, to which it is now her mission to lead the lovers. In this vision of a non-Christian afterlife, the boat enters the safe, uterine waters of a "windless waveless lake," fed by "four great cataracts," the four rivers of the biblical paradise (4806–7). Hanging in the sky is the spherical Temple of the Spirit, a new womb, a womb of the mind, a womb or source of new revolution, and Laon and Cythna take their places in it as inspiring thoughts, as influences.

Yet Shelley manifests a certain incongruous resistance to that ideal. The poem closes with a dissonant simile in which the Temple is a new earth and the boat is the moon, "drawn nearer and more near" (4816). Although the line finishes with the boat finding its haven, strictly in the terms of the simile, Laon and Cythna will never reach their goal, or if they do, it will be a catastrophe. Shelley has not quite been able to come up with a fiction of regression that he can feel comfortable with. His strong urge toward freedom and autonomy impedes his vision of a merging even into a structure that is supposed to be the very source and emblem of freedom and autonomy.

This last-second equivocation manifests itself in a second way. If Laon and Cythna are joining the great ones of the past in a common project, then their association with them should be one of joy, not anxiety. Yet on the voyage to the Temple, the homes of the great dead are "Cyclopean piles" atop a high canyon (4762). Why Cyclopean? And why does Shelley write that those houses "frowned" over "the bright waves" around their "dark foundations" (4763–64)? "Cyclopean" is an architectural term for a style of building in which "huge blocks of stone are fitted closely together and without mortar";[20] but it would be difficult not to think beyond this sense of the word to the cannibalistic giant who threatens travelers on great odysseys. In totemism, the sons devour the body of the father-animal and incorporate his greatness. But in Shelley's image the situation is reversed; those inspiring spiritual fathers of the Temple threaten to devour the sons. In Hesiod, the Cyclopes are master builders who also helped forge Zeus's thunderbolts and fought with him against the Titans, their own race. The adjective "Cyclopean" seems strikingly inappropriate, revealing that Shelley is not fully reconciled to his own ideal of a past that nourishes rather than devours us.

Indeed, the poem is marked in general by the way in which it unwittingly complicates its own poetic myths. I am not suggesting, like William Ulmer, that those myths are devalued by contradiction. For Ulmer, the poem's ideals are undermined by the traces they contain of hierarchy, violence, and sexism.[21] I am concerned to show, rather, how psychological complexity may accompany poetic concepts that yet remain moving, thoughtful, and valuable and how Shelley is engaged in an ongoing creative process, working out poetic themes in a ferment of fantasies, anxieties, conflicts, and conscious ideas. In *Laon and Cythna* Shelley attempts a work of major synthesis, but its inspiring Temple stands in its wholeness as an image of a poetic and psychological intactness that he has not yet attained.

We can see another example of such complication in the poem's myth of language. *Laon and Cythna* proposes that the hero of words, whether a poet like Laon or a prophet and political orator like Cythna, can achieve an ideal relationship with an audience; that he or she can do with language what heroes ordinarily do with force or cunning—so Cythna "with strong speech tore the veil that hid" Liberty (3523); and that those words can survive death to shape history in the future. Those who heard the *Alastor* Poet could only "interpret half the woe / That wasted him" (267–68), but when Cythna addresses the multitudes, her voice "Pour[s] forth her inmost soul" (2277) and moves "To rapture like her own all listening hearts" (2280). The *Alastor* Poet's words were both inspired and scattered into oblivion by the wind, but Cythna's voice is "as a mountain stream" (2281); speech itself attains the power of a natural force, as it sweeps "withered leaves" (2282), her listeners, through a beautiful

metamorphosis. Her words are echoed by her followers until they be-
come "one universal sound, / Like a volcano's voice" (3497–98).

But Laon, Cythna, and the hermit, another virtuoso speaker, are
not the only masters of communication in the poem. Othman him-
self is an adept of signs, summoning his allies with secret signals, and
the Christian priest is a speaker of spellbinding force, stimulating
hate as well as Cythna could stimulate love. The power of language is
consequently not in itself good. In *Prometheus Unbound* the battle will
also be waged on the level of language, but there Shelley will be con-
cerned with the understanding of important words rather than sheer
eloquence.

Further, in the poem's dedicatory verses Shelley fears not being
able to reach his own ideal of speech. He ends the dedication by
imagining "no response to my cry" and men stamping "with fury
blind / On his pure name who loves them" (119–21). This anticipa-
tion of failure makes a poignant contrast to an immediately preced-
ing passage, in which Godwin is a great voice that gathers up the wis-
dom of three thousand years: "And the tumultuous world stood
mute to hear it, / As some lone man who in a desert hears / The
music of his home" (111–13).

But the dream of communication is complicated not only by the
potential eloquence of evil and the anxiety of not matching the great
voices of the past. Like the vegetarianism that Cythna promotes to re-
place the eating of flesh in the new age of equality, the dream of lan-
guage is a benevolent oral ideal, horrifyingly parodied by the poem's
recurrent imagery of cannibalism. Both lovers hallucinate devouring
each other's corpse; their power of speech, as well as their desire to
merge, is doubled by a savage fantasy of oral aggression and incor-
poration.[22] They become like the "unholy men" who devour the athe-
ists at the pyre (4209). The dream of language is a dream of master-
ing and transforming oral impulses, or at least eliminating the
"unholy" ones, those that return to the mind in times of madness.
This is a poem the primal symbol of which, we remember, is a pair of
animals biting and poisoning each other.

Laon and Cythna also complicates its prime theme of a political
failure purified of despair. The poem begins and ends with a defeat,
but in the second defeat Shelley attempts to give grounds for hope.
Yet it remains important that the poem is unable to imagine present
worldly success. Earthly failure in the poem even has its own glory. In-
deed, transcendence, regression, and the beauty of dying for a cause

seem finally more compelling than earthly success. So martyrs come to the pyre to commit suicide for Liberty, dying "with moan / Like love" (4222–23). Baker writes, "The will to self-sacrifice is stronger than the will to survive and triumph" (82). But what accounts for the will to self-sacrifice?

Whatever else plays a role in the failure to find earthly success, we have to attribute a portion of responsibility to the incest motif. Unlike Tristan and Isolde, René and Amelia, or most of the other inherently doomed couples in the literature of eros, Laon and Cythna don't conceive of their passion as wrong or tragic; the narrative is free of a Werther-like guilt and sorrow. It also is sufficiently provocative that the lovers do find transcendent bliss and an ultimate status as inspiring symbols for the rest of humanity. But what we can call freedom we can also call conspicuous absence. As J. Hillis Miller puts it, "The union of Laon and Cythna is paid for when they are burned at the stake" (242). As a story of incest *Laon and Cythna* cannot be a story with a happy ending in this world.[23] The will to self-sacrifice is, more precisely, a will to the martyrdom that unifies in a single fire forbidden consummation and self-punishment. By virtue of its commitment to incest, *Laon and Cythna*, while it seeks to alleviate failure, also generates it.

Another of the poem's major themes is equality, including equality of the sexes. For William Veeder, Cythna is merely an "instrument" and a "projection" of Laon (55–56). I think Baker takes us deeper into the poem, though, when, just the opposite, he calls Laon a "mere shadow" of Cythna (81). Indeed, after its incestuous character the most provocative aspect of the relationship is that the more conventional forms of active heroism belong to Cythna. It is she who steals the horse, or the sexual power, from tyrannical authority. It is also in her development that Shelley portrays an emergence from discipleship into autonomy. In counseling Laon that all is not lost despite the tyrant's return, she even becomes the teacher of her teacher. Laone is both the female and the aggressive side of Laon. Richard Holmes, who admires the couple as equals, remarks elsewhere that Shelley often assigned masculine roles to his heroines and passive ones to his heroes. Holmes speaks of this, vaguely, in terms of "bisexuality and androgynous creative powers."[24] One might argue that Shelley is trying to strengthen the female side of the partnership to compensate for the male bias of his culture. But I would suggest that in assigning the aggressiveness to the female side of his dyadic hero, Shelley is accepting that aggressiveness only enough to associate it with the mirror-self. Meanwhile Laon, the original ego, preserves a certain detachment and innocence, while still sharing the advantages of his double's aggressiveness.

The character of the child is relevant here. Cythna gives birth after her rape by Othman, which in turn occurs after Laon has had a sexual dream about her, flying through the air with her clasped to his bosom (1145–47). Laon is the spiritual and symbolic father, but Othman is the paternal tyrant Lust that plants the seed. In one sense, Laon steals the father's child for his own, but in another sense Othman is a substitute father, giving Laon a child while taking on the psychic burden of sexual aggressiveness and physical lust. Shelley was an actual father several times over by the time he wrote *Laon and Cythna*, but in this poetic fantasy he is still unable to imagine the ideal self as the father, although he is struggling toward such a conception.

But the poem's deepest myth is the separation of good and evil, embodied in an ontological conflict between two equal powers. Cythna's faith is that "Evil with evil, good with good must wind / In bands of union, which no power may sever: / They must bring forth their kind, and be divided never!" (3709–11). Her faith is not only that, as in Freud's prayer in *Civilization and its Discontents*, Eros might "assert himself in the struggle with his equally immortal adversary" (*SE*, 21:145), but even more that, like the tares and wheat of the apocalyptic harvest in Jesus's parable (Matthew 13:30), good and evil are clearly separable. But in fact Shelley makes it difficult for us to tell the difference between the two when, after establishing serpent and eagle as symbols of good and evil, he then proceeds to use them with the opposite significations and to do so with a seemingly perverse persistence. Poison is "a snake in flowers" (383), fear and lust are "two dark serpents" (701), Custom is a serpent (3439), hate and guile are twin serpents (4078), hate grips the heart like a snake enfolding a bird (3379–87), Othman is a "toothless snake" (1941), his allies are wolves and serpents (3854), his senators have eyes like "hungry snakes" (4443), and his assassins are "rabid snakes" attacking a child who feeds them (1774). The winged earth and revolutionary America (3693, 4423), on the other hand, are like eagles, and Cythna addresses the rebels after their apparent victory as "new-fledged Eagles" (2183). Bird and serpent even appear together with conventional results as when Cythna is a "charmed bird that haunts the serpent's den" (1080) and when in a revolutionary sculpture a winged figure, looking calmly at the sun as eagles are supposed to, crushes the "obscene worm" of Faith beneath his feet (2168). Brian Wilkie (130) and James Rieger (103) defend such reversals, arguing that after the first canto Shelley returns from a vision of eternity to the scene of fallen, conventional perception. But after the opening canto the entire story is told by Laon and Cythna, who in every other way see things in the true, or Shelleyan, perspective. The reversal seems like a thoroughgoing self-subversion, a poetic parapraxis; it seems as if Shelley forgot the novel symbolism he developed in the opening canto.

Laon and Cythna, then, in its argument presents good and evil as clear antitheses and in the imagery of bird and serpent presents them as inextricably intertwined. The attempt to separate them is the poem's chief strategy of defense. While *Alastor* is a romance of regression, *Laon and Cythna* is a romance of projection. In Laon's early sexual dream, he is sitting with Cythna at the threshold of a cave when he hears shrieks from "The cavern's secret depths" (1143). As he flies away with her, "Legions of foul and ghastly shapes" pluck at her (1149). Then he wakes to find her being kidnapped by Othman's henchmen. The threat is first deep inside the cavern, or within Laon, then outside; his desire for his sister is projected onto Othman, the "hyena lust" (989).[25] Afterward, imprisoned naked on the phallic column, unable to escape from his own tormented sexuality, he hallucinates "Legions" of "Foul, ceaseless shadows," which look like him (1309, 1311); and in his vision of eating Cythna's corpse, he becomes the hyena lust. Later, Laon's sexuality emerges in a form that is both idealized and physical, but this is only after lust and rape in the form of Othman have proleptically cleared the way for it. That is, after Othman's sexuality even incest can seem pure.

The women of the Golden City seek refuge "from the oppressor's wrath, / Or the caresses of his sated lust" (1587–88). Othman is Wrath as well as Lust. Laon is a man preternaturally free from anger, and it is easy to forget, since the poem never again refers to the fact, that he once killed three men. That, not incest, is the literal reason for his punishment on the column. But even though Laon's act can be justified, this is a poem that bends over backward to advocate nonviolence. In the original incident Cythna urges Laon not to despair, for she sees her seizure as a way to penetrate the Golden City and begin her work among its slaves, but he ignores her and kills the three "with one impulse" (1194). He is then schooled in nonviolence by the hermit, and we see no more of such impulses in him; even when he fights desperately against the counterrevolution, he does so in shame. While the active, rebellious Cythna, with her gifted leadership, is the projected form of good aggressiveness in the poem, Othman is the repository of the sheer anger, hate, and violence that Laon himself originally expressed.

The heroes of *Laon and Cythna* live in a dualistic world of sublime eros and self-sacrificing altruism, on the one hand, and, on the other, unspeakable cruelty, pestilence, rape, infanticide, and cannibalism—projected forms of the lust and violence that are felt to be tyrants within the self. Defending Othman against the vengeance of the rebels, Laon says, "Is there one who ne'er / In secret thought has wished another's ill?— / Are ye all pure?" (2017–19). Laon says that the victims of Othman's assassins forgive their murderers; Cythna forgives time for its changes; and, liberating the mariners from their own past crimes, she says, "Reproach not thine own soul, but know thyself, / Nor hate another's crime, nor loathe thine own" (3388–89). But in the poem as a whole forgiveness of evil in the self, as opposed to evil in others, remains a dream.

Together with Liberty and Equality, the poem celebrates Fraternity. "We all are brethren," Laon tells the assassins (1812). The double of Laon, whose poetry makes brothers of his listeners, is the fratricidal first man, and Laon himself becomes a fratricide when he participates in the killing of "human brethren" (2462). In this context we can understand his elliptically described relationship with the friend who betrays him and to whom he is later reconciled. Here too the poem seeks to convert brotherly hostility into brotherly love, although it finally kills off the friend in battle. Shelley's intense, ambivalent feelings about Byron and Hogg no doubt contribute to the poem's portrayal of the friend and of brotherly love and brotherly anger in general. But in addition, if we are all "sons of one great mother" (817), then the "brother" is anyone like ourselves with whom we must share the mother. A sculpture celebrating the revolution shows a mother nursing an infant and a basilisk (2161–63). The poisonous basilisk, the destructive sibling, is peacefully transformed in this emblem of revolutionary fraternity.[26]

When the first man, who "alone, / Stood on the verge of chaos" (352–53), kills his brother, one may wonder where that brother suddenly comes from. The first man may be the elder brother, thus a murderous precursor. But in a literal reading he is a solitary who has just been created. A solitary first man could kill his brother if his "brother" was part of himself, the dark *semblable* that the ego cannot forgive and would like to kill off by projection. So the infant and the deadly basilisk may be seen not only as siblings but as two sides of the same being. The wish for fraternity is a wish for reconciliation with the self as well as with others.

Laon and Cythna seeks to establish a family of brothers with the Earth as mother and no father. But although the father appears negatively as the tyrant and ambivalently as the inspiring and Cyclopean good ones of the past, he also appears positively as the hermit. This mild father inspires Laon to prevent the revolution from becoming violent, and he also rescues him from the column of lust. The good father saves him from his own passions.

As for the mother in the poem, her role is much less visible but ultimately more complex than that of sister, brother, or father. Indeed, the idea of the mother is as pivotal here as the similarly muted idea of the father was in *Alastor*. Where does the mother appear in the poem? The Earth is several times described as an ideal mother, and Cythna celebrates a "Spirit" that is the "Mother and soul of all to which is given / The light of life" (2197–99). In addition, Laon's first recollections are of maternal sweetness and nourishment. But we also meet a mother who throws her children onto the sacrificial pyre (4207), and the most vivid mother in the poem is the grotesque Pestilence. Laon's homeland is Argolis, a curious authorial choice. Argolis was the home of the treacherous and murderous Clytemnaestra, who dreamed of her son Orestes as a snake suckling at her bosom.[27] In the allusion to ancient Argolis the destructive and hated mother appears in Laon's idyllic childhood before Othman comes on the scene. In its exploration of aggression, *Laon and Cythna* goes back beyond oedipal revolt and sibling rivalry to the earlier war between infant and mother, between the devouring, poisoning, or denying mother and the biting infant. That biting is the prototype of the oral aggression I described earlier as the double of the oral power of poetry and eloquence in the poem.

Aeschylus describes Clytemnaestra as a viper and Agamemnon as an eagle;[28] their personal conflict also embodies a struggle between the old religion of the earth mother and the new religion of the sky father. But in Clytemnaestra's nightmare of Orestes, the serpent-son who is supposed to be the champion of the mother turns against her, an omen of the upheaval in which the father triumphs over the mother. The allusion in the epigraph to Hyperboreas is suggestive in this context. Hyperboreas, "beyond the north," is where Apollo spent his winters when he shared with Dionysos the shrine of Dephi. He had taken over Delphi from the mother goddess after killing the serpent who guarded it.[29] The allusion to Hyperboreas brings into play the attempt to master or wrest power from the mother or even to flee from her, beyond the north, beyond all mortal nature, her world. We can understand here the inconsistency in the symbol of the serpent. Something in Shelley does not want to be the phallic subordinate of the Great Mother.

There is an additional reason why the mother is, in part, bad in *Laon and Cythna*. Laon's punishment on the column after his sexual dream is marked particularly by starvation. Similarly, after their actual lovemaking, the lovers are hungry—Cythna has not eaten for two days—and Laon rides down to the plain for food. He finds a fountain made undrinkable by blood and also the mother Pestilence, who tells him, "this bosom dry, / Once fed two babes," now dead (2767–68). She takes him to the feast of "Famine, my paramour" (2781): three heaps of bread surrounded by a ring of dead infants. The movement from sexuality to famine suggests an archaic anxiety. The onset of genitality takes the child away from its original image of the mother as nourisher. When the son becomes phallic, the breast becomes dry and the baby dies. Here punishment for sexuality comes from the mother, not the father. At its peak of joy, however, the poem expresses a wish that even a basilisk, a monster, might not be rejected by the nourishing mother. Shelley once complained in a letter, "I am regarded . . . as a rare prodigy of crime & pollution whose look even might infect," like a basilisk (2:94). That the impulse toward liberation from authority and toward erotic liberation leads to a conflict with the mother is an unresolved problem in the poem. How can we have the advantages of both genital maturity and the pregenital, dyadic relation to the mother? Incest is the poem's experimental answer, and it doesn't work, at least in this world.

When Laon enters the Golden City to sacrifice himself for Cythna, he stops a would-be assassin, saying, "What hast thou to do / With me, poor wretch?" (4400–4401). Laon is paralleled to Jesus at several points: the quasi-crucifixion on the mountain, the ethic of forgiveness, the pacifism, the voluntary entry into the dangerous capital. But this particular allusion takes us into the psychological center of the poem. Jesus said these words—in the King James version,

"What have I to do with thee?" (John 2:4)—to his mother, declaring his independence from mortal nature; Laon says them to an assassin, declaring his independence from violence. But in the parallelism of the allusion, the mother becomes violence. The allusion thus reinforces the shadowy sense of the mother in the poem as an aggressor against the child. But if the mother is violence, by the same figure violence is also a mother; and, indeed, aggression, or negation, is the rejected mother of *Laon and Cythna*, its source of inspiration. In the opening canto the twin genii of good and evil "burst the womb of inessential Nought" (351). Negativity is the primal mother of the poem's universe; and in this poem, which takes as its primal scene and symbol the violent conflict of two animals, aggression is vital in the poem's political protest, its moral defiance, and its quest for intellectual freedom and literary autonomy. We also see aggression in its poetic and psychological reliance upon the primitive aggressive strategy of projection, or expulsion. In Laon's wish to rise above aggression, we see the poem's wish to be resurrected from its own source of poetic vitality.

Ambivalence over regression gave *Alastor* both its richness and its disturbing irresolution. Similarly, the conflict over aggression gives *Laon and Cythna* an unruly depth and a richness of inner energy that it might not have attained had it been more ideologically undisturbed and less self-subverting, but it also suggests that in the poem's quasi-Manichaean vision and its desire for a complete transcendence of aggression Shelley has not yet found a poetic myth adequate to the deep needs and recognitions of his total sensibility.

P. M. S. Dawson cites Robert Nozick to explicate Shelley's political vision: we need to know our wishful fantasies, Nozick suggests, in order to understand what will satisfy us.[30] *Laon and Cythna* tells us what our fantasies are. More than that, it makes the shocking proposal that incestuous fantasy calls us ever higher in the fight against evil; indeed, incestuous wishes become the nourishing source of sympathy, idealism, and humanistic reform. *Laon and Cythna* eroticizes revolution without, however, resolving problems within eros. It associates political ideals with deep psychic impulses but leaves those impulses at least partly in the realm of the ego-dystonic, almost wholly so in the case of the aggressive impulses. It is not that the poem's myths of equality, inspiration, and undefeatable struggle break apart. Rather, Shelley is able to take them only to a certain point. He can keep the quest going, but he can't envision a positive conclusion to it. To go further, to imagine successful revolutionary change without the problems associated with aggression and to imagine realized ideal eros without the problems associated with regression, he would have to do more than express wishes and anxieties; he would have to work with them, which is what he does in *Prometheus Unbound*.

10

Prometheus Unbound:
The Prometheus Myth

PROMETHEUS, SAYS JANE HARRISON, IS THE "ARCH-TITAN."[1] CHILDREN of Mother Earth and Father Sky, the Titans have been commonly thought of as proud, violent, rebellious, virile, even Priapic, beings, who were recurrently punished for overreaching themselves.[2] "They are constantly being driven down below the earth to nethermost Tartarus and always re-emerging," Harrison writes. "The very violence and persistence with which they are sent down below show that they belong up above. They rebound like divine india-rubber balls."[3] They are like repressed, or irrepressible, energies.[4]

But it is not only Shelley's identification with rebellious forces that made Prometheus an ideal subject for him. Prometheus was a great sufferer; Mary Shelley notes that in the year he wrote what he called his "lyrical drama," Shelley was also contemplating "lyrical dramas" based on the tormented life of Tasso and the book of Job (*H*, 270–71). Prometheus was also a hero of words, the herald of the Titans; Norman O. Brown notes that the herald was originally the leader of magic rituals and that the crafts of messenger and bard, two kinds of speakers, descend from this single function (31). The culture-bringer and, according to the meaning of his name, the Forethinker, Prometheus was also a hero of mind. Gaston Bachelard identifies an "Oedipus complex of the life of the intellect," called the Prometheus complex, which drives us to know more than our fathers and teachers.[5] But if Prometheus is the one who seeks to know, he is also the one who already does know. The *Alastor* Poet, like the riddle-solver Oedipus, was a pursuer of secrets. But Prometheus is the holder of secret knowledge; he knows from his mother—Themis, the Earth, the Goddess of Delphi—that the sea nymph Thetis, whom Zeus is pursuing, will bear a child stronger than his father. Prometheus fills an ideal role for Shelley; he knows what even the king of the gods is curious about.

The peculiar condition of belatedness in the Prometheus myth also has Shelleyan resonance. Zeus and Prometheus were actually cousins, but Prometheus is like a rebellious son to the father of the gods; in Hesiod, Zeus even married Prometheus's mother, Themis.[6] Also, as a thief of fire rather than one who possessed it originally, Prometheus is a latecomer who overcomes his belatedness. At the same time, Prometheus is fatherlike as well as sonlike: as a Titan, he is part of an older order than Zeus's Olympians, and he also helped bring Zeus to power; as the creator of the first men, he is a father to humanity. Prometheus is a positive contrast to the *puer senex,* not a youth wasted into an old man like the *Alastor* Poet but a hero who combines the attractions of the youthful position with fatherly priority and power.

Furthermore, Prometheus has the kind of doubleness that haunted Shelley. The benefactor of humanity, Prometheus is also responsible for Pandora and her evils. C. Kerényi calls him "the corrupter and savior."[7] With his brother, Epimetheus, he makes up an unfortunately inseparable pair, Forethought and Afterthought, trickster and dupe. Yet Kerényi points out that Prometheus himself lacks forethought in misjudging the consequences of his acts.[8] We have seen Shelley's concern with the "intertexture of good and evil" (*Essay on the Punishment of Death, C,* 156). In the preface to *Laon and Cythna* "violent and malignant passions . . . are ever on the watch to mingle with . . . the most beneficial innovations" (*E,* 2:47). In the *Essay on the Devil and Devils,* we live in a universe "where evil and good are inextricably entangled" and "tendencies to happiness and preservation are forever baffled by misery and decay" (*C,* 266).

Prometheus seems as emblematic of that entanglement as any character in Western myth, and judgments of him have varied widely. As far back as the early church fathers, Prometheus was compared to Christ;[9] and for Goethe, he was a new and better creator, making humanity in his own compassionate image.[10] But for Rousseau, he was the spoiler, "a God inimical to man's repose."[11] For Nietzsche, the story of Prometheus exemplifies the unhappiness of Western culture, which envisions "at the heart of things" a tragic "contrariety": "an interpenetration of several worlds, as for instance a divine and a human, each individually in the right but each, as it encroaches upon the other, having to suffer for its individuality"; the heroic striver inevitably "comes up against that primordial contradiction and learns both to sin and to suffer" (64).

In Aeschylus the doubleness of Prometheus is particularly rich. In *Prometheus Bound* Zeus is the rightful ruler of the world, but he is a new god, and, as Hephaestus says, "every ruler is harsh whose rule is new" (line 35). Furthermore, he has planned to destroy the present race of men and create a new one, and only Prometheus has dared to resist him. Prometheus, however, "gave honors to mortals beyond what was just" (30). Perhaps what Prometheus surrenders to when he finally gives up the secret is less Zeus than the Necessity and Justice beyond Zeus. Nietzsche speaks of the "profound Aeschylean longing for *justice*," of the poet's "central tenet . . . in which Moira, as eternal justice, is seen enthroned above men and gods alike" (62).

Shelley too conceives of an eternal Necessity or Justice beyond all tyrants—in *Prometheus Unbound* it is called Demogorgon—but not one that would ever induce his Prometheus to give up his rebellion. As he explains in his preface, he "was averse from a catastrophe so feeble as that of reconciling the Champion with the Oppressor of mankind" and appalled by the concept of Prometheus "unsaying his high language, and quailing before his successful and perfidious adversary" (*R*, 206). Yet Shelley himself had regarded Prometheus ambivalently in the past. In *The Retrospect*, an *Alastor*-like career is portrayed in Promethean terms: the poem's speaker once yearned "to seize the wings of morn, / And where its vital fires were born / To soar" (73–75), but now a "ceaseless flame" preys on his "withered vitals" (41–42). In the vegetarian mythology of *Queen Mab*, Prometheus stands at the very source of human evil: Prometheus, representing humanity, "applied fire to culinary purposes; thus inventing an expedient for screening from his disgust the horrors of the shambles. From this moment his vitals were devoured by the vulture of disease. . . . All vice arose from the ruin of healthful innocence. Tyranny, superstition, commerce, and inequality, were then first known, when reason vainly attempted to guide the wanderings of exacerbated passion" (*E*, 1:409).

It is a major purpose of the play's preface to unbind Prometheus from these and the other negative treatments of him. "The only imaginary being resembling in any degree Prometheus, is Satan,"

Shelley writes, and in a tone that combines the inflammatory and the innocent he calls Prometheus "a more poetical character than Satan because, in addition to courage and majesty and firm and patient opposition to omnipotent force, he is susceptible of being described as exempt from the taints of ambition, envy, revenge, and a desire for personal aggrandisement, which in the Hero of *Paradise Lost,* interfere with the interest." Moreover, the ambiguity of Milton's treatment of Satan is morally, as well as aesthetically, corrupting because it induces us to accept evil, "to weigh his faults with his wrongs and to excuse the former because the latter exceed all measure." But Prometheus is a Satan cleansed of aggression and self-glorification, "the type of the highest perfection of moral and intellectual nature, impelled by the purest and the truest motives to the best and noblest ends" (*R,* 206–7).

Having compared Prometheus to Satan, Shelley goes on in the play to make him Christlike in certain respects. Shelley is trying to create a new hero, at once loving and titanically aspiring, who will encompass and surpass the two dominant, and antithetical, figures in Miltonic and Western myth. He is a better Satan, a better Christ, and also a better Prometheus. Prometheus in the play is a genius who rises out of the gulf of error. He is not only the former self-betrayer, or "Proteus," of Aeschylus and the former inventor of evil of *Queen Mab;* he is also the former doomed hero of anger and rebellion in Shelley's poetry, the Ahasuerus or Zastrozzi figure. In the comparison to Satan, Prometheus assumes and then casts off the intertexture of good and evil. In *Prometheus Unbound,* Shelley rejects the tragic vision of "contrariety" at "the heart of things" in favor of a vision of liberation not only from evil and tyranny but also from the ego-dystonic elements of the mind that opposes them. He tries to separate the morbid from the ideal not by repressing it, as in *Athanase,* or by projecting it, as in *Laon and Cythna,* but by making it a corrigible part of the hero's character.

In addition to making Prometheus a rebel to the end and a victor and cleansing his character of fury and vengeance, Shelley radically revises the original myth by changing its attitude toward women. He makes Prometheus a romantic lover, even a dreaming Adam. More generally, in positively portraying the feminine, he brings out certain repressed elements in the original myth. Karl Abraham wrote that the myth of Prometheus, in which women are "mentioned only incidentally," and which is based on the drilling of a stick into a disk to make fire, celebrates "masculine procreative power as the main principle of life" (200). Yet Prometheus has close ties to a female divinity, his mother, Themis, the daughter of Gaea, the primordial earth mother. Themis appears in Greek culture sometimes as Earth herself—in *Prometheus Bound* Themis is another name of Gaea—and sometimes as Law; in Homer's Olympian mythology, she has the seemingly minor function of assembling the gods. Kerényi interprets her as "the earthly maternal principle, which protects and brings forth growth and fruit."[12] For Jane Harrison, "She is the force that brings and binds men together, she is 'herd instinct,' the collective conscience, the social sanction."[13] Whether figured as the earth or the group, the mother of Prometheus embodies the Dionysiac principle of de-individuation, and even in the Olympian reduction of her role, she preserves her function of bringing individuals together into oneness. Prometheus has his roots in an older, pre-Olympian order of culture, in which the earth goddess is the center of worship and the mother is the center of family structure.

The Titans, however, were intermediary beings, who, Harrison writes, "seem early to have left their earth-nature behind them and climbed one step up the ladder to heaven,"[14] and among them Prometheus had the closest connections to the new Olympian order. He sided with Zeus in the war of the Titans against the Olympians and convinced his mother to do so as well.[15] The maleness of the Promethean myth might itself be a sign of this Titan's peculiar transitional position; he is a being of the archaic mother made over in the image of the new fathers and serving in his defeat as testimony to their power.

What Robert Graves calls Hesiod's "antifeminist fable" of Pandora, with its diatribe against "the deadly race and tribe of women,"[16] brings to the surface a theme in the myth, in which the power of earth, woman, and the mother is a force to be conquered. Aeschylus, although a partisan of patriarchal Zeus, treats the mother more sympathetically, envisioning an end to the wars of father against son and male against female but all under the dominion of the father. In *The Oresteia*, after the murdering Clytemnaestra is killed and the rule of the mother symbolically ended, Aeschylus makes a place for the maternal principle within the new regime of the father, converting the terrifying Erinyes into the benign Eumenides.[17] In *Prometheus Bound* he gives us not Pandora but Io, who, as Kerényi puts it, "suffers and displays the absolute defenselessness of woman in the order of Zeus."[18] In that order, the consorts of divinity are chiefly young maidens, sometimes treated in a sacrificial manner. Conversely, in the order of the Great Mother, the consorts of divinity were young males, also treated sacrificially, the dying and reviving fertility heroes. In the religion of earth, kings succeeded each other in violent struggles, like the priests of Frazer's Golden Bough, or Agamemnon and Aegisthus. The secret of Themis, we might say, is that Zeus might be no more than another sacrificial king in a matrilinear, earth-centered order, to be replaced by a younger and stronger version of the subordinate male principle.[19]

Barbara Gelpi argues that Harrison, despite her attraction to the older maternal order, ultimately agrees with the conciliatory Aeschylus that the development from a mother-centered to a father-centered culture is necessary. Shelley, Gelpi writes, challenges that necessity.[20] Indeed, in his drastic revision of the myth, Shelley goes straight to its underlying antifeminism: he makes the father a tyrant and idealizes woman. In place of Pandora and the pitiable Io, he gives us Asia, a female creative power who is necessary to humanity's salvation. I would suggest, however, that Shelley's treatment does contain ambivalent elements. R. D. Laing sees the rock on which the original Prometheus is bound and the eagle that devours his liver "as two aspects of the mother, to whom one is chained . . . and by whom one is devoured. . . . The devouring eagle and the entrails, renewed only to be devoured again, are together a nightmarish inversion of the normal cycle of feeding" (174). For Arthur Wormhoudt that hostility survives in Shelley: while Asia is a good mother, the Earth, Prometheus's literal mother, is a denying, unsatisfying mother.[21] Shelley critics have excoriated Wormhoudt, but we should be open to the possibility of ambivalence toward the mother when we have found it elsewhere in Shelley.[22] I will suggest, however, that it is less the denying than the overwhelming mother that is at issue. The mother in *Prometheus Unbound* is a strong power with which one must both ally oneself and struggle.[23]

The prefatory matter of the play includes another figure, in addition to Satan and the Prometheus of Aeschylus, against whom Shelley plays off his hero. The title page of the 1820 *Prometheus* volume includes an epigraph from Aeschylus's lost *Epigoni:* "Audisne Haec, Amphiariae, Sub Terram Abdite?"[24] Amphiaraus was a seer who opposed the war of the Seven against Thebes because he foresaw a dis-

astrous defeat, including his own death. Finally joining the attack, he
was pursued by a fierce opponent and saved from a disgraceful death
by Zeus, who split the ground with a thunderbolt. Swallowed up into
the earth, Amphiaraus lived on as a famous oracle and, in Kerényi's
words, "a chthonian god of healing."[25] The chthonians, dwelling in
the earth, were associated with both fertility and the souls of the
dead, the precursors.[26]

Shelley came upon Aeschylus's line in Cicero, where it is a rebuke
to a student who could not live up to his teacher's stoical doctrines:
"Do you hear this, Amphiaraus, hidden under the earth?" Bloom
finds two meanings in the epigraph. First, Shelley contrasts Am-
phiaraus's defeatism to the stoical endurance of his own Prometh-
eus. Second, he contrasts "the Zeus-defying Prometheus and the
Zeus-fearing Amphiaraus," to challenge "a multiplicity of orthodox
poets," including Aeschylus and the Lake Poets.[27] Confirmation of
this reading comes in Shelley's notebook, where the line is addressed
"To the Ghost of Aeschylus."[28] Shelley turns Aeschylus's line against
its author. But if Amphiaraus yields to the father, he is also under the
power of the mother, swallowed up into the earth. His situation is
suggestive of Wordsworth, not only in that Wordsworth was, to Shel-
ley, a Protean turncoat now serving orthodoxy but also in that he was
the great poet of the theme of enclosure within nature, the creator
of Lucy, "Rolled round in earth's diurnal course, / With rocks, and
stones, and trees," and Margaret, who at the end of *The Ruined Cot-
tage* becomes a modern version of a chthonian deity, nourishing us
spiritually from her place of rest in "the calm earth."[29] In Amphiaraus
we can see the wish to rejoin the mother carried to an unacceptable
extreme.

Max Muller said that fire was "the son of two pieces of wood" and
that "it devoured its father and mother."[30] In *Prometheus Unbound*,
Shelley tells the story of both Prometheus and Asia emerging from
parental figures into their own maturity. But although he imagines
an unbinding from the mother as well as from the father, at the
same time he wants to retain a connection to the mother's power.
The original Prometheus, as we have seen, was a transitional figure,
hovering between humans and gods, Titans and Olympians, earth
mother and sky father. Indeed, in his role as herald he was one who,
as Kerényi puts it, traveled "eternally back and forth, connecting
antithetical realms."[31] The freedom that Shelley imagines is inter-
nal, as well as external, and involves in part a psychic mobility, a

traveling back and forth between antithetical positions toward the mother.

But before *Prometheus Unbound* takes up the struggle with the good mother, it must deal with the bad father, and we turn now to the conflict of Prometheus and Jupiter that opens the play.

11

Prometheus Unbound:
Act 1

PROMETHEUS UNBOUND BEGINS IN RAGE.[1] THE SETTING, WITH ITS "RA-
VINE of Icy Rocks" and its glaciers (*R*, 209), recalls the description
Shelley wrote of the Alps while traveling through Savoy: "The scene is
like that described in the 'Prometheus' of Aeschylus—Vast rifts & cav-
erns in the granite precipices—wintry mountains, with ice & snow
above . . ."; he goes on to speak of the "tyranny" of the mountains
over the impoverished, disease-ridden inhabitants of the valley be-
low.[2] The tyrannical mountain-demon against whom Prometheus
rages in his opening speech is God, king, father, any male authority.
The theme of his first words, however, is his own freedom; he ad-
dresses Jupiter as "Monarch" of "all Spirits / But One" and claims that
he too has an empire, even if it is one of "torture and solitude," that
he reigns "O'er mine own misery and thy vain revenge" (1–2, 14, 11).

His autonomy and self-mastery, however, are unrealized ideals.
His anger has fueled his endurance, but in "Three thousand years of
sleep-unsheltered hours" it has not advanced him toward liberation
(12). In *Alastor* Shelley explored an ego controlled by regression;
here he explores an ego controlled by aggression. Prometheus calls
himself "eyeless in hate" (9); this blind prophet is no visionary Tire-
sias or Milton but is blinded by his own fury. For three thousand years
he has been immobilized creatively as well as physically, unable to go
beyond reiterating his rage over and over. His claims to autonomy
are questioned by their very wording. Richard Cronin points out that
in the passage "Whilst me, who am thy foe, eyeless in hate, / Hast
thou made reign and triumph, to thy scorn, / O'er mine own misery"
(9–11), either Prometheus or Jupiter could be making the other

130

reign, either could be scorning the other, and either could be eye-less in hate (137–38). In this blurring of pronouns, we see that Prometheus has not succeeded in clearly differentiating himself from Jupiter; the hatred he uses to struggle against, in Leon Wald-off's terms, being incorporated into Jupiter's world (83) is ironically what makes them similar.

Prometheus's defiance is accompanied by intense physical agony. Earthquakes "wrench the rivets" in his "quivering wounds" (39). This play begins with the sparagmos—"the tearing apart of the sacrificial body," Northrop Frye calls it[3]—that, as in *Prometheus Bound,* typically comes at the end of a classical tragedy. In Shelley's sparagmos, Prometheus is symbolically penetrated and feminized, as the glaciers "pierce" him with their spears (31), and he is devoured, as the chains "Eat" into his bones (33). Arthur Wormhoudt observes that the pas-sage suggests suffering caused by the mother, as well as the father (88–89). Prometheus, for example, is angry at nature for ignoring his pain: "Have [the] deaf waves not heard my agony?" (29). He is "Nailed" to a "wintry" and "dead" mountain (20–21) as if crucified on a cold, denying breast. The rage at the father awakens all the ar-chaic angers. As the play opens, Prometheus is not only imprisoned by a tyrant; he is also imprisoned in a nightmare of genital and oral aggression, of assaults upon the sense of self and the sense of bodily integrity, of victimization by monstrous parental forces. As seen in his exquisite consciousness of types of pain, he is also imprisoned in his own masochism.[4] "Pain, pain ever, forever!" is his refrain (23, 30), and its repetition is the poetic sign of his failure to advance.

The anger of Milton's great hero of righteous aggression, Sam-son, finds its consummation in a glorious, self-destructive act of re-venge. But the angry opening words of Prometheus climax in a radi-cal change, a Shelleyan version of the peripateia, or reversal of the expected, in classical tragedy. Thus far Prometheus has been experi-encing time as an agonizingly slow succession of pain-filled moments. "And yet," he suddenly says, "to me welcome is Day and Night"; for that succession of "wingless, crawling Hours" will bring the one hour that "Shall drag thee, cruel King, to kiss the blood / From these pale feet, which then might trample thee / If they disdained not such a prostrate slave" (44, 48, 50–52). The classical peripateia advances the hero toward his destruction. In this constructive reversal, Prometh-eus first affirms the time that has been torturing him and then envi-sions a turnaround in which the master and the slave trade places.

How can we account for his faith in time, and why does that faith appear just at this moment?

Donald Reiman compares the Hours of Prometheus's speech to the Horae of classical myth (*R*, 211). Daughters of Zeus and Themis, the Horae were fertility spirits, personifications of the seasons. C. Kerényi writes that the Horae, "rhythmic periods of the world's unfolding," symbolize "an ideal—lawful, just, peaceful—world order" and embody the "belief that a just order has its natural foundation in Themis, the earthly maternal principle."[5] At the furthest reaches of his rage, Prometheus touches something more primal than disappointment and fury. In his reversal we see the emergence of a deep, ultimate belief in a maternal ideal. That it appears just after images of suffering that express, in addition to rage at the father, anger at the mother is suggestive. The good mother follows the bad mother into the poem as if by reaction formation. That new sense of the mother brings with it power as well as goodness. Prometheus compares the liberating hour to "some dark Priest" dragging "the reluctant victim" to his death (49), and in this simile we can glimpse the savage priest-kings of the Golden Bough, guardians of the Goddess and her sacred space, murderously succeeding each other.[6] In his peripateia, Prometheus asserts that the archaic order of the mother has priority over Jupiter's paternal order, that Jupiter is merely a subordinate of the Great Mother.

At this point a second and greater reversal occurs. The victim has envisioned restraining himself from inflicting physical pain on his oppressor: he will "Disdain" to trample Jupiter (53). But that disdain still implies a barely nonviolent sadism; Prometheus will be nonviolent not because he rejects violence but because Jupiter is too contemptible to be crushed physically. To be liberated here is to have the opportunity to even a score. But then he says,

> Disdain? Ah no! I pity thee.—What Ruin
> Will hunt thee undefended through the wide Heaven!
> How will thy soul, cloven to its depth with terror,
> Gape like a Hell within! I speak in grief
> Not exultation, for I hate no more.
>
> (53–57)

Although the Hour will release Prometheus from Jupiter, he must release himself from rage. In his act of self-correction we see a saving form of belatedness, a second chance, the beginnings of a rebirth. How does this change come about?

Prometheus says that "misery made me wise" (58), but this seems like a vague afterthought or rationalization. The change seems sudden and inexplicable. "It does not appear that [Prometheus] had to struggle with his hatred," Frederick Pottle writes. "Reaching for it one day, he found it evaporated."[7] But we saw a similar change in *Laon and Cythna*. When Laon steered the revolution he had inspired away from violence, he was, in effect, checking his own aggression. The pattern of building up aggression against the father figure to the point of violence and then sacrificing it is common in Shelley in cases in which the aggression cannot be attributed to a safely remote stand-in like Ahasuerus or Beatrice Cenci. *The Mask of Anarchy*, for another example, culminates with a speech in which Mother Earth calls upon the men of England to revolt, reminds them of their reasons to be angry, focuses their attention on their own passion for vengeance, and finally says, "Do not thus when ye are strong" (196). Passive resistance for Shelley is not only resistance of external aggression with nonviolent methods but also resistance of a tremendous charge of internal aggression. The ultimate source of Prometheus's reversal is not time, knowledge, or suffering but the extremity of his own hatred. When his vengeful and sadistic feelings reach an unacceptable level and when the gratification of those feelings seems a realistic and imminent possibility, he recoils to an opposite extreme.[8]

What exactly is the pity that Prometheus's hatred turns into? Rousseau called pity a "gentle voice" of compassion that enables men to be more than monsters.[9] For Rousseau, pity is the "maternal law," Jacques Derrida observes, "illustrated archetypically by the relationship between mother and child" (173). But Ross Woodman writes that Prometheus's pity is actually "related to a lingering desire for revenge"; after he pities Jupiter he goes on to imagine what Jupiter's ruin will be like (110). Pity may normatively contain an aggressive element. Derrida writes that for Rousseau "We neither can nor should feel the pain of others immediately and absolutely, for such an interiorization or identification would be dangerous and destructive . . . one protects oneself, and holds the evil at arm's length" (190). In Blake, pity can be a mask for cruelty: "Pity would be no more / If we did not make somebody Poor"; "The Ox in the slaughter house moans . . . [Urizen] wept, & he called it Pity."[10] In Aeschylus,

Prometheus is "pitiable" and Jupiter is "pitiless" (248, 242). The one who gives or withholds pity is in a superior position. The attitude into which Prometheus recoils in his peripateia offers both continuity with and discontinuity from the original hatred. Michael Ferber writes that "pity seems to undermine the very basis of Jupiter's existence" (69). That is because in pitying Jupiter, Prometheus identifies both with the primal mother's power over male rulers like Jupiter and with her dyadic capacity for sympathy and goodness, which is alien to Jupiter's purely sadistic aggressiveness. This double pity responds to the demands of a contradictory state of mind, in which both hatred and submission are intolerable.

Here the play takes still another strange turn. Prometheus says, "The Curse / Once breathed on thee I would recall" (58-59), both "revoke" and "remember." Prometheus claims to be "changed so that aught evil wish / Is dead within, although no memory be / Of what is hate" (70–72). Why does he wish to remember what he has just repudiated? Shelley senses that aggression that has been forgotten has merely been driven out of consciousness and may continue to be obstructive. But there is an additional reason that he now launches his play into what might seem a lengthy and superfluous diversion, the search for the exact words of the lost curse.

In his preface Shelley writes that the imagery of his drama is "drawn from the operations of the human mind, or from those external actions by which they are expressed" (*R*, 207). Indeed, *Prometheus Unbound* is frequently conceived of as a drama of the mind or even a drama in the mind. But it is also a study of the insufficiency of purely internal change. In *Lines written among the Euganean Hills*, "love or reason cannot change / The despot's rage, the slave's revenge" (234–35); in *Prometheus Unbound*, they can do so but not by themselves. As several critics have argued, the play's special field of action is not thinking or feeling but language. Prometheus, we are told in act 2, "gave man speech, and speech created thought" (4.72). To change the world Prometheus must change his words. Kim Blank puts it well, saying that "it is through words that Prometheus is bound and unbound"; Blank writes that in the play "power resides . . . in the performative action of words" (145, 144). What needs to be added is that Shelley's vision of language has a strange, magical quality. In that vision, words are like things or physical forces. Once they have gotten out into the world they will continue to influence reality until they are taken out of the world or replaced by other words. Oscar

Firkins writes of Shelley's way of materializing the abstract; love, thought, and soul take on a quasi-physical being in his poetry (34–35, 60), and so too, we can add, does language.

Milton Wilson finds in Aeschylus a source for what he calls the play's "primitive belief in the effective power of words to produce the thing which they invoke" (62). He cites S. M. Adams, who found in *Prometheus Bound* "a deliberate throwback to a magic ritual . . . in which words are potent—helpful or injurious . . . words could *do* things."[11] Wilson writes that Shelley uses this archaic principle for dramatic purposes only, but I am suggesting that he makes it into a myth of the power of poetry. While we can see in that myth the primitive magic that made curses deadly and good words propitious, we can also see in it an infantile fantasy of omnipotence through vocalization, the child's cry that brings whatever is desired. The myth of the power of language in the play reaches back for both the potency of archaic words and the potency of preverbal orality, the medium of expression, pleasure, and survival for the child in the dyad.

That is why Shelley's concern is specifically with spoken language. Prometheus gave man speech. Marjory Bald called Prometheus "a voice rather than a man,"[12] and R. A. Holland, more sympathetically, wrote in 1876 that in Shelley's speculative world the "inhabitants must be spectral, often formless, sometimes only voices."[13] We need to eliminate the "only," for Shelley in *Prometheus Unbound* offers us a vision in which human beings are essentially speaking or singing presences. In the play, voices often emerge from a shadowy, radiant, or phantasmal setting that impedes visualization. This style, often characterized as abstract, has its own sensory presence, one that appeals primarily to the ear. It is a style that seeks the power of the preoedipal mother and her world.

But Shelley's myth of poetry has a progressive, as well as a regressive, dimension. The language of Prometheus is literally a language not of childlike cries and ritualistic formulas but of considered adult words. Shelley's myth of words is an example of extreme Romantic humanism, a vision of a world in which humanity has taken over some of the power of the God of Genesis, who creates heaven and earth with his voice, and the God of John, who creates the world with his Word. Shaped by speech and song, the Promethean world is specifically a poet's world. Shelley's exuberant creation of verse forms in the play (thirty-six different rhymed forms, according to Vida Scudder)[14] is part of a general celebration of man's oral, verbal power in general and the poet's in particular. At the origin of the fallen world of *Prometheus Unbound* is a forgotten speech, or repressed poem. The entire process of renovation begins with an act of verbal self-criticism, as Prometheus reflects on the wrong sound of a word, "disdain," that he has just spoken. Daniel Hughes studies "the development of Prometheus as an increasingly capable poet";[15] Kim Blank calls the curse "a corrupt poem that must be revised" (146); and Susan Hawk Brisman analyzes Shelley's search in the play for "a new language of the sublime," one, purified of Satanic tragedy and self-destructiveness, that can bring about a new form of consciousness (52). That new language is the end of a metamorphosis of orality. Prometheus begins in Shelley as the flesh-eating villain of *Queen Mab*; he then becomes the cursing and devoured rebel of the opening diatribe; and from there he develops through act 1 to become a benevolent and creative prophet. In Shelley's thematic treatment of language we find a strange and powerful mixture of magic and sublimation, narcissism and adaptation.

"A voice / Is wanting," Asia is told in act 2 (4.115–16). The wanting voice is, in context, both a desiring voice and a missing voice. In Act 1, as well, a voice is wanting as Prometheus wishes to recall the lost curse. The problem in acts 1 and 2 is to find the right words, and in the play's world of language the search for the right words is an epic adventure.

Like the narrator of *Alastor*, Prometheus first calls on his "brethren" in nature (130), asking them to return his words to him. But instead the voices of nature tell him only of the violence they suffered because of the curse. The elements of nature are like younger, frightened, helpless siblings, whom Prometheus champions against an oppressive father. He next calls on his mother, Earth, for help, but although she remembers the curse, preserving it as a "treasured spell" (184), she will not speak it for fear that Jupiter "Should hear, and link me to some wheel of pain / More torturing than the one whereon I roll" (141–42)—an allusion to the torture-wheel on which Ixion was punished in Hades. The Earth is a victim who needs her son's protection, and, far from the all-knowing Themis of the original myth, she lacks not only his prophetic conviction of future victory but also his saving recognition of the limitations of the hatred that consumes both of them. She is, nevertheless, the oedipal mother in league with the son against the tyrannical father. The allusion to Ixion reinforces the oedipal quality of the relationship: Ixion mur-

dered his father and tried to seduce Zeus's wife. In Shelley's trans-
formation, the mother, not the son, is on the wheel; she is on the
son's side in truth, not just in his fantasy, and is even punished for it.

At last, in one of the most important instances of doubleness in
Shelley's poetry, Earth does reveal a way for the lost words to be
found. "Ere Babylon was dust," she says,

> The Magus Zoroaster, my dead child,
> Met his own image walking in the garden.
> That apparition, sole of men, he saw.
> For know there are two worlds of life and death:
> One that which thou beholdest, but the other
> Is underneath the grave, where do inhabit
> The shadows of all forms that think and live.
>
>   (191–98)

In memory, St. Augustine says, "I meet myself"; "I remember myself
and what I have done, when and where I did it, and the state of my
mind at the time" (215). But Augustine is speaking of common
memory. Shelley's Zoroaster met himself in an uncommon way; he is
the sole of men to have descended to a deep realm of reflections. In
Earth's second world, where we can find the ego-dystonic as well as
the forgotten, Shelley gives us his clearest portrayal of an uncon-
scious. But this world also includes "all that faith creates, or love de-
sires"; it is a storehouse of dreams and "light imaginings" (201, 200).
In this shadow world the concepts of the unconscious and the Ro-
mantic imagination touch each other.[16]

Jane Harrison tells us that at the time of Zoroaster, in the sixth
century BCE, Persian religion infused Greek culture with elements
of magic, mysticism, and nature-worship, contributing to the Orphic
revival of the old Dionysian religion of Earth.[17] Shelley's Zoroaster is
Earth's child, a magus of the archaic mother, a preoedipal son, who
still has access to the mother's power. He is also Earth's dead child, a
nature-worshipper who after meeting his own image went on, in ef-
fect, to rejoin the mother and become a chthonian divinity like Am-
phiaraus, exercising power from within the mother's body. Prometh-
eus will duplicate the unique feat of the great magus Zoroaster, but
unlike Zoroaster he is a god. He will be the first to meet his image
without dying, without being absorbed into the mother. Indeed, his
encounter with a series of images or versions of himself will lead to
his rebirth.

He is not quite ready for his own image, though. Given the choice of any shadow to call up, he asks for the Phantasm of Jupiter, for he does not wish evil to "pass again / My lips, or those of aught resembling me" (219–20). He wants to know what he once was, but he still wants to keep it at a bearable distance. A certain degree of projection is still necessary to him.

As the Phantasm of Jupiter arises, Ione and Panthea, sisters of Asia who tend Prometheus during his captivity, describe for us the dreadful "Shape" (233). Ione and Panthea are intermediaries not only between Prometheus and Asia but also between the action and us; they perform a choral function of witnessing and interpreting from a common, as opposed to heroic, point of view. Douglas Bush calls Ione, Panthea, and Asia a "seraglio of feminine abstractions" and "a wife and two sisters-in-law, a typical Shelleyan household."[18] It would be more accurate to think of Ione and Panthea as Claire Clairmont and Mary, say, with Asia as the ideal beyond both of them. Ione and Panthea represent the best love that Prometheus can have in the world of Jupiter, the realistic object choice, the good but less than absolutely ideal woman the son can have after the passing of the preoedipal and the oedipal mother. The name Panthea appears in *The Faerie Queene*, where it is mentioned just after the Red Crosse Knight has his sublime vision of the New Jerusalem with its towers stretching into the stars. Until then, the Faerie Queene's capital, Cleopolis, seemed to him the most beautiful city and its crystal tower, Panthea, "the brightest thing that was"; but now "this great citty that does far surpas, / And this bright angels towre quite dims that towre of glas" (1.10.58.6, 8–9). This is the relationship of Asia to her younger sisters.

John Bailey complained that in *Prometheus Unbound* "one person seems to fade into another,"[19] and critics have found it especially difficult to distinguish Ione and Panthea. In their responses to the action Ione and Panthea can be differentiated to some extent. Typically, when some new phenomenon appears, Ione has a vague sense of a presence but doesn't know what to make of it, while Panthea sees it more clearly, perhaps identifying it. When the Phantasm of Jupiter appears, Ione senses "A Shape, a throng of sounds" (226), and Panthea, more specifically, hears whirlwind and earthquake and sees the Shape's scepter and robe. Susan Hawk Brisman (78–79) observes that at one point Ione feels her spirit to be "mingled" with Panthea's (2.1.102) and that Panthea's identity, in turn, is lost in her function as Asia's shadow or Prometheus's echo. Bailey does have a point, but it is the play's point. Ione and Panthea, daughters of Ocean, live on the threshold between the oceanic and clear identity. They function as intermediaries between the ego and the undifferentiated. Later in act 1 when Earth's spirits of consolation depart, Panthea says, "Canst thou speak, sister? all my words are drowned" (758). With a fine reversal Shelley has the usually less perceptive and articulate Ione respond, "Their beauty gives me voice" (759). The two sisters stand on the border between articulation and dissolving, and the same phenomenon can provoke self-expression in one and self-loss in the other. Most often, we find them struggling away from the oceanic but, at the same time, able to experience the realm of distinct identity only tenuously. The ideal of the play, as we will see, is the coming together of a strong sense of self with a strong sense of the oceanic.

In a mirror-image of the original event, the Phantasm of Jupiter now delivers the curse to Prometheus: "Fiend, I defy thee!" (262). In this proto-Pirandellian reversal, Prometheus becomes the fiend and curses himself; in spite of his attempt at avoidance, he finds himself, in effect, facing his own image. As the Phantasm goes on, it becomes clear that Prometheus's current condition is a fulfillment of his own words: "All that thou canst inflict I bid thee do" (263). In the curse Prometheus calls down upon himself "Ghastly disease and frenzying fear" (267). He gives Jupiter power over the rest of the world and tells him how to use it: "Aye, do thy worst. Thou art Omnipotent" (272). The Phantasm is reciting the articles of a new constitution. After specifying punishments for himself, mankind, and even "those I love" (277), Prometheus calls down suffering on Jupiter. Jupiter's "Infinity" will be a "robe of envenomed agony" like the one that killed Hercules, and his "Omnipotence" "a crown of pain" around his "dissolving brain" like Jesus's crown of thorns and the fatal crown that Medea gave Jason's new wife, Creusa (288–91).[20] Like Milton's Satan, Jupiter will fall "through boundless space and time" and will be condemned to see his evil deeds produce good (301, 293).[21] In opposing the vengeful Jupiter, Prometheus ironically identifies with three figures of appalling vengefulness: Medea, Milton's God (in the Shelleyan reading of him), and the rapist Nessus, source of the robe that killed Hercules. Conversely, the curse associates Jupiter with Jesus and Satan, both of whom the play elsewhere associates with Prometheus, and also with Hercules, who later appears in the play on Prometheus's side.

These allusions intensify the sense of Prometheus's original moral and emotional confusion. Indeed, we can see the curse as a desperate attempt to sort out that confusion. Prometheus in the curse is a Manichaean, as Shelley himself in *Laon and Cythna* tried to be, seeing evil and good as separate twin powers. But in the repetition and reversal of the curse Shelley brings the entanglement that was latent and subversive in *Laon and Cythna* under the reflective capacities of the ego. The authority enthroned by the curse now appears as a projection of an intolerable side of Prometheus's own nature. In a similar situation, Blake's Divine Man, Albion, falls "upon his face prostrate" and speaks "Idolatrous to his own Shadow," which has risen "from his wearied intellect."[22] In Blake the part of the self that is externalized and deified is variably its weariness (that is, to Blake, its passivity or femininity), its reason, or its sense of sin. In *Prometheus Unbound*, aggression is the chief disruptive element in the soul.

Introducing her underworld, Earth tells Prometheus that he may call up "Thine own ghost, or the ghost of Jupiter, / Hades or Typhon" (211–12). Typhon, a son of Earth, was a monster of 100 serpentine heads, who fathered the Sphinx and Prometheus's eagle and who waged a ferocious rebellion against Jupiter himself. In *Prometheus Unbound*, Prometheus identifies with this destructive and impetuous monster, who, now blasted by Zeus's lightning, lies beneath the volcano Etna but will one day burst forth in "boiling wrath" (371). Typhon is a violent, mindless version of Prometheus, and in the projections of the curse, Prometheus tries to rid himself of the Typhon-side of his own titanic being.

But Jupiter is a lightning rod to ground all the ego-dystonic elements within Shelley's sensibility, including feelings associated with the mother. Jupiter's infinity is a poisoned robe, his brain dissolves, and his culminating punishment is to fall through boundlessness. Fear of regression, as well as fear of aggression, goes into the making of this monster-god. And so does a dreadful masochism.[23] The primal scene in the world of the play is one of defiant surrender. It is as if Prometheus is saying in the curse, "Go ahead and castrate me. I'll still defy you and see you destroyed in the end."

When Prometheus has heard the curse, he says to Earth, "Were these my words, O Parent? . . . It doth repent me: words are quick and vain; / Grief for awhile is blind, and so was mine. / I wish no living thing to suffer pain" (302–5). The power of words in the play is ideally not one that is inescapable but one that we can activate or deactivate. Indeed, the Promethean myth of speech stresses not only the power of language but, even more, a power over language.

Earth immediately interprets the recantation as a surrender and expects that she will now be overwhelmed by an unrestrained Jupiter. She herself is locked into the old Promethean perspective, in which anything but anger and hatred is weakness. Prometheus, however, recants his anger and hatred, not his opposition. He liberates that opposition from what made it "eyeless." We should note that he actually speaks not of his hatred but of his grief. Grief is a response to loss. What emerges beneath the more evident rage against the tyranny of the father is a deep, sorrow-born rage over the loss of the mother. The issue of the mother, arising occasionally thus far, is one that the play will eventually have to confront.

The mythic Prometheus established the rites of sacrifice, dividing the offering at Mecone between gods and humans. Shelley's Prometheus makes the founding sacrifice of a new culture in renouncing his curse, as he also made the founding sacrifice of the old culture in cutting Jupiter out of himself. The renunciation of the curse does not eliminate aggression but completes its transformation into an adaptive, constructive, and clearly focused force. Aggression in Prometheus reaches that sublimated form in stages, appearing first in the defiance and masochism of the curse, then in the ambivalent pity, then in the repression of the curse, then in the detachment of the returned curse from the self, then in the self-correction, and finally in the continued and purified resistance that emerges from the recantation.[24]

The *Alastor* Poet reached the origin but was swallowed up in it; there was no second chance for him. Prometheus returns to the source to change, to rectify, to be reborn. We can contrast this vision of the past to that of Coleridge, whose Ancient Mariner will never be fully liberated from his old, terrible moment of aggression and whose Kubla Khan, even in the midst of the paradise he creates, hears "Ancestral voices prophesying war" (30). According to *Prometheus Unbound,* the ancestral voices need not haunt us forever.

Jupiter immediately tests Prometheus's new attitude by sending Mercury to extract the fatal secret. The confrontation of Prometheus and Mercury has a rich mythological background. "As a craftsman-god, Hermes is endowed with the essential traits of the mythological type of culture hero, of which there is no finer example than the Greek Prometheus," writes Norman O. Brown in *Hermes the Thief.* "Like Prometheus, Hermes is represented as 'pre-eminently intelligent' [and] as a friend of mankind" (22). Drawing on Brown, Susan Hawk Brisman calls the two gods doubles (63). Brown quotes one writer who calls Hermes "the little Prometheus," notes that both are tricksters, and observes that, as a herald like Prometheus, Hermes was an expert in "word-magic" (78, 24, 31). As Kerényi shows, the two gods are even associated with the same ceremony: Prometheus, the thief of fire, was the first to sacrifice an ox, while Hermes stole the oxen of Apollo, invented a new way of kindling fire, and established the sacrifice to the Olympians.[25] Edgar Wind observes that Hermes was also the "god of the probing intellect," a keeper of "'Hermetic' knowledge," a knower of secrets (122).

In Aeschylus, Prometheus calls Hermes "the lackey of the Gods," and Hermes calls Prometheus a madman (954, 977). Shelley's Mercury, by contrast, tries to be gently persuasive and laments his mission: "Awful Sufferer! / To thee unwilling, most unwillingly / I come" (352–54). He claims to hate himself for what he must do, wishes that they "might be spared—I to inflict / And thou to suffer!" and, finally, when his powers of persuasion are exhausted, says, "I must obey his words and thine—alas! / Most heavily remorse hangs at my heart!" (410–11, 435–36). Such lines, especially the clever "unwilling, most unwillingly," could be read by an actor to seem unctuous and hypocritical. But we miss the full power of this episode unless we see that Mercury is truly divided. In view of his mythological background, he is an Olympianized Prometheus, a rebel—as in the *Homeric Hymn to Mercury* that Shelley translated—who becomes a servant of established power. He is a Proteus, and Stuart Curran is right when he calls him a Lake Poet (149). Mercury is what Prometheus might become. He must meet and overcome this compromised version of himself just as he overcame a blindly destructive version of himself in the Phantasm of Jupiter.

For Mercury, the issue that entangles Jupiter and Prometheus is one of will and can be readily resolved by an act of volition: "Let the will kneel within thy haughty heart" (378). Aeschylus's Prometheus tells Hermes, "Let it not cross your mind that I will turn / womanish-minded from my fixed decision" (1003–4). Milton's Samson, in contrast, yields the fatal secret of his power to a woman and becomes "Unmanly": "foul effeminacy held me yok't" (*Samson Agonistes*, 417, 410).

Idealizing woman and holding a more complex view of passivity than Milton or Aeschylus, Shelley does not have Prometheus explicitly equate yielding the secret words with the shame of becoming a woman. But he does present his refusal to submit as something that goes beyond simple conscious volition: "Submission, thou dost know, I cannot try" (395). As has been pointed out, his words are reminiscent of those attributed to Martin Luther before the Diet of Worms: "Here I stand—I cannot do otherwise." It is as if submission is alien to Prometheus's nature, or as if giving in on this issue is tantamount to a complete surrender of his being.

While not submitting, however, Prometheus does, in a way, reveal the secret. In fact, in the following exchange he reveals it twice:

> *Mercury:*　　Thou knowest not the period of Jove's power?
> *Prometheus:* I know but this, that it must come.
> *Mercury:*　　　　　　　　　　　　　　　　Alas!
> 　　　　　Thou canst not count thy years to come of pain?
> *Prometheus:* They last while Jove must reign, nor more, nor less
> 　　　　　Do I desire or fear.
>
> 　　　　　　　　　　　　　　　　　　　　　(412–16)

Mercury expects a precise prediction of the future, but what the prophet gives him is a truth about the future based on the strength of his own conviction, and this may be all that Shelley's Prometheus really is able to say. In contrast to his original material, Shelley never mentions that Prometheus learned from his mother that Jupiter would fall. Prometheus's prophecy comes purely from within. His secret, his source of power, is his visionary faith and understanding, his imagination. Prometheus is like Blake's Isaiah, in *The Marriage of Heaven and Hell,* who, when Blake asks him, "Does a firm perswasion that a thing is so, make it so?" replies, "All poets believe that it does, & in ages of imagination this firm perswasion removed mountains" (pl. 12).

Prometheus and Mercury have clashing concepts not only of will and prophecy but also of time and the mind. Mercury says that Prometheus is helpless "Against the Omnipotent, as yon clear lamps / That measure and divide the weary years / From which there is no refuge, long have taught" (362–64). In the world of Jupiter, the heavenly bodies teach us that we are subordinate to a fixed external order. When Mercury asks how long Prometheus can stand to wait for Jupiter's fall, time seems overwhelming:

> Yet pause, and plunge
> Into Eternity, where recorded time,
> Even all that we imagine, age on age,
> Seems but a point, and the reluctant mind
> Flags wearily in its unending flight
> Till it sink, dizzy, blind, lost, shelterless;
> Perchance it has not numbered the slow years
> Which thou must spend in torture, unreprieved.
>
> (416–23)

But for Prometheus the mind does not dissolve in trying to follow time; rather it remains unchanged as "the retributive hour" approaches, ever nearer even as they speak (406). And when Mercury suggests that Prometheus offer Jupiter the "benefits" of the secret, the Titan says, "Evil minds / Change good to their own nature" (379–80). The mind has primacy over its objects, as it does over time.

The interview concludes with Prometheus subverting Mercury's conceptions one more time. Mercury says, "Alas! I wonder at, yet pity thee" (428). He has made the mistake of choosing to play with Prometheus's favorite nonviolent weapon. Prometheus answers, "Pity the self-despising slaves of Heaven, / Not me, within whose mind sits peace serene" (429–30). Pity the ones, like Mercury, who have given up what is most valuable in themselves and cannot endure themselves for it.

Prometheus tells Mercury, "Behold! Heaven lowers under thy Father's frown" (409). Mercury, literally Jupiter's son, is the child with the father; Prometheus is the child with the mother, and not only the helpless Earth but the Great Mother, Hora, Necessity, Themis, a primal, preoedipal mother. In *Queen Mab* the self was ideally integrated with Necessity as a nursling with a mother. But here Prometheus internalizes that mother; his secret—his prophetic conviction, the source of his power over Jupiter—is the mother within him. As Waldoff suggests, Prometheus seems to equate submission to Jupiter with castration (87). But if asking Prometheus to give up the secret is like asking a boy to give up his penis, it is also like asking a child to give up its mother; and while the castration fantasy was operating all during Prometheus's captivity, the maternal fantasy is a new element in his opposition. At the same time, the mother within rather than outside, as in *Queen Mab*, is the mother whose power is part of Prometheus's own power, an *Ananke* subordinated to his own creativity. Shelley expresses a wish to have access to some giant external power, a Mont Blanc, an Hour, something that must, to be effective, remain larger and greater than oneself, and at the same time expresses a second wish for the individual mind to be, as Satan in *Paradise Lost* put it, "its own place" (1.254). We can see in *Prometheus Unbound* a struggle to master a benevolent Necessity.

In fact, Prometheus's next antagonists are the creatures who in *Prometheus Bound* are called "the steersmen of necessity": "the remembering Furies" (515–16). The Furies, however, do not appear onstage in *Prometheus Bound;* Shelley took his Furies from *The Eumenides,* against the advice of his cousin Tom Medwin, who thought Might and Violence from *Prometheus Bound* would have been more suitable as Prometheus's tormentors.[26] But Shelley was right in his sense that the Furies belonged in his play. The Furies, or Erinyes, were female demons who punished offenses against blood relations. They championed parents against children and elder siblings against younger—thus precursors against latecomers—but above all they avenged the wronged mother. As Kerényi puts it, "They represented the Scolding Mother."[27] They were born from the earth and the blood of the mutilated Uranus, that is, from the mother after the castration of the father; both Aeschylus and Shelley call them daughters of "Mother Night."[28] In Shelley's Furies, both winged and serpentine, we meet again the winged snake, here with its components not in conflict but in dreadful unity. Marija Gimbutas writes that the neolithic mother goddess frequently appears as bird and serpent, both "as separate figures and as a single divinity" (42); the monster is often the divinity transfigured by repression. Wormhoudt sees in the Furies the phallic mother (93); in this fantasy, as Wormhoudt writes, the child responds to oral frustration by seeking a substitute breast in his own body and finds one in the penis, which he then projects back onto the mother (10).[29] In rebelling against the Olympian order of the father, Prometheus moves back into the chthonian, mother-dominated order, but such a move reawakens old anger and anxiety concerning the mother.[30] The Furies are indeed relevant to the play. Now that Prometheus has mastered the manifest conflict with the father, he must confront an unacknowledged, or repressed, conflict with the mother, his ally and source of strength.

The classical Furies were often three sisters, and Aeschylus's are a "company" (*The Eumenides,* 46), but Shelley's come in numberless "legions" (462), and they are also "shapeless" (472). Prometheus calls them "many fearful natures in one name" (458). Their amorphousness is a frightening version of the oceanic or Dionysian sense of form that characterizes the archaic world of the mother.[31] "Whilst I behold such execrable shapes," Prometheus says, "Methinks I grow like what I contemplate / And laugh and stare in loathsome sympathy" (449–51). Faced with the threat of an ego-dissolving influence, Prometheus's challenge is to retain his singleness, or sense of self, and particularly his newfound identity as an antithetical hero beyond Satanic hatred. Maintaining his sense of self against the bad father in the Mercury interview is less difficult than maintaining it against the bad mother.

What kind of new torture can the Furies inflict on Prometheus? He is a god and has already endured 3,000 years of agony. The question is also one of literary originality. How can Shelley's Furies in their methods be more than a copy of Aeschylus's? They begin their work by asking Prometheus if he expects them to rend him "bone from bone . . . / And nerve from nerve" (475–76). Already used to physical suffering, Prometheus is unmoved. Stepping up their attack, they ask him if he expects them to "be dread thought beneath thy brain / And foul desire round thine astonished heart" (488–89). Against this threat of being tormented by the nightmarish fears and impulses of his own unconscious, Prometheus asserts an Apollonian sense of mastery and self-possession: "Yet am I king over myself, and rule / The torturing and conflicting throngs within / As Jove rules you when Hell grows mutinous" (492–94). Here is a key point in the play. Some readers find it ironic that Shelley invokes an Olympian, monarchical ideal of control. Ulmer writes that Shelley's wording "reintroduces rule in Shelley's anarchist world" (100). Dawson argues that Shelley distinguishes between inner and outer control, but Ulmer answers that such distinctions "merely divide Shelley's model of authority into obverse complements: each remains a form of rule inherently misplaced in a world of anarchism" (100).[32] Shelley, however, not only does make a persistent distinction between the rule of others, an evil, and both inner and communal self-rule, a good, but he also treats the rule of others as a perversion of self-rule, rather than as a model of all types of rule. The curse gives Jupiter power "O'er all things but thyself" (273). The Furies refer to "Kingly conclaves stern and cold" (530) and then seven lines later call Prometheus "The stern of thought." Tyranny is a displaced and hypertrophied form of a desirable kind of sternness or firmness. A vision in which all kinds of mastery, control, and authority are conflated and repudiated and in which the ego is treated negatively is not Shelley's vision. The argument of this book is that his vision includes both Dionysian and Apollonian elements. In *Long Walk to Freedom*, Nelson Mandela repeatedly stresses that a freedom fighter needs self-control.[33] *Prometheus Unbound* is closer in spirit to Nelson Mandela than to Lacan or Foucault. In his sonnet *To the Republic of Benevento* (also called *Political Greatness*), Shelley writes:

> Man who man would be,
> Must rule the empire of himself; in it
> Must be supreme, establishing his throne
> On vanquished will,—quelling the anarchy
> Of hopes and fears,—being himself alone.—
>   (10–14)

The Furies, however, will be more than the torments of Prometheus's personal unconscious, and Prometheus will need another kind of self-control to resist them. They now tell Prometheus that human suffering is the product not of his curse but of his love and his benevolent acts:

> Dost thou boast the clear knowledge thou waken'dst for man?
> Then was kindled within him a thirst which outran
> Those perishing waters: a thirst of fierce fever,
> Hope, love, doubt, desire—which consume him forever.
>   (542–45)

The special torment reserved for Prometheus is a moral and political one. The taunt of the Furies is that the Promethean imagination, far from satisfying man's oral need, makes it unquenchable, that the story of Prometheus is ultimately the story of *Alastor*. The Furies answer Prometheus's vision of a necessity in which evil must fall with a vision of a necessity in which pure impulses must lead to destructive results.

They cite two examples of this tragic disjunction of ideals and consequences. The first is Jesus:

> One came forth, of gentle worth,
> Smiling on the sanguine earth;
> His words outlived him, like swift poison
> Withering up truth, peace and pity.
>   (546–49)

The second example is the French Revolution: "a disenchanted Na-
tion / Springs like day from desolation"; but before long "kindred
murder kin! / 'Tis the vintage-time for Death and Sin" (567–68, 573–
74). The Furies are effective because their vision is an arguable one.
There is something in it of Swift, as, for example, when Gulliver says
of certain appealing Lilliputian regulations, "In relating these and
the following laws, I would only be understood to mean the original
institutions, and not the most scandalous corruptions into which
these people are fallen by the degenerate nature of man" (49). With
their story of spiritual and political failure, the Furies could turn a
less intensely Romantic idealist than Prometheus into a Swiftian con-
servative.

A single Fury now speaks, another negative version of himself for
Prometheus to confront: after facing rage in the Phantasm of Jupiter
and compromise in Mercury, he must face despair. The Fury shows
him "A woeful sight—a youth / With patient looks nailed to a cruci-
fix" (584–85). Prometheus has already implicitly confronted the pre-
cursor of his rebelliousness, Satan; here, he must confront the pre-
cursor of his patient suffering, Jesus. The Fury says, "Those who do
endure / Deep wrongs for man, and scorn and chains, but heap /
Thousand-fold torment on themselves and him" (594–96). First
Prometheus was tortured by the possibility that his love and ideal-
ism might have destructive effects. Now he is tortured by the possi-
bility that his suffering and endurance might actually increase hu-
man misery.

But the last Fury has not quite unveiled its ultimate torture. Here
is a dark little parody of the *Hymn to Intellectual Beauty* with its unseen
fair Spirit: "Blood thou canst see, and fire; and canst hear groans; /
Worse things, unheard, unseen, remain behind" (616–17). Those
worse things are inward; the Fury introduces a survey of the inner
self with an image of oral destruction: "In each human heart terror
survives / The ravin it has gorged" (618–19). Inside us is an introject
of not the good mother but, as Gelpi says, the terrible, cannibalistic
mother (153–54). In Yeats's rewriting in *The Second Coming* of the last
Fury's speech, "The best lack all conviction, while the worst / Are full
of passionate intensity" (7–8); Shelley is concerned only with the
best, with those elements in humanity from which renovation might
be expected to come: "the loftiest fear / All that they would disdain
to think were true"; "They dare not devise good for man's estate, /
And yet they know not that they do not dare" (619–20, 623–24). We

might think of Wordsworth's "The good die first," Arnold's "the best are silent now" (*Stanzas from the Grande Chartreuse,* 114), even perhaps the first section of Allen Ginsberg's *Howl.* Shelley, however, puts the sentiment into the mouth of a Fury.

The torture continues:

> The good want power, but to weep barren tears.
> The powerful goodness want: worse need for them.
> The wise want love, and those who love want wisdom;
> And all best things are thus confused to ill.
>
> (625–28)

In this moral chaos, good and evil are not only inextricable; they are indistinguishable. "Many are strong and rich,—and would be just," the Fury goes on, "But live among their suffering fellow men / As if none felt" (629–31). And it closes by flinging in Prometheus's face the words of Jesus about his crucifiers: "they know not what they do" (631). Here Prometheus is being crucified not by Jupiter but by those on his own side, the potentially good, who are doing nothing. The source of Prometheus's strength has been his "secret," his inner being, where a belief in regeneration could exist even in the midst of total outer misery. But the Fury lays waste humanity's inner being, portraying it as paralyzingly confounded. Nothing sustaining can be expected from the defeated and insensitive heart described by the last Fury.

The Furies are Shelley's counterpart of Spenser's Despair, with his arguments so convincing that Red Crosse is persuaded to try to kill himself. They are a voice within us that insists that what has been in the past must continue to be in the future, that humanity is inadequate to the demands made upon it by Promethean ideals, that Promethean knowledge must always be undermined by a kind of ignorance: he too was one who knew not what he did.

Prometheus replies to this last speech, "Thy words are like a cloud of winged snakes" (632)—or like the Furies themselves. No physical torment can surprise Prometheus, but in this world in which language and poetry have a primal power, he is vulnerable to words, and so that is the form the Furies take for him. Yet Prometheus goes on to pity those not tortured by the Fury's words; and at this the astonished Fury vanishes. Once more the act of pity is a reversal of perspective in which the victim defeats the aggressor. With pity Prometheus asserts his superiority over the Fury and detaches himself from its dark vision. At the same time, more than in the cases of Prometheus's pitying of Jupiter and Mercury, his pitying of the Furies and those like them who are insensitive to or cynical about human unhappiness contains not only aggression but also compassion for those who, without knowing it, are in need.

But if the Furies vanish, their effects remain, because they have been torturing Prometheus with realistic possibilities. Indeed, Prometheus has been reduced to a state of agony much like that in which he first appeared, as he reiterates the cry of misery from his opening speech: "Alas! pain, pain ever, forever!" (635). Even so, he reaffirms his commitment to humanity and his sensitivity to its suffering, no matter what torture that stance may cause him. Wormhoudt characterizes his condition at this point as a "masochistic orgy" (95). We should recall, however, Aeschylus's Prometheus, who cries, "This my body / let Him raise up on high and dash it down / into black Tartarus," to which Hermes replies, "These are a madman's words" (1049–50, 1056). Shelley's Prometheus, by contrast, is undergoing a tempering and strengthening of his revolutionary attitude; he is confronting the dark potentialities of his own idealism, and he is using that knowledge to prepare himself for the continuing struggle. In the terms of *Paradise Lost*, the Furies have tried to bring forth evil out of his good, and now he tries to bring forth good out of their evil. "The sights with which thou torturest," Prometheus tells them, "gird my soul / With new endurance, till the hour arrives / When they shall be no types of things which are" (643–45).

To comfort her newly wounded champion, Earth now calls up spirits of her own, "Gentle guides," who, in contrast to the Furies' portrayal of inner terror and confusion, breathe "The atmosphere of human thought" and "sicken not" (673, 676, 675). They are Eumenides, representatives of the good preoedipal mother. In them the oceanic does not threaten but actually enhances the sense of self: from the "boundless element" of thought they "bear the prophecy / Which begins and ends in thee" (689–91). They bring back to Prometheus the contours of his heroic identity.

The Spirits foresee a future based on not the failures of the past but the most promising signs of the present. The Furies spoke of "red gulphs of war" (527), but the first of the Spirits brings news of ongoing battles against tyranny and "creeds outworn" (697). The Furies spoke of "kindred murder[ing] kin" (573), but the Second Spirit reports an astonishing example of self-sacrifice: it has just witnessed a naval battle in which, after a storm devastated both fleets, one sailor gave up his plank to an enemy, "then plunged aside to die" (722). The Third Spirit tells of a sage dreaming the same dream "Which had kindled long ago / Pity, eloquence and woe" (729–30). Readers have suggested that Shelley was thinking of one particular philosopher or another, but the dream represents what to Shelley is the essence of philosophical wisdom throughout the ages, a fundamental sensitivity to human unhappiness and a vision of something better. Despite the Furies' insistence on the failure of the loftiest, that wisdom still persists in the world.

The Fourth Spirit sings of the poet, who, rather than pursuing "mortal blisses,"

> feeds on the aerial kisses
> Of shapes that haunt thought's wildernesses.
> He will watch from dawn to gloom
> The lake-reflected sun illume
> The yellow bees i' the ivy-bloom
> Nor heed nor see, what things they be;
> But from these create he can
> Forms more real than living man,
> Nurslings of immortality!
>
> (740–49)

The persistence of the poetic imagination is a fourth cause for hope. Seeking aerial kisses rather than mortal blisses, this particular poet has something of the *Alastor* Poet in him, but unlike the latter he has creative power. This poet is not a Blakean, corroding nature with his fires to display "the infinite which was hid."[34] More gently, he watches the beauties of nature, and from them he creates a greater reality.

The Four Spirits reassert the sense of the good mother and find in that sense intimations of renewal. They celebrate transformations of orality—the rebel's defiant "cry" (700), the self-sacrificer's "sigh" (720), the sage's eloquence, the poet's "nurslings of immortality"—that might make a world far different from the one made by the curse. Two additional Spirits arrive to report whether Love too still appears in the world. The Fifth Spirit has seen a winged and "planet-crested Shape" "Scattering the liquid joy of life," but "hollow Ruin yawned behind" with its trophies, "Great Sages bound in madness, /

And headless patriots and pale youths who perished unupbraiding"
—like the passive *Alastor* Poet (765–66, 768–69). Even so, for the Fifth
Spirit the sight of Prometheus turns "the worst I saw to recollected
gladness" (771).

No memory of original joy can mitigate the vision of the Sixth
Spirit, however, one of Shelley's darkest versions of Adam's dream:

> Ah, sister! Desolation is a delicate thing:
> It walks not on the Earth, it floats not on the air,
> But treads with silent footstep, and fans with silent wing
> The tender hopes which in their hearts the best and gentlest bear,
> Who soothed to false repose by the fanning plumes above
> And the music-stirring motion of its soft and busy feet,
> Dream visions of aerial joy, and call the monster, Love,
> And wake, and find the shadow Pain—as he whom now we greet.
>
> (772–79)

Ruin is not the pursuer but the reality of Love. Readers have com-
pared the passage to the speech in *The Symposium* in which Agathon
strangely uses the description of the terrible goddess Ate in *The Iliad*
to praise the sensitivity of Love. Here is Shelley's translation:

> For Homer says, that the goddess Calamity is delicate, and that her
> feet are tender. "Her feet are soft," he says, "for she treads not upon
> the ground, but makes her path upon the heads of men." He gives as
> an evidence of her tenderness, that she walks not upon that which is
> hard, but that which is soft. The same evidence is sufficient to make
> manifest the tenderness of Love.[35]

Agathon leaves out the most damaging part of the allusion: in Latti-
more's translation of *The Iliad*, Ate "walks the air above men's heads
/ and leads them astray. She has entangled others before me" (19.93–
94).[36] The speaker is Agamemnon, who is blaming Ate for his disas-
trous infatuation with Briseis. Indeed, Agamemnon describes Ate as
"Erinys the mist-walking," a Fury, an avenging *Alastor*-like spirit, who
"caught my heart in savage delusion" (87–88). The Sixth Spirit brings
to the surface the full association of Love and Desolation that Aga-
thon suppresses.

In the songs of the Fifth and Sixth Spirits the difference between
consolation and torture almost breaks down, as these "Eumenides"
confirm the vision of the Furies, although in a sorrowing, not mock-

ing, tone. In a closing chorus, however, the other Spirits see Ruin as "Love's shadow" not inherently but only "now" (780). They have seen "Wisdom, Justice, Love and Peace, / . . . struggle to increase," and those are signs of a coming spring, as certain to them "as soft winds be / To shepherd boys" (796–99). Shelley suggests that we need knowledge of what he called "sad reality"[37] but that we also need pastoral optimism. The Spirits, together, do not deny the vision of the Furies; they deny its absoluteness. And they close with a final reassertion of their faith in "the prophecy / Which begins and ends in thee" (799–800)—which is also a faith that beginnings and endings need not be incongruous, that good can come from good.

After Prometheus has faced and rejected a series of negative images of himself—the vengeful Jupiter, the compromising Mercury, the Furies of despair—the Spirits reflect for him a positive sense of what he has meant to others and what he might fully become: the prophet of reform, empathy, nourishing wisdom, and far-reaching creativity. He is not quite convinced by the Spirits; nevertheless, they have succeeded in turning his mind in a new direction, as important and dramatic as the turn from hatred in the first speech: "How fair these air-born shapes! and yet I feel / Most vain all hope but love, and thou art far, / Asia!" (807–9). He cannot believe in Love as a capitalized abstraction or a universal force, but he can believe in love as a particular relationship. Only once before in the play has Prometheus thought of Asia and then only in passing to contrast Earth's unresponsiveness to his memories of wandering "With Asia, drinking life from her loved eyes" (123). Now, however, he addresses Asia directly, thinking of her as a current although distant reality. This thought of Asia, as quietly and even diffidently as Prometheus expresses it, is the culminating moment of Act 1. With it his transformation is complete, and his role in the process of liberation has reached its successful conclusion. The closing moments of the act will refine and strengthen the thought of Asia.

Prometheus goes on to recall his relationship with Asia in a striking image: "Asia! who when my being overflowed / Wert like a golden chalice to bright wine / Which else had sunk into the thirsty dust" (809–11). Gelpi finds in this image "a startlingly crude expression of a phallocentrism that makes women the passive vessels for male autoerotic ejaculation" (166). She also finds in the image a less "unpleasant" sense in which mother and infant flow into each other's identities (166). But her first reading remains pertinent: the image *is* blatantly phallocentric, and yet, if we place it in context, it may not seem as objectionable as she says. To conceive of all reality or all gender relations in phallocentric terms is not the same as simply fantasizing about sexual pleasure in phallocentric terms, as Prometheus is doing. The fantasy, in addition, is part of a series. First, love appears in the preoedipal terms of Prometheus's drinking life from Asia's eyes. Then it appears in the oedipal terms of the planet-crested shape pursued by Ruin. The phallocentric fantasy of overflowing wine and chalice, an adolescent male fantasy on the border between autoerotism and intercourse, represents not maturity but growth toward it.

That new image of love, however, is expressed as a memory rather than an anticipation, and as Prometheus continues, the thought of Asia is overcome by quiet sorrow and extreme weariness. He sees himself at a final crossroads, where he might either "Be what it is my destiny to be, / The saviour and the strength of suffering man, / Or sink into the original gulph of things" (816–18). But Panthea encourages and develops his new turn of mind: "Hast thou forgotten one who watches thee?"; "Asia waits in that far Indian vale, / The scene of her sad exile" (821, 826–27). Asia may be far, but she is a present possibility, and she is herself a suffering subject. Panthea speaks of "her transforming presence—which would fade / If it were mingled not with thine" (832–33). The image of mingled presences and the thought of lovers' need for each other make Asia seem even closer and also bring into the play a fuller, more mature and mutual concept of love beyond that of fountain and chalice. Panthea then puts Prometheus's tentative and tenuous thought into action and departs for Asia's vale.

Act 1 has shown us the purification, chastening, and strengthening of an idealistic and revolutionary stance and the building up step by step of an effective creative power. Prometheus has moved from a self-crippling hatred of Jupiter through pity of his various enemies to love not of his enemies but of Asia. At first he could imagine only Jupiter; now he imagines Asia, and in both cases what he imagines becomes his reality. His aggression has been transformed from the wish to inflict injury on and enjoy power over an adversary into conviction, resistance, endurance, and the maintenance of an ideal and an ideal self against all threats. Good has been tested and honed by exposure not only to external evil but also to the evil within the self and, beyond that, to the possible evil within good itself.

Act 1 begins in the negative way Bloom calls typical of belated poetic openings, with a limitation or contraction, the recantation of the curse, and it ends with a representation or expansion, the naming of Asia.[38] Indeed, the entire course of act 1 is a process of education that Prometheus must go through to bring him from the oral aggression of the first lines to that one word. The Veiled Maid was nameless and unnameable to the Poet; she was a purely oceanic being. Asia has an identity, a self, a name. At the end of *Jerusalem*, Blake's renovated Human Forms cry out "the Name of their Emanations they are named Jerusalem" (pl. 99, line 5). The Human Forms name Jerusalem in joyous recognition of her presence. Asia is still absent, but her name is a creative word that sets in motion her actualization in Prometheus's life; it is a counterspell to the curse; it is a new poem. Earlier, Prometheus had to recall something from being; now he recalls something into being. In both cases a missing word or voice is found.

The pattern of act 1 is triumphant, but the tone of the conclusion is not. At the outset Prometheus was filled with furious energy; now he is exhausted and, as at the end of *Samson Agonistes*, the mood is one of "all passion spent" (1758). But although his current passivity is, in part, a real debility, it also veils a new sense of the active in him; the recantation and the turn toward Asia are his first creative acts since his imprisonment. At the same time he has become passive in a positive way. His imaginative faith in a process that will in good time bring about his release is a Shelleyan version of Wordsworthian wise passiveness. His restraint from vengeance is also a passive trait. To gain in freedom, initiative, and control, Prometheus must become less seemingly active. But passiveness in the play is not wholly good as it is. In his last speech Prometheus is left in suspense between a progressive, active impulse to assume his destiny as the strength of suffering man and a regressive, passive impulse to sleep and to sink into the original gulf of things. Here the passive is associated with despair and self-loss, as it is in the *Stanzas written in Dejection, near Naples*: "I could lie down like a tired child . . . and hear the Sea / Breathe o'er my dying brain its last monotony" (30, 35–36). The existence of these two contrary impulses is still an incompletely resolved problem in the play. To be active without domination and self-warping destructiveness and to be passive without self-loss and a sense of defeat: progress has been made toward these ideals but they have not yet been fully realized. While act 1 centered on the transformation of aggression, act 2 will center on the transformation of regression.

12

Prometheus Unbound:
Act 2

"Nothing of all these evils hath befall'n me / But justly," says Milton's Samson, accusing himself of having "betray'd" God's mystery "to a woman." The chorus tells him, "Therefore God's universal law / Gave to the man despotic power / Over his female in due awe."[1]

In other precursors of Prometheus like Jesus and Milton's Satan, misogyny may not be so strident as this; but Jesus—whose words "Woman, what have I to do with thee?" (John 2:4) represent a rejection of not only Mary but the mother in general, including Mother Earth—and Satan, who was the parthenogenetic parent and narcissistic lover of Sin, are male principles without female counterparts. Making Prometheus a lover, elevating the prestige of traditionally feminine qualities like love, pity, and passiveness, and giving the entire second act to Asia together constitute one of Shelley's most radical transformations of his material. Prometheus is not a narcissistic but an anaclitic hero; he both needs and desires otherness, both for help and for love. Indeed, a fantasy of being rescued by a woman is at work in *Prometheus Unbound*; in act 2 the heroine goes off to save the imprisoned hero and even confronts a monster along the way. Asia is also a subject in her own right and must undergo her own process of growth. Her vale is filled with beauty flowing from "her transforming presence" (act 1.832); she will eventually transform the world, but now she is only a local spirit of place or fertility goddess investing a solitary vale with flowers (1.829); she will eventually become a better Aphrodite, as Prometheus had to become a better Jesus and Satan.

John Todhunter called Prometheus "the divine imagination, the father-force, which creates and re-creates the universe by its marriage with the divine idea, or mother-force, Asia."[2] But in act 2 Prometheus is as much an object of Asia's imagination as in act 1 she is of his. While Prometheus embodies the prophetic imagination, fixed on one great, clear ideal, Asia embodies a fantastic and aesthetic imagination, open to all possibilities, particularly involved with dreams, intimations, reveries, and art.[3] In the play's vision, we need both kinds of imagination for our liberation from Jupiter's world. But Prometheus and Asia are indeed like a primal father and mother. Occupying the precipice and vale of the Indian Caucasus, the cosmic mountain of origins, they are our dispossessed ideal parents. In Keats's *Lamia*, Hermes and his nymph are ideal lovers who can realize a perfect eros that must always haunt and elude mortals. Prometheus and Asia are ideal lovers who are also our once and future parents and can provide a model of what we ourselves might at least partially attain.

Asia's vale, like the *Alastor* Poet's, is a place of dreams; the act opens with her celebrating the beginning of spring, which arrives like "the memory of a dream" (2.1.8). But unlike *Alastor*, act 2 tells the story of a dream coming to realization. In a passage of delicate complexity that sets the theme for the act, Asia describes the first moments of morning and the coming of Panthea: "The point of one white star is quivering still / Deep in the orange light of widening morn"; reflected in a lake, "now it wanes—it gleams again," until at last it disappears in the also-quivering "roseate sunlight" just as she hears Panthea approaching (17–18, 21, 25). The dreamed, the anticipated, the imagined is emerging into external reality.

Yet the theme of emergence is modified by a note of loss, as Asia follows the gradual waning of the white star until finally "'Tis lost!" (24). A beginning, in this scene, is an end of something else, and something valued. The morning star, Venus, is the distant ideal of love in the dark winter of Jupiter's reign. In Asia's dawn the joy of a long-awaited emergence is shadowed by a reluctance to be born, to give up the perfect beauty of unrealized imaginings. Lost as well is the total moment of which the star is a part, a moment of special Shelleyan beauty, in which we have what we desire as an ideal imagining and at the same time as a real possibility on the verge of actualization.

Still, the predominant drive in Asia is away from that moment and toward full emergence. Panthea is "Too long desired, too long delaying" (15); "How late thou art!" (32). In his own opening soliloquy, Prometheus surveyed the "wingless, crawling Hours" (1.48); Asia exclaims, "How like death-worms the wingless moments crawl!" (2.1.16). While Prometheus is patient before the slow crawl of time, impatience is one of Asia's character traits. Prometheus looks forward to the moment of ripeness with firm conviction, while Asia wants it to happen now. Both attitudes are necessary to the process of liberation. Asia's impatience, nevertheless, reveals a certain lack in her. Prometheus, the prophet, knows and masters time; it is like something contained within him. For Asia, who is like a spirit of place, time is external. Attentive to outer process, waiting for Panthea, living, as she says, by Prometheus's soul (31), Asia is passive and dependent. She has forgotten her true power, as Prometheus had his own at the beginning of act 1. Venus is now a force external to her, a star to which she bids farewell, a goddess, a lost mother. At the end of the act she herself will be Venus.

Yet in a certain way the star is not lost, for it reappears in Panthea's eyes, which Asia describes as "Like stars" (29). Losing the star in reality, she holds onto it tenaciously with her imagination. In *Alastor*, the mother makes her final symbolic appearance in the moon that sinks as the Poet dies. For Asia, love and vitality do not vanish with the sinking star; the love associated with the mother reappears in another person in the world.

The theme of a tenuous emergence into actuality continues in the dialogue of Asia and Panthea, which concerns dreams. Panthea has had two dreams but has forgotten one. Adam woke to find his dream true; here, without God's help, the passage from dream to truth is gradual and arduous. It begins with a struggle to remember, not what was spoken, as in act 1, but what was prior to consciousness.

The dream that Panthea reports is an Adam's dream from a female point of view. In it, Prometheus appears in his original glory, and the love from his eyes "wrapt me in its all-dissolving power" (76); then, as she gradually awakens, she hears him say Asia's name. This dream of ecstatic dissolution, unlike the *Alastor* Poet's, is not in conflict with waking thought, words, and other people but rather is helped to realization by all three. Ione, in Panthea's report, now wakes up, "trouble[d]" by "something sweet" (94, 98), haunted by mysterious desire, and confused by a feeling of self-loss, as if Panthea has stolen her spirit by some enchantment and mixed it with her own. In response to Ione's feelings and her own, Panthea "fled" to Asia (108). *Sehnsucht*; a strengthening of the oceanic feeling; a need to understand one's dreams and one's vague sweet and troubling feelings; and eros, in the form of one person's sexual or, as in the case of Ione and Panthea, affectionate impulse toward another: all these contribute to Panthea's voyage and thus to the liberation of Prometheus and the transformation of the world. So too does the awareness that others are having the same feelings.

During Panthea's narration, Asia asks her to lift her eyes so that she can "read thy dream," and in her sister's eyes, Asia sees "a shade—a shape—'tis He" (56, 120). To read the dream is also to interpret it, and in Asia's interpretation, what began as something within another person's mind and then became words that "Are as the air" (109) now becomes not only a vision that Asia can see for herself but also a sign of a coming reality: "Say not those smiles that we shall meet again?" (124). But Asia also sees something else: "What shape is that between us? Its rude hair / Roughens the wind that lifts it, its regard / Is wild and quick" (127–29). The dream will not simply come true by itself; an obstacle stands in the way. The vision of renewal is not a fantasy but an inspiration and a challenge. Yet in Asia's mood of enthusiastic anticipation the obstacle seems one that can be overcome: the shape is "a thing of air / For through its grey robe gleams the golden dew" (129–30). That dew is compared to "stars the noon has quenched not" (131); the lost star of love appears once again, now associated with Prometheus; primal, dyadic love is transferred for Asia from mother to sister to lover. On the exact meaning of the shape there is little agreement,[4] but its riddling obscurity is exactly its essence. Panthea recognizes it as her other dream when it speaks the words "Follow, follow" (131). In the second dream, we see dreams in general as not visions but forgotten or repressed shapes, rough, wild, and obscure, and also as summonings. The first dream is a radiant wish; the second is a compelling mystery that calls upon us to follow—in context, both to figure it out and to pursue the first dream.

But as mysterious as dreams may be in *Prometheus Unbound*, they can be remembered, expressed, and shared; far from alienating us from others, as in *Alastor*, dreams seem to be potentially communal forms, bringing us closer together.[5] Panthea now begins to remember her second dream, in which a "lightning-blasted almond tree" (135) blossoms before a wintry wind blows down its new flowers; but on its leaves appear the words "O *follow, follow!*" (141). The dream now moves from one mind to another, as it reminds Asia of a similar, forgotten dream of her own, in which the words "*Follow, O follow!*"

(153) appeared on the vanishing shadows of morning clouds. In the image of the early-blooming almond tree the beginnings of new life rise unexpectedly out of what has been blasted by Jupiter, and then that new birth is itself blasted. The destroying wind comes from the "Scythian wilderness" in the north, where it is still wintry when spring comes to Asia's vale (136); in *Laon and Cythna,* "dreary winter leads / Out of his Scythian cave, a savage train" of frosts and storms (3651–52, *E,* 2:214). A flowering in one corner of Jupiter's world is destroyed by the winter that is still general. But Asia is told to follow those seemingly devastated first impulses toward renewal. More generally, she is told to follow the lost. The whole scene has been concerned with ephemeral visitations of beauty and the pursuit of vanished and forgotten things of value. In the *Hymn to Intellectual Beauty* Shelley writes of a nourishing maternal source that comes and goes, leaving us desolate in its absence. Asia is called upon to follow such an intermittent presence when it disappears. Wordsworth in the *Immortality Ode* is grateful that the newborn infant experiences "obstinate questionings / Of sense and outward things, / Fallings from us, vanishings" (145–47) and retains "Those shadowy recollections" that keep the original glory alive in him (153). Asia is asked, in effect, to question the vanishings and follow her shadowy recollections. She is asked to follow a spirit of earliness, or, in the non-pejorative sense in which I have been using the word, to regress.[6]

But Asia is also pursuing a dream beyond her sheltered vale. In the poetic myth of act 2 the regressive and the progressive work together; a pursuit of the oceanic is also a pursuit of realization in the world of object love. And if Asia is asked to follow the mother, she is also asked to become the mother. In the second dream, the words appear on the almond leaves "as the blue bells / Of Hyacinth tell Apollo's written grief" (139–40). Hyacinth, the youth loved by Apollo and killed when the jealous North Wind guided Apollo's discus into him, seems originally to have been a pre-Hellenic god, a dying-and-reviving vegetation deity like Adonis.[7] Blowing down flowers, the Scythian wind from the north is a scythelike castrating force of the type that cut down fertility heroes. Asia, who began the act watching the planet Venus fade away, is now asked to be like Venus and the other maternal fertility goddesses who followed their consorts to the underworld to bring them back.[8]

The call to follow is taken up by still another form of evanescence, echoes, which "fade away" (169). Indeed, the lost star that is associated with the mother and that reappeared in Panthea's eyes and then in the dream of Prometheus now appears in the echoes, who compare themselves to "dew-stars" (168). Like the *Alastor* Poet, Asia follows a vision of what once was; unlike him, she opens herself to transferences and recreations of that lost ideal in the actual world. The echoes call upon the sisters to follow their receding voices out of common nature—"As the song floats, thou pursue / Where the wild-bee never flew" (179–80)—to a confrontation in the chthonic darkness: "In the world unknown / Sleeps a voice unspoken" (190–91). Asia is asked to follow the vanishing oceanic sound into a silence that is not, as in *Alastor*, a final loss but the potentiality of speech.

In this scene Shelley is redefining the imagined, the felt, the obscurely glimpsed or heard or desired as the possible, and he is suggesting that we must follow dreams, inexpressible intimations, visitations of beauty, for within our attention to such phenomena is a subversive tendency of regression to the mother that can help overthrow the paternal reign of Jupiter. Asia is asked to be passive, to follow the beautiful wherever it might take her. At the same time, her following has an active element; it is a chosen pursuit of a dream of renewal, and at the end of the scene Asia has become assertive and decisive: "Come, sweet Panthea—link thy hand in mine, / And follow, ere the voices fade away" (207–8). In that the echoes, which at first seem to come from "some being / Around the crags" (164–65), are actually echoes of the sisters' own dream, the sisters are following something in themselves. The echoes "mock" the sisters (163); this much-loved and ambiguous Shelleyan word means "to deride by imitation." Asia is teased out of her vale by the alien manifestation, the projection, of something unknown within her, including her own active impulse to go, her own power. Through following the vanishing, she is on the way to finding what has vanished or been repressed in herself.

In scene 2, the echoes have led Asia and Panthea into a forest of laurels and other evergreens, "curtained out from Heaven's wide blue" (4). The Oceanids are leaving the Olympian realm for the chthonian territory of the mother goddess, with its perpetual dark life and its inspiring, narcotic laurel that was sacred to the goddess at Delphi. A. M. D. Hughes compares the forest to the grove of the Eumenides in Colonus, home of Dionysos, where Oedipus finally finds repose. There "The sweet, sojourning nightingale / Murmurs all night long";[9] Shelley's forest is also a place of nightingales, who in the darkness sing even at noon. The singing and especially the sounds that "overflow" (39)—for Shelley, Firkins notes, "The kinship of sound and water was an inexhaustible stimulus" (120)—suggest early orality. When one of the singers "with bliss or sadness fails," another "lifts on high / The wings of the weak melody" (26, 32–33); their music keeps renewing itself in the cyclical rhythms of a maternal world.

But the echoes are leading to something still more compelling, drawing

> By Demogorgon's mighty law
> With melting rapture or sweet awe,
> All spirits on that secret way,
> As inland boats are driven to Ocean
> Down streams made strong with mountain-thaw.
>   (43–47)

Within our sensations of beauty is a deep providence; music is leading Asia back to its own source. Demogorgon's mighty law is Necessity, the "law of fixed and inviolable sequences," as Wasserman puts it (317). But it is also an oceanic impulse, a natural force like gravity, sweeping through the world, making things thaw and melt, leading toward an ever deeper and earlier sense of the mother.

Unlike the laws of Jupiter, Demogorgon's law compels us not with brute force and punishment but with rapture and sweet awe. Shelleyan Necessity includes everything in our existence that, even at our most Promethean, is beyond our control: inner, irrational forces; natural, historical, and social forces; mighty laws of cause and effect; cycles of mutability. But although the Oceanids are driven through the forest by a wind from "the breathing Earth," they believe they are obeying the "sweet desires within" (52, 56). What the Oceanids are compelled to do is also what they wish to do.

A chorus of spirits has been singing about the passage of the sisters through the forest, and now two listening fauns wonder where that music is coming from. As half-animal and nonindividualized fertility figures and as companions of Dionysos, fauns are appropriate inhabitants of this regressive realm. Compared to their lusty originals, Shelley's fauns are mild-mannered and refined; Firkins calls them "emasculated" (82). In one draft the fauns, against tradition, are even female.[10] Shelley is trying hard to make the Dionysian gentle and benevolent. The fauns "imagine" (64) that the singing spirits live in the bubbles that rise from the "oozy bottom" of forest pools (73). When the bubbles burst, the "fiery air" within them flies through the air "like meteors," which the spirits ride until they "glide" into the water again (77, 79, 81). This is the will o' the wisp—methane, "formed," as Holmes writes, "from decaying organic matter, which spontaneously combusts on contact with oxygen" (493)—a common symbol of romantic delusion, but here a symbol of the delicate, fleeting, easily dismissed sensations and imaginings that Asia must take seriously. In the spirits of the will o' the wisp, as in the nightingales, we see a process of perpetual cyclical transformation like that of the archaic world of the mother goddess. The traditionally illusory marsh gas is here not mistaken for something else; in its mere exemplification of cyclical process it is subversive of Jupiter's patriarchal reign. And, as in the rising and falling of the nightingales' song, music expresses that process, as it also expresses an oceanic impulse. Scene 2 is sometimes characterized as a lyrical interlude;[11] its subject, however, is the meaning and power of lyricism itself.

The fauns also speak of another inhabitant of the forest, Silenus, who, if they don't milk his goats, will not sing his songs "Of fate and chance and God, and Chaos old, / And love, and the chained Titan's woful doom / And how he shall be loosed" (92-94). Wasserman sees in the background of Shelley's necessitarian cycles in scene 2 Virgil's Sixth *Eclogue*, in which Silenus sings the songs the Fauns speak of.[12] That Silenus is typically sly and intoxicated, but Shelley gives a milder, more regressive cast to his orality: he will be cross if his goats aren't milked (90). Here again Shelley both establishes the regressive and the Dionysian and tries to make them unthreatening. Accordingly, he leaves out of the list of Silenus's songs several subjects that Virgil's Silenus sings about: the mad passion of Pasiphaë; the devouring Scylla, "a lovely woman with a ring of howling monsters round her waist";[13] and the original melancholy nightingale, the raped and maimed Philomela.

As the next scene begins, however, the dangerous side of regression appears. The sound has carried the Oceanids out of the forest onto a pinnacle, entry to "the realm / Of Demogorgon," like a volcano from which "oracular vapour is hurled up" (3.1–2, 4). The Dionysian quality in the voyage becomes explicit: "Lonely men . . . wandering in their youth," Panthea says, drink "That maddening wine of life," and become wild and deluded "Like Maenads" (5, 7, 9).

Panthea on the cosmic mountain sees illusion, *Alastor*-like solitude, and destructiveness: regression out of the ego's control. But she is serving as a lightning rod to attract the anxiety of the oceanic, leaving Asia free to be unambivalently exhilarated: "Fit throne for such a Power! Magnificent!" (11). To her, the morning mist is like "Ocean's dazzling spray" around "some Atlantic islet" (30–31). In Panthea's re-vision of that simile, the "sea of mist" rises around "foodless men wrecked on some oozy isle" (43, 46). For her, the ego is threatened by both denial of nourishment and oceanic regression, by too little and too much. But no ambivalence is assigned to Asia. Her wonder and adoration extend to the entire "glorious" earth, and even if "evil stain" it, she "could fall down and worship" it (12, 14, 16). Her mis-sion, however, is not to end her journey and fall down in reverence before a world still imperfect and unchanged. Moreover, the earth is to be protected, not worshipped. In moving away from a supernatu-ralism in which it has projected its own proper power, humanity might fall into a naturalism in which it projects its power just as effec-tively. But at the end of Asia's celebration the mind enters the scene —and the mind at its most defiantly active and Promethean: as the mountain snow is gathered "Flake after flake" into an avalanche, so

> in Heaven-defying minds
> ... thought by thought is piled, till some great truth
> Is loosened, and the nations echo round
> Shaken to their roots: as do the mountains now.
>   (39–42)

The tremendous landscape becomes an illustration of the human mind's own power—a power that Asia herself has not yet realized.

Led by singing spirits, Asia now enters the abyss, accepting what Fogle calls "a dizzying vertical downward plunging" (95). Daniel Hughes calls this fall "terrifying,"[14] but remarkably no terror is at-tributed to Asia. Shelley creates, as he did not in *Alastor*, a figure in whom regression is psychologically acceptable, partly because the figure, female and not explicitly a poet, is sufficiently distanced from Shelley himself; partly because she is not alone, with the spirits to "guide" her (90) and a "bright form beside thee" (92), Panthea, to accompany her and to validate her visions as more than private; and, especially, because her regression is part of a total process in which the ego is becoming stronger. It is a provisional regression with a pro-gressive goal.

This is not to say that the descent is gentle. The music of the spirits becomes a whirlpool, taking Asia "Through the veil" (59), which other Shelleyan poems have associated with dying: "Lift not the painted veil which those who live / Call Life" (*R*, 327). Asia descends "Through the shade of Sleep," beyond any familiar level of regression; "Through the cloudy strife / Of Death and of Life" and "the bar / Of things which seem and are," beyond any differentiation, "Where there is One pervading, One alone" (56–60, 79). There "A spell is treasured but for thee alone" (88). The spirits tell Asia to

> Resist not the weakness—
> Such strength is in meekness—
> That the Eternal, the Immortal,
> Must unloose through life's portal
> The snake-like Doom coiled underneath his throne.
> (93–97)

Her weakness will lead to a tremendous release of power, even Doom, a Last Judgment. Asia's weakness is her wise passiveness, her receptivity, her capacity to regress, to be carried away, to be inspired, to be influenced. Such weakness is the particular strength of her character. One might say that Panthea is not weak enough for Asia's kind of greatness.

In scene 4 Asia is given the chance to fulfill the fantasy of total knowledge that has driven and frustrated prior Shelleyan heroes. She and her sister stand before a throne in the Cave of Demogorgon, the very center and origin of existence. Panthea sees "a mighty Darkness / Filling the seat of power," and that "shapeless" spirit says, "Ask what thou wouldst know" (2–3, 5, 7).

Mysterious and alien in appearance, Demogorgon is what is other to humanity. In Demogorgon Shelley acknowledges an ultimate limitation; despite humanity's titanic capacities, something remains beyond its knowledge and control. He represents the great forces and patterns of nature and history to which we are, or feel, inescapably subject. He is Necessity, the way things work. At the same time, as Wasserman puts it, he represents "infinite potentiality," which is why he is shapeless (319, 333). He is the process by which the potential becomes actual and the actual returns to potentiality. He is an otherness inside us, as well as outside; the many caves in Shelley's poetry are often caves of thought, and Demogorgon is what he called in the "Lionel" notebook fragment the monster in the labyrinth of the mind.[15] In act 1, Prometheus confronted the aspect of the unconscious that concerned his own experience; in Demogorgon Asia confronts the aspect of the unconscious that concerns human experience in general; he is the very sense of a strangeness, an unknown, within us.

In his literary provenance, Demogorgon is a riddle of origins come to life. Two themes in particular recur in his history. The first is that, as Boccaccio says, he is "the ancient father of all the gentile and the pagan gods,"[16] being himself without parents. He is the father beyond the sky god, the father who makes all other fathers seem belated; Lucan says that he has "witchcraft power over all the gods."[17] The second theme is that his name, like Yahweh's, is dreadful and forbidden. But unlike Yahweh, he often seems to be in his very essence something not to be said. In *Paradise Lost* it is "the dreaded name / Of Demogorgon" (2.964–65) that stands beside the throne of Chaos, as if the name were a full being. According to Lucan, his name could cause earthquakes;[18] Peacock, in his summary of Boccaccio, says, "This awful Power was so sacred among the Arcadians that it was held impious to pronounce his name. The impious, however, who made less scruple about pronouncing it, are said to have found it of great virtue in magical incantations."[19] A virtual symbol of the primitive idea of the power of language, Demogorgon is an appropriate primal power for the world of *Prometheus Unbound.* Indeed, he seems to have originated as a verbal error, a medieval spelling mistake for Plato's cosmic creator, Demiourgos or Demiourgon, according to H. N. Brailsford, or a conflation of "the monstrous terrifying Gorgon and the great Craftsman, Demiourgos," according to Gilbert Highet.[20] Boccaccio thought of him as a theological mistake, "he whom the Ancients in their error, for sake of a beginning, called the first god."[21] Demogorgon is a name for a beginning or a name by which a beginning is made, a mystification that both clears the way for new forward developments and stops things from developing backward in an infinite regression.

In the song of descent, Eternity has a "snake-like Doom coiled underneath his throne" (3.97); in act 3, Demogorgon will call himself Eternity, while Jupiter will compare him to a snake (1.72). In the *Essay on the Devil and Devils,* Shelley writes that "In Egypt the Serpent was an hieroglyphic of eternity" (*C,* 274). In Demogorgon we find the serpent of fertility and regeneration and also the serpent of secrets, "the oracular beast of the earth-oracle," as Jane Harrison puts it.[22] We find the snake who is the mythic form of heroes, kings, and daemons in the chthonic realm of the earth goddess. We find the Python-like guardian of the omphalos, the navel of the earth, as the sacred stone of the Delphic oracle was called.[23] But, as I have noted, the serpent was a form commonly taken not only by the male companion of the archaic goddess but also, before that, by the goddess herself.[24]

The name Delphi may be derived from *delphys*, or "womb," also the origin of the name of a female snake, Delphyne, who once guarded the oracle.[25] Harrison tells us that "Doom" is philologically identical with Themis, the earth mother and the personification of law.[26] Part of the riddle of Demogorgon is his gender. He is traditionally a father, and I follow convention by using the masculine pronoun, but the total image of Shelley's cave of Demogorgon includes female and maternal elements. At the end of the play Demogorgon refers to "Eternity, / Mother of many acts and hours" (4.565–66). Rieger, while acknowledging that the divine principle in Shelley is typically female, as in Intellectual Beauty, ridicules the notion that Demogorgon might here be referring to himself and insists that he is male (153). But too many associations, even beyond the serpentine and Delphic ones, lead us to think the contrary. The mother is the presence we would expect at the end of a deep regressive voyage. Northrop Frye writes that the descending hero of romance goes "down into a dark and labyrinthine world of caves and shadows which is also either the bowels and belly of an earth-monster, or the womb of an earth-mother, or both."[27] Demogorgon is the primal other, and the primal other in our experience is the mother. Demogorgon is Necessity, a goddess for the Greeks, the mother of the world for Shelley; as Necessity, Demogorgon is the primal might of the mother, not her goodness but her sheer power and authority, her necessity, seemingly absolute, in the infant's life. Demogorgon is the sense of the mother as a neutral giver and withholder of supplies.

But if Demogorgon suggests the maternal, it remains important that the figure is referred to once, seemingly, as female ("Eternity, / The Mother"), once as male (Doom is coiled underneath "his" throne" [2.3.97]), and twice as neuter ("its throne" [2.4.151]; "we feel it is / A living Spirit" [2.4.6–7]). There are several possible reasons that Demogorgon is not explicitly female. First, Shelley is taking a traditionally male figure and investing it unconsciously with the sense of the mother. Furthermore, Demogorgon is an amorphous being representing a stage of childhood development prior to a clear sense of sexual differentiation. Then, too, not making the figure explicitly female is a way of denying that Demogorgon represents ego-dystonic feelings about the mother. In addition, in its confusion, or shapelessness, of gender, Demogorgon intensifies a similar condition in the sources and analogues. The serpent of Delphi is male in some stories and female in others, and Baker points out that in Boccaccio Demogorgon is accompanied by Eternity, "an aged goddess encircled by a snake" (116). In the Temple of Venus in *The Faerie Queene,* Spenser shows us the idol Venus, entwined by the Ouroboros, the snake with its tail in its mouth, emblem of eternal natural cycle. This hermaphroditic Venus is "Both male and female, both under one name: / She syre and mother is her selfe alone, / Begets and eke conceives, we needeth other none" (4.10.41.7–9). Similarly, Demogorgon is the mother as an all-powerful, all-comprehending, self-sufficient force, in whom the male power exists in an unclearly differentiated, subordinate mode. But the combination of serpent and woman, together with the name, also points toward the Gorgon Medusa. Wormhoudt sees Demogorgon as the preoedipal phallic mother (99). The Furies too are formless, serpentine females. In each of the first two acts a nightmarish image of the mother must be confronted.

Spenser uses the image of the hermaphrodite to describe not only his Venus but also the embrace of Scudamour and Amoret at the end of book 3.[28] We can see the combination of male and female in Demogorgon further in terms of an embracing couple. Fontenrose writes that there were originally a male and female pair of dragons guarding Delphi, just as in creation myths there are often a pair of primordial chaos demons, like the Babylonian Apsu and Tiamat, the fresh water and the salt water.[29] In addition to his other resonances, Demogorgon is the mysterious combination at the origin, the mother together with the father. In this case, that enigmatic "shape" may have especially disturbing undertones. Wasserman sees not only Virgil's Fourth *Eclogue* but also the descent to the underworld in *The Aeneid,* book 6, as important sources of Asia's voyage.[30] Nearly 40 percent of Silenus's song of creation in the Fourth *Eclogue* deals with Pasiphaë and her bull;[31] the story of Pasiphaë also appears near the beginning of book 6 of *The Aeneid,* and later in that book Pasiphaë appears again in the underworld.[32] In the "Lionel" fragment, in which Shelley speaks of "the monster of his thought," he alludes to the story that begins with Pasiphaë: "If we could for the sake of some truth [as] fair as Ariadne vanquish the monster of his thought, I fear lest we should find no thread to guide us back thro the labyrinths."[33] The monster of thought is the product, or symbol, of a monstrous primal scene. Combined in Demogorgon are anxieties of the mother as a Pasiphaë, as a phallic mother, as a neutral or unloving preoedipal power, as a primal formlessness or chaos.

But given all this, and given the terror traditionally associated with this deity, Demogorgon is a remarkably mild figure in scene 4. In act 2, in general, mildness is found where terror is expected. Shelley dreams that the center of the labyrinth will turn out to be not so dreadful after all. He dreams too of an accessible source; unlike the elusive Spirit of Intellectual Beauty and the unreachable Power of Mont Blanc, Demogorgon can be confronted and even spoken to. Above all, Demogorgon exists in Shelley not only because Shelley senses an otherness in our existence but also because he wants there to be a helping power outside us. In *Queen Mab* the beneficence of Necessity is a given; in the cave of Demogorgon, however, it must be gained. If Demogorgon is less intimidating than we expect, he still remains a giant power that must be mastered; his primacy must be reduced, and his potentially destructive energy must be put to creative use. Lucan says that Demogorgon "looks on the Gorgon's face unveiled" and "lashes the cowering Fury with her own scourge";[34] in scene 4 the most terrible of demons becomes a terror to other demons, as Medusa becomes in the hands of Perseus.

Within the play Asia is the agency by which Demogorgon is mastered. Her interview with him is a version of the battle with the dragon, and she plays the role of Apollo, who not only defeats the dragon but also takes over its power. But Asia also considers Demogorgon a wise counselor, and her confrontation with him is a struggle for knowledge. If Asia is the ego trying to master inner and outer power, she is also the curious, questioning child confronting the enigmatic parent-power at the source. In still another sense she is the good mother facing the strong mother, whose strength may be used for good or ill. Fontenrose reminds us that in traditional myth "She who appears as Chaos-Hag and first mother is closely related to or identical with the great goddess of love and fertility, who often appears as the champion's sister or wife" (466).

Both male and female, both father and mother, both the possible and the necessary, Demogorgon is potentiality specifically as the opposite of what is; he is the perpetual antithesis; he is always the other. From a childlike point of view, like Asia's, he is like a parent; from a parental point of view, like Jupiter's in act 3, he is a child. And as process, he is that which can turn one contrary into another, Love into Ruin, for example, or the reverse. Yeats, wondering why Demogorgon, "whose task is beneficent," should "bear so terrible a shape," commented that something "again and again forced [Shelley] to balance the object of desire . . . with nightmare."[35] But in Demogorgon Shelley tries to master that compulsion by embodying such doubleness in a single, coherent figure and portraying the figure's transformation into a servant of goodness.

"A mighty Darkness / Filling the seat of power" (2–3), Demogorgon is the psychic darkness of mystery or repression. But that darkness is also the absence of an anticipated greatness. That Demogorgon fills the seat might imply that he is its provisional, not its original or rightful, holder. Where we expected power, there is really nothing there, or at least hardly what we expected. Indeed, historically Demogorgon should never have come into existence; he was a mistake; this symbol of Necessity is himself unnecessary. At the same time, out of this mistake arose a poetic tradition. The mighty darkness is both an absence in the place of expected authority and an absence out of which new creation comes. In one more form of doubleness, Demogorgon embodies at once a demythologizing skepticism and a romantic, mythologizing richness.

In her questions to Demogorgon, Asia tries to determine responsibility for the way things are, but Demogorgon's answers merely repeat what is commonly thought, forcing her to further questions:

Asia:	Who made the living world?	
Dem:		God.
Asia:		Who made all
	That it contains? . . .	
Dem:	God, Almighty God.	

(9–11)

When she asks who made evil, the answer changes: "He reigns" (28). Asia twice asks who reigns, even passing through a stage of Promethean fury: "Utter his name—a world pining in pain / Asks but his name; curses shall drag him down" (29–30). This moment of anger, while partly a reprise of a mistake, is also a positive, transitional development in a character who is wisely passive in her receptiveness to influence but unwisely passive in her total dependence on it. Despite her aggressiveness, Demogorgon repeats, "He reigns" (31). This is an oracle who throws the petitioner's questions back at her. He is like a machine, with Asia searching for the right button.

To break the impasse, Asia is forced to become more active; she tries to figure out for herself how things got to be the way they are. She recalls that the world was first ruled by Saturn, "from whose throne / Time fell, an envious shadow" (33–34), and whose reign, while one of "calm joy" (36), was also one of frustration. Saturn's subjects yearned for knowledge, power, and love, "For thirst of which they fainted" (43). Rousseau believed that only a catastrophe could force man to abandon his "natural indolence" for "the labors, and the miseries that are inseparable from the state of society."[36] But where Rousseau sees indolence at the base of human nature, Shelley sees *Sehnsucht*.

Saturn, however, is a lethargic ruler, who "refused / The birthright" of his subjects (38–39). In response, Prometheus "Gave wisdom, which is strength, to Jupiter" and "Clothed him with the dominion of wide Heaven" (44, 46). Saturn's subjects had also longed for love, but Prometheus apotheosizes the aggressive, Jupiter side of himself and ignores, or exiles, the Asia side. He is thus responsible for the evils that Jupiter brings: famine, toil, death, war, and "fierce wants" (55).

To alleviate these miseries, he tames fire and unveils the mysteries of "herbs and springs" to heal disease (85); he teaches human beings "to rule" sailing ships (92) and gives them science, which undermines superstition. If Prometheus now gives humans good forms of mastery and aggression, he also, belatedly, gives them forms of eros. He "bind[s]" the human heart with love (63) and reveals the secrets of navigation, so bringing together distant peoples. Aeschylus's Prometheus gives humanity writing (460–61), but Asia's gives "speech, and speech created thought, / Which is the measure of the Universe" (72–73). Here is a characteristic Shelleyan shift to the oral; here too is an optimistic vision of the primacy of the mind and the complete adequacy of language. Asia describes two more gifts, unmentioned in Aeschylus. One is music, which "lifted up the listening spirit / Until it walked ... / Godlike, o'er the clear billows of sweet sound" (77–79). The other is sculpture, in which artists surpassed "The human form, till marble grew divine" (82). The influence of art is such that mothers, gazing on that beauty, give birth to children who reflect it (83–84). Art is a Promethean gift to bring out the god-like potential of human beings.

Human experience has thus been shaped by the two sides of Prometheus working against each other. Why is there such a split in the first place? Why does Prometheus delegate power to Jupiter? In Asia's story of Prometheus's gifts, progression is associated with aggression: getting beyond Saturn's indolence involves mastery and rule, including "Self-empire" (42); Prometheus "tortured to his will / Iron and gold, the slaves and signs of power" (68—69). Wisdom is associated with strength, and strength is associated with sadism and tyranny. In Prometheus's surrender of authority, we can see not only a repressed need for a father, something consciously inconceivable to Shelley, but also a refusal to be a power and a projection of the impulse to mastery.

The story of Saturn suggests another dimension of that refusal. The Roman Saturn was a fertility god and presided over the Golden Age, but the Greek Kronos, with whom he was identified, was far from either idyllic or indolent; he castrated his father in his mother's bed to get power, and he devoured his children to keep it. Shelley's "envious shadow" Time, or Kronos with a sickle, is the negative double of Shelley's indolent king of the Golden Age, and his envy is oedipal. To be aggressive is thus to be a castrating, power-crazed usurper. In Asia's story, unacceptable aggression is first split off as a "shadow," and then, when aggression is felt to be necessary but is still unacceptable, it is further projected and enthroned as Jupiter. Jupiter is Prometheus's failed way of being aggressive without, as it were, soiling himself with the responsibility for it.[37]

Yet Asia still hasn't learned what she wants to know: "But who rains down / Evil?" (100–101). The evil she speaks of is something that remains with us after all Prometheus's "alleviations," as an "immedicable plague," which "drives [man] on / The wreck of his own will, the scorn of Earth, / The outcast, the abandoned, the alone" (98, 101, 103–5). Asia now envisions a deep human solitude and self-destructiveness that cannot be attributed to Jupiter or to Prometheus's specific creative error. The imagination leads to evil not only through some rectifiable mistake but, more deeply, through something inherent in itself; there is a dark, inevitable double within creativity. The Furies must be faced again in act 2. This is a thematic way of describing the immedicable evil. Asia's story suggests an additional way.

In that story, Time is the first evil. The child eventually associates time with its competitors, or "envious shadows," like the castrating father,[38] but its sense of time begins in the suspenseful absence of the mother. Saturn's subjects, fainting with thirst for knowledge, power, and self-empire, seek Apollonian goals partly as fulfillments of impulses toward development and partly as substitutes for a lost oral gratification. From Jupiter they receive "famine" (50), but Prometheus, as Wormhoudt suggests, becomes a good mother, a prolific giver (101). The theme of orality runs through his gifts: speech; song; love, "the wine of life" (65); mothers drinking love as they gaze at beautiful statues (83); Disease drinking medicine and falling asleep (86).

Among his gifts are two remedies for suffering, Nepenthe and Moly, which are mentioned in *Comus*. Milton compares the potion offered by the Dionysian Comus to Nepenthe, the drug of oblivion; he compares the antidote against Comus to Moly, the drug of clear-sightedness and self-possession that Odysseus used as an antidote to Circe's spells.[39] Moly and Nepenthe suggest contrary impulses in relation to regression. At the end of Asia's story, we see man, "the abandoned," as "The wreck of his own will," not certain whether his will is to go forward or backward, away from the mother or toward her. The immedicable evil of human unhappiness, which is not explained by Jupiter and the story of the father, appears rooted in the ambiguity of the mother and the doubleness of our attitude toward her.

"Whom called'st thou God?" Asia now asks (112).

Demogorgon answers in a line that plainly reveals Asia's primacy in a dialogue in which she has conceived of herself as the subordinate one: "I spoke but as ye speak" (112). If she is dissatisfied with his answers, she must blame her own questions. Demogorgon then reiterates that "Jove is the supreme of living things" (113); that is, it would be futile to seek a greater father figure, a monotheistic creator-ruler, beyond him. As words of hate were retracted in act 1, so the word "God" is retracted here, the word by which creative power is surrendered and an unwise passiveness accepted.

Asia still persists: "Who is the master of the slave?" (114). And Demogorgon's response brings her to the very nadir of obscurity: "If the Abysm / Could vomit forth its secrets:—but a voice / Is wanting, the deep truth is imageless" (114–16). Why exactly is the deep truth imageless? If evil is an eternal potentiality within good, then no single, finite image of evil would express its nature as a possibility, as a double. Yet the skepticism of Demogorgon's response goes further, dogmatically placing origins and answers beyond the reach of any formulations we can possibly make. In this case, speech and thought are *not* the measure of the universe.

But in one sense, skepticism serves as a screen. If we take into consideration Shelley's choice of metaphor, then we have to say that a secret that has to be vomited forth is not one that anybody would be eager to discover. Especially in the context of the scene's concern with orality, to compare the secret to vomit is to describe it symbolically as something bad that has been ingested or as something gone wrong in the process of taking in nourishment. The entire scene suggests that one answer to all Asia's questions is the mother: the mother is the God, the source of good and evil, the "master" of Prometheus as well as of Jupiter. The skeptical myth of language then saves us from the danger that if language were totally capable we would discover what in Shelley would be intolerable: that the mother is a source of anxiety and the object of an aggression deeper and earlier than the aggression against the father. Instead of nourishing us, the mother is making us ill, poisoning us. In this sense, it is not that we can't know but that we don't want to—especially in a part of the play, act 2, that is supposed to be celebrating the feminine. The Abysm is an unconscious that Shelley seeks to keep unconscious. Asia celebrates Prometheus for revealing secrets to human beings and for making available the power "Hidden beneath the mountains and the waves" (71), but in Demogorgon's lines, withholding a secret may be desirable. We can see in Shelley, the poet of curiosity, four different impulses associated with secrets: an impulse to know or steal the secrets of others, an impulse to keep secrets from others, an impulse to know one's own secrets, and an impulse to keep one's own secrets from oneself.

It is not immediately clear how Demogorgon gets from his assertion that the deep truth is imageless to his next statement:

> For what would it avail to bid thee gaze
> On the revolving world? what to bid speak
> Fate, Time, Occasion, Chance and Change? To these
> All things are subject but eternal Love.
>
> (117–20)

How do we get from the absence of truth to the presence of Love? Pottle sees no contradiction between the two parts of Demogorgon's speech. We are told that the problem is unsolvable; we are then told so much of the truth as it is possible to tell.[40] We might say, "That's all we know and all we need to know." Still, Demogorgon's rhetoric is jarring with its ambiguous transition "for" and its seemingly contradictory assertions that speaking and seeing are first impossible and then only unavailing. We see here less a seamless logical argument than an imaginative and psychological dialectic. We see a strong defensive recoil from ultimate negation into positive mythmaking. The romance of eros saves Shelley from the abyss of skepticism, as elsewhere the detachment of skepticism saves him from the oceanic abyss of romance. We can also see in the passage an act of aggression, in which all prior words and images are exposed as having nothing to do with the deep truth; this unnaming clears the way for Shelley's own poetic myth or new naming.

But in addition, in the voiceless, imageless abyss we can see a state of being prior to the distinctions of words and separate images, the "eternal Silence" of the *Immortality Ode* (159), identifiable with "that immortal sea / Which brought us hither" (167–68). The Abysm and Eternal Love are negative and positive visions of the primal mother, and in finding the former at the end of a regressive voyage Asia also finds the latter, or its immanence. The turn in Demogorgon's speech has something of the quality of the turn at the end of *The Inferno*, in which Dante climbs through "the point to which all gravities are drawn"[41] and suddenly finds above and below reversed as he emerges from the lowest pit of Hell. In Dante, however, Hell remains Hell; in Shelley, the reversal of perspective transforms the abyss into the oceanic, or Love.

Demogorgon's speech does more than elevate Love, or the good mother, over Jupiter. Insofar as Demogorgon includes "Fate, Time, Occasion, Chance, and Change," he is granting the power of Love over himself. In Demogorgon's speech, eros is established as the greatest power in the "revolving world," something beyond ambivalence and mutability, or revolving; it replaces Demogorgon at the center of the world. The good mother overcomes the mother as sheer primal power, as impersonal necessity. Moreover, the might of the mother is placed at the disposal of her goodness. In act 1 Ruin followed Love "destroyingly" (781), but in act 2 Love tracks Ruin to its lair, and there Ruin surrenders its power. Prometheus endures the Furies and dispels them, but Asia gains their power for herself.

If we can't know the ultimate secrets, how can we know as much as we do, that Love is not subject to Fate and Change? Asia tells Demogorgon: "So much I asked before, and my heart gave / The response thou hast given; and of such truths / Each to itself must be the oracle" (121–23). In *Paradise Regained,* the "Oracles are ceast" at Delphi, for God "sends his Spirit of Truth henceforth to dwell / In pious Hearts, an inward Oracle / To all truth requisite for men to know" (1.456, 462–64). Shelley eliminates God from this formulation. Asia now trusts her own feelings and intuitions as a source of truth. In one sense, the voice of Demogorgon is lacking, and the desiring voice of Asia fills the void. In another sense, her true voice is itself the unspoken voice she has been seeking to awaken. Asia has pursued that missing voice through nightingales and echoes, and now she finds herself as the source of the echoes.

Now in her final question, the first one she asks in her own proper voice, Asia becomes a new kind of petitioner: "One more demand . . . and do thou answer me / As my own soul would answer, did it know / That which I ask" (124–26). This question is a demand, and the questioner directs what the answer is to be: "Prometheus shall arise / Henceforth the Sun of this rejoicing world: / When shall the destined hour arrive?" (126–28). And the answer is "Behold!" (128). That is, "Right now!" Demogorgon's frustrating answers cross off the wrong questions one by one until she finds the right one. This is the question proper to her own nature, the question of the heart, of desire, of impatience and impetuousness, the question in which the wanting voice articulates what it wants. And Demogorgon's answer is, as always, a reflection of Asia's own words.

The *Alastor* Poet vanished into the origin, but Asia transforms both the origin and herself. Like Prometheus, Asia has forgotten something about herself, her identity as Love and her power; and like Prometheus she regains what she has lost through a confrontation with a disembodied voice from the world of shadows and dark universal process. At the source, Asia becomes the source. As Eternal Love and the spirit of the good mother, she assumes power; as an individual, she gains an active self to complement her wise receptiveness and a strengthened ego to complement her Dionysian tendency toward regression. As in the case of Prometheus, her self-transformation includes correction and change. And as in the case of Prometheus, it also includes internalization. Asia seeks a creator, an evil, and an authority all outside her, and she finds inner ones; she recalls what she has projected. But although Prometheus's liberation is now a matter of inner conviction for her, she must still ask "when" because time as a process remains outside her. Demogorgon is that which must always be outer to the soul, an inalienable otherness; this is a limitation of human power, but it is also what enables Demogorgon to function as a strong aid to humanity.

At the end of the interview, Time—the first evil, the envious shadow, the absent mother, the castrating father—is changed. First Demogorgon says that Love is not subject to it, and then in the "Behold!" that he utters at Love's command, it becomes a desired "now." Indeed, what Asia literally beholds is an image of time, for the Oceanids see a rush of chariots driven by "the immortal Hours," or Horae (140). Asia's question releases the forces of the mother.

Jupiter and Mercury were helpless before the mystery of time, but Asia uses time as her vehicle. Actually, the Hour that Asia has been seeking has two vehicles. While Demogorgon ascends to Jupiter in a chariot of wrath, the "Daughter of Ocean" (168) is invited to ascend to Prometheus in a shell. In the two cars, we see the two sides of the powerful mother, strength and gentleness, necessity and love. We also see a way in which Shelley can make use of aggression and keep a certain distance from it. Aphrodite was born of the severed genitals of Uranus fallen into the sea; here Asia enters Aphrodite's famous shell to be reborn as Eternal Love while, separately, Jupiter will be overcome by a new, more acceptable version of castrating Kronos, or Time.

Act 2 began with a dream in which Prometheus recovers his unfallen glory. In the final scene of act 2 Asia recovers her own unfallen glory. "How thou art changed!" exclaims Panthea; "I scarce endure / The radiance of thy beauty" (16-18). Commentators have reminded us of the unveiling of Beatrice in *The Purgatorio*, and in *The Paradiso* Beatrice herself tells Dante, "Were I to smile . . . / You would be turned to ash, as Semele was."[42] The unbearable glory that once belonged to Jupiter now belongs to Asia, but in her it causes, Panthea says, "Some good change / . . . in the elements which suffer / Thy presence thus unveiled" (18–20). Asia is returning to what she originally was in her Venus-like birth, when, as Panthea recalls, the water "Was cloven at thy uprise, and thou didst stand / Within a veined shell, which floated on / Over the calm floor of the crystal sea" (22–24). But as quickly as she becomes the Venus of common myth, she surpasses her: love "Burst from thee, and illumined Earth and

Heaven" (28). Asia began the act as a local nymph, whose influence was limited to her own vale; now she is a divine creative power, the Aphrodite of the pre-Olympian mother religion. But her response to Panthea makes clear that the love she now embodies is still human, emotional, and personal:

> Thy words are sweeter than aught else but his
> Whose echoes they are—yet all love is sweet,
> Given or returned; common as light is love
> And its familiar voice wearies not ever.
>
> (38–41)

We are not moving up a ladder of love; rather, the love that we know now is expanding in presence and power.

Now the world, in the form of a singing voice in the air, responds to Asia. Here are the first lines of one of Shelley's most controversial lyrics:

> Life of Life! thy lips enkindle
>   With their love the breath between them
> And thy smiles before they dwindle
>   Make the cold air fire; then screen them
> In those looks where whoso gazes
> Faints, entangled in their mazes.
>
> Child of Light! thy limbs are burning
>   Through the vest which seems to hide them.
>
> (48–55)

This is the poem that, according to Bush, makes "all good Shelleyans face the east"[43]—and provokes everybody else to satire. Tennyson reportedly said that Shelley "seems to go up into the air and burst!"[44] "How could one draw such a picture?" Stephen Spender asks.[45] But that is the point of the lyric. Shelley is trying to describe something that has not been seen before and that cannot be seen with our present visual powers. He is, further, imagining a risen body and what, following Gaston Bachelard, we might call a new materialization of the world composed of luminosity, music, and soaring lightness.[46] At the same time, that new vision has its roots in a world anterior to that of the perspectival eye with its clear differentiation of self and other. Here, in the breaking down of such a separation, the gazer is entangled in what he gazes at. In the radiance that dissolves all distinctions, the synesthetic merging of the senses, and the melting of solid matter into "liquid splendour" (63), Shelley is giving us an appearance as "seen" through the oceanic feeling, which here, as in the *Immortality Ode*, is the Life of Life, "the fountain-light of all our day" (*Ode*, 155).

The song of the Voice in the Air ends with loss and failure:

> Lamp of Earth! where'er thou movest
>   Its dim shapes are clad with brightness
> And the souls of whom thou lovest
>   Walk upon the winds with lightness
> Till they fail, as I am failing,
> . . . Dizzy, lost . . . yet unbewailing!
>
> (66–71)

But this is an ecstatic or orgasmic self-loss, a pleasurable dissolution, and it follows a Dionysian transport in which the souls loved by Asia know the soaring feelings that Phyllis Greenacre identifies as characteristic of the phallic phase and know as well even earlier infantile feelings of omnipotence.[47]

Asia responds to the Voice in the Air with a lyric that is equally extreme in content but different in style, not frenzied and rapturous but measured and serene. It is one of the themes of this book that the oceanic feeling drives some of Shelley's finest poetic achievements and also that one of the inner dramas of his poetry is the struggle to bring that regressive impulse into the service of the ego. Here is one of Shelley's greatest attempts to give poetic expression to the regressive, oceanic impulse and one of his most interesting efforts to shape or master it. In "Life of Life," Asia was a mother; here she is like a fetus in the womb:

> My soul is an enchanted Boat
>   Which, like a sleeping swan, doth float
> Upon the silver waves of thy sweet singing,
>   And thine doth like an Angel sit
>   Beside the helm conducting it
> Whilst all the winds with melody are singing.
>
> (72–77)

To listen, in this song, is not only to float but also to undertake a meandering, hypnogogic journey. As the lyric develops, its regressive imagery intensifies, as does the association of music and the oceanic. Originally prompted by the "liquid responses" of the echoes (2.1.171), Asia follows music until she becomes part of it. "Like one in slumber bound," she descends "Into a Sea profound, of everspreading sound" (2.5.82, 84). At the same time, her guiding Spirit "lifts its pinions / In Music's most serene dominions" (85–86). Asia's slow, heavy song of descent and the Voice's fast, dizzying song of ascent keep each other in check. Shelley uses two regressive forces against each other and so keeps a regressive motion, Asia's voyage, going on an even keel. Together Asia and her pilot "sail on, away, afar, / Without a course—without a star— / But by the instinct of sweet Music driven" (88–90).

In the final stanza, regression becomes explicit:

> We have past Age's icy caves,
>   And Manhood's dark and tossing waves
> And Youth's smooth ocean, smiling to betray;
>   Beyond the glassy gulphs we flee
>   Of shadow-peopled Infancy,
> Through Death and Birth, to a diviner day.
>   (98–103)

Why does Death come first where we would logically expect Birth as the next stage after Infancy? We may expect a regression so extreme as this, a reversal of time that takes us back beyond birth, to be a death; but in this case what should be oblivion and annihilation turns out to be new life. That final passageway of Death and Birth is another perspectival turning, like that at the bottom of Dante's Hell.[48]

In these lines the development of life is a transformation of water from "glassy gulphs" to "smooth ocean" to "dark and tossing waves" to "icy caves." The oceanic feeling, which lies behind our visionary ideals, finally freezes up in age, and perhaps in adulthood it is a rebellious force that can cause tempests. In youth it is perilous to those like the *Alastor* Poet who see only its "smooth" side. The mirroring waters of infancy suggest primal narcissism; the infant lives with its dyadic reflection; to go through that mirror is to reunite with that double and enter the uterine world in the water.

In the "diviner day" beyond the world of natural process, Asia finds

> A Paradise of vaulted bowers
> Lit by downward-gazing flowers
> And watery paths that wind between
> Wildernesses calm and green,
> Peopled by shapes too bright to see,
> And rest, having beheld—somewhat like thee,
> Which walk upon the sea, and chaunt melodiously!
>
> (104–10)

Asia does not return from the underworld to the common world in the usual heroic pattern but keeps on regressing until she reaches repose.

Why can Asia, unlike the *Alastor* Poet, find a nondestructive repose among the bowers and the narcissi? The love that Shelley seeks to regenerate the world is a regressive and seemingly spiritualizing force that leads away from the world; why does that not seem problematic here? Asia does "flee" back to this uterine paradise, but unlike, say, Blake's Thel, who also flees back to Innocence, she is not fleeing from anything.[49] The oceanic here is wholly without anxiety of self-loss or threats of any kind. In Asia's song, "abysses" (80) are part of a beautiful landscape; wildernesses are "calm" (107). There is nothing maenadic about Asia's song; it combines the Dionysian with the tranquil.

At the end of the *Ode to Liberty* the poet's voice fails like a shot swan and like a "drowner" (285). Drowning was a theme in Shelley's poetry and, of course, in his life; he was a passionate sailor who never learned to swim, and Rieger has written at length about his impulse toward death by water (221–36). In Asia's song, however, the bright shapes can walk on the water; with that Christlike ability there need be no fear of the oceanic. In the last line the bright shapes are also chanting. Voice doesn't fail here as it does in *Alastor*, the *Ode to Liberty*, and "Life of Life." Asia can enter the ocean without, like the Voice in the Air, becoming "lost forever" (65). Her complete adventure is, at base, a dream of the ego: in the cave of Demogorgon she gains a strong sense of self, strong enough so that she can then undergo an experience of deeply regressive character without destruction or even anxiety. Asia can do with impunity what the *Alastor* Poet must die for.

Asia's boat, unlike the *Alastor* Poet's, also has a helmsman. Hers is an oceanic voyage with another; she has both Dionysian bliss and the guidance of a pilot; she sings to a "thou," who in turn celebrates her. In her song we see both primal narcissism and object love. It is important that Asia's paradise, unlike the *Alastor* Poet's, is "peopled," and it is also important that the bright shapes, when compared to the Voice in the Air, are "somewhat like thee," not identical; here is a gentle but definite assertion of difference in the midst of oceanic connection. The context of mutuality and otherness helps make the oceanic and the regressive appear acceptable, safe, and serene.

But the most important factor in that serenity is that the return to the womb is not the conclusion of the play. Asia's regression is part of a total story. In her part of that story, love, liberated to develop into the fullness of its being, becomes a nourishing plenitude at the base of life, an answer to the problem of diminishing supplies, something evermore about to be. But Asia does not exist in isolation; while she sings of an oceanic regression she is outwardly in the midst of an ascent through the air to meet Prometheus.

In the reunion of Prometheus and Asia the mutually exclusive opposites of the Furies—wisdom and love, power and goodness—come together. But that reunion is enacted within each character as well as between them, as each takes on qualities associated with the other. If Prometheus is associated with thought, then thought in act 1 must receive an emotional education, purging itself of hatred and allying itself to love. If Asia is associated with the emotions, then the emotional life in act 2 must receive an intellectual education and come to the knowledge of its own strong role in the world.[50] While Prometheus embodies a necessary negative capacity of sensibility, associated with discontinuity, rebellion, and righteous wrath, Asia embodies a necessary affirmative capacity. But Prometheus, at first concerned only with Jupiter, must turn positively toward Asia, while Asia, at first concerned only with Prometheus, must say no to Jupiter and the beliefs that keep him in power.

But there is another relationship between Prometheus and Asia besides reunification. The legislative, revolutionary, progressive function of the culture-bringer Prometheus and Asia's regressive function need each other as contraries. It is Asia's role to regress and Prometheus's to be aggressive and progressive. Asia embodies an impulse toward the oneness of oceanic communion, while Prometheus embodies an impulse toward the oneness of the sole self, and together these contrary impulses defend against the contrary anxieties of separation and dissolution. Asia and Prometheus sustain us in opposite ways, one giving nourishment and the other strengthening the separate ego.

Thus in acts 1 and 2 aggression and regression are mastered and channeled ultimately through being brought into relation with each other. The impulse toward what some readers call transcendence, what I have been calling the oceanic feeling or primary narcissism, is kept as a term in a dialectic. However we may define Prometheus and Asia, it is necessary for Shelley to maintain two principles and keep them flowing together and moving apart. In the very form of that relationship both the ego and the oceanic are cultivated.

At the end of act 2 that dual movement of merger and differentiation is, however, still implicit; Asia is still only on her way to Prometheus, and Jupiter is still on his throne. Regression is regarded serenely, but it is also dominant, and as we end act 2 we have lost sight of the progressive impulse and of the mortal world that Prometheus is supposed to save. It will be the job of the remaining two acts to work out fully the union and the dialectic that are now emerging.

13

Prometheus Unbound:
Act 3

IN ITS DIALECTICAL RHYTHM, THE PLAY NOW TURNS FROM THE ETHE-
real to the political, from regression to aggression, from the apotheo-
sis of Asia to the dethroning of Jupiter. The third act begins with an-
other of the play's errors of understanding, indeed with its climactic
Epimethean mistake. Jupiter in Heaven is awaiting a "fatal Child, the
terror of the Earth," ascending "from Demogorgon's throne" to
"trample out the spark" of man's rebellious soul once and for all
(3.1.19, 48, 24). Jupiter is parodying Virgil's "Messianic" *Eclogue:* "The
Firstborn of the New Age is already on his way," "dear child of the
gods, great increment of Jove."[1] He acts as if Demogorgon could be
subject to tyranny as he is to Love, as if the father could command
the maternal power of Necessity.

Jupiter tells Thetis that the mighty spirit of the child "unbodied
now / Between us, floats, felt although unbeheld, / Waiting the in-
carnation" (44–46). It is as if he were awaiting a visitation of Intellec-
tual Beauty. In an attack on Christianity, Shelley shows Jupiter ex-
ploiting the oceanic feeling for tyrannical purposes. Jupiter also
parodies the paradisal imagery and the recovery of primal orality that
we find in Shelley's passages of elation:

> Pour forth Heaven's wine, Idaean Ganymede,
> And let it fill the daedal cups like fire
> And from the flower-inwoven soil divine
> Ye all triumphant harmonies arise

"Like music from Elysian winds" (25–28, 33). Jupiter seems like a di-
abolical, projected form of Shelley's own Dionysian impulses. At the

same time, the allusion to Ganymede reminds us that this father is, like the original oedipal father, Laius, a rapist of children.[2]

The doubling of Shelleyan ideals is particularly noticeable when Jupiter reminds Thetis of the conception of their child,

> When thou didst cry, "Insufferable might!
> God! spare me! I sustain not the quick flames,
> The penetrating presence; all my being,
> Like him whom the Numidian seps did thaw
> Into a dew with poison, is dissolved."
>
> (37–41)

A sea goddess like Asia, Thetis is the oceanic mother subdued and diminished by the sky god; we might think of Ingres's 1811 painting of an importunate Thetis and a huge, impassive Jupiter, who does not even seem aware of her presence. Shelley's Thetis, even more, is the violated, helpless oedipal mother. She is also like Semele, the earth mother of Thrace,[3] and in her devastation we see a dark double of the good dissolutions of the last scene of act 2. The seps was a serpent whose poison worked so thoroughly that the body of its victim totally disappeared. In the lines on Thetis, Shelley portrays a dissolution that attends not regression but aggressive male sexuality; the phallus of the rapist-father, the Tyrant Lust, rampaging over women and boys, poisons and dissolves. The union of Jupiter and Thetis, in which the female is conquered and absorbed by the male, is a nightmarish primal scene to contrast with the union of Prometheus and Asia, which has been anticipated by the relationship of Asia and the Voice in the Air.[4]

As he hears Demogorgon's chariot "thundering up / Olympus" (50–51), Jupiter cries, "Victory!" (49). He forgets that thunder is supposed to go down from Olympus; his own aggression is returning upon him. And when the chariot arrives, he is shocked by what he sees: "Awful Shape, what art thou?" (51).

Demogorgon answers,

> Eternity—demand no direr name.
> Descend, and follow me down the abyss;
> I am thy child, as thou wert Saturn's child,
> Mightier than thee . . .
>
> (52–55)

This messianic child comes not to fulfill but to overthrow the father. Just as Jupiter's authoritarianism was the child of Saturn's lassitude, so the child of his violent aggression is the revolution that dethrones him. But the Epimethean Jupiter, like Prometheus in his own Epimethean stage, cannot recognize potential consequences; even after Demogorgon identifies himself, Jupiter can only repeat, "What then art thou?" (69). Like a vulture and a snake "twisted in inextricable fight," the two sink together into "the bottomless void" (73, 76). In this revision of *Paradise Lost,* God himself is thrown into what Milton called the "bottomless pit" (6.866). Demogorgon tells Jupiter that they will "dwell together / Henceforth in darkness" (55–56). What appears void to Jupiter is a state of potentiality in which he will dwell together with the force that transforms the potential and the actual into each other.

Demogorgon overcomes Jupiter in several ways. He is a serpentine process of change, which may come upon us as mutability or as the necessitarian chain of cause and effect or which we may actively try to invoke as revision. He is not only, as Eternity, a totality that is larger than Jupiter and that sweeps him away; he is also a dialectical condition in which no single entity can be without a contrary. As a perpetual other, Demogorgon subverts any sense of omnipotence, Jupiter's particular kind of narcissism. Although I will suggest some direr identities than "Eternity," all of Demogorgon's names must be provisional. In his fluid identity, Demogorgon is the threat that there is something that in a dreadful way is evermore about to be.

Jupiter's defeat has additional resonance. Jupiter's semen poisons Thetis and brings about his own downfall; the sexual father is punished through his own lust. And if Demogorgon includes among his many implications the power of the Gorgon's head, interpreted by Freud as the dread of castration felt by the viewer of the mother's forbidden genitals, then here that power is turned against the lord of the primal scene himself. "Lift thy lightnings not," Demogorgon tells him (56): we might further say that, deprived of his lightning, he is castrated by his child, as Uranus was by Kronos. Bearing Prometheus's aggression against the father, Demogorgon leaves Prometheus himself free from guilt. Necessity here is that which is necessary but not acceptable. Jupiter, Demogorgon, and Asia all serve to draw aggression away from Prometheus.

In the comparison of Demogorgon to a snake (72), we see once again the serpentine guardian of the mother, or even the mother herself in the form of a chaos dragon. Thus, insofar as Demogorgon is also the surrogate of Prometheus, we can see in the inextricable vulture and serpent a destructive embrace of the father by the son and mother identified together, a violent revision of the primal scene, in which the father is conquered. Perhaps in the vanishing of Demogorgon into the "shoreless sea" (74) we can see the sacrifice or repression of a power with homosexual intimations after it has done its work. And if Demogorgon represents the terrible aspect of the preoedipal mother, the shoreless sea suggests the mother's oceanic realm as oblivion rather than potentiality or nourishment. Among the "direr names" of Demogorgon are, in effect, Oedipus, Medusa, Kronos the castrator, the anti-Olympian monster Typhon, or Prometheus's own projected rage and violence, and Ganymede, or the homosexual identification with the mother; and "Eternity" itself is the uterine abyss into which Jupiter disappears. Jupiter falls "Dizzily down" (81) like the Voice in the Air, but this is a negative, not a pleasurable, failure. The end of his Dionysian dissolutions is to be dissolved himself.[5] As a destructive force, Eternity, or the full oceanic power of the mother, is the child of Jupiter's Olympian aggression against Earth and woman. We might think of his fall as the revenge of the sea goddess Thetis.

Yet we can see in Jupiter's ambition to be omnipotent and in his rape of Thetis an extreme and aberrant form of an attempt to reduce the power of the oceanic mother and achieve autonomy. Here too Jupiter seems like a Mr. Hyde version of Shelley himself, representing in projected and monstrous form one tendency in Shelley's attitude toward the mother. And Jupiter is indeed ruined through woman, that is, through Thetis. If Demogorgon is the vehicle of aggression toward the father, Jupiter is the vehicle of aggression toward the mother, and for Shelley, champion of woman, "the hated mother" would be a direr name than any of the others. In Jupiter and Demogorgon we can see a father in combat with an oedipal son and a paternal tyrant in combat with a saving maternal power; we can also see a woman-hater, a rapist and a lover of boys, in combat with a female monster, and, in addition, a child in combat with a mother, an orally aggressive child, the angry biter of the no longer caring and productive but still all-powerful preoedipal mother.

In this scene the old father and the old mother, inextricably bound, disappear together. Both of them are scapegoats and are sacrificed. The scene of Jupiter's fall embodies a complex wish: that the powerful mother might return to bring down the father, that this overwhelming mother might then herself disappear, and that the violent psychic conflicts of the Jovian age might be laid to rest.

After Jupiter's final screams, a giant peacefulness enters the play. In sharp contrast to the intensities of quest, torment, and struggle that have dominated thus far, and even in contrast to the bliss of Asia's transformation, the mood of scene 2 is relaxed and even casual. A new way of speaking accompanies this change of mood. In act 1 speech took forms appropriate to a fallen world of oppression, alienation, and suffering: the soliloquy, the curse, the brutal interrogation, the lament, the verbal assault, and, a small island in a sea of misery, the song of consolation and hope. In act 2, in a threshold world suffused with portents, speech took the forms of the dream report and the haunting, mysterious song; then in the final scenes we heard the philosophical dialogue, the oracular message, and the song of ecstasy and liberation. Now after Jupiter's last ragings, we hear conversation. For the first time in the play, characters simply talk together. That type of ordinary interaction has not been possible in the intensely burdened world of Prometheus's captivity and so seems a precious achievement.

While the task of the play up through the first scene of act 3 is to imagine how Jupiter might be gotten rid of, the task of the second half of the play is to imagine what the world would be like without him. In the remainder of act 3 Shelley gives us a series of views of the transformed world, in which different observers perceive the new world in their own different ways. Through these reports, Shelley suggests that the new world is a world of others and their individual perspectives. In the aftermath of Asia's transformation, Shelley is emphasizing the Apollonian rather than the Dionysian.

In scene 2, Apollo and Ocean appear "near the Shore" of "the Island Atlantis" (*R*, 257). We have moved from the shoreless sea to the shore of an island, a location that combines the sea and safety. Moreover, this particular island is Atlantis, the flooded land, here securely above the water. The return of an ancient utopia sets the stage for Shelley's own paradisal images. These images will be radically new, but Apollo and Ocean are familiar figures. Shelley wants to keep us in a recognizable world so that we can identify with his great transformation.[6] Meeting at the beginning of the sun's daily journey, Apollo and Ocean, Olympian and Titan, are friends; beneath the old conflicts, now ended, lies a basic peace. Ocean and Apollo also suggest the maternal and paternal worlds, the chaos monster and the principle of order, the oceanic feeling and the autonomous ego that rises high out of the water like the sun. In this scene the sun does not drown in the water; nor does its illumination pose any threat to the older, darker world.

Ocean announces that "Henceforth the fields" of the sea "will heave, unstain'd with blood / Beneath the uplifting winds—like plains of corn" (18–20). Shelley emphasizes the improvement of earthly life rather than a voyage away from it to a "diviner day" (2.5.103). Compared to fields and to plains of corn, the sea becomes as safe as the land; figuratively, it is brought under cultivation, or tamed. This new sea "will flow / Round many-peopled continents and round / Fortunate isles" (3.2.21–23). It will not overwhelm but serve and nourish.

The scene closes with one of Shelley's most quietly moving passages. Ocean says, "The loud Deep calls me home even now, to feed it / With azure calm out of the emerald urns," and as "A sound of waves is heard," he adds, "It is the unpastured Sea hung'ring for Calm. / Peace, Monster—I come now! Farewell" (41–42, 49–50), to which Apollo responds, "Farewell," the two great powers together completing the iambic pentameter line. Locock reads "unpastured" as "unfed," and Forman finds the word with that connotation in a draft of *The Mask of Anarchy*.[7] The sea is like a hungry infant, and in this vision it will be satisfied. Bloom speaks of Ocean's "fatherliness,"[8] and Apollo, who refers to himself as the sun's "guide" (37), is also a paternal figure. In contrast to Jupiter, these fathers are likable and trustworthy; they are gods who work for humanity. Also, they do not threaten the primacy of Prometheus and Asia, the children: Ocean refers to Asia as "mighty" (47). While strong and capable, they are content to be secondary.

Shelley also uses "unpastured," as Locock reminds us, in *Adonais*, in which the dead hero "Dare[d] the unpastured dragon in his den" (238).[9] In addition to being the clamorous, hungry child, the sea remains the chaos monster, the womb, the id, the Dionysian, the regressive, the power of the preoedipal mother, primal narcissism, all that the sea suggests in Shelley, and all of which can be monstrous, as well as compelling, for him. But here, as Bloom notes, when Ocean calls the sea "Monster," he is speaking with affection.[10] Shelley is imagining a condition in which what has appeared in the play as Demogorgon and even as the frightening Furies could be regarded with a familiar love.

It is the sea itself that has been the central subject of scene 2. The new sea that Shelley imagines is as much a reaction to Asia's sublime but problematically extreme regression to a diviner day and the dizzying speed and flight of the Voice in the Air as it is to Jupiter's destructive sense of the oceanic.

In scene 3 Hercules makes a brief appearance to perform the actual unbinding of Prometheus. The famous rescuer who won Alcestis back from death and tore Theseus loose from a seat in the underworld is limited to a minor, anticlimactic action. It is not force but imagination and love that play the leading roles in the liberation from Jupiter.[11] At the same time Shelley need not have introduced Hercules at all. But his presence contributes to Shelley's theme that the quest for liberation is not the solitary Byronic struggle of one hero against the world; while inspired and led by Prometheus, it is carried out by a coalition of forces playing more and less important parts but all making their contributions. As in *Laon and Cythna,* with its immortal senate of great minds inspiring reform on earth, and the *Defence of Poetry,* with its poets from all ages writing one great epic, Shelley dreams of a community working together to create paradise.

More important than his act of unbinding is Hercules' declaration that strength "Minister[s], like a slave" "To wisdom, courage, and long suffering love" (3.4, 2). Prometheus calls these words "sweeter even" than his new freedom (5), because they contradict the Furies' insistence that power and wisdom cannot dwell together. They are sweet even more because they acknowledge the primacy of wisdom over strength, as Demogorgon acknowledged the primacy of love over Necessity. The laboring Hercules was the same kind of figure as Prometheus, the kind that Apollo and Ocean are in scene 2, the pre-Olympian deity or hero who worked and often suffered for humanity; Hercules, Harrison writes, strove to "cleanse the earth for man from monsters."[12] The strength with which Hercules mastered monsters and tyrants, however, was often uncontrolled; he also killed good people, even his own children. The mastering capacity itself needs to be mastered. Hercules here willingly subordinates his strength to the Promethean qualities that will ensure its constructive expression. We can see in this subordination a reaction to the violent upsurge of Demogorgon, a capping of aggression after it has served its purpose.

Prometheus now describes to Asia and her sisters the life they will all lead together. They will live in a cave, which in Greek religion, as W. K. C. Guthrie writes, was the typical chthonian shrine, as the temple, often elevated, was the typical Olympian shrine (222). Moving from mountaintop to cave, Prometheus returns from the high Olympian world of the fathers to the deep chthonian world of the mothers and also to what René Spitz calls the primal organ of perception, the oral cavity.[13] But caves were also the lairs of dragons and chaos monsters, like Demogorgon, whose worship, Boccaccio writes, began in the darkness of caves.[14] In *Prometheus Unbound* the monsters in the cave are overcome: Demogorgon is mastered by Asia, and Prometheus masters his own inner monster, his raging Typhon, who also lived in a cave.[15] Then the hero enters the cave to live in it; his entry into the maternal world, although it is partly a return to a lost state, is partly like the coming of Apollo to take over the shrine of the mother to use it for his own purposes.

The paradise that the Titans enter is a chastened one. In the cave, Prometheus says, "We will sit and talk of time and change / As the world ebbs and flows, ourselves unchanged— / What can hide man from Mutability?" (23–25). In maintaining mutability, Shelley is trying to create a story of renovation that is not pure wish-dream. In the cave, "We will entangle buds and flowers, and beams / Which twinkle on the fountain's brim, and make / Strange combinations out of common things" (30–32). Holmes, who thinks that in acts 3 and 4 "the poem completely disintegrates," calls Prometheus's new life a "jaded exile" (507); Cronin speaks of the Titan's "plans to make daisy-chains" (155). But the mildness and anticlimactic relaxation of the new state is a response to the agonized conflicts of the Jovian world, and also to the Jovian concept of divinity as an intimidating, brutal force. More important, the new life is one of art. After Jupiter, the imagination is free to explore and discover, and a renewed capacity for wonder and inventiveness can find the strange and beautiful in "common things." Bloom, though, complains that Shelley's paradise lacks the spirit of Blake's Eden, where the life of art and intellect is an exhilarating clash of contraries.[16] But Shelley had a strong need for serenity, and he also had a different attitude toward regression, passivity, and aggressive conflict from Blake.

And yet there *is* poetic conflict in the picture of the paradise in act 3: it is Shelley's struggle to keep his renovation a transformation, not a transcendence. Following Jupiter's fall, the conflict between regression and progression becomes, in effect, the major dramatic action of the play. Like the vision of the sea in scene 2, the vision of mild regression in the cave is a reaction not only to the torments of Jupiter's world but also to the extreme regression of Asia and the

Voice in the Air. In their cave, the Titans will "Weave harmonies divine, yet ever new, / From difference sweet" (38-39), and Shelley's effort in the scene is to make sure that "difference sweet" is preserved, that harmony does not become oceanic oneness.

The Titans not only create art but are visited by human art, "the progeny immortal / Of Painting, Sculpture, and rapt Poesy, / And arts, though unimagined, yet to be" (54–56). As in Blake's "Proverbs of Hell," "Eternity is in love with the productions of time" (pl. 7). Unlike Jupiter, these gods watch humanity's growth approvingly; they are like loving parents, precursors who encourage the latecomers. The Titans are not only an audience for human art but also inspire it. Prometheus attributes human improvement to the "virtue" of the cave (63); the cave is the womb of humanity's art, with the progeny of Sculpture and Poesy ultimately emerging from the wonder, the playfulness, and the imaginative exploration within it.

The pastoral life in the cave is thus only part of a total paradisal structure, of a dialectic in which the gods regress and humanity progresses. The dialectic now moves outward toward ordinary humanity, as Prometheus gives the Spirit of the Hour a shell belonging to Asia to carry around the world, "Loosening its mighty music" (81), announcing the fall of Jupiter. What exactly does the world hear from this Shelleyan version of Gabriel's martial trumpet? Ione compares its azure and silver lining to "lulled music sleeping there" (73). In the sound of the sea that is the shell's apocalyptic music and in the synesthetic description of that visible, lulled music, Shelley images the oceanic feeling, which is now released into the common world. The shell is the vehicle of Asia, like the shell in which she floated to shore at her birth and the chariot of "ivory shell" (2.4.157) in which she ascends to meet Prometheus, and it announces the return to power of the primal mother.[17]

Prometheus now turns to his "Mother Earth," kissing the ground (84). In response, the angry, barren, misunderstanding figure of act 1 is filled with new life and joy. Prometheus becomes a nurturer even to his own mother. In her rejuvenation, the Earth becomes a good, capable mother with "many children fair / Folded in my sustaining arms" (90–91), and her transformation, as Wormhoudt notes, is described in oral images (105): her creatures will take from her "sweet nutriment" (96); flowers at night will "suck unwithering hues in their repose" (102). Regression will be replenishment, not loss of self.

Yet together with these images of regression, almost as if drawn along by them, comes death: a newly gentle death, "the last embrace of her / Who takes the life she gave, even as a mother / Folding her child, says, 'Leave me not again!' " (105–7). This death is a consummation of regressive eros, like the death of the *Alastor* Poet. But Asia protests: "O mother! wherefore speak the name of death? / Cease they to love and move and breathe and speak / Who die?" (108–10). With that question, Shelley changes the meaning of death from the extreme form of regression to the extreme form of mutability, from an intimation of transcendent oneness to a reminder of the recognizable world.

Earth tells Asia that only "the uncommunicating dead" can understand death (112); one secret of the transformed world must remain obscure. Nevertheless, Earth does go on to hint at a reassuring answer to Asia's question: "Death is the veil which those who live call life: / They sleep—and it is lifted" (113–14). To live in the new world is to live with the unconfirmable feeling that there is something evermore about to be. But while we wait to find out for certain, the world will be one of "mild variety" and "seasons mild" (115), rather than a "wheel of pain" (act 1.141). There will be no eternal spring, no oneness, but the mutable will become a beautiful multiplicity.

The cave where the Titans will live belongs to Earth and is filled with her inspiring spirit, and to lead them there she calls up her "torch-bearer" (148), a spirit who appears as a winged child like Eros. This guiding principle of regression will light the company beyond "Bacchic Nysa, Maenad-haunted mountain" (154)—a traditional birthplace of Dionysos, the Maenads being originally the nymphs who nursed him—to a pool that reflects a temple, now deserted but once dedicated to Prometheus; the cave is beside that temple. We recall Guthrie's point that the classical Greek temple and the cave represent opposed forms of worship, and Shelley's temple, "Distinct with column, arch and architrave" and adorned with "Praxitilean" sculpture seems very much a classical, Olympian place of worship (162, 165). In the Promethean temple and Earth's cave, Olympian and chthonian are parts of a total harmonious structure. The regressive Spirit of the Earth takes us back to the dyadic reflection in the water and the uterine cave and, at the same time, forward to the temple of the culture-bringer. Prometheus will live in a cave and be worshipped in a temple; the art in that temple will be inspired by the power within the cave; regression can be a source of cultural advances.

To this temple, youths once carried a lamp, Prometheus's symbol, just as Prometheus himself has borne the "torch of hope" "To this far goal of Time" (171, 174). E. B. Hungerford explains that the Athenians honored the Firebringer Prometheus with a race called the Lampadephoria, in which the winner had to cross the finish line with a torch still unextinguished (197). The far goal of time, now reached, is a renovated earth and a renovated humanity, yet the passage suggests that this renewal is haunted by humanity's desire for something more, oneness, immortality; for the runners of the Lampadephoria are compared not only to Prometheus, who bore the torch of hope to the far goal of time, but also to those who bear it "Into the grave across the night of life" (172). Shelley tries to contain primal glory within the cave, to tap it as a power that could drive earthly renovation. But it is a force that tends to make even the renewed earth seem like a "night of life." In contrast to the harmony of cave and temple, the closing juxtaposition of the two torch-races—one to renovation, one beyond it into the grave—is dissonant and unstable. In Freud's story of Prometheus, restraint is necessary to keep fire alive;[18] in Shelley, restraint is necessary to keep Promethean fire from consuming the world it seeks to renovate.

Scene 4 begins with Ione and Panthea describing the mysterious Spirit of the Earth, which, Ione says, "is not Earthly" (1). We can see in this winged child a return to beginnings, an emblem of renewal itself. At home in the places of regression, it plays in the sea, high in the air, in "cities while men sleep" (12). Before Jupiter's reign, the Spirit called Asia mother and drank "the liquid light / Out of her eyes," yet Asia is not the Spirit's actual mother, and "whence it sprung it knew not" (17–18, 23). Todhunter writes that "Prometheus and Asia are probably his parents."[19] But even though Prometheus fills the place of adoptive father, he is not called father and remains in the background during this scene. He is the shadowy, muted father of a mother-centered culture or of its parallel in the life of the individual, early infancy. He is also the father who stands benignly in the background while Asia tells the Spirit, "I love thee, gentlest being, and henceforth / Can cherish thee unenvied" (30–31); he is the father who will not be an envious and castrating intruder, like Time in Asia's account of origins in act 2. Prometheus and the Spirit are also the two forms of the male companion of the traditional mother goddess, the adult lover and the child. At this point, the regressive impulse is dominant, and so the Spirit takes center stage. Like Eros or the young Dionysos, the Spirit is a version of what Kerényi calls "the Primordial Child [in] the world of the Mother."[20] In the divine child Kerényi sees a symbol of a "still completely undifferentiated state," sometimes expressed, as in Dionysos's case, in a bisexual nature.[21] Shelley's Spirit too is an oceanic figure, a child of Asia and not, a Spirit of the Earth and yet not earthly.

For Bloom the Spirit is "perhaps the least successful creation in the entire drama," a creature out of "Namby-Pamby land."[22] Compared to such versions of the divine child as the messianic child of Virgil's Fourth *Eclogue*, the "Infant God" of Milton's *Nativity Ode*, the "Mighty Prophet" of Wordsworth's *Immortality Ode*, and the vigorous upstart of Shelley's own translation of the *Homeric Hymn to Mercury*, the Spirit is certainly a small figure. However, in act 3 Shelley is trying to domesticate the sublime, make the strange familiar, not astonish us but assure and convince us, not consume the present but build between the present and a promised world a bridge that we can imagine passing over. We also have to understand the Spirit in the context of the theme of childhood that Shelley has been developing since the beginning of the act. There Jupiter is expecting a child of terror; he gets a metaphorical child and terror too, ironically directed at himself. But the Spirit is the actual, rather than metaphorical, child, the new beginning that Jupiter could never father. That beginning appears as an "Awful Shape" to those who are threatened by it (3.1.51) and a harmless, playful child to those who yearn for it. Although a shadowy father, Prometheus is still a truly creative force, who, in contrast to Jupiter, can father something new.

Indeed, the downfall of Jupiter seems to release positive concepts of fathering, like Ocean's care of the childlike waves and Prometheus's love for the "progeny" of the arts, sublimated offspring. Psychologically, however, the situation may be quite different. Prometheus's relationship to the Spirit is like Laon's relationship to Cythna's child. Just as the Tyrant Lust is the scapegoat for Laon's genitality, so too Jupiter, the great fathering force of classical mythology, embodies in a demonic form the sexuality that is not clear in Prometheus's character as a father. We might say that Jupiter and Thetis in the rape scene not only parody the union of Prometheus and Asia but also act it out. We might say that figuratively Jupiter and Thetis are the biological parents of the Spirit of the Earth. Shelley must work his way past an ego-dystonic sense of the father's aggressive genitality before he can give us a brighter vision of mature sexuality.

Finally, in attempting to understand the Spirit, we must note that Shelley's divine child is not intended to be a complete ideal. Hardly a Mighty Prophet, it "idly reasoned what it saw" (22), and it admits to Asia that "a child / Cannot be wise like thee" (33–34). However, it also says, "I am grown wiser" on this day "And happier too, happier and wiser both" (33, 35). Embodying a sense of beginnings rather than achieved finalities, it is in the first stage of an education in which, in contrast to the education, say, of the Ancient Mariner's Wedding Guest, wisdom and happiness will increase together. The Spirit of the Earth embodies a turning point; it functions as a limit of regression, a limit well this side of dissolution, and in it rejuvenescence turns back toward growth.

As the Spirit reports his impressions of the new world, we see the change in the Earth, or mother, from the child's point of view. Formerly his travels through nature were impeded by "toads and snakes and loathly worms" and "boughs / That bore ill berries" (36–38). The mother was a poisoner, her swarm of reptiles suggesting the dreadful serpents associated with the Furies and the Gorgons. In the past too his heart was sickened by the "foul masks" that hid man (44) and even more by woman, "ugliest of all things evil . . . When false or frowning" (46, 49). Of all creatures in the world of Jupiter, it seems, women were most deformed by that world. But the passage is also speaking of female mutability and rejection, or the treachery of the mother, as the ugliest of evils.

Passing through a city, the Spirit hears the apocalyptic sound of the shell, "A long long sound, as it would never end" (57). His response is in keeping with the infinite, oceanic quality of this music that signals the return of the good mother: hiding in a fountain to observe people's reactions, he becomes a fetus in the womb. The reactions he sees, however, are not marked by regression; just the opposite, the music wakes people from sleep. As they gather in wonder in the streets, "Those ugly human shapes and visages" floated away into the air, and "those / From whom they past seemed mild and lovely forms / After some foul disguise had fallen" (65, 68–70). While this unveiling seems a radical transformation, Shelley portrays it in the same understated rhetoric that characterized the Apollo-Ocean scene. With the disguises fallen, all "Were somewhat changed—and after brief surprise / And greetings of delighted wonder, all / Went to their sleep again" (71–73). "Somewhat" and "brief" are fine strategic touches. Only a small difference separates our world from par-

adise; it is all possible. No one is consumed by radiance. The trans-
figured men and women even go back to sleep.

Nature too loses its foul disguise; even the reptiles appear beauti-
ful: "All things had put their evil nature off" (77). The Spirit is par-
ticularly elated to see "two azure halcyons clinging downward / And
thinning one bright bunch of amber berries," nightshade but no
longer poisonous (80–81). The halcyons, or kingfishers, are now veg-
etarians;[23] both mother and child, Earth and birds, have lost their
oral aggression. But why are the birds upside down? Their inverted
posture is an indication that the renovation does not erase individual
characteristics, for kingfishers are known for plunging straight down-
ward into the water after prey. Shelley is being careful to show that
individual identity is not lost in the new state of being.

But the Spirit says that "the happiest change of all" (85) is his re-
union with Asia. They will never part, she responds, until his "chaste
Sister / Who guides the frozen and inconstant moon" comes to love
him (86–87). The Spirit asks if the Moon will love him "as Asia loves
Prometheus" (90). Here Prometheus does appear as a fatherly figure
of a mature, positively represented sexuality. "Peace, Wanton," Asia
answers, "thou art yet not old enough," and she jokes about his pre-
genital sexuality: "Think ye, by gazing on each other's eyes / To mul-
tiply your lovely selves?" (91–93). Some readers have lamented this
bit of banter, but it serves two functions: in taking a deliberately anti-
sublime tone, Shelley is again reining in his own extremist impulses,
and in joking about pregenitality, he is acknowledging that regres-
sive eros is not the complete and final goal of the Promethean reno-
vation. In this conversational interlude, Shelley is moving the youth-
ful spirit of renovation toward maturity.

That development continues as the Spirit of the Hour returns to
make its report, which as William N. Guthrie notes, offers a mature
perspective on the transformation in contrast to the Spirit of the
Earth's childlike perspective.[24] It also offers a more ecstatic perspec-
tive: after the oceanic power of the shell filled the world, the Hour
says, the very air and the sunlight "were transformed / As if the sense
of love dissolved in them / Had folded itself round the sphered
world" (101–3).

As the Spirit of the Hour descends to earth after its work, its
horses return to "their birthplace in the sun," where they will live
"Pasturing flowers of vegetable fire," while its chariot will be en-
shrined in a temple, where sculptures of the horses, "Yoked" to the

chariot "by an amphisbaenic snake," will "mock" their former flight (108, 110, 119–20). At this point the Hour reacts as if it has gotten carried away: "Alas, / Whither has wandered now my partial tongue?" (121–22). Why must it apologize for its description of the temple in the sun?

Linking sculpted horses to the real chariot, the amphisbaena holds together art and actuality. In the sculpted horses' mocking of the actual flight, however, art and life may diverge as much as they come together, for *mock* suggests "surpass," not merely "copy." The Spirit of the Hour has fallen under the spell of pastoral repose, primal orality (the edible flowers of vegetable fire), the return to the place of birth, the oceanic radiance of the "bright and liquid sky" to which the temple lies "open" (118). It must pull itself up short and continue to let gravity take it to earth. The Hour's "alas" expresses its sadness at having to leave the ideal state of being it has just described. Even more, it expresses two Shelleyan sorrows: a sorrow that what the play's preface called the "beautiful idealisms" of poetry may only, in the end, mock the possibilities of life; and a sorrow that the regressive and progressive tendencies can only be yoked by continued, renewed effort. The two-headed amphisbaena is an appropriate emblem for the Spirit's uneasy looking in opposite directions at once.[25]

On the earth the Spirit of the Hour reports its disappointment at first "not to see / Such mighty change as I had felt within / Expressed in outward things" (128–30). Shelley returns to the rhetoric of understatement. Soon, though, the Spirit begins to understand that the world is deeply changed: "thrones were kingless, and men walked / One with the other even as spirits do, / None fawned, none trampled" (131–33). In addition,

> hate, disdain or fear,
> Self-love or self-contempt on human brows
> No more inscribed, as o'er the gate of hell,
> "All hope abandon, ye who enter here."
> (133–36)

"Myself am Hell," Milton's Satan said, proudly asserting his autonomy (*Paradise Lost*, 4.75). The unreformed Prometheus might have echoed him, but for the common person under Jupiter's reign Dante's line was a better motto. Enslaved outwardly, he was also enslaved inwardly: "the subject of a tyrant's will / Became, worse fate, the abject of his own, / Which spurred him, like an outspent horse, to death" (139–41). A "soul self-consumed" (146), a being of "self-love," "self-contempt," and "self-mistrust" (152), Jovian man was torn by destructive doubleness. But now, "None talked that common, false, cold, hollow talk / Which makes the heart deny the *yes* it breathes" (149–50). In the new world of act 3 the individual self is not dissolved but made whole. And in what is deeply a poet's apocalypse, the self's language is no longer in conflict with its inner being. Most dramatically transformed are women, now "Speaking the wisdom once they could not think, / Looking emotions once they feared to feel / And changed to all which once they dared not be" (157–59). If women become equal members of a progressive society, they also, symbolically, become good mothers, "radiant forms" raining "fresh light and dew / On the wide earth" (154–55). The transformation becomes ever deeper and more sweeping. The accoutrements of tyranny and faith "Stand, not o'erthrown, but unregarded now" (179), relics of oppression that have lost their power to influence us: the old gods "Frown, mouldering fast, o'er their abandoned shrines" (189). The Hour's report of the downfall of the old gods and tyrants builds to a climactic image of aggression:

> The painted veil, by those who were, called life,
> Which mimicked, as with colours idly spread,
> All men believed and hoped, is torn aside—
> The loathsome mask has fallen . . .
>
> (190–93)

Earth spoke of mortal life as a veil of "rainbow-skirted showers" (3.3.116), not "colours idly spread," much less a "loathsome mask." The Hour's report has built up to a mood of Dionysian rapture; as in the passage on the sun, an impulse to transcend the earth threatens to overwhelm the commitment to transform it. But Shelley is struggling to master and shape that surging intensity. Behind the "loathsome mask" is not Asia's ocean or death or the abysm but something recognizable: "the man remains" (193). Man is radically different; he is "Sceptreless, free, uncircumscribed"; he is "Exempt from awe, worship, degree;—the King / Over himself" (194, 196–97). But he is man still, and "but man" is the Spirit's repeated assurance (194, 197). The vision has become Apollonian. Man is "just, gentle, wise," but he has not been refined beyond recognition: "Passionless? no—yet free from guilt or pain" (197–98).

The Hour's report now brings the conflicts of act 3—between restraint and ecstasy, progression and regression, transformation and transcendence, Apollo and Dionysos—to a culmination. Earlier the Spirit of the Hour's horses were "exempt" from toil, women were "exempt" from old customs, humanity was "Exempt" from the worship of external authority (109, 156, 196). Now the report climaxes with a lack of exemption: man is "Nor yet exempt, though ruling them like slaves, / From chance and death and mutability" (200–201). The "yet" holds open the prospect of achieving that exemption in an afterlife, but it is on this life that the Spirit of the Hour focuses. Like Asia, the new man has power over those elements of existence that are associated with Demogorgon. What does it mean to be not exempt from death, yet ruling it like a slave? We might say that human beings now see death as a last embrace; that while desiring more than the earth can offer, they can still affirm earthly existence; that they are now able, like Asia, to use Demogorgon as a source of energy, to move Necessity for their own purposes; or that while they must die they will no longer be driven to death by a self-destructive will, by a need for self-punishment, by a death wish.

The final three lines of act 3 help us understand further this paradoxical power. Chance, death, and mutability are

> The clogs of that which else might oversoar
> The loftiest star of unascended Heaven,
> Pinnacled dim in the intense inane.
>
> (202–4)

In these lines Shelley tries to check the paradisal vision from carrying us away into nothingness. Here is a further way in which man rules the chance, death, and mutability to which he is subject: he turns them from limitations into, in Wordsworth's terms, "The anchor of [his] purest thoughts."[26] They save him from losing himself in the infinite; they keep him from being transformed out of human existence. Shelley wants the infinite with the dim star in it, not by itself. His vision in act 3 is that both the ego and the oceanic can be strengthened together, with the ego, finally, in ascendancy.[27]

The Spirit of the Hour's survey of the new humanity begins in disappointment and ends with an acknowledgment of limitation, but both are parts of a strategy of restraint and understatement with which Shelley tries to keep the desire to transform the world from overflowing into the desire to transcend it, and to keep the regressive impulse harnessed to progressive ends. But such limitation is only one kind of purified aggression or constructive mastery. Another kind—capability, the power to do things—remains to be dramatized.

I have been suggesting that to read Shelley is to observe him restlessly trying to position his contraries in relation to each other in order for him to have two things he wants or to avoid the dangers of two things he both wants and fears. This continual positioning and repositioning does not characteristically result in static structures but rather in liminal or dialectical structures in which there is passage back and forth, whether defensive recoil or free mobility. In *Prometheus Unbound*, his most ambitiously optimistic poem, Shelley tries to position his contraries to yield the happiest possible results. At the end of act 3 this has not yet happened. A sense of free passage back and forth, although longed for, is finally less in evidence than a danger of flying off in opposite directions. The Dionysian impulse, while successfully contained, is not yet content to be part of a dialectical process. Shelley's quest for a poetic formulation to satisfy contrary impulses must be continued in a fourth act.

14

Prometheus Unbound:
Act 4

SHELLEY CONSIDERED *PROMETHEUS UNBOUND* COMPLETE IN THREE ACTS
and sent it off in that form to his publisher, but several months later
he added the fourth act, a "sublime after-thought" to some readers,[1]
an Epimethean blunder to others. A. A. Jack wrote that "with [this]
choric song of joy and harmony the world in which we live is so little
in touch that so far from the words having interest to human beings,
they have scarcely even meaning."[2] But without act 4, something in-
herent in the drama and in Shelley's own sensibility would be left un-
said. Without this choric song Shelley's "lyrical drama" would not
reach the level to which its orality tends and which the songs of Asia's
transfiguration anticipate.[3] Carl Woodring writes that by the end of
act 3 most of the goals of Godwin, Mary Wollstonecraft, and other
radical thinkers of the Enlightenment have been achieved (302); but
Shelley was always a votary of Romance as well as of Reason, and in
the last act he gives free play to his spirits, voices, daemons, and vi-
sions in a beneficent Walpurgisnacht.

The third act ends in a conspicuous absence in another way. In
that act Shelley tries to be measured and restrained, and we never get
a climactic spirit of joy commensurate with a liberation from Jupiter's
world of suffering. But now in act 4 comes the deferred festival of re-
joicing; now Shelley moves from understatement to hyperbole, from
restraint to release, from the conversational to the rhapsodic. In act 3
we see through multiple individual perspectives; in act 4 we see
through the oceanic feeling. While act 3 is comparable to Act 1 in its
Apollonian stress on the self and its focus on aggression, act 4 is com-
parable to act 2 in its Dionysian stress on ecstasy and regression. Act

4 thus fills out the play's dialectical balance, strengthening its ongo-
ing interplay of contraries. We can see that interplay within each of
the final two acts as well. If act 3 stresses progressive change in the so-
cial world, it also includes regression into the cave. If act 4 stresses
the Dionysian in its ecstatic music, it also includes Apollonian and
humanistic tendencies. To trace the details of that interplay is to fol-
low the deep melody of this lyrical drama.

Act 4 is needed, perhaps above all, to complete Shelley's engage-
ment with the oceanic. Act 3 ends with Shelley saving his renovated
humanity from the intense inane. In act 4 Shelley soars beyond the
clogs, undertaking a poetic voyage somewhat like Asia's voyage in the
last song of act 2 into a realm where it has seemed that humanity and
earthly nature could not survive. We might say that the ego must be
strengthened in act 3 before it can give itself safely and affirmatively
to the regressive and Dionysian in act 4. But at the beginning of the
act the Dionysian is still problematic. The world is filled with rejoic-
ing spirits possessed "By the Storm of delight, by the panic of glee"
(44), and it may be difficult for readers of such words as "storm" and
"panic" not to think of mania in the midst of ecstasy. In act 3 Shelley
tried to contain the Bacchic or Pan-ic possession; in act 4 he tries to
shape it from within.

Prometheus and Asia are absent from act 4. In one sense, they
have been internalized within humanity and nature, and their spirits,
no longer exiled, pervade the universe. Literally, however, they are
absent because they are consummating their love; as is often noted,
the cosmic festival is the epithalamial celebration of their reunion
and also a symbolic form of it. Within the cave a new primal scene for
a new state of being is taking place. Prometheus and Asia are like ar-
chaic fertility figures, on whose love the eros of all humanity and na-
ture depends. They are also the children who have taken over the
primal scene.

Outside the cave Ione and Panthea serve once again as our guides
and surrogates in the visionary action, as ordinary faculties of per-
ception confronting the marvelous. They measure the capacity of a
human audience to keep up with the great transformation. They are
Shelley's lifeline to the world of the ego.

The act opens with the funeral of the bad father, the "Father of
many a cancelled year," as the "Spectres" of the "dead Hours" "bear
Time to his tomb in eternity" and are themselves driven from the sky
(11–14). A Chorus of Hours now awakens out of a prenatal existence.

Carl Grabo finds it "not easy to explain the reappearance of the Hours," since Shelley has made a point of killing off not just the past but Time.[4] But what Shelley kills off is the particular sense of time that we usually identify with Time itself: time as the father, the reaper, the castrator; time as clock-time; time as what it was on the Caucasus, a pain-filled succession of "wingless, crawling Hours" (1.48); what it was to Mercury, an external immensity that overwhelms the mind; and what it was in Asia's narrative, an envious intruder. Those old Hours are replaced not by timelessness but by a new sense of time. The new Hours move quickly, as they "Weave the dance on the floor of the breeze," and then slowly, as they "Enchant the Day that too swiftly flees" (4.69, 71). They are dancers, as the Horae traditionally were, and, now fast, now slow, they change with desire and give pleasure instead of frustration.[5]

The past Hours also represent an old sense of the mother as not a nourisher but a devourer: "Once the hungry Hours were hounds / Which chased the Day, like a bleeding deer" (73–74). There are two groups of Horae in act 4, the bad mothers, who are gotten rid of along with the bad father, and the good mothers, who now "weave the mystic measure / Of music and dance" (77–78). Jane Harrison tells us that the Horae, the basic temporal divisions of the world order, were originally divided into two categories, like the seasons: "the fruitful and the fruitless."[6] It is also the Horae, she writes, who bring in the Year-Festival, which celebrates the annual rebirth of the Kouros, the Dionysian hero of the mother religions, the new man.[7] Act 4 is a Shelleyan version of such a festival. The old time was pervaded by a sense of the father and the bad mother, the new time by a sense of the good mother and the powerful child in league with her. Thus, the Hours now dance together with the Spirits of the Human Mind. In that dance, Wasserman writes, time, instead of ruling the mind, is interwoven with it.[8] Specifically, I would suggest, time becomes what it is for an artist, who transforms time into rhythm and timing, who uses time to organize the elements of a work, who shapes and plays with time itself.

The liberated Spirits of the Mind are now "free to dive or soar or run," to fill the sky vacated by Jupiter (137). The clogs are removed, and they want to outsoar the stars, but when they do, they don't vanish into the intense inane: "We'll pass the Eyes / Of the starry skies / Into the hoar Deep to colonize," chasing away "Death, Chaos, and Night" (141–44). The Spirits fly away from the earth not to transcend but to humanize. "Colonize" follows such words as "empire" and "king" in the play in a transformation of language, in which the idea of mastery is not abandoned but redefined from mastery of other human beings to mastery of disturbing elements within the self, mastery of our own potentialities, mastery of what is outside our common humanity and restricts or threatens it.

The idea of artistic time now becomes explicit as the Hours choreograph the closing movement of the dance: "Break the dance and scatter the song— / Let some depart and some remain" (175–76). One Semichorus of Spirits will go off "beyond Heaven" to "build a new earth and sea," while the other will be held by "the inchantments of Earth" (161, 164, 162). Dividing the dance, Shelley satisfies both his contrary impulses. In addition, each group of Spirits includes the quality of the other: the transcendental Spirits will bring forth plants and creatures, Apollonian individual forms, from chaos, and the earthbound Spirits will infuse the world with the Dionysian "music of our sweet mirth" (174).

The Hours and Spirits fly off, leaving Ione and Panthea to witness the spectacular central visions of the last act: the chariots of the Spirit of the Moon and the Spirit of the Earth. In *Poetry and Repression,* Bloom traces the history of the visionary chariot as a representation of divine power from Ezekiel and Revelation to the *Purgatorio,* in which Beatrice rides in the Chariot of the Church Triumphant, and *Paradise Lost,* in which Christ rides the Chariot of Paternal Deity (83–93). Ezekiel's chariot has the form of four "living creatures" (1:5), or cherubim. Cherubim were originally Mesopotamian winged dragons that guarded treasures and special places; they were thus like the Python of Delphi and Fontenrose's other chaos monsters; and so in Psalm 18, when God "rode upon a cherub and did fly" (10), he is, like Apollo, adapting for his own use the power of the old mother religions.

Shelley's chariots belong to a sequence within the play that begins with the chariots of Asia and Demogorgon. Asia's chariot, like Dante's, contains a female figure of power, but Asia is not a guide to a higher paternal divinity; she herself is the divinity. The chariot of Demogorgon is an even more striking departure from tradition because here the cherub acts on its own. In Demogorgon Shelley returns the cherub to its maternal origins; the old chaos monster takes back the supremacy it lost to the sky god; the power of the mother is used to overcome Paternal Deity.

But the divine chariots in act 4 hold neither a paternal deity nor a maternal one; they hold two children. The regressive impulse of the entire play culminates in these visions of the Spirits of the Earth and the Moon as, in effect, infants in cradles or even embryos in the womb. Here is a hyperbolic counterpart to the understated child-spirit of act 3. Here is the Primordial Child of the ancient rites and myths, the young year, the young god, the child-companion of the mother goddess. However, if these infants symbolize a return to potentiality, they also symbolize an emergence from potentiality, and we will be watching them mature. In an image of birth, the two chariots emerge from two openings in the forest, and they "float upon / The Ocean-like inchantment of strong sound" (202–3). Like Asia in her regression, the chariots float on a sea of music, but unlike Asia, they are floating into our world, not out of it.

Ione, in the first vision, sees "a chariot like that thinnest boat / In which the Mother of the Months is borne" (206–7)—"the new Moon, / With the old Moon in her arms," in the lines from the *Ballad of Sir Patrick Spens* that Coleridge used as an epigraph to *Dejection: An Ode.* Inside the chariot is an infant with a white face "like the whiteness of bright snow" and wings like "sunny frost": "Its limbs gleam white" within "its white robe"; its hair has "the brightness of white light" (220–24). This preternatural whiteness is literally the cold and life-less brilliance of the moon. For Daniel Hughes, it suggests a state of "magnificently unresolved possibility—the condition of being before the 'staining' process of existence takes over."[9] It also suggests the whiteness of milk, or, in effect, the state in which milk is of supreme importance. The whiteness of the infant passenger is difficult to distinguish from the whiteness of its chariot, the new moon, the reborn form of the old moon-mother. In addition, the chariot figuratively bears the mother of the months but literally bears the winged infant. Ione's vision is a divine image of the dyad, in which the child is as close to the mother as it is possible to get while still retaining a distinct being. At the same time, the child actively guides the chariot with "a quivering moonbeam" (231). While celebrating infancy and the dyad, Ione's vision thus contains an impulse toward mature independence and power.

The chariot of the Spirit of the Earth, in Panthea's description of the second vision, is "A sphere, which is as many thousand spheres," "Purple and azure, white and green and golden," "Sphere within sphere" (238, 242–43). The two chariots suggest the white radiance of oneness and the abundance and ever-changing diversity of living actuality. They also suggest two senses of potentiality or imagination —the sheer openness of possibility, on the one hand, and all the possibilities, on the other—and two poetic capacities—the capacity to insert a blank page into the world and its givens and the capacity to conceive of the multitude of things that might go on it. But if the swift and complex motion of the spheres as "they whirl / Over each other with a thousand motions" (246–47) embodies an increase in activity and energy over the first chariot, it also embodies an increase in Dionysian or regressive vertigo. The orbs whirl "with the force of self-destroying swiftness," and the chariot "Grinds the bright brook into an azure mist / Of elemental subtlety, like light" (249, 254–55); the bright brook, already an oceanic phenomenon, is transformed, both destructively and beautifully, into an even more regressive state. Similarly,

> the wild odour of the forest flowers,
> The music of the living grass and air,
> The emerald light of leaf-entangled beams
> Round [the Chariot's] intense, yet self-conflicting speed,
> Seem kneaded into one aerial mass
> Which drowns the sense. . . .
>
> (256–61)

Fogle sees in these lines "the consummation toward which the Shelleyan synesthesia continually strives: a blending of all sensations into one mystical, ineffable, supersensuous harmony" (132). But I would question whether Shelley is entirely happy about this, for the oneness beyond images is produced by grinding and kneading; in addition, in the "self-conflicting speed" we can see a return of the "self-destroying swiftness." In this passage, regression is pleasurable but overwhelming; the sense is drowned.

It is just at this point, where all form is lost, that the most distinct form in the entire vision is introduced: the rider within the chariot, the child within the regressive state of being. The Spirit of the Earth is not only a distinct form but also a tranquil one, calmly sleeping and smiling in the center of the wild spinning. The child's sleep also contains a libidinal or progressive impulse toward waking life: in a version of Adam's dream, the child is "Like one who talks of what he loves in dream" (268). In another way too Shelley reassures us that the child's sleep is nothing to worry about: Ione interrupts Panthea's description to observe of the child, "'Tis only mocking the Orb's harmony" (269). This line offers us detachment in reaction to an extremity of Dionysian regression. The sleeping is a satisfied repose, not a drowning.

We also see an active, aggressive element in the child, for a star on its forehead shoots beams "Like swords of azure fire, or golden spears" that "Pierce the dark soil" and "Make bare the secrets of the Earth's deep heart" (271, 278–79). The child's curiosity about the mother is combined with its aggressive and genital impulses toward her.[10] Within the mother the beams reveal wealth and sustenance, "unimagined gems" (281), "Wells of unfathomed fire, and water-springs / Whence the great Sea, even as a child, is fed" (284–85). Here is the ultimate source of supplies. But suddenly Shelley unlooses a passage of devastation. The beams reveal the wreckage of "cancelled cycles" and the relics of violence: "gorgon-headed targes," "sepulchred emblems / Of dead Destruction, ruin within ruin" (289, 291, 294–95). "Ruin within ruin" parodies "Sphere within sphere"; inside the mother is her destructive double, her "gorgon-headed" self. The earth is packed with waste, the fragments of an old culture of thanatos: "Jammed in the hard black deep" are "monstrous works and uncouth skeletons," "The anatomies of unknown winged things," and "serpents, bony chains" (302, 299, 303, 305).[11]

As the passage progresses, it seems that we are going deeper into the earth and further into its past, and in one sense the beams are penetrating into more and more deeply repressed feelings toward the mother. But the prehistoric anatomies and serpents lie "over" the weapons and wrecked cities (302), which in turn lie above the gems and wells in "the Earth's deep heart" (279). The beams reveal the chronology of a relationship that begins in abundance and then moves forward in time, or upward, to the cancellation of the infantile cycles of the dyad and to the child's sense of the mother's hostility as she seems increasingly alien and monstrous and increasingly complicated by serpentine or phallic elements. In this sense the "unknown winged things" are closer to the surface, or the present, than the nourishing "watersprings."

Over the primeval beasts lie even worse terrors, "jagged alligator" and "earth-convulsing behemoth" (309–10), which

> on the slimy shores
> And weed-overgrown continents of Earth,
> Increased and multiplied like summer worms
> On an abandoned corpse . . .
>   (311–14)

The child's sense of the mother's destructiveness comprehends the oral (the "jagged alligators"), the anal ("the slimy shores, / And weed-overgrown continents"), and the primal scene (the worms multiplying on the corpse).

The phantasmagoric vision of the Earth's interior comes to a stunning close. When all the land becomes a dead body festering with monstrous serpents, "the blue globe / Wrapt Deluge round it," and the monsters "Yelled, gaspt and were abolished; or some God / Whose throne was in a Comet, past, and cried— / 'Be not!'—and like my words they were no more" (314–18). The child's light reveals an archaic age of horror suddenly abolished, and now separated from us by the surface of the globe or an apocalyptic deluge or the border between the conscious and unconscious realms of the mind. What has been repressed is the sense of the destructive mother and the child's own violent anger at her. Both the monsters and Panthea's words that have been describing them vanish. The repressive "Be not" has two senses: "Let there be not such a mother" and "Let there be not such words about the mother."

What of the God on the passing comet? This saving force of repression is "some" God, an unknown divinity, not the God worshipped as Jupiter. By itself, the image of the blue globe wrapping deluge around the festering corpse gives us a flood of biblical proportions but without the Bible's transcendent God. It is as if Shelley is trying to imagine the primal, oceanic mother overcoming the destructive mother. But the latter may be too strong and the idea of deluge too ambivalent for him to be satisfied with that imagining alone. He has to go on to imagine salvation from outside the mother-child dyad. And so the father comes back to rescue us from the mother, who earlier rescued us from the tyranny of the father. The romance of the regressive impulse is ended through a positive identification with the father. In the chariot visions Shelley comes to a limit of regression and turns back toward new growth.

The father's function in act 4 is to help free the child from the mother, not to become a new authority, and having accomplished that purpose he disappears, leaving the Earth and the Moon as the primal powers in the scene. We now move not away from Dionysian ecstasy but to a new form of it as the Earth and Moon enter into a mating dance. From regression and primal narcissism, we move to genitality. Moreover, the Earth and Moon become speakers. Reborn in their chariots, they are now maturing in a new reality.

The Earth is filled with a "boundless, overflowing, bursting gladness," which shoots forth "like a beam," a phallic impulse aimed now at not the mother but the Moon; it "penetrates [her] frozen frame," not aggressively but erotically, "With love" and "deep melody" (320, 327–28, 330). The phallic power of the father was threatening, punishing, even poisoning; now in the Earth's possession it gives warmth and pleasure. Indeed, Earth remembers the old "Sceptred Curse" "battering and blending" "my children's bones, / . . . to one void mass" (338, 342–43). Bloom writes that the Earth has "no consistent role or sex,"[12] and Earth does sound here like the old Mother, as Jupiter is remembered destroying everything "Which finds a grave or cradle in my bosom" (348). In a draft, Earth refers to man as "my latest born my most beloved."[13] The Earth is analogous to the Bacchic male, the Kouros, the young male in the religion of the goddess, and a figure simultaneously important as a lover and as the child of a mother. Thus the Earth oscillates in its relation to the female, sometimes merging back into the dyad and even sounding like the mother herself, sometimes emerging into a genital relationship with a separate female—although still an incestuous one, a sister. Radically unlike the Bacchic male, however, Shelley's Earth is not a subordinate to the female but an equal.

The Earth's new love engenders in the Moon "unexpected birth," and "living shapes upon [her] bosom move" (360, 365). That same love "interpenetrates" the Earth itself, waking "a life in the forgotten dead" (370, 374), and a storm rises "Out of the lampless caves of unimagined being" (378). Dionysos was a chthonic god of the dead, as well as a god of fertility. The power of the dead, or repressed, now unimagined primal mother bursts into the world of the father, overwhelming "Hate and Fear and Pain, light-vanquished shadows" (381). Having unloosed the dark, stormy spirit of Dionysos, Shelley now shapes it into Apollonian illumination.

Accordingly, Shelley introduces humanity into his celestial raptures, as Earth celebrates the new, Promethean man. The new man is compared to a leprous child, "Who follows a sick beast to some warm cleft / Of rocks, through which the might of healing springs is poured" and then, cured, returns to its mother (389–90). Wasserman points out that this is the legend of Bladud and the founding of Bath. He writes that in typical fashion Shelley is detaching the myth from its "inherited contexts" and thereby universalizing it to use it as a beautiful pattern of thought.[14] But unless we do pay attention to the inherited context we will miss a significant point in the passage. In the original legend Bladud is not a child but a king. In Shelley's version the child's mother is like the foster-mother Earth in the *Immortality Ode*, the well-meaning but helpless post-narcissistic mother. The healing water in the warm cleft is the oceanic power of the primal mother. To be cured is to become like a passive child and return to the "immortal sea / Which brought us hither." At the same time, the conspicuously absent kingship of Bladud suggests an active male power that the child does not have.

That quickly changes. The new man is part of a whole but one other than the dyad: "Man, oh, not men! a chain of linked thought, / Of love and might to be divided not" (394-95). The pivotal word in this couplet is "might"; with that word we have left the representation of man as a child with his mother. Now man is pictured instead

> Compelling the elements with adamantine stress—
> As the Sun rules, even with a tyrant's gaze,
> The unquiet Republic of the maze
> Of Planets, struggling fierce towards Heaven's free wilderness.
>   (396–99)

Here is an extreme instance of Shelley's programmatic transfiguration of the language of power; according to these lines, the elements are held within the cosmos by a certain kind of mastery, without which the world would, through its own regressive impulses, dissolve into the "intense inane." But this is a mastery that neither crushes its subjects nor absorbs them into itself; rather it holds them in their individual orbits; it is a tyranny that creates a republic. To see in this image the model of a political system, however, would be to follow the path of Jupiter toward the dark shadow of mastery, to transform the gravitational rule of the sun over the planets, the rule of the ego over the elements of the self, or the rule of humanity over the inanimate elements of the outer world into the rule of one person or group over others.

Together with might Shelley stresses control. Humanity will now be "one harmonious Soul of many a soul / Whose nature is its own divine controul" (400–401). Without God or king, man is self-governing, and he also governs his own "mean passions" and "selfish cares" (406–7). Man has replaced both father and mother as the central active power in the world, and "All things confess his strength" (412). That strength manifests itself not in any Jovian aggression but in art and language. In another form of self-mastery, the new man gains control of his unexpressed, even inchoate imaginings: "Through the cold mass / Of marble and of colour his dreams pass," and common language becomes "a perpetual Orphic song, / Which rules with Daedal harmony a throng / Of thoughts and forms, which else senseless and shapeless were" (412–13, 415–17). In the "Lionel" notebook fragment in which Shelley speaks of finding a thread that could lead us through the labyrinths of a complex mind,[15] he was identifying with a hero who depended on a woman, the Ariadne who provided the thread. But in the image of "Daedal harmony" he identifies with the fatherly builder of the labyrinth.

In the conclusion of the Earth's song, Shelley moves from humanity's mastery over itself to its mastery over the outer world. He speaks of science and technology in romantic and visionary terms, but at a deeper level he speaks of taking over the father's power. The lightning that belonged to Jupiter is now man's "slave" (418). The stars "pass before [man's] eye, are numbered, and roll on!" (420); in Psalm 147, it is God who numbers the stars (4).[16] And it is God in Psalm 18 who "did fly upon the wings of the wind" (10), but here "The Tempest is [man's] steed—he strides the air" (421). The song ends with a figure of not technological development but pure knowledge: "And the abyss shouts from her depth laid bare, / 'Heaven, hast thou secrets? Man unveils me, I have none' " (422–23). The insatiable curiosity of the child and the Promethean curiosity of the adult are completely and benignly satisfied. This last image asserts power over both father, or heaven, and mother, or abyss, and it also claims the father's privilege of unveiling the mother.

As the duet of Earth and Moon continues, the accent shifts from the shaping ego and the progress of humanity to a gradual building up of Dionysian ecstasy. Like the abyss, the Moon too is unveiled, as the "shadow of white Death" passes from her, and "paramours" wander through her bowers (424, 428). She now sees "All suns and constellations shower" on the Earth "a light, a life, a power," which, in turn, it pours on her (440–41). The Earth, to her, is both a source and a recipient of supplies. The passage suggests a wish to have the advantages of both mature genitality and infantile nourishment, to live in two states of being at once. Such doubleness now takes another form. Spinning "beneath [his] pyramid of night" into an "enchanted sleep," the Earth compares himself to "a youth lulled in love-dreams faintly sighing, / Under the shadow of his beauty lying"

(444, 446–48). Since Shelley is referring to the nocturnal shadow of the earth, "his beauty" could mean "his own beauty," but it could also mean the beautiful otherness he dreams of in his Adam's dream. Is the Earth about to awaken to his Eve, or is he, in the midst of his dance with the Moon, returning to an archaic state of blissful self-absorption? The dreaming Earth is also "Murmuring victorious joy" (446). Is sexual love, for him, a sublime self-exaltation? It is important that the image of the Earth giving and receiving supplies is the Moon's vision of the Earth's experience. The Moon sees eros in terms of object love and relationship, while the Earth—who has never yet referred to the Moon except in the ambiguous terms of "his beauty"—sees eros in terms of autonomy and narcissism.

But out of these competing inflections of eros comes an image of intercourse in the Moon's next speech:

> As in the soft and sweet eclipse
> When soul meets soul on lovers' lips,
> High hearts are calm and brightest eyes are dull;
> So when thy shadow falls on me
> Then am I mute and still—by thee
> Covered; of thy love, Orb most beautiful,
> Full, oh, too full!
>
> (450–56)

In this darkness and passivity the Moon finds not self-annihilation but plenitude and serenity. The whirling of the Earth, however, begins to gain ascendancy over the Moon's calmness; the verse itself speeds up, the lines shortening. The Moon pictures the Earth "speeding round the Sun" (457) and herself whirling with him:

> I, thy chrystal paramour,
> Borne beside thee by a power
> Like the polar Paradise,
> Magnet-like, of lovers' eyes.
>
> (463–66)

Gravity and electromagnetic attraction are transformed into the eros that, Freud wrote, "holds all living things together."[17] And conversely eros assumes something like the ubiquitous material being and the physical power that gravity and magnetism now have; it becomes the natural law of a new state of being. But the anxiety that often attends

Shelleyan speed also appears; love becomes intoxication, and the Moon's passivity becomes increasingly extreme:

> I, a most enamoured maiden
> Whose weak brain is overladen
> With the pleasure of her love—
> Maniac-like around thee move,
> Gazing, an insatiate bride,
> On thy form from every side
> Like a Maenad round the cup
> Which Agave lifted up.
> (467–74)

Ecstasy becomes mania; the regressive impulse threatens to carry us away in frenzy. In his *Notes on Sculptures in Rome and Florence* Shelley describes Maenads in "their tempestuous dance" with heads "thrown back" and "looking up to Heaven" in a state "beyond insanity" and refers to one of them as "Agave with the head of Pentheus" (*C,* 349). In the Moon's lines the impulse toward the "intense inane" takes over, accompanied by dreadful violence in the allusion to a mother who killed her son.[18]

How does Shelley respond to this destructiveness in the ecstatic and the regressive? Here is a crucial point in his poetic handling of the oceanic feeling in act 4. He doesn't follow Pentheus and his own Jupiter, who tried to suppress it. He doesn't even respond with Apollonian images of self-rule. The Moon tells the Earth:

> Brother, whereso'er thou soarest
> I must hurry, whirl and follow
> Through the Heavens wide and hollow,
> Sheltered by the warm embrace
> Of thy soul, from hungry space.
> (476–80)

In Anton Ehrenzweig's account of the creative process, the artist must undergo an inner experience of dedifferentiation but, unlike the psychotic, finds within the dedifferentiated not a frightening chaos but an enveloping womb.[19] The warm embrace of the Earth serves that enveloping function, keeping the Moon from the intense inane and keeping the mother from becoming a devouring monster, "hungry space." Jupiter, in contrast, with neither object love nor a positive sense of the mother, was "drunk up / By thirsty nothing" (350–51).

After this turning point, orality and passiveness appear positively. The Moon drinks from her sight of the Earth "Beauty, majesty, and might" (482), and she grows like what she looks upon but "As a lover" does (483) or as a "mist / Glows . . . amethyst" on a "western mountain," "When the sunset sleeps / Upon its snow" (488–92). The Earth adds, "And the weak day weeps / That it should be so" (493–94). That he completes the Moon's quatrain represents poetically a change in his character. Formerly involved in his own ecstasy, now he is responding to her. Now we see the full development of object love from its narcissistic origins in the chariot. For the first time the Earth directly addresses the Moon: "O gentle Moon, the voice of thy delight / Falls on me like thy clear and tender light / Soothing the seaman" (495–97). After the eclipse of intercourse, after the ecstatic whirling, comes a first and tender recognition of otherness for the Earth. And now the Earth receives from the Moon, her gentleness soothing his intensity, "Charming the tyger Joy, whose tramplings fierce / Made wounds, which need thy balm" (501–2). In the tiger joy we see the aggressiveness and sexuality of the father, which the son has appropriated. Indeed, in a draft it was "the eagle joy."[20] But even in the Earth's benevolent possession, the fatherly power is troubling to its possessor. The Earth keeps the Moon from dissolving in regression; the Moon keeps the Earth from dissolving in aggression. Each gives to the other a deep calm. That reciprocity is the achievement of a course of development that begins with the entrance of the infants in their chariots. And in the reciprocity and serenity of the lovers, act 4 has reached one of its deep goals, the purification of extremities of aggression, narcissism, and regression in the Dionysian spirit.

But the Dionysian spirit is not the whole of Shelley, and the play cannot end quite yet. Ione and Panthea have been witnessing these ecstasies, and now, like Keats after listening to the nightingale, they return to their sole selves. Panthea's sole self, however, is hardly "forlorn": "I rise as from a bath of sparkling water, / A bath of azure light, among dark rocks, / Out of the stream of sound" (503–5). Ione, on the other hand, laments that she and her sister cannot keep up with the visionary music: "Ah me, sweet sister, / The stream of sound has ebbed away from us / And you pretend to rise out of its wave" (505–7). The sisters embody alternative Shelleyan responses to the oceanic, Panthea actively emerging from it, Ione stranded by its with-drawal; but although Shelley makes Ione's case strongly, Panthea's view is the one he will develop. The closing movement of the play is Apollonian. Now after the celestial ecstasies, Shelley portrays the new world as not an ocean of music but an order.

That order must include all the elements of the drama, and so Demogorgon now makes his third appearance. Panthea says, "A mighty Power, which is as Darkness, / Is rising out of Earth" "like eclipse" (510–11, 513). We move from radiance to darkness, from the heights to a power that has been associated with the abyss. Demogorgon serves as a gravitational force, bringing the action down to an earthly level, modifying the transcendental tendency of eros and imagination with his own ethos of material process. Act 4 thus far has celebrated what may be; Demogorgon embodies what must be: otherness, process, *Ananke.* His sober presence provides an anchor for the whirling, flying beings of act 4. Demogorgon characteristically embodies the opposite of what is, functioning as a balancing force when things get too heavily weighted on one side; he is figuratively the child of the revels, as the revels are of the restraint of act 3. His preternatural darkness is also the primordial mystery and power of the mother and, since he is a figure of combined male and female associations, that of the primal scene, as well: his eclipse doubles the ecstatic eclipse of the Earth and the Moon in their mating rites. Ultimately it is not enough for Shelley to stress the benevolence of the Dionysian, the mother, the oceanic, and to create a new and benign primal scene; he also wishes to integrate their dark side, to put the terrible power of Demogorgon to use.

Demogorgon is also, as he was in act 2, a voice: the Oceanids hear "A universal sound like words" (518). The words of the Oceanids when the Earth and Moon disappeared fell from them like "clear soft dew" (508), a remnant of the oceanic, a lyrical language that expressed passing beauty. Demogorgon's language, in contrast, is one that names and calls into being, like the divine voice of Genesis: "Thou, Earth, calm empire of a happy Soul" (519). In a measured style that answers the rhapsodies and the "self-destroying swiftness" that have gone before, Demogorgon calls the roll of the cosmos. He is recalling the renovated universe back to a point at which it has not ebbed away. Acknowledging his authority, the Earth says, "I hear,—I am as a drop of dew that dies!" (523). Demogorgon is performing an Apollonian task of redifferentiation, as he names the individual parts of the universe and describes their distinct characteristics. But he is separating things in a way that is compatible with the erotic tendency toward oneness, for he is assembling the separate parts into a community. The "universal sound like words" is a language that the entire cosmos understands.

After the Earth and Moon, Demogorgon addresses the heavens: "Ye Kings of suns and stars, Daemons and Gods" (529). Shelley's heavens are cleansed of what he called in the *Defence of Poetry* the "modern mythology" of Christianity (*R*, 527), but they are still rich with romance presences. A "Voice from above" responds: "Our great Republic hears . . . we are blest, and bless" (533). The heavens are still a domain of plenitude, although not a domain that is superior to Earth; these heavens exist in reciprocity with the rest of the cosmos, blessing and being blessed. From the heavens Demogorgon turns to the abyss, bringing into his assembly the "happy Dead," of whose condition not even the "brightest verse" can inform us with certainty (534). In this acknowledgment of the continuing presence of death and its secrets, Shelley returns to the restrained mode of act 3, in which he tried to make his paradise seem possible by not claiming too much for it. Yet we are given the immense assurance that the dead, able to respond to Demogorgon, have some form of sentience and are even happy. The roll call culminates as humanity is drawn into the gathering, and the response to Demogorgon's address to humanity is given by "All." Essential to the religion of the original Olympians, Jane Harrison writes, was a differentiation of human from nonhuman,[21] but Demogorgon's Apollonian act of separating culminates in humanity's joining with the rest of the cosmos.

With Demogorgon's arrival we have moved from love to law, from Venus to Themis, from the nourishing aspect of the mother to the strong. Themis, Harrison writes, is "collective conscience" transformed into "Law and abstract Right," the rules and conventions of the group crystallized into the "set, fixed, settled,"[22] and in the sermon that now closes the play, Demogorgon gives the community he has assembled its law. He begins by recapitulating the events of the liberation: "This is the Day which down the void Abysm / At the Earth-born's spell yawns for Heaven's Despotism, / And Conquest is dragged Captive through the Deep" (554–56). Jupiter is overcome or swallowed by the day, by time or the Hour, or by the void abysm, the mother in her destructive, retributive guise. That has happened

"At the Earth-born's spell"; Prometheus's change of words has brought about the "correct moment," as Kerényi defines Hora.[23] The lines assert the triumph of the mother but assign ultimate credit to the son. A new maternal figure then comes into being, the mother in her nourishing, protective role: "Love from its awful throne of patient power / In the wise heart" "springs / And folds over the world its healing wings" (557–58, 560–61). In the world of Jupiter, the good mother may continue to live within us, both inspiring us and sustained by us, until she can emerge to assume power in the world at large.

What becomes of Jupiter after his fall? "Destruction's strength" is now imprisoned in a "pit" (564), kept there by the Promethean qualities of "Gentleness, Virtue, Wisdom and Endurance" (563). Nevertheless, it can still break out of its confinement for "with infirm hand, Eternity, / Mother of many acts and hours" may "free / The serpent that would clasp her with his length" (565–67). It seems that we must always live with the prophecy of a fatal child; yet if the reminder that Jupiter may return limits the paradisal transformation, it also, like the reminder in act 3 that death and mutability still exist, makes that transformation more credible to the Enlightenment skepticism within both Shelley's anticipated audience and his own sensibility. It also functions to keep the joyful members of the universe from getting carried away, to bring them down to sobriety.

How, exactly, could Jupiter return? In Demogorgon's lines, it is the infirmity of Eternity, the "mother of many acts and hours," that brings about the end of paradise. Eternity has a tendency to become Mutability; Eternity herself cannot keep the necessary virtues and endurance; she cannot keep herself from becoming the bad mother. The serpent, however, also plays a role in Demogorgon's warning. In its clasping of Eternity we can see the extreme aggressive sexuality that we saw in Jupiter's rape of Thetis. The bursting loose of Destruction is the return of the old parents Jupiter and Earth, Lust and Weakness. But if the serpent is the rapist father, it is also the fatal child. The embrace of snake and maternal Eternity has oedipal connotations; we recall the serpent of *Laon and Cythna* coiled at the breast of the woman by the sea (289–306, *E,* 2:71–72). In what way can the snake be both the oedipal son and the old father? The child's wish to "clasp" the mother brings the father into play in several ways: the child is emulating the father; he is, because of his oedipal wish, afraid of the father; and, in Shelley's case, he is projecting the aggressive element in his desire, his lust, onto the father. The tyrannical Jupiter and the defiant, wronged Prometheus come into being together once again.

The ideal love of the Earth and Moon can thus give way in favor of love as it used to be, oedipal trespass and conflict, leading to the outbreak of Destruction; and Prometheus can be transformed back into the unpurified Satanic serpent. And the blame for this is placed on the infirmity of the mother, Eternity, who could not help freeing, or arousing, the serpent, who could not help being sexually attractive to both son and father, or, worse, who was too weak to keep from turning from nourisher into seducer. An archaic disappointment in and anger at the mother is one element in Demogorgon's complex warning about the future.

But the lines also tell another version of this story. Eternity is not the only appearance of the mother in Demogorgon's sermon. We remember the bird of love that "folds over the world its healing wings" (561), and we recognize two old Shelleyan antagonists, the bird and the serpent, back for another battle. But now there is a reversal. In act 3, in Demogorgon's struggle with Jupiter, the serpent championed the spirit of the mother against the bird of the ruling father. Now the good mother has taken over and in the form of the bird enfolds the world. Yet if this is a healing, protective image, it may also be, from the viewpoint of any impulse toward freedom and autonomy, a restricting one. After all, the serpent in Demogorgon's lines is the one who is under the mother's power, the one who is restrained or liberated by her. It may be the bird in Demogorgon's first stanza that calls up the rebellious, attacking serpent in the second. Jupiter followed Saturn and his maternal age of innocence and passivity; Eternity followed Jupiter, bringing back the mother; now Jupiter follows Eternity in a continuing cycle of rebellions against the influence of the father and the influence of the mother.

But the full ambivalence of both the serpent and the mother in Demogorgon's warning does not appear until we consult a passage outside the play: in a canceled line from the *Defence of Poetry* Shelley wrote that poetry "is the Serpent which clasps eternity."[24] How are Poetry and Jupiter congruous? To clasp Eternity is to seek to be immortal, to seek to be the primal father, to seek to know the primal mother and have power over her. It is the Promethean wish itself—to actualize potentiality, to be free, to be the most that humanity can be and, even more, the most that humanity can imagine—that may shatter the paradise that Prometheus himself has inspired. Demogorgon is suggesting that autonomy and the order of the mother may indeed not be compatible, that it may be impossible to be nourished and healed by the primal mother and at the same time have power over her.

To return to the good mother is thus to return from the actuality of Jupiter to his potentiality. It is to return to the Python that always accompanies the goddess, to the other side of the good mother, the chaos monster. It is to return to the possibility of an endless series of battles between old and young serpent-kings or fathers and sons in the domain of the goddess. And most of all it is to return to the common, inevitable impulse toward liberation from even the good mother, toward the child's assertion of his own ambitions.

But all this does not mean that Demogorgon is telling humanity that in the long run there may be nothing new. He is giving humanity new knowledge, which is significant in a drama in which the central character is specifically a hero of consciousness, famous for his knowledge of the future. Demogorgon's warning plunges us into a vision in which good and evil inevitably double each other, in which each is always potential within the other. Demogorgon reminds us that there will always be an other. In *Laon and Cythna* Shelley tried to separate good and evil by projection, and, as we saw, good remained haunted by the shadowy double it sought to escape. But here the double is exposed. It is not rendered powerless, but it no longer influences humanity from an unconscious state. That anything is possible, that what we imagine can become real, is inspiring in the old world and chastening in the new. And it is the price we must pay for a new world that will not settle into stasis and lassitude, that has endless reserves, and will always contain something still unspoken and unbeheld. A world in which there will always be potential and otherness is one in which Jupiter is never abolished.

Even so, there has been a radical break with the past. The ages of Saturn and Jupiter had to come to an end; the new age *may* come to an end: Demogorgon says, "if" Eternity should free the serpent (565). To be Prometheus is to be able to anticipate, to know the fullness of potential, to be, to a certain extent, the master of the future by knowing what may happen as well as what must happen. But Shelley goes further. Demogorgon now explains how humanity can keep from falling back into the old cycles. If Jupiter does break loose,

These are the spells by which to reassume
An empire o'er the disentangled Doom.

To suffer woes which Hope thinks infinite;
To forgive wrongs darker than Death or Night;
    To defy Power, which seems Omnipotent;
To love, and bear; to hope, till Hope creates
From its own wreck the thing it contemplates;
    Neither to change nor falter nor repent;
This, like thy glory, Titan! is to be
Good, great and joyous, beautiful and free;
This is alone Life, Joy, Empire and Victory.

                         (568–78)

On the notebook draft of the *Ode to the West Wind* is a Greek line pointed out by Neville Rogers and translated by him as follows: "By virtue I, a mortal, vanquish thee, a mighty god."[25] The line, from Euripides' *Hercules Furens*, is spoken by Amphitryon against Zeus, the divine father who is his sexual rival. In Demogorgon's sermon too humanity vanquishes Jupiter by "virtue," by, if we combine meanings of the word, morality that has become power, by a unique and potent combination of defiance and forgiveness and by a hope that, in a version of the Romantic imagination, is so strong that it can make itself come true. Raffaelo Piccoli noted in these lines a resemblance to Byron's *Prometheus*, in which the hero opposes "The ruling principle of Hate, / Which for its pleasure doth create / The things it may annihilate."[26] Shelley revises the Hate that creates in order to annihilate into the Hope that can create beyond annihilation. In that revision, the imagination is the father's power of destruction transformed into the son's power of creation. But if the Hope-Imagination of Demogorgon's sermon embodies the usurped and purified power of the father, it is also an introjected and sublimated form of the mother's capacity to create life. In *The Mask of Anarchy*, Hope is a trampled maiden who rises from her devastation as an apocalyptic mother to inspire the makers of a new world. The creative imagination is a power that must be taken from both the mother and the father.

Demogorgon's last lines bring the action down from the spheres into the world of human, ethical behavior. Wordsworth called nature in *Tintern Abbey* "The anchor of my purest thoughts" (109); for Shelley, politics and morality are the anchor of his purest thoughts. The redifferentiation that takes place in the roll call culminates in the re-constitution of an ideal Promethean self that all human beings may attain. Under Jupiter human beings knew "self-contempt"; here they know self-esteem, a sense of capability, a sense of reserves within the ego. To be such a self, to have such power within oneself, is alone the Empire and Victory that eluded Jupiter. The word "empire" appears in the last line of each of the two last stanzas, and in the second case it receives extra emphasis as it expands the normal iambic line into an alexandrine: "This is alone Life, Joy, Empire and Victory." Humanity now has empire over Jupiter and the process that produces him. Thus, after gathering power in the roll call, Demogorgon hands it over to humanity, giving humanity the spells to control destruction. We recall Demogorgon's similar handing over of power to Asia in act 2. It seems to be a major function of Demogorgon in the drama to abdicate and to place his maternal power at the disposal of humanity and its champions.

In act 2 a "spell" was "treasured" in the cave of Demogorgon (3.88). The sermon is didactic poetry, but it is also romance; in it humanity learns magical formulas or incantations from a divinity associated with the mother-religion. The virtues are forms of behavior infused with Dionysian energy, forms of behavior in which the primal mother acts together with us. To call them spells is also to remind us of the magical power of words in the play; human beings at the end are weavers of spells, who work their magic in language and whose moral and political gestures are poems, acts of creation, in the large sense. The Apollonian stress of the final lines does not destroy the oceanic feeling but shapes and masters it and makes it available. Shelley envisions a Dionysian poetic power, which comes from the mother, within a strong Apollonian self.

The dialectician, Socrates said, can see the one and the many.[27] In this play, in the most positive vision in Shelley's poetry, our conflicting impulses need not tear us apart, as in *Alastor*, but can be shaped into a creative whole. *Prometheus Unbound* is a form of moving parts in constant interaction, filled with interplay, cycle, oscillation, defensive move and countermove, and that very form is the model of a sensibility that feels itself evermore about to be.

III
UNTOLD THOUGHTS

15

"The Right Road
to Paradise"

Jerome McGann sees Shelley in his last poems giving up "the dream of a deified earth" and the quest for a supernatural absolute in favor of a Keatsian "attempt to come to terms with experience in all its forms, positive and negative"; now he is "committed to the world as men know it." At the same time, McGann observes, "Old habits of thinking and feeling are not easily tossed aside."[1] I would suggest, however, that they still dominate Shelley's sensibility. We find him jotting down in his notebook in 1822 the following passage from *The Republic*: "He, then, who believes in beautiful things, but neither believes in beauty itself nor is able to follow when someone tries to guide him to the knowledge of it—do you think that his life is a dream or a waking?"[2] In a letter in this period, he writes of his enthusiasm for *Faust* and its romantic quest for an absolute:

> I have been reading over & over again Faust, & always with sensations which no other composition excites. It deepens the gloom & augments the rapidity of the ideas, & would therefore seem to be an unfit study for any person who is a prey to the reproaches of memory, & the delusions of an imagination not to be restrained.—And yet the pleasure of sympathizing with emotions known only to few, although they derive their sole charm from despair & scorn of the narrow good we can attain in our present state, seems more than to cure the pain which belongs to them.—Perhaps all discontent with the *less* (to use a Platonic sophism) supposes the sense of a just claim to the *greater*, & that we admirers of Faust are in the right road to Paradise. (*L*, 2:406)

The Romantic imagination is embattled; delusion and painful memory impinge upon it; but he is still committed to it. In *The Zucca*, written, according to Mary Shelley, in January 1822, he echoes *Alastor*: "I loved, I know not what—but this low sphere / And all that it contains, contains not thee" (20–21, *H*, 665).[3]

He did, however, at this time love Jane Williams, and in a sequence of lyrics to and about her he worked out another version of Adam's dream.[4] He wrote in a letter that Jane was "the exact antitype of the lady I described in the Sensitive-plant—though this must have been a *pure anticipated cognition* as it was written a year before I knew her" (2:438). The lady who presides over the garden in *The Sensitive-Plant* is an ideal maternal figure, without whose care there is only destruction. Similarly, in *To Jane: The Recollection*, Jane is "the centre" of a "magic circle": "*one* fair form that filled with love / The lifeless atmosphere" (49–52). She is also an ideal sexual object, and a dangerous adulterous and oedipal one, another man's wife; in *The Magnetic Lady to Her Patient*, Shelley tells her that what would cure his suffering would also kill him: "And as I must on earth abide / Awhile yet, tempt me not to break / My chain" (43–45).[5] A letter he wrote in June 1822 about sailing with Jane and Edward Williams suggests that he imagined his relationship with her in Faustian terms:

> Williams is captain, and we drive along this delightful bay in the evening wind, under the summer moon, until earth appears another world. Jane brings her guitar, and if the past and the future could be obliterated, the present would content me so well that I could say with Faust to the passing moment, 'Remain, thou, thou art so beautiful.' (*L*, 2:434–35)

According to his bargain with Mephistopheles, Faust would die when he found a moment beautiful enough to satisfy him.

Rousseau wrote, "Even in our keenest pleasures there is scarcely a single moment of which the heart could truthfully say: 'Would that this moment could last for ever!'" Before Shelley, he searched for "a sufficient, complete and perfect happiness which leaves no emptiness to be filled in the soul."[6] In a direct engagement with Rousseau and in a dark anticipation of Freud, who analyzed from a realistic viewpoint that insufficiency in the midst of common happiness, Shelley wrote *The Triumph of Life*, his last Adam's dream, and one that explores not wishful fantasies but anxious ones.

16

A Dream
of Life

THE NARRATOR OF *THE TRIUMPH OF LIFE*, BEFORE HIS DREAM VISION, has lain awake all night, suffering from "thoughts which must remain untold" (21). What untold thoughts Shelley the man may have had in mind we cannot know, but insofar as the poem itself has untold thoughts, they must, at least in part, have to do with aggression, because the dream that follows is a nightmare of violence. The emblem of that violence is a triumphal procession crushing everything in its path. In a letter from Rome, Shelley describes such a procession portrayed on the arch of Constantine, with "captives in every attitude of humiliation & slavery" and "the conqueror . . . riding over the crushed multitudes who writhe under his horses hoofs" (2:86).

The Triumph of Life begins, however, with a seemingly good triumph, a benevolent upsurge of male joy and strength: "Swift as a spirit hastening to his task / Of glory and of good, the Sun sprang forth / Rejoicing in his splendour" (1-3). We may think of Blake's portrait of the rising sun as a god of youthful energy, *Glad Day,* or of Milton's strong man rising after sleep in *Areopagitica.* The world that Shelley's sun awakens is filled with harmony and love: flowers open "Their trembling eyelids to the kiss of day" (10).

Even so, the scene is not unambiguously ideal, with suggestions of religious orthodoxy: the sound of the ocean is an "orison," the mountains are like "altars," the flowers are like "censers," and they burn "inconsumably" like the burning bush of Exodus (7, 5, 11, 13). The ambiguity intensifies as the parts of the world rise "as the Sun their father rose, to bear / Their portion of the toil which he of old / Took as his own and then imposed on them" (18–20). In drafts of the opening, the flowers pay tribute to God, and "Every successive region slowly rose / Out of the death of daily life, and bore / It's [*sic*] portion in the ruin of repose."[1]

The narrator enters the poem in opposition to the sunrise; "as wakeful as the stars" all night, he now lies down with "faint limbs" beneath an old tree on a mountainside, and he has turned away from the new day: "before me fled / The night; behind me rose the day; the Deep / Was at my feet, and Heaven above my head" (22, 24, 26–28).[2] Barbara Schapiro writes that he "is unable to identify or ally himself with the father; he is unable to realize or fully assert his male identity" (25). What must be added is that the male image in these lines only becomes fatherly; at first the sun is youthful, not paternal. In one draft it even rises amid an imagery of infancy: night scatters clouds "to swathe in its bright birth / In fleecy snow & gold the infant day."[3] And while at the outset the sun hastens to his task, now the toil that was his he imposes on his children. One problem, or untold thought, in the opening is the instability of the male image: it seems hard to keep an image of male joy and strength from sliding into one of paternal orthodoxy and imposition.

With his faint limbs the narrator is differentiated from male strength. He identifies with the stars as opposed to the sun, children as opposed to the father. In "a strange trance," he sees the scene through a "transparent" shade, like "a veil of light" "drawn / O'er evening hills" (29, 31–33); his imagination transforms dawn to twilight. And then he has a sensation of déjà vu:

> and I knew
>
> That I had felt the freshness of that dawn,
> Bathed in the same cold dew my brow and hair
> And sate as thus upon that slope of lawn
>
> Under the self same bough, and heard as there
> The birds, the fountains and the Ocean hold
> Sweet talk in music through the enamoured air.
>
> (33–39)

This is the original scene but with the dominating presence of the sun now missing. In his trance the narrator has transformed the world of the father into the world of the mother, and he now remembers the freshness of a different dawn, the early paradise of love on the "slope" of the mother's breast. But one word in this revision of the original scene does not fit: "cold." In the manuscript, the dew was "sweet."[4] Here is a small expression of ambivalence about the mother and her world. The sound of "cold" now returns in the introduction's final line: "And then a Vision on my brain was rolled" (40). The trance was gentle and delicate, but in the last line having a vision is like being run over. The vision itself is like the triumphal procession that is its subject. In the prelude to the vision, then, an attractive image of youthful male assertion is replaced by an ambivalent image of paternal power. In reaction, the narrator's imagination arises as a force of regression to the mother. But a touch of ambivalence toward the mother appears, and this is the secret link that suddenly turns the imagination from a delicate veil into a crushing vehicle of nightmare. Perhaps the central untold thought that generates the dream, the thought that the poet cannot tell himself, much less us, is that his deepest hostility is toward not the father but the mother.

In his dream vision the narrator finds himself "beside a public way" (43). His imagination, unlike the *Alastor* Poet's, has led him not far away from common humanity but into its midst. In this new scene, the dewy green slope is replaced by "summer dust" (44); the "glimmer" of evening hills (33) becomes an "evening gleam" infested with gnatlike swarms of humanity (46); the fountains and ocean become a "mighty torrent" of people (53). The new vision thus begins as a nightmarish parody of the idyllic trance that the narrator has just experienced. The world of the good mother has turned into the world of the bad mother. Here all individuality is dissolved, for each member of the crowd is merely "One of the million leaves of summer's bier" (51). The leaves in *Ode to the West Wind* were "multitudes" swept by a known power in a process that had positive ends (5); but here "none seemed to know / Whither he went, or whence he came, or why / He made one of the multitude" (47–49). In this fury of "motions which each other crost" (62), some are "flying from the thing they feared and some / Seeking the object of another's fear" (54–55). Some walk "mournfully within the gloom / Of their own shadow" (58–59), while others flee from their shadow "as it were a ghost" (60). Others "Pursued or shunned the shadows the clouds threw" (63). In these crossed motions the narrator is observing ambivalence itself.

The ultimate object of that ambivalence soon becomes clear, as the narrator sees "a cold glare" obscuring "The Sun as he the stars"

(77, 79). The source of the "icy" light is a chariot carrying a hooded, ancient "Shape" and guided by a blinded "Janus-visaged Shadow" driving a team of winged "Shapes" so dazzling that they cannot be seen (78, 87, 94, 96). Thus Shelley brings back the divine chariots of Ezekiel, Dante, and Milton, as well as his own chariots of Queen Mab, Asia, and the Spirits of the Moon and the Earth. In this new chariot, with its appalling radiance and wild careening, we see Shelley's favorite imagery turned destructive. The driver has four faces and would be able to see "all that is, has been, or will be" (104) but, blinded in every direction, embodies, rather than prophetic knowledge, the inability to know whence and whither, the questions that keep recurring in the poem. The chariot was formerly a vehicle of liberation and benevolent new power; now it reminds Shelley of "some conqueror's advance" in "Imperial Rome" (112–13). Bloom, analyzing the poem as a struggle with the *Immortality Ode*, writes that only the chariot, in which the visionary chariot of Ezekiel is assimilated to the chariot of a Roman triumph, truly belonged to Shelley: "After seven years of struggle with Wordsworth's poetry [since *Alastor*], Shelley's work still battled to keep itself from being flooded out by the precursor's."[5] But is even the chariot wholly free from the influence of Wordsworth? In the *Immortality Ode* the child moves further and further away from his glory as he plays games in which he makes believe he is an adult,

> Filling from time to time his "humorous stage"
> With all the Persons, down to palsied Age,
> That Life brings with her in her equipage;
>> As if his whole vocation
>> Were endless imitation.
>
> (103–7)

Life's equipage becomes Shelley's crushing chariot. Endless imitation is humanity's lot in *The Triumph of Life;* the traditional chariot is an emblem of tradition itself. First the narrator had a sense of déjà vu, and now the past returns like a juggernaut.

But although that past is associated with the literary fathers, in the end the father is not the source of the dreadful icy glare. Shelley compares the chariot to the "young Moon" bearing "The ghost of her dead Mother" (79, 84). In *Prometheus Unbound*, act 4, the mother-infant dyad, symbolized by the new moon with the old moon in its arms, heralded a great new age that was opposed to the rule of the

father. The narrator of *The Triumph of Life* gets his wish for a return
to night, but it is a night dominated by a moon-mother who does
to the sun-father what he did to the star-children: with a light "in-
tenser than the noon," the sun's strongest light (77), she blots him
out—we might say, castrates him. In a draft the shape in the chariot
wears a cloud like "a widows veil."[6] This vague, clouded figure is
modeled on Milton's Death, who, Reiman points out, had a crown
on "what seem'd his head";[7] Shelley revises the line to "what seemed
the head" (91). In this figure, Shelley gives us the first openly and
unambiguously destructive female principle in his poetry. As Bar-
bara Schapiro notes, the recurrent winged chariot in Shelley sug-
gests the womb (26); here the womb-symbol is associated with ag-
gression and conquest. The Shadow on the beam is a dark version of
the guide or companion—the child—who often appears with Shel-
ley's mother figures. The Necessity that in *Queen Mab* was a benefi-
cent mother and that in *Prometheus Unbound* was a neutral power
that could be mastered by humanity and activated for its good is in
The Triumph of Life a terrible *Ananke* that grinds humanity into the
dust.

The "captive multitude" around the chariot includes all who knew
"power / Or misery," who attained greatness "By actions or by suffer-
ing," who experienced "weal or woe," who achieved "fame or infamy"
(119–23, 125). The masters and the victims, the active and the pas-
sive, the happy and the unhappy, the good and the bad have all come
to the same end. Distinctions are lost, opposites equated, in this pri-
mal horde of the mother, a dark version of the oneness of primal
narcissism.

The procession includes

> All but the sacred few who could not tame
> Their spirits to the Conqueror, but as soon
> As they had touched the world with living flame
>
> Fled back like eagles to their native noon.
>   (128–31)

In this vision, there can be no Prometheus. Those who have fire must
either lose it in the chariot's glare or escape from the world like the
Alastor Poet. Also exempt are those who rejected earthly power and
wealth, Shelley specifying "they of Athens and Jerusalem" (134).
Socrates and Jesus seem singled out not only for their resistance to

worldly temptations but also for their moral purity and childlike in-
nocence and their allegiance to inwardness and spirit. That they are
distinguished from the "ribald crowd" around the chariot (136) sug-
gests that the sexual purity, perhaps the pregenital quality, of Jesus
and of Socrates' ideal of love is also important.[8]

What follows, indeed, is a dark vision of intercourse inspired by
the monster-goddess in the chariot. The "maniac dance" turns "ob-
scene" (110, 137): "Convulsed" by a mischievous "fierce spirit," young
men and women "Kindle" until, "like two clouds into one vale im-
pelled," they mingle "their lightnings" and "die in rain," and "the
fiery band which held / Their natures, snaps" with a tingling "shock":
"One falls, and then another in the path / Senseless, nor is the deso-
lation single" (144–45, 152, 155–60). Orgasm is physically a giant elec-
tric shock and psychologically a snapping of what holds us together.
In place of a blending into one soul, as in *Laon and Cythna* and
Epipsychidion, sex is a mutual "desolation." And after the chariot runs
over the lovers, no "trace" is left of them "But as of foam after the
Ocean's wrath / Is spent upon the desert shore" (162–64). Ejacula-
tion is an act of aggression, and intercourse is a nearly self-annihilat-
ing expense of supplies.

The destruction of the young is at least "bright" (154). The old
limp "with limbs decayed / To reach the car of light," which is leav-
ing them far behind (167–68). Yet still "They wheel" round and
round (171) in what a draft calls their "Mocking" of youth.[9] At last
they "fulfill / Their work" (172–73); either they achieve with labor
what the young achieve with frenzy, or their futile mocking of sex
reaches its own closure, its nadir of expense and exhaustion, its anti-
climax, as it were. Then they too sink into the dust, "And frost in
these performs what fire in those" (175). So the old ironically do
find themselves at last in the same state as the young.

Appalled by this "sad pageantry" (176), the narrator asks aloud,
"What is this? / Whose shape is that within the car?" Why "is all here
amiss" (177–79). "Who is the mistress of the mystery?" he asks in a
draft.[10]

"Life," answers a voice that comes from what seemed a twisted
"old root" but now turns out to be "one of that deluded crew" (180,
182, 184). The white grass hanging from the "root" is his hair, and he
has holes in place of eyes. This is a grotesque parody of a characteris-
tic Wordsworthian moment, as in *The Leech Gatherer* when an appar-
ent rock turns out to be an old man, a creature living in a Wordswor-

thian state of grace on the borderline between humanity and nature and able to serve as a wise guide. Offering to explain the terrible pageant, Shelley's man-root is a guide too, a blind guide to a blinding vision of a blind force. He now reveals his identity:

> "And if the spark with which Heaven lit my spirit
> Earth had with purer nutriment supplied

> "Corruption would not now thus much inherit
> Of what was once Rousseau . . ."
>
> (201–4)

The passage oscillates in assigning responsibility now to the destructive mother, who does not nourish us properly, now to the erring subject, who says that he might have "well forborne" to follow the chariot (189). But he can still be defiant: "If I have been extinguished, yet there rise / A thousand beacons from the spark I bore" (206–7)—one of whom is Shelley himself. Rousseau is a father, like the eclipsed paternal sun, come to tell how his fire was extinguished.

But before he tells his own story, he answers the narrator's questions about the identity of the chariot's captives, describing them as the "Wise" and "great," "they who wore / Mitres and helms and crowns" (208–10). The strong ones, the influences, are revealed as mere slaves of the Great Mother. It is surprising to find the wise listed among the powerful, to whom in *Laon and Cythna* they were antithetical; but in this passage, just as bishops, warriors, and kings achieve their particular forms of conquest, so the wise achieve "thought's empire over thought" (211). In *Prometheus Unbound*, Prometheus "Gave wisdom, which is strength, to Jupiter" (2.4.44); here too intellect is associated with aggression. But the great sages, who controlled other minds, have been undone by their own ultimate inadequacies of thought and mastery: "their lore / Taught them not this—to know themselves; their might / Could not repress the mutiny within" (211–13). Edward Duffy takes these lines, and the entire poem, as a critique of Enlightenment rationality.[11] But the poem's implications are both more general and more personal. *The Triumph of Life* is Shelley's *Civilization and its Discontents*, and it studies the blindness of humanity to its own deepest motives. It also examines the mutinous elements that have troubled Shelley's own conscious wisdom or poetic myths: the deep rage, for example, and in particular the rage against the mother.

Rousseau points out among the captives a prototypical figure of aggression and power, Napoleon, the "Child of a fierce hour," whom opportunity carried "on its eagle's pinion to the peak / From which a thousand climbers have before / Fall'n" (217, 222–24). Rousseau was destroyed in part by an inadequate mother, who did not have pure enough nutriment; Napoleon had a different kind of mother, a fierce hour, the opportunity in his revolutionary times in France. Seeking "to win / The world" and falling from a peak others had failed to climb, Napoleon is a figure of oedipal ambition and defeat (217–18). While Rousseau's Earth is a neglectful or incompetent nourisher, Napoleon's predatory, eaglelike hour, or Hora, is an oedipal mother who sweeps her child to danger and destruction.

Meditating on Napoleon, the narrator grieves that "God made irreconcilable / Good and the means of good" (230–31). Adam would never be able to realize his dream without transforming it into something destructive. Were the Furies right after all? "The good want power, but to weep barren tears. / The powerful goodness want" (*Prometheus Unbound*, 1.625–26). *The Triumph of Life* makes this vision even darker because the word "God" takes away any question of human choice and error. The Furies embodied fears that Shelley felt throughout his career; Prometheus was able to master those fears, but this narrator is no Prometheus. In addition, while the Furies were associated with the bad mother, manifestations of the good mother appeared even in Jupiter's world, but thus far in *The Triumph of Life* there is no strong sense of the good mother to alleviate a bleak and melancholic vision.[12] The God who makes goodness and power antithetical is a bad father in complicity with the bad mother.

Rousseau now points out other figures of greatness: "Voltaire, / Frederic, and Kant, Catherine, and Leopold, / Chained hoary anarchs, demagogue and sage" (235–37). Here again thought and power are allied. In a canceled passage, Rousseau himself is classed with Voltaire,[13] but in revision he sharply distinguishes his own case as unique:

> "For in the battle Life and they did wage
>   She remained conqueror—I was overcome
> By my own heart alone, which neither age
>
> "Nor tears nor infamy nor now the tomb
> Could temper to its object."
>
> (239–43)

The other captives of Life were defeated because their hearts sought objects within Life's realm, but Rousseau's heart was defeated by its own transcendent desire, its *Sehnsucht.* Although he failed to find fulfillment, his defeat, like the *Alastor* Poet's, was glorious; he did not fall as a thousand others had fallen but in a way that was his alone.

Even Shelley's great favorite Plato is chained to the chariot, as he "Expiates the joy and woe his master knew not; / That star that ruled his doom was far too fair" (255–56). Plato, who loved the boy he called Aster, is conquered because unlike Socrates, for whom eros was spiritual, and unlike Rousseau, for whom eros was beyond any object, he thought he could find a "flower of Heaven" in life (257).[14]

After Plato come Aristotle and Alexander, another coupling of wisdom and aggression, with Aristotle "Throned" in the thoughts of men long after his death (267). Even now he would have kept "The jealous keys of truth's eternal doors" (268) if not for Bacon, whose "lightning" spirit forced "the Proteus shape of Nature" to "unbar the caves that held / The treasure of [its] secrets" (270–73). Bloom calls this passage an "intrusion" and a blemish.[15] Reiman tries to integrate it into the poem, finding in it an allusion to Spenser's Mammon and thus to Bacon's weakness for money.[16] But it is difficult to see in the actual passage any derogation of Bacon. In fact, he is not one of the captives; the passage refers to his "spirit" (269), not, as in Plato's case, "All that is mortal of" him (254). If the passage seems to intrude, it is because it is positive. Bacon is a heroic discoverer of secrets and a knower of deep origins, who wrote, "Human knowledge and human power meet in one; for where the cause is not known the effect cannot be produced."[17] Truth is a treasure hidden in caves, and Bacon is a lightninglike aggressor who delves into Mother Earth; he is like Odysseus, who forced the sea god Proteus to give him information. In this passage we get a brief glimpse of mastery of, rather than by, the mother.

The next figures pointed out by Rousseau also seem positively portrayed, although, unlike Bacon, they are among the captives: "See the great bards of old"—in a draft "Homer & his brethren"[18]— "who inly quelled / The passions which they sung" (274–75). If they are such conquerors, why are they prisoners of the chariot? Rousseau contrasts these ancient bards with himself:

> "their living melody
> Tempers its own contagion to the vein

"Of those who are infected with it—I
Have suffered what I wrote, or viler pain!—

"And so my words were seeds of misery—
Even as the deeds of others . . ."

(276–81)

Great poems "infect" us, and when we "catch" them they seem to speak precisely to our own situations and emotions. The Greek artists, Shelley writes in the *Notes on Sculptures*, "turned all things—superstition, prejudice, murder, madness—to Beauty" (*C*, 349). They could do this, *The Triumph* suggests, because they had mastered their own passions. Rousseau, in contrast, wrote about passions that obsessed him and that he lived out, and his art made his readers as unhappy as he was. Classical poetry is both a disease and a medicine, while Rousseau's writing was only a disease. The metaphor of contagion, however, is still provocative. In *Prometheus Unbound*, Shelley used "contagion" to refer to Dionysian frenzy (2.3.10). While thematically asserting a positive sense of poetry, the passage expresses a fear that the imagination, classical or romantic, may have a destructive force, as irresistible and ambiguous as Bacchic intoxication, as irresistible even as a disease, and it also expresses a fear that no poetry can fully transcend or quell the mutiny within or save its author from being chained to the chariot of Life.

The narrator defends Rousseau against his own self-condemnation, saying that his words cannot be compared to the deeds of the true tyrants who now appear among the captives: "the heirs / Of Caesar's crime"; the "murderous" founders of "many a sceptre bearing line"; the medieval popes, "shadows between Man and god," quenching "the true Sun" (284–86, 289, 292). Rousseau, called in this passage the "leader" (293) like Dante's Virgil, acknowledges that the power of the tyrants was "But to destroy," while he was one who "created, even / If it be but a world of agony" (293–95). Rousseau doesn't want to be confused with usurping, phallic scepter-bearers, oedipal sons, who extinguish the father. In the joint objections of Rousseau and the narrator, we can sense Shelley defending himself against the anxiety that words and thoughts may be deeds of aggression or expressions of oedipal ambition. But Bacon too was an oedipal aggressor against the father, Aristotle, and the mother, Nature. In this sequence we can recognize both a wish to be like Bacon and a fear that to be like Bacon is to be like Caesar.

After Bacon symbolically invades and conquers the mother, Life does not appear in the poem until Shelley begins a new sequence thirty lines later. In the present sequence, the father appears as a good, quenched sun and as a good Virgilian leader but also as a criminal Caesar. When good fathers come into the poem, bad ones do too. But the poem's deepest quarrel is not with the father. Now in its final movement, the poem turns back to the mother. It also turns to regression as a defense against the aggressive or Baconian impulse within the self. In this closing movement, Rousseau will appear not as a leader or father but as a youth.

The narrator now asks the poem's central questions in reference not to the procession but to his guide's part in it: "Whence camest thou and whither goest thou? / How did thy course begin . . . and why?" (296–97). The confession that follows in answer is not a Rousseauistic autobiography but a Shelleyan one, a romance of a life.[19] It opens in April, "When all the forest tops began to burn / With kindling green," with Rousseau in a partly sleeping state—"I found myself asleep"—in a cavern within a mountain, an enclosed, maternal world (309–11). From the cavern comes a "rivulet" (314), the sound of which induces a sweet and total forgetfulness; in that "oblivious spell" (331), "A sleeping mother there would dream not of / The only child who died upon her breast" and "a king would mourn no more / The crown of which his brow was dispossest" (321–24). Rousseau answers the narrator's insistent curiosity with a celebration of the beauties of oblivion.

Schapiro sees in this sequence a "regressive return to the womb" (29). But Rousseau's cavern is a womblike state, not the womb itself, for he has the sense of an earlier state of being: he feels unsure "Whether my life had been before that sleep / The Heaven which I imagine, or a Hell" (332–33). The repose Rousseau describes, asleep in some sense and yet aware, is like latency. Before that repose, the metaphors in the passage suggest, a mother and a child were tragically separated, and a king—the child as center of the world—was replaced by his rival. Rousseau likes to imagine that childhood before latency was Heaven, but it may have been a Hell of preoedipal and oedipal traumas. The repression in latency appears as a psychic return to the paradise of the womb. The April prime, when Rousseau wakes up from this maternal world, is not birth but adolescence, a time of kindling in the "forest tops," a time of phallic awakening.

The scene in which Rousseau arises retains "a gentle trace / Of light diviner than the common Sun" and, at the same time, is "filled with many sounds woven into one / Oblivious melody, confusing sense" (337–38, 340–41). "Oblivious" now suggests not quasi-uterine repose but obscurity and disturbance. In this state, in which a haunting sense of a past paradise is mingled with the new and confusing, Rousseau has an Adam's dream. It begins with his witnessing an act of conception, as "the Sun's image radiantly intense / Burned on the waters of the well" and "emerald fire" fills the forest (345–46, 348), Rousseau's adolescent sexuality begins with an awareness of the sexuality of great powers. At first the forest tops burned; now the whole forest is aflame, as the world is charged with new eros. Then, just as the diviner light, the sense of the primal mother, was eclipsed by the stronger light of the genital father, that father is now replaced by a new female power:

> "there stood
>
> "Amid the sun, as he amid the blaze
>   Of his own glory, on the vibrating
>   Floor of the fountain, paved with flashing rays,
>
> "A shape all light . . ."
>
> (348–52)

In a draft, the figure is "A Woman."[20] In the conception of the Witch of Atlas and, behind it, the conception of Spenser's Amoret and Belphoebe, the sun impregnates a nymph or maiden associated with water; here the sun impregnates the water itself, and the result is a "shape."[21] That shape may be more than any individual mortal female, a glory that invests many forms, including particular women, including ideals in general. But the shape also has ambiguous connotations. Located on the "vibrating" floor of the fountain, it suggests instability; on a floor, it suggests the low, not the high and the ideal; at the bottom of the water, it suggests drowning. Above all, it is called a "shape" like the figure in the Car of Life. The radiance of such female ideals as the transformed Asia and the visionary "Being" of *Epipsychidion* (190) transcends shape, but the brilliance of this unidentifiable shape serves to obscure exactly what shape it is or even if it has any reality beyond the "flashing rays." That it begins as a reflection suggests that it belongs to the world of secondary things, like shadows, but, as a reflection, it also suggests the Shelleyan ideal of the uterine world in the water. As a figure in the water, it suggests nature, but as a preternatural vision, it also suggests imagination. Beyond both, it suggests a certain mysterious and glorious sense of the female, based in the early mother but refracted through the eros of adolescence.

The Shape is preceded by a rainbow: on the grass "Iris her many coloured-scarf had drawn" (357). Iris, goddess of the rainbow, was the herald of Juno, goddess of marriage and subordinate to a ruling male.[22] Shelley's rainbow heralds anything but the peace traditionally associated with rainbows and a very different kind of female power from Juno. In the manuscript beneath the Iris line, Shelley writes a mysterious word that Reiman reads as "devi." Reiman also reads those letters earlier in the manuscript at a point where Rousseau is unable to explain why his life has taken its particular unhappy course (line 303).[23] Perhaps these apparently mystifying letters mean exactly what they say. As the Hindu Devi, or "goddess," the powerful female principle that appears both in benevolent and malevolent forms, the letters might suggest what Iris's rainbow heralds and what has caused Rousseau's sorrows and failures.[24]

Bearing a "chrystal glass" of Nepenthe (358), the Shape, although associated with Rousseau's adolescent sexual impulses, is also associated with a return to the sleep from which he awoke. Rousseau moves from an oblivious spell to an oblivious confusion to Nepenthe. Regression is as overwhelmingly powerful a tendency in his story as aggression was in the story of the chariot. He stands as an extreme case of what Ferenczi and Róheim point to as a norm, the investment of genitality with an impulse to return to the womb.[25] But the Shape's crystal glass gives the Nepenthe sinister overtones. Reiman notes that Milton's Comus offers travelers a "Crystal Glass" of "orient liquor," which Comus claims surpasses Nepenthe but which seduces those who drink it away from virtue and God.[26] Comus's mother was Circe, who was a daughter of the sun god and a sea nymph and who herself possessed a "charmed Cup" (51).

The Shape now begins to move with a "fierce splendour," recalling the "splendour" of the chariot and the "fierce song" and "fierce" dance of its followers, who were possessed by a "fierce spirit" (359, 87, 110, 137, 145). But she also glides along the rivulet "with palms so tender / Their tread broke not the mirror of its billow" (361–62). The curious use of "palms" for "soles" may reflect an impulse toward a stage of development before the clear discrimination of bodily parts, or a stage when soles are indeed as tender as palms and when, as crawlers, we do move on our palms.[27] Bending forward until "Her fair hair swept the bosom of the stream" (365), she is not only becoming rainbowlike herself but is also moving toward repose on the maternal bosom. At the same time her motion is described in upright, phallic terms: she is "As one enamoured . . . upborne in dream," seems "to tread the waves with feet which kist / The dancing foam," and is compared to dew ascending "Between two rocks, athwart the rising moon" (367, 370–71, 380). Her movements express Rousseau's attraction to both regression and genitality. The foot, the part of the Shape that dominates the description, is a common symbol of the phallus, and "treading" is the sexual intercourse of birds: Chaucer's Chauntecleer "fethered Pertelote twenty tyme, / And trad hire eke as ofte, er it was pryme" (3177–78). With its treading feet and its arched, concave posture, head bent to the water, the riddling Shape suggests both a penis and a vulva, at once male impulses and their female object.

She herself is dancing "to the ceaseless song / Of leaves and winds and waves and birds and bees" (375–76), that is, to the music of nature, the realm of the mother and also of what we proverbially refer to as the birds and the bees. Her dancing is at first "sweet" (378), but then her feet

> "seemed as they moved, to blot
> The thoughts of him who gazed on them, and soon
>
> "All that was seemed as if it had been not—
> As if the gazer's mind was strewn beneath
> Her feet like embers, and she, thought by thought,
>
> "Trampled its fires into the dust of death,
> As Day upon the threshold of the east
> Treads out the lamps of night . . ."
>
> (383–90)

Aggression enters the story of Rousseau. The Shape has become like the chariot of Life.

The trampling and extinguishing of thought is part of a process of obliteration that, Paul de Man suggests, is at the center of not only Rousseau's story but the whole poem: "Each of the episodes forgets the knowledge achieved by the forgetting that precedes it" (65). He analyzes this process in terms of epistemology and language, writing of the Shape with her dancing "measure" (line 377) as a principle of poetry or signification, creating illusions of meaning and then defeating them (59–60). Studying the poem psychologically, I would say that the poem portrays the erasure of thought because the particular thoughts that it deals with are disturbing. "Untold" thoughts keep the narrator awake, and the sight of the procession makes his heart sick with "one sad thought" (299). At the same time, I would suggest that erasure in this episode is invested with the same regressive, oceanic impulse that is characteristically attended by both attraction and anxiety in Shelley and that has been driving Rousseau's story from oblivion to oblivion.[28]

A new movement of obliteration now begins, as for the first time Rousseau speaks to the Shape. As he does, he describes himself as "between desire and shame / Suspended" (394-95). Nothing in the manifest text of Rousseau's story up to this point can account for the word "shame," but shame competes with desire when desire has forbidden or oedipal undertones. In that oedipal state of mind, and facing a sphinxlike figure, Rousseau asks the questions of the poem:

> "'If, as it doth seem,
> Thou comest from the realm without a name,
>
> "'Into this valley of perpetual dream,
> Shew whence I came, and where I am, and why—
> Pass not away upon the passing stream.'"
> (395–99)

It might seem odd that he doesn't ask the Shape who she is but asks instead about himself. His questions express the primal-scene puzzle: where did I come from? They also express the dizzying, dreamlike mystery of differentiation, the sudden onset of self-consciousness. Rousseau asks questions about himself because being a self is a new and strange sensation. As for the Shape, she seems to come from the realm without a name for she herself is inherently nameless. To name her would be to give her an identity that since it is oedipal needs to be kept repressed. In addition, she has associations with the preoedipal mother and thus with the realm of the nameless as not the repressed but the undifferentiated.

In response, the Shape tells Rousseau, "Arise and quench thy thirst" (400). Her offer of the cup is a response to what Rousseau, behind his questions of identity and origin, is most deeply asking for: nourishment, a return to the mother. His questions are an attempt to prolong the presence of the passing Shape and the passing liquid with which she is associated, to undo his sense of a separate self, to regress to the blissful oblivion of the breast.

When he drinks, he undergoes a dramatic transformation, and here erasure becomes explicitly oceanic:

> "And suddenly my brain became as sand
>
> "Where the first wave had more than half erased
> The track of deer on desert Labrador,
>   Whilst the fierce wolf from which they fled amazed
>
> "Leaves his stamp visibly upon the shore
>   Until the second bursts . . . "
>
> (405–10)

The psychoanalyst Otto Isakower described the sensation of sandiness that some people experience in the process of falling asleep.[29] In that context the simile of the beach confirms the regressive implications in the act of drinking. In the *Immortality Ode*, to return in spirit to childhood is to journey back to a shore where children play before the immortal sea. Rousseau, however, returns to a deserted, desertlike beach where wolves try to devour deer before an ocean of obliterating waves. In the sudden simile of Labrador, a place of isolation, we can see a movement to an extreme of separation, exactly the state that Rousseau was trying to avoid when he asked the Shape to "Pass not away upon the passing stream." In his attempt to return to the breast, the drinker confirms that the breast has been lost forever.[30]

According to the simile, the drink gives Rousseau the feeling of something having been erased, as is appropriate for Nepenthe. The tracks of the animals, however, are still partly visible, or, as Shelley first wrote, "legible."[31] We remember the "trace" like foam on a desert shore left by the wild dancers around the car (162) and the "gentle trace" of divine light that Rousseau perceives upon awakening (337). In the 1821 *Fragment of an Unfinished Drama*, a character's dream becomes "Like a child's legend on the tideless sand, / Which the first foam erases half, and half / Leaves legible" (152–54, *H*, 486). The world of the poem is like a partly ruined text, haunting in its obscurity; it is a world in which signs are specifically signs of the past, and we live among the vestiges of giant traumas and blisses. The world of the *Immortality Ode* is also one of incomplete erasure:

> Not in entire forgetfulness,
> And not in utter nakedness,
> But trailing clouds of glory do we come
> From God, who is our home.
> (62–65)

In Wordsworth, the trace of memory brings us back into revitalizing contact with the immortal sea. But the traces on Rousseau's shore are desolating.

In *Laon and Cythna*, Shelley in effect revises Spenser's Sonnet 75— "One day I wrote her name upon the strand, / But came the waves and washed it away" (1–2): Cythna, in her ocean cavern, finds within herself "One mind, the type of all, the moveless wave / Whose calm reflects all moving things" (3104–5, *E*, 2:191) and invents new symbols to accompany her new intellectual power:

> "And on the sand would I make signs to range
> These woofs, as they were woven, of my thought;
> Clear, elemental shapes, whose smallest change
> A subtler language within language wrought."
> (3109–12)

The narrator of *The Triumph of Life* and Rousseau are readers of the half-legible traces that are given to them. Cythna is a writer, a creator of tracks, a maker of spells rather than one who is spellbound. And the spell she makes is a language that has contact with the oceanic "one mind" but that is also within "language," that has contact with the world of differentiation. That kind of mastery seems out of range in the story of Rousseau.

What exactly is erased on the shore of Labrador? The tracks are footprints, reminding us of the treading and trampling of the Shape. Yeats found in the scene of the wolf and the deer "violent . . . longing and desire."[32] "Labrador," Shelley's symbolic state of desertion, is where we read the signs of the primal scene, of sex perceived as trampling, of the sexual father and mother as predator and victim. And since in the archaic logic of primal-scene fantasy the mother can be both victim and accomplice, to read those signs is to confirm that the mother has deserted us. The waves of oblivion wipe out the tracks of the primal scene and of aggressive genital sexuality; regression, that is, wipes out aggression—but incompletely. The disturbing elements of the mind cannot be totally eradicated, at least partly because the impulses Rousseau would like to erase he would also like to pursue; the vision is rooted not only in shame but also in desire. Then too regression cannot completely erase aggression because it too contains aggressive elements: the wolf and deer suggest, as well as sexual aggression, a preoedipal oral aggression. Rousseau drinks the potion in an act of wishful orality and then experiences the sense of a destructive orality.

Now like another wave on that Labrador shore, "a new Vision never seen before" bursts on Rousseau's sight, making the "fair shape" fade, just as "veil by veil the silent splendour drops / From Lucifer" at dawn (411–14). The Shape, which earlier made "the night a dream" (393), is herself overcome by a new sunlike brilliance and is identified with the last star of night, what Yeats called Shelley's "Star of infinite desire."[33] Reiman asks the essential question: "If the 'shape all light' is a seductress, if she was associated on her appearance with symbols of limited human vision . . . why does she, after Rousseau has drunk of the cup and seen the vision of evil, suddenly become associated with the morning . . . star and with love?"[34] What Rousseau describes as the unveiling of the morning star refers paradoxically to its being hidden, or veiled, by a greater light. When the Shape is half-erased, she becomes purely good. In particular, her aggressive and sexual qualities have been erased; her oedipal intricacy has been veiled, leaving her good preoedipal qualities. Rousseau can now still feel "the presence of that fairest planet / Although unseen" and sense its light, which is "like the scent / Of a jonquil" or the song of a shepherd or "the caress / That turned his weary slumber to content" (416–17, 419–20, 422–23). The shepherd suggests an early world of pastoral innocence; the jonquil is a member of the narcissus family. As the light of Venus is compared to a scent, then a song, and then a caress, we return through synesthesia toward oneness. And perhaps, insofar as the female Shape is compared to the male Lucifer, that includes a regressive lack of sexual differentiation. Above all, the Shape has become something felt though unseen, the characteristic condition of the Shelleyan ideal. Thus we have seen an ambiguous presence develop into the Spirit of Beauty by being half erased. The repression of the mother's bad qualities has produced an idealized mother. The process is also a splitting. When Rousseau is separated from the mother figure through the act of drinking, she divides into good and bad forms. In place of the original fair Shape with its "fierce splendour" we have a veiled splendor and an onrushing, blinding fierceness, an aggressive wolflike vision pursuing and trying to annihilate an innocent, deerlike vision.

And so, despite the new light, Rousseau still knows "The presence of that shape which on the stream / Moved, as I moved along the wilderness":

> "The ghost of a forgotten form of sleep,
> A light from Heaven whose half extinguished beam
>
> "Through the sick day in which we wake to weep
> Glimmers forever sought, forever lost."
> (425–26, 428–31)

So begins the *Alastor*-quest, the romance pursuit of the visionary ideal. The Shape now reminds Rousseau of a "forgotten form of sleep," the oceanic repose in the womb. She moves as Rousseau moves, his double in a dyadic intimacy. When her light is "half extinguished," it becomes a "light from Heaven."

In *Alastor*, however, the bad mother did not appear as a separate figure. Rousseau now sees the source of the severe new light: a "cold bright car" accompanied by "stunning music" and a "loud million" that "Fiercely extolled the fortune of her star," as if that car were "from some dread war / Triumphantly returning" (434–38). What dread war? The next image tells us: over her "wind-winged pavilion" Iris has built an "arch of victory" (441, 439); the rainbow becomes a triumphal arch, a transformation that undoes the antithesis just established between the fair Shape and the cold new light, for Iris and her rainbow also heralded the Shape.[35] The new vision has a tempestuous "splendour" (444) that recalls the fair Shape's "fierce splendour," and the star whose fortune the loud million extols recalls the star associated with the veiled Shape. So after attempting to separate the two visions, the text conflates them. When the oedipal mother is eclipsed, the ideal elements of the preoedipal mother appear, but then what have been most deeply repressed, the negative elements of the preoedipal mother, also make their appearance. In effect, the

chariot of Life is returning triumphantly from the dread conflicts of
the preoedipal period.

We can pursue the sense of the bad preoedipal mother further in
the passage. In "stunning music" Reiman sees an allusion to the
"stunning sounds" that Satan hears during his voyage through Chaos
in *Paradise Lost* (2.952).[36] Milton's description of Chaos in book 2
hovers behind the present passage of *The Triumph* at several points.
Shelley locates his rainbow-arch in the "wilderness" (443), a word
Milton uses for Chaos (943). Shelley's "wind-winged pavilion" (441)
is reminiscent of the "dark Pavilion" that Satan visits in Chaos (960),
and among the figures in that pavilion is "the dreaded name / Of
Demogorgon" (964–65). Shelley's Life is a destructive and tyrannical
version of what he earlier called Demogorgon and before that Ne-
cessity, "Mother of the World." Life, like Demogorgon, embodies the
sheer power of the preoedipal mother, felt by the very young child to
be behind all things that happen, and the even more elemental
power of the mother as origin. Milton's Chaos is "A dark / Illimitable
Ocean" (891–92), a state of battling "embryon Atoms" (900), "The
Womb of Nature and perhaps her Grave" (911), and the atmosphere
around Life is a purely dreadful version of that maternal source.
Those "embryon atoms" now make their appearance, as the crowd
surrounding the car "Seemed in that light like atomies that dance /
Within a sunbeam" (446–47). Individuality is lost in the oceanic one-
ness around Life: "all like bubbles on an eddying flood / Fell into the
same track at last and were / Borne onward" (458–60). In *Paradise
Lost*, Satan establishes a "track" "Over the dark Abyss" and its "boiling
Gulf" (1025, 1027), but the track of Life is Shelley's equivalent of
chaos itself.[37]

Rousseau too "among the multitude / Was swept" (460–61). How-
ever, he also describes himself as actively joining the tumultuous
flood: into "The thickest billows of the living storm / I plunged, and
bared my bosom" to "that cold light," as if trying to become one with
it (466–68). Why does he forsake the fair Shape? It seems that, seek-
ing radiance, he follows the brightest light; that, offered two forms of
regression, a beautiful, solitary, narcissistic quest and a merger into
the Dionysian torrent, he chooses the more immediate, popular, sen-
sational alternative. But if Rousseau seems guilty of an error, we need
to remember that the drink offered by the fair Shape has led to her
own fading and replacement by Life, and that the poem has been
striving to make Life and the originally ambiguous Shape appear as

antitheses even as it entangles them. The wishful myth of *The Triumph of Life*, and the manifest theme of Rousseau's story, is that the maternal Shapes are different figures, but the deep story that the poem tells is that they are split forms of the same being, that to follow the fair Shape is inevitably to join the crowd around the chariot. It is less distressing to believe that Rousseau betrays his own vision, that we make a wrong choice, than to believe that the mother betrays us.

In *The Triumph of Life* Dante has been implicitly present in the image of the chariot, in the vision of an infernal state, and, pervasively, in the use of terza rima; at this point he enters the poem explicitly: in "that mysterious dell" through which the chariot is now passing, a "wonder" appears

"worthy of the rhyme

"Of him whom from the lowest depths of Hell
Through every Paradise and through all glory
Love led serene, and who returned to tell

"In words of hate and awe the wondrous story
How all things are transfigured, except Love."

(470–76)

The Love that is the ultimate theme of Dante's story is "the Love that moves the Sun and the other stars," or God,[38] but it is Beatrice who literally led Dante through every paradise. Shelley transforms Dante's fatherly ideal into a female ideal. Indeed, Rousseau goes on to associate that guiding Love with "The sphere whose light is melody to lovers," or Venus (479). "How all things are transfigured, except Love," in addition, echoes Demogorgon's confirmation to Asia that to "Fate, Time, Occasion, Chance and Change . . . / All things are subject but eternal Love" (*Prometheus Unbound*, 2.4.119–20). Just when the fair Shape loses itself in the glare of the chariot, just when it is driven back into a disturbing confusion with that from which the poem tries to differentiate it, a new female ideal appears in a leap to the transcendent. But if Dante appears as the authoritative source for that ideal, he also appears as the father to be challenged by the ambitious son: "I will now write something worthy of Dante," Shelley announces.

In the climactic vision to which Dante helps move the poem, the scene of blinding brightness is suddenly "grey with phantoms,"

"Shadows of shadows," like "A flock of vampire-bats before the glare / Of the tropic sun" (482, 488, 484–85). The simile of the vampire-bats characterizes the shadows as creatures of oral aggression. They are also compared to "eaglets" (489) and "elves" (490), or young and small creatures. The "mysterious dell" with its childlike multitudes thronging about the maternal glare is a nightmarish version of the world to which regressive impulses call us.

The dell is a realm of power as well as regression. Some of the shadows make a "cradle" in "kingly mantles," or "upon the tiar / Of pontiffs sate like vultures," or played in nests within the crown on "A baby's or an idiot's brow" (495–500). In this cluster of cradle, nests, vultures, and play, childlikeness is mingled with oral aggression. But these kings and pontiffs are only "worms" with a "delegated power" (504, 503). The true powers are female skeletonlike birds, who "Sate hatching their bare brood under the shade / Of demon wings" (501–2). The paternal authorities are, like the male consorts of the Great Goddess and the kings in her cultures, phallic serpents, and here mere worms. These small devourers of carrion, these babies and idiots, are, like the vampire-bats and eaglets, predatory infants in the world of the demonic mother.

Other shadows suggest blasted promise, falling like tears "On fairest bosoms and the sunniest hair," extinguishing "the youthful glow" (512–13). The source of all the shadows now appears: "each one / Of that great crowd sent forth incessantly / These shadows, numerous" (526–28). With Rousseau's description of the complex process by which the shadows fall from the dancers, the poem reaches the heart of its melancholic vision. He first observes that

> "From every form the beauty slowly waned,

> "From every firmest limb and fairest face
> The strength and freshness fell like dust, and left
> The action and the shape without the grace

> "Of life . . ."

(519–23)

The life of life, the influence and nourishment of the good mother, falls away. The mother now appears explicitly: "in the eyes where once hope shone / Desire like a lioness bereft / Of its last cub, glared ere it died" (524–26). The lioness, who cares whether or not her child lives, is the good mother, but the good mother dies in the passage. On closer inspection, however, the lioness has a certain ambiguity: she glares, like the car of Life; and she is identified with desire, which, in Rousseau's "desire and shame" (394), has been associated with a troubled, oedipal ambivalence. Furthermore, that she somehow lost her cub brings her competence and goodness into question. Another type of separation appears in the passage, as well: the loss of strength of "every firmest limb" suggests castration. In a draft Shelley wrote, "manliest firmest limb."[39] Also in a draft the glaring lioness "turned to stone / Its object & itself."[40] This lioness has a Medusa-like power. Here is castration charged to the mother, not the father.

Like "dead leaves blown / . . . from a poplar tree" (528–29), all the shadows that fall from a person are similar: "Each, like himself and like each other were" (530). But once detached from their source, they lose their original form and become "Obscure clouds": "And of this stuff the car's creative ray / Wrought all the busy phantoms that were there / As the sun shapes the clouds" (532–35). The glare of Life parodies the visionary splendor that Wordsworth in the *Immortality Ode* called the "master light of all our seeing" (156); in this case the great light is the source of our nonseeing, since the chariot's "creative ray" specifically creates obstacles to sight. And what we cannot see, above all, is that the phantoms we live among are our own shadows given an independent, animate existence.

Rousseau now formulates the production of the shadows as a falling of "Mask after mask" (536). In *Prometheus Unbound*, evil and ugliness fell from people like masks (3.4.40–70). In the opening of *The Triumph* "the mask / Of darkness fell" from the Earth as the Sun sprang forth (3–4). But in the unmasking carried out under the influence of the mother Life, there is a perpetual falling of disguises without any final revelation or any end to ugliness. Unmasking becomes a purgatorial torment.[41]

The production of the phantoms has thus been described in two different ways, as a sending forth of masks and shadows and as a waning or falling of beauty and strength, but Rousseau goes on to treat these divergent processes as one: the exhausted dancers fall by the wayside, and those fall soonest from whom "most shadows past / And least of strength and beauty did abide" (542–43). In sending forth the shadows, we lose our good qualities. Here is the psyche producing replica after replica of itself and at the same time continually experiencing loss. We see both separation from the mother—the loss of strength, the loss of the Life of Life—and a constant compensatory attempt to create a new dyad by producing a shadow. Thus we have the passive description of losing beauty and strength and the active description of sending forth shadows.

In these "Fallings from us, vanishings," to use Wordsworth's terms from the *Immortality Ode* (147), we lose supplies; instead of taking in nourishment, there is a constant streaming out of us of all manner of things. The shadows, as suggested above, are also like lost phalluses; here particularly, the loss of the shadow, a seemingly detachable part of us, and the loss of strength seem congruent. In the incessant falling of the shadows, we can see a psyche compulsively repeating in symbolic form two primal forms of separation: detachment from the mother and castration. We can see a third primal separation, as well: the shadows that "stained" the track of Life (517), that are compared to dust and dead leaves, and that are "moulded" as if they were physical substance (532) also seem excremental. Phallic, oral, and anal forms of loss and also of aggression—trampling, biting, defecating—all come into play in the "mysterious dell." That this endless fragmentation and dismemberment occurs in the valley of the mother suggests the picture of preoedipal conflict drawn by Melanie Klein, a maelstrom of aggression, in which the infant, in anger at the denying breast, fantasizes tearing the mother to pieces and being torn to pieces by her in return. Shelley's valley of shadows, with its vampire-bats and its parts of the self constantly coming loose, has something of the atmosphere of this "paranoid-schizoid" stage of development. Klein calls it schizoid because the infant cannot reconcile its sense of the good, fulfilling breast with its sense of the hostile, frustrating, persecuting breast, a condition similar to the opposition between the fair Shape and Life.[42]

But among all the psychological implications of the episode of the shadows, perhaps the central one for our understanding of the poem is the idea of projection. In the image of the self incessantly casting out parts of itself we see a defense that doesn't work as it should. Projection is supposed to rid us of the bad, but in this episode good and bad, strength and shadow, are connected, and thus as the bad is expelled, the good also falls away. The defense of projection becomes enervating, dismembering; through it we lose vital substance; intended to save us, it leads us into an inferno.

Throughout the poem, we have seen an attempt to split the good mother from the bad, and over and over we have seen the poem undoing that splitting, bringing the good mother and the bad into disturbing connection. So as we expel the mother, we find we have lost something of value, and as we cleave to her in reaction, embracing the glare of the chariot, we find new reasons for expelling her. And so the process of casting off shadows is endless. In the episode of the shadows the poem criticizes its own method; at the climax of its nightmare it reveals for us the workings and results of projection; it exposes its own magic. And in unmasking itself, it also reveals that its masks, or shadows, or defenses, are inseparable from its strength and beauty. Perhaps this is one reason why the poem now comes to an end. It has exposed and subverted its own principle of forward motion, of narrative and psychic mobility, the life of its life. It has found itself trapped by its own saving agency. It has nowhere to go.

But perhaps the poem's great display of unmasking, its wonder worthy of Dante, is itself a defense. Shelley's vision of the shadows is often related to Lucretius's portrayal of a stream of replicas flowing from all objects.[43] For Lucretius, sensation is caused by the striking of these replicas against the senses. But Shelley turns Lucretius's account of knowing into a vision of unknowing, for his shadows are a force of obfuscation, creating a premature evening as they gather before the glare of Life (484–86). If Shelley's defenses do not succeed in preserving the fair Shape or saving us from the vision of Life as our ultimate reality, they still keep us from knowing, at the manifest level of the poem, that we are talking about the mother. John Munder Ross writes that "at times sons and daughters will do almost anything" to protect their deep idealizations of the father (305); a similar point can be made about Shelley and the mother. Shelley sacrifices his defenses in order to maintain them at a deeper level; he pulls them back to the last possible line. Here is a second reason why the poem now ends: Life must be maintained as a mysterious figure. Thus the narrator responds to Rousseau's narrative with a final repetition of the poem's compulsive question: " 'Then, what is Life?' I said" (544). After all the unmasking, we see that one mask has been left on. The poem maintains its last myth, that the question is unanswerable.

It does so even as Rousseau tries to respond in the manuscript's last lines:

> "Then, what is Life?" I said . . . the cripple cast
>   His eye upon the car which now had rolled
>   Onward, as if that look must be the last,
>
> And answered. . . . "Happy those for whom the fold
>   Of
>
> (544–48)

Rousseau's experience in the maternal valley ends in exhaustion and crippling, or castration. But "must" in the third line suggests that he is still not free from the spell of Life: although now blind, he looks after the departing car longingly. We still want life, and we still love the mother, no matter what they have been. Or perhaps to be overcome by the mother still exerts a Dionysian and masochistic compulsion.

In his last words Rousseau seems to be contrasting the destiny of the regressive, visionary questers and the aggressive conquerors with some happier lot. What kind of happiness might he be referring to? Perhaps those might be happy who do not feel and imagine too exquisitely, who seek achievable goals, who accept an experience within the "fold" of the ordinary. But by calling his destructive principle Life, Shelley seems to rule out the possibility of common happiness. Perhaps only the fold of death could offer us happiness. But Rousseau is dead and still suffering. Perhaps only those could be happy who, in a thorough skepticism and stoicism, could cast a cold eye on life and all its allures, including knowledge, power, fame, rainbows, poetry, and sexual pleasure. But what kind of fold would those detached ones fit into? Perhaps Shelley remembers in the middle of a line that the poem has already told us that there are no happy others; everybody is conquered by Life except Jesus, Socrates, and those who enter the fold of death early.

Reiman sees another suggestion in "fold": "In his late poetry Shelley more and more frequently drew upon the Christian metaphor of the shepherd as a symbol of human salvation, usually using in conjunction the symbol of Venus as Hesperus, the evening star, which, appearing when the shepherd led his sheep to the fold at the end of the day, Milton had called the 'folding-star.' "[44] Reiman adduces examples from *Epipsychidion* ("love's folding-star" [374]) and *Hellas* ("the folding star of Bethlehem" [231]); in *Hellas* too "Freedom and Peace" "follow Love's folding star / To the Evening-land" of America (1029–30). Reiman concludes that Rousseau "might have continued with an affirmative use of 'fold' as the sheepfold into which were gathered followers of the 'folding-star' of Love."[45] But perhaps the reason that Rousseau did not continue in this way is that it was no longer possible in the logic of the poem to use ideal Love as an antithesis to Life. To do so would only be to cycle back and forth between the split images of the purely good mother and the purely bad mother. Even by itself, however, the folding star is not without its ambiguities. Reiman refers us to Milton's line "The Star that bids the Shepherd fold."[46] But this is the first line spoken by the Dionysian seducer Comus, who goes on to say that now that the folding star "the top of Heav'n doth hold," the "gilded Car of Day / His glowing Axle doth allay / In the steep *Atlantic* stream" (93–97). The apex of Venus is the drowning nadir of the sun; now is the time for the enchanter's revels and for witches. Stopping dramatically in the middle of a prepositional phrase, Rousseau, or Shelley, realizes, it seems, that it would be futile to appeal to an ideal that has already been undone, that "fold / Of" could only be completed by a fatally ambiguous grammatical object, a Love that shades into Life. It is as if the very word "fold"—an enclosure, a crease, a hollow, a refuge in the night—cuts the poem off; despite everything in the poem before this, Shelley cannot help imagining happiness in terms of entering a female. That the implications of "fold" include paper and pages even makes the act of writing seem like entering a female. The last few lines are important not because they might have led somewhere but because they suggest why they did not and thus reinforce our understanding that the poem has reached its end.

Instead of continuing to write, Shelley turned over the page of his notebook and drew a sail.[47] We may take this scribbling as the poem's final punctuation and as a confirmation that no more poetry is possible in *The Triumph of Life*. And yet that sail also suggests casually and pictorially exactly what Shelley has just refrained from suggesting formally and poetically: it suggests a beautiful regression, another magical Shelleyan boat ride, a floating on the uterine waters. It brings back the lines, quoted above, that he wrote about sailing on the Bay of Lerici shortly before, on June 18: "Williams is captain, and we drive along this delightful bay in the evening wind, under the summer moon, until earth appears another world. Jane brings her guitar, and if the past and the future could be obliterated, the present would content me so well that I could say with Faust to the passing moment, 'Remain, thou, thou art so beautiful'" (*L*, 2:435–36).

The Romantic imagination has been exposed and defeated in *The Triumph of Life*, but beyond the logic of a particular poem, it continues to dream.

But the logic of this poem that recounts a dream vision has been a dream logic all along. *The Triumph of Life* may seem a work of exposure, irony, and skepticism; it may seem on the surface a palinode; it may seem an antiromance. But the infernal nightmare and the paradisal dream are both extreme imaginings. With its vision of female depredation, defeated maleness, and all-but-complete human failure, *The Triumph* is as fantastic as the fantasies it calls into question. As Wallace Stevens wrote, "The adherents of the imagination are mystics to begin with and pass from one mysticism to another" (116).

17

Shelley's Rousseau
and Shelley's Dante

I HAVE BEEN STUDYING *THE TRIUMPH OF LIFE* AS A POEM IN WHICH THE
father is swept aside by the mother with not good results as in *Prometheus Unbound* but devastating ones. Yet the father plays a more extensive role in *The Triumph* than the poem's manifest concern with
spectacular female figures of power might indicate. While Shelley
tried in *Alastor* to ignore or circumvent the father and in *Prometheus Unbound* to depose and replace him, in *The Triumph of Life* he makes
complex psychological use of him, in part identifying with him, in
part treating him as a scapegoat, and in part seeking his help. We can
trace the details of this engagement in Shelley's relations with the literary forebears most overtly present in the work, Rousseau, Petrarch,
and Dante.

The figure Shelley chose to be the central character in *The Triumph of Life* has been regarded by critics from Irving Babbitt to Derrida as the father of European Romanticism, or the culprit chiefly responsible for it. In Shelley's England, as Edward Duffy has shown, he
already had that dual status. He was regarded as the father of the
French Revolution by both its sympathizers and its detractors. He was
identified, often disparagingly, with the celebration of nature and
the celebration of feeling, or sensibility. He was identified with the
Enlightenment, again both positively and negatively, and at the same
time he was, in Duffy's words, "an escapist dreamer" (45). He inspired dramatic ambivalence not only in his English audience as a
whole but also in individual readers. *The Quarterly Review* attacked his
social criticism but was enraptured by his sentiment; Mary Wollstonecraft admired his concepts of reason and virtue but was ap-

palled by his "voluptuous reveries" and his portrayal of women; the *Monthly Review* wrote that he combined "the most elevated senti-ments with the lowest propensities."[1] Byron in *Childe Harold*, Duffy writes, captures the full ambivalence toward Rousseau, attributing to him "vanity, sophistry, self-pity, emotional masochism, eloquence, verbal wizardry, sensibility, idealism, sensuality, paranoia, insanity, so-cial and political revolution, and selfishness."[2] But with all that, Rous-seau in *Childe Harold* is "all fire," and his "oracles . . . set the world in flame, / Nor ceased to burn till kingdoms were no more."[3]

Shelley's comments on Rousseau in his essays and letters are al-most wholly positive. The exceptions come early: he wrote in 1811 that the *Confessions* "are either a disgrace to the confessor or a string of falsehoods, probably the latter" (*L*, 1:84) and in 1812 that Rous-seau "gave licence by his writings, to passions that only incapacitate and contract the human heart," thus contributing to the failure of the French Revolution (*M*, 52). But otherwise Rousseau appears as one of Shelley's heroes. In 1811 he grouped Rousseau with Voltaire, Hume, Franklin, and Adam Smith as Deists whose lives were "char-acterised by the strictest morality" (*L*, 1:51), a sharp contrast to the remark about the *Confessions*. In *Queen Mab* he approvingly cited Rousseau's idea that for civilized man "those arts which are essential to his very being are held in the greatest contempt" (*E*, 1:365). But it was in 1816 on his visit to Lac Leman that Shelley's enthusiasm for Rousseau caught fire, and it was *La Nouvelle Héloïse* that excited him. He wrote to Peacock, "This journey has been on every account de-lightful, but most especially, because then I first knew the divine beauty of Rousseau's imagination, as it exhibits itself in Julie" (*L*, 1:480). Exploring the lake becomes a voyage into the world of Rous-seau's novel: "I read Julie all day . . . surrounded by the scenes which it has so wonderfully peopled"; those scenes and characters were cre-ated by "a mind so powerfully bright as to cast a shade of falsehood on the records that are called reality" (485). When he and Byron vis-ited Gibbon's house, Byron "gathered some acacia leaves to preserve in remembrance of him. I refrained from doing so, fearing to out-rage the greater and more sacred name of Rousseau; the contempla-tion of whose imperishable creations had left no vacancy in my heart for mortal things" (487–88). A few days later Shelley wrote, "Rous-seau is indeed in my mind the greatest man the world has produced since Milton" (*L*, 1:494). In *A Philosophical View of Reform* Rousseau's ideas on equality are favorably compared to those of Jesus Christ (*C*,

253). In the *Defence of Poetry* he is classed with Ariosto, Tasso, Shakespeare, Spenser, and Calderón as authors who "celebrated the dominion of love" (*R*, 526).

Elsewhere in the *Defence* Shelley groups him with Locke, Hume, Gibbon, and Voltaire as a practical reasoner but explains in a footnote that he has only been following Peacock's classification, for "Rousseau was essentially a poet. The others, even Voltaire, were mere reasoners" (*R*, 530). That Rousseau was both an Enlightenment reasoner engaged in skeptical and progressive analysis and a "poet" plunged into passions and fantasies reflects a similar doubleness in Shelley's own sensibility. But if the poetic side of Rousseau most interested Shelley, his "reasoning" too was marked by themes that Shelley was to take up. Rousseau assumed, as Northrop Frye puts it, "that civilization was a purely human artifact, something that man had made, could unmake, could subject to his own criticism, and was at all times entirely responsible for."[4] Rousseau envisioned a new man in *Emile*, as Shelley did in *Prometheus*, and among the characteristics of Rousseau's new man is his originality: "There is no one in the world so little given to imitation as Emile."[5] Indeed, Rousseau was a seeker of origins in general, speculating on the beginnings of music, language, inequality. While sharing Rousseau's fascination with sources, however, Shelley did not share his vision of culture as a falling away from natural origins. A thinking man is not for Shelley "a depraved animal."[6] Rousseau's Prometheus, the inventor of science, is "a God inimical to man's repose";[7] he is like the Furies' Prometheus. Rousseau provides an antitext to the *Defence of Poetry*, with its faith in the mutual progress of morality and art; for Rousseau, as art and science grow, so do luxury, uselessness, and vice.[8] For Rousseau, even more, goodness and society are incompatible, for with socialization came the inequality of rich and poor, powerful and weak, master and slave.[9] As the antidote to the disease of civilization, he offers the pleasures of solitude in nature, a private return to origins. On his island of Saint-Pierre, Rousseau wishes "to have no more traffic with mortal men."[10] Drifting in his boat, he is overwhelmed with joy and cries out, "O Nature! O my mother! I am here under your sole protection. Here there is no cunning and rascally man to thrust himself between us."[11] No oedipal father, we might say. If Rousseau's vision of solitude is in conflict with Shelley's vision of utopia and love, it does contain a powerful regressive tendency that would be compelling to Shelley.

Rousseau also expresses an ambivalence about feeling and imagination that we have observed in the author of *Alastor* and *The Triumph of Life*. A poet of love, who could say, "Few men have sighed as I have," but could also say that his "passions have forever destroyed [his] original simplicity," Rousseau was both the great mythologist of Romantic feeling and its critic.[12] In the *Confessions* he calls the sensitive heart both his gift and his misfortune (19). Derrida has pointed out a similar conflict in his treatment of the imagination (185). In the *Essay on the Origin of Languages*, Rousseau writes, "He who imagines nothing feels only himself; in the midst of mankind he is alone."[13] But in the *Discourse on Inequality*, "The imagination, which wreaks such havoc among us, does not speak to Savage hearts," which are completely satisfied by nature (164). In *Emile*, "The world of reality has its bounds, the world of imagination is boundless; as we cannot enlarge the one, let us restrict the other; for all the sufferings which really make us miserable arise from the difference between the real and the imaginary."[14] In the works of Rousseau the eighteenth-century debate over imagination is acted out in a single mind.

Much about the *Confessions* might have fascinated Shelley, and much apparently did disgust him. In the *Confessions* he would have seen his own interest in self-knowledge carried out in epic terms. Duffy quotes Hazlitt that "Rousseau was the first who held the torch . . . to the hidden chambers of the mind of man," and for Hazlitt this was a political act. Until Rousseau, "birth and wealth and power were all in all . . . and what there was in the man himself was never asked," but Rousseau, "like another Prometheus, breathed into [man's] nostrils the breath of a new and intellectual life, enraging the Gods of the earth, and made him feel what is due to himself and his fellows."[15] But Hazlitt also writes that "Rousseau, in all his writings, never once lost sight of himself," and for Shelley, egoism, or the "principle of Self," was something to be fought, not displayed and exploited.[16] And while Shelley portrayed the quest for self-knowledge in idealized terms, the *Confessions* has a comical crudeness and frankness that are antithetical to Shelley's style. Rousseau portrays himself not only as a Sensitive-Plant but also as a charlatan, a rascal, and a buffoon. When Hogg suggested that he and Shelley write something together, Shelley responded that Hogg should write it himself—"I am sure *I* could not"—remarking that the only comparable work would be "The Confessions of Rousseau" (*L*, 1:84). The *Confessions* is the antitext to such poems of subjectivity as *Alastor*, *Athanase*, and *Epipsychidion*.

This is nowhere more apparent than in Rousseau's candid treatment of sex, and not just heterosexuality. While Shelley in *Alastor* gives us a sublime onanistic fantasy, Rousseau talks freely about masturbation, and he does so in a way that is lyrical as well as realistic and comical. In particular contrast to Shelley is Rousseau's way of being lyrical and earthy, idealizing and de-idealizing, at the same time. Ariel himself could be earthy, as in *Swellfoot the Tyrant* and the translations of *The Cyclops* and the Walpurgisnacht scene of *Faust*, but only in carefully delimited ways, as in aggressive satire or translation; comical rowdiness was not allowed to contaminate the sublime or Shelley's most cherished self-images.[17]

Rousseau also brings to the surface things that Shelley was not aware he was writing about. The worship of a maternal principle that is latent in Shelley is manifest in Rousseau: "O Nature! O my mother!" Derrida writes that in *Emile* "All evil comes from the fact that 'women have ceased to be mothers, they do not and will not return to their duty.'"[18] And while Shelley idealizes sibling incest, Rousseau creates an aura of parental incest in his sexual affair with Madame de Warens, whom he calls *Maman*. On the theme of the mother, Rousseau's text reads like Shelley's unconscious.

The crucial part of the *Confessions* for the study of *The Triumph of Life*, as Reiman first pointed out, is the episode on the conception of *La Nouvelle Héloïse*.[19] Rousseau tells us that in his midforties he grew dissatisfied in his longtime affair with Thérese Le Vasseur, who fulfilled his sexual needs but not his need "for a companionship as intimate as possible": "This singular need was such that the most intimate physical union could not fulfil it; only two souls in the same body would have sufficed. Failing that, I always felt a void" (386). He laments, "How could it be that with such inflammable feelings, with a heart entirely moulded for love, I had not at least once burned with love for a definite object?" (396). He tries to satisfy his need in reverie—"The impossibility of attaining the real persons precipitated me into the land of chimeras" (398)—and out of such fantasy came Julie and a lover with whom he identified, St. Preux. Instead of plunging into his imaginings like the *Alastor* Poet, he tries to bring them to life through writing. He chooses as a setting "that lake around which my heart has never ceased to wander" and particularly "that part of its shores, which my wishes long ago chose as my dwelling-place," his mother's birthplace (401). The ideal love is localized in the archaic maternal landscape. Thus Rousseau comes to write a book that he calls contrary to his literary impulses, so much so that he feels "shame at so fully and openly going back on myself" (404); he had been violently against "effeminate books" of "love and languor" (405), and then he wrote one. He is like Spenser's Arthur, who scorned love as a pursuit contrary to the manly virtues of a soldier and then fell asleep and had his Adam's dream.[20]

It was just "at the height of my reveries" that he fell in love with the Countess d'Houdetot, now the mistress of his friend Saint-Lambert: "I saw my Julie in Mme d'Houdetot, and soon I saw only Mme d'Houdetot, but endowed with all the perfections with which I had just embellished the idol of my heart" (402, 410). That the relationship is triangular is essential to its sublimity: "To complete my undoing, she talked to me of Saint-Lambert like a passionate lover. How contagious is the power of love!" (410). He "swallowed the poisoned cup" (410)—as Reiman points out, like Shelley's Rousseau drinking from the cup of Nepenthe.[21] Shelley's Rousseau was suspended between desire and shame before the fair Shape (394), and just as shame attended the conception of *La Nouvelle Héloïse*, so "Shame, the companion of crime," fills Rousseau before the countess (410). After he declares his love, his feelings become even more rapturous and tormented, but "The vehemence of my passion of itself kept it within bounds. . . . to have soiled that divine image would have been to destroy it" (413). They embrace once: "What an embrace! But that was all" (414). This relationship was both his ruination and his paradise lost: "Such was the sole amorous gratification of a man whose temperament was at the same time the most inflammable and the most timid that Nature can ever have created. Such were the last happy days that were dealt out to me upon earth" (415).

Thus from a reverie two intertwining paths lead out to actuality, one to the Countess d'Houdetot and the other to *La Nouvelle Héloïse*. In the novel the lovers not only share a sublime kiss in an arbor but also eventually sleep together, and the novel spends much of its energy defending them for doing so. St. Preux is not a seducer but a "sensitive soul," a hero of *Sehnsucht* with "limitless desires" (71–72), and he and Julie are "two beautiful souls" who "left nature's hand made for each other" (163). Standing between them is the tyrannical authority of Julie's father, who tries to "form or break" what only nature should determine, the "conjugal tie" (163). Yet it is also nature that impels Julie to forsake St. Preux, for to betray her natural tie to her father by making him miserable "would follow me as my torment every instant of my life" (176).

The husband Julie chooses, Wolmar, is a man of not feeling but reason, not extremism but temperateness. He characterizes himself as a detached spectator with a "love of order" and "a cold heart," but he is also fair, objective, and as free from prejudice as from passion (317). Wolmar brings St. Preux into the household and tries to cure him of his intoxication; he envisions an ideal life for all three, in which Julie will be made happy by having St. Preux near her as a friend. Indeed, as Duffy suggests, Wolmar tries to cure him of his imagination, encouraging him to see that he is in love with an image in his mind (103). Wolmar, Duffy argues, freezes the novel: "The handing over of his novel to the Wolmar ethos must have struck Shelley not as Rousseau's ascent to judicious reasonableness but as his descent from the imaginative to the didactic, a falling out of poetry and into the 'mere reason' of the Enlightenment" (104). Rousseau, in this reading, is an Aeschylus, reconciling the champion of imagination and love with their oppressor.

It is possible that Shelley thought of the novel in these terms. Wolmar's methods do approach the monstrous: at one point he tests the former lovers by having them repeat their first kiss in the arbor. But there are other ways to see the later stages of the novel. The presence in the story of Julie's father frees Wolmar from the burden of being the representative of antinatural authority. St. Preux and Julie fall in love in a state of nature, which is ended by her father, but, as Wolmar's wife, Julie creates a new state of nature, a garden called Elysium, where, she says, "nature has done everything, but under my direction, and there is nothing here which I have not ordered" (305). In her garden she masters nature in a way that increases its beauty. The novel's moral ideal is expressed in Julie, not Wolmar, as she tries to integrate the claims of Wolmar and St. Preux.

"People stifle great passions," Julie writes; "rarely do they purify them" (393). How do people purify a passion? Not by imposing reason on it but by opposing to it another passion, such as a passion for virtue or for domesticity. In the taming of St. Preux, we can also see a less manifest passion at work. From a Shelleyan viewpoint, what might be particularly, although unconsciously, compelling about the later part of the novel is the way in which St. Preux falls back into an oedipal triangle, although this time with a good father, who is a loving friend and guide: St. Preux reports that he takes pleasure "in considering myself as a child of the house" (345), and he tells Wolmar that he is the eldest of the latter's children (360). Regression to an ideal childhood is the reward for the symbolic castration that Rousseau's Abelard must undergo for his Héloïse.

Yet the ideal vision of Elysium and of purified passion does not finally work out in the lives of these people, and this too might have made the later part of the novel interesting to Shelley. In a deathbed letter to St. Preux, Julie confesses, "I have for a long time deluded myself. . . . You had thought me cured of my love for you, and I thought I was too" (405), but "I am dying in this sweet hope, only too happy to purchase at the price of my life the right of loving you forever without crime and of telling you so one more time" (407). Far from a didactic treatise in which cold Enlightenment reason conquers passion, *La Nouvelle Héloïse* is an eighteenth-century *Civilization and its Discontents*. But it is one with a special romantic twist. Julie dies in saving her child from drowning. Nature—eros, maternal passion, and water, the primal maternal realm—asserts its power over attempts to govern it and claims Julie as its own. The novel ends not with the survivors joining together, as she had wished, "to take her place as mother" (397), but with her friend Claire yearning to join her in death and even the fatherly Wolmar left like a child dependent on the female power (408–9). Julie had hoped that her children would now receive Claire as their mother; she and Wolmar had hoped that St. Preux would marry Claire; they had hoped that love could be happily transformed into friendship. But in the novel the dream of ideal metamorphoses and substitutions fades before the stubborn persistence of original desires.

How is Shelley using Rousseau poetically in *The Triumph of Life*? Critics have tended to treat Rousseau as the villain of the piece. For Jean Hall, he has a "time-ridden sensibility" that misinterprets the good Shape as a bad presence (159). For Duffy, he is a figure whose imagination, love, and sympathy are curtailed by "egotism" and Enlightenment "pride of intellect" (133). For McGann, he makes the error of scorning the common earth and dreaming of an Absolute.[22] For Bloom, just the opposite, he is the poet of nature, "confessing his errors of vision so that others may not follow him into slavery."[23] In all these treatments, we lose the idealized sense of Rousseau as one who did not give in to life in the ways others gave in. Bloom's reading has balance, however; he sees Rousseau as a Virgil-figure whose natural humanism is replaced by Shelley's apocalyptic humanism in the same way that in *The Divine Comedy* Virgil's paganism is replaced by Dante's Christianity.[24]

But to this I would add that Virgil was both what Dante had to surpass and his model. E. R. Curtius writes that for Dante, Virgil was rhetoric, was the art of writing itself (357), and for Shelley, Rousseau was Romanticism, a rhetoric of imagination, the heart, and political renovation. Rousseau in the poem is also Shelley's spiritual father, subsuming Wordsworth and Godwin; in *The Triumph of Life* Shelley confronts the source of his own sensibility and ideals. Rousseau is the good father, as opposed to Jupiter or Othman. He is also the good father gone bad, the ex-revolutionary who turned away from society. He is, as well, the failed father who cannot answer our questions, who cannot save us. He cannot be what the divine "Guide" and "Author" was in the first dream of Milton's Adam, the one who can explain "who I was, or where, or from what cause" (*Paradise Lost,* 8.298, 317, 270). Rousseau himself vainly has to ask "whence I came, and where I am, and why" (398). He is, in addition, the crippled and blinded father, castrated by the mother.

Rousseau in the poem embodies a vision of the self as well as the father. He is the spirit of romance, idealization, romantic extremism. He is the part of Shelley that would plunge into his visions and pursue a love affair with Jane Williams. He is an Adam totally committed to realizing his imaginings, whatever the consequences. He is also the spirit of regression, the worshipper not finally of nature but of the mother; he is the one who actually does drink of the mother's liquid. But, destroyed in the poem by female Shapes, he also embodies Shelley's negative feelings about woman. From another angle, he is the dying god in the world of the mother goddess.

In the poem the father Rousseau is expelled or sacrificed. Shelley attempts to make him into an old order. Like the French Revolution in *Laon and Cythna* and Milton's Satan in *Prometheus Unbound,* he is both what inspires Shelley and what he needs to correct. Rousseau is also the scapegoat punished for embodying Shelley's own disturbing fantasies. Like the Maniac in *Julian and Maddalo* and the *Alastor* Poet, he is a cherished part of Shelley that Shelley must present to us in projected form. The sacrifice of Rousseau is another version of the rejection of romance that must be made before romance can live again.

Rousseau's status as a double of the narrator helps us understand further Shelley's use of him. Since the narrator is "I," everything about Rousseau is rhetorically rendered "not-I"; but since Rousseau is partly a poetic self-representation, we can see in the poem an instance of Neil Hertz's "end-of-the-line" situation, in which authors try to stabilize a sense of self or differentiation by creating structures of doubleness that make us analyze subtle differences and thereby focus on difference itself.[25] In a poetic world of collapsing distinctions, one in which Life and the fair Shape are difficult to keep from a nightmarish conflation, as are the blind Shadow guiding the chariot and the blind guide Rousseau, the doubling of the narrator and Rousseau functions to keep difference, or the ego, alive, to defend against merger. The double, as the psychoanalyst Irvine Schiffer puts it, can be "an insurance against destruction" (98), a need not to be underestimated in a poem in which the self is exposed to the full power of the mother, conceived of as harsh and overwhelming, and in which Shelley subjects aspects of himself and his poetic mythology to severe attack. The full weight of danger and damage can fall on one self-representation, and yet Shelley can still envision a continuation of life and safety because of a second self-representation. And if Hertz and Freudian psychoanalysis give us paradigms for understanding Shelley's doubling, so too does Greek mythology; for just as the head of the Medusa became not a threat but an advantage to Perseus once he saw its reflection in his shield, so it may be Shelley's hope that the regressive energy embodied in Rousseau can be mastered and purified by being contained within a structure of doubleness. We do not look directly at it but see it mediated, in a story within a story told by a character who is in part a reflection of the narrator and of the author.

To understand further Shelley's attempt to master and purify the image of Rousseau, we need to attend to Shelley's use of the two other generating influences and pervasive presences in *The Triumph of Life*, Petrarch and Dante. In Petrarch, Shelley returns to an early exemplar of romantic love, indeed to perhaps the poet most closely identified with the theme of idealized and unattainable love and its pleasurable melancholy. Petrarch's poems, Shelley writes in the *Defence*, "are as spells which unseal the inmost enchanted fountains of the delight which is in the grief of Love" (*R*, 525). In Petrarch, Shelley returns to the near-origins of the tradition of *La Nouvelle Héloïse*; he returns to the cultural roots and the cultural authority of his own infatuation with Jane Williams. Petrarch's Laura is the heroine of not only the Sonnets but also the *Trionfi*, and that work opens with *The Triumph of Love*, in which the narrator is captured by Laura and compelled to join a procession of sufferers on their way to the realm of Venus. Love, however, is not the only relevant theme Shelley would have found in Petrarch. Thomas Bergin writes that the landscape in which Petrarch sets Laura is "more lovingly portrayed than any the world of poetry had beheld before his time"; Laura "becomes one with nature" (167–68). Petrarch was also the author of *The Ascent of Mont Ventoux*, the first account of climbing a mountain for the beauty of the view. Petrarch lies behind Rousseau in the joining of romantic love with love of nature, two versions of the worship of a female principle. In thus going behind Rousseau to Rousseau's origins, Shelley achieves a measure of detachment from and power over him and what he represents.

Shelley seems to have been particularly fond of *The Triumph of Death*,[26] in which Laura herself is conquered, one of many victims of Death, who appears as a lady in black. Laura's death is described in elaborate and graphic detail, but she returns to describe dying as the experience of "one in exyle his owne countre to see."[27] The vision of death as a return to the source may have interested Shelley, although more relevant to *The Triumph of Life* may be the portrayal of aggression by a female figure. Aggression itself is essential to the *Trionfi* in its scheme of successive conquests: Love conquers Man, Chastity conquers Love, Death conquers Chastity, Fame conquers Death, Time conquers Fame, and Divinity conquers Time. In effect Shelley places the regressive story of Rousseau within the aggressive format of Petrarch, so countering one disturbing impulse with another and thus modifying its power.

The presence of Petrarch has connotations of aggression in another way. Petrarch was Dante's younger contemporary. In the preface to *Prometheus Unbound*, defending himself against anticipated charges of imitation, Shelley wrote, "There is a similarity between Homer and Hesiod, between Aeschylus and Euripides, between Virgil and Horace, between Dante and Petrarch, between Shakespeare and Fletcher, between Dryden and Pope," or, we can add, between Wordsworth/Rousseau and Shelley. "If this similarity be the result of imitation, I am willing to confess that I have imitated" (*R*, 208). Shelley thus exonerates the junior member of each relationship. Petrarch was not only a latecomer but a particularly successful one;

his work at first outstripped Dante's in popularity. He was also an audacious latecomer: among the lovers chained to Cupid's chariot in the first *Triumph* are Dante and Beatrice; the precursor is swallowed up into the latecomer's poetic mythology, as Rousseau is in Shelley's.

Or so the latecomer might like it to appear. In the final triumph of Divinity over Time, Petrarch imagines that "In that endles glory we shal beholde and se / My fayre swete lady, of whome so much I write, / More beauteous then the sonne in his hyest light."[28] Bergin writes that Petrarch sees Laura in the closing lines "precisely as Dante saw Beatrice" (151), and for Shelley too Dante towers behind Petrarch: in the *Defence of Poetry* Shelley writes, "Dante understood the secret things of love even more than Petrarch," and "His apotheosis of Beatrice in Paradise . . . is the most glorious imagination of modern poetry" (*R*, 525–26). Furthermore, the terza rima that Shelley uses in *The Triumph of Life* and that he used earlier in *Athanase* and the *Ode to the West Wind* is really Dante's form, not Petrarch's; Petrarch too in the *Trionfi* was writing in Dante's verse form. That verse form announces Dante's contextualizing presence at every moment in *The Triumph of Life.*

Bloom writes that Shelley at the end of his career turns to Dante as an answer to Milton.[29] Strictly in terms of *The Triumph of Life*, I would say that he turns to Dante as an answer to Rousseau. The two are counters in several ways. Dante, within his poem, found his ideal woman; Rousseau did not. Rousseau is carried away by his passions and in the *Confessions* is mired in earthly problems and anxieties; Dante has a transcendent serenity. Rousseau is the "poet" of incestuous and masturbatory fantasy; Dante's imaginings of love are even more intensely idealized than Rousseau's, but they are free from any morbidity. Rousseau acts out his fantasies, in a disturbing conjunction of words and deeds; Dante is the great poet of sublimation, but an ideal sublimation that is pure gain and promises a satisfaction of our deepest impulses. Shelley in *The Triumph of Life* uses Dante to control or contain Rousseau, and the containment is ubiquitous and literal in the sense that the story of Rousseau is framed within the terza rima that embodies Dante's magic power. As Julie used one passion to master another, Shelley tries to use one poetic imagination to master another.

Thus if Dante functions as a fatherly precursor for Shelley to try, like Petrarch, to surpass—we recall Shelley's ambition to show us "a wonder worthy of the rhyme" of Dante (471)—he also functions as a good, strong father to oppose the failed father Rousseau and to master the regressive and incestuous energies of the son, which Rousseau also embodies. He is the ego ideal, which, as Heinz Kohut puts it, is "related to drive control," while at the same time "arousing our love and admiration."[30] But Shelley's Dante is not Dante's Dante; in order to serve as a Shelleyan ideal, Dante must be revised. This is evident in Shelley's handling of the terza rima, as Reiman points out: "Whereas Dante tends to make the tercet a closed unit like the couplet of Pope, Shelley emphasizes the interweaving of rhymes to develop long periods, the meaning rushing breathlessly from tercet to tercet."[31] Shelley makes the terza rima more Dionysian. But he also revises Dante in vision as well as in style. The divine Love that Shelley's Dante follows and celebrates is not the father but the mother. The answer to Rousseau's failed regressiveness is a deeper regressiveness. Shelley's Dante is of Rousseau's party without knowing it. But he is a better Rousseau, for while Shelley's Rousseau follows ambiguous expressions of his ideal in the natural world and is himself filled with equivocation, Shelley's Dante embodies a transcendent regression to the primal glory. But can Shelley still have Dante's mastery and serenity when he eliminates the Christianity and the patriarchalism with which Dante contextualizes his worship of a female principle?

Let us consider one of the poem's specific references to Dante, the episode in which Rousseau follows the fair Shape along the stream, alluding to Dante's similar following of Matilda in the Earthly Paradise.[32] Shelley's Matilda-like Shape, the woman who can walk upon the water, is a female savior and also embodies a vision of regression without drowning. In Dante, Matilda's appearance is followed by the Triumphal Chariot of the Church; then Beatrice appears; then Matilda immerses Dante in the waters of Lethe, which obliterate his memories of sin, and the waters of Eunoë, which strengthen his memories of good; then Dante, in the closing lines of the *Purgatorio*,

> . . . came back from those holiest waters new,
> remade, reborn, like a sun-wakened tree
> that spreads new foliage to the Spring dew
>
> in sweetest freshness, healed of Winter's scars;
> perfect, pure, and ready for the Stars.[33]

In *The Triumph of Life*, the Matilda-figure is followed by the chariot of Life. Beatrice never appears. Rousseau is immersed only in the billows of the throng. God plays no role. The poem never emerges from purgatory into paradise. Shelley's use of Matilda and the divine chariot expresses a wish for a Dante-like transformation, a wish to rise above the tragic experience of Rousseau, but at the same time a rejection of Dante's Christian and patriarchal means of achieving that transformation. It expresses a persistent vision of redemption through the female, the mother, regression; yet, as the Matilda-like Shape is replaced by the terrible chariot, it also expresses a skepticism or an anxiety about that vision. A better Rousseau cannot overcome the problems of *The Triumph of Life*.

But a saving fantasy of Dante does remain part of the total vision of the poem. In part, Dante is simply there in the poem as a good fatherly presence, to which a certain childlike sense of safety is attached. Rousseau is the father who is too human, too like the son, while Dante is the father who is superior and magical; and there was no such presence in the world of *Alastor*. But additionally, in the terza rima and in the allusion to his "rhyme," Dante appears in the poem as a poet. The character Rousseau is not a near-mute like the *Alastor* Poet; he is a storyteller but a tortured, confessional one, a writer whose words were "seeds of misery" (280). Dante too is the poet as personal quester, one who followed Love from "Hell / Through every Paradise" (472–73), but he is also the poet as artist, as maker of wonders and rhymes. It is Dante as poet that contextualizes Rousseau's regressive energy. The active, mastering ego in the form of the poetic imagination contains and purifies the regressive imagination, and the aggressive one as well, in *The Triumph of Life*. In Rousseau contextualized by Dante or ultimately by Shelley the poet, we see regression in the service of the ego; in Rousseau alone, we see regression controlling the ego. The ego is partly unconscious, partly constituted by fantasies, wishes, anxieties, and defenses, and fantasies also invest poetic form and style. In *The Triumph of Life* these fantasies concern not only the father but also the mother. The artist, Anton Ehrenzweig writes, finds in the energies of the unconscious not a frightening chaos or swallowing void but an enveloping womb.[34] Dante and his terza rima contain Rousseau—the Dionysian energy, the destroyed hero, the dying god, the sacrifice to the mother—as in a womb. In *The Triumph of Life* Shelley finds, or recreates, both the good father and the good mother in poetry itself.

"The only relief I find springs from the composition of poetry," he wrote in 1821, "which necessitates contemplations that lift me above the stormy mist of sensations which are my habitual place of abode" (*L*, 2:296). At the end the imagination—specifically the poetic imagination—is still saving to Shelley, at least until that last, empty hemistich.

18

Imagination and
the Heart

I<small>N THE CONCLUDING SECTIONS OF THIS STUDY</small> I <small>WISH TO DISCUSS WITH</small> reference to Shelley's writing in general four elements of *The Triumph of Life* that bear on the concept of imagination. The first is feeling: Rousseau is overcome not by Life but by his own heart. Shelley's heroes and lyric speakers are characterized by the extremism and intensity of their emotions, but he was also, as he wrote to Godwin, "not a stranger to the immense complexity of human feelings" (*L*, 1:243). His poetry combines emotional extremism with emotional conflict and ambivalence. In the story of Asia, he dreams that the heart might be our oracle, that we might follow our feelings and impulses to paradise. But often he portrays our feelings and impulses—sexual, aggressive, and regressive—as dangerous and the heart as filled with labyrinthine riddles and ambiguities.

Desire, for example, appears as Asia's yearning for Prometheus and as "The desire of the moth for the star,"[1] as both a life force and a sublime death drive. Closely allied to desire is hope, which in *Prometheus Unbound* successfully "creates / From its own wreck the thing it contemplates" (4.573–74) but which in *Alastor* is interchangeable with despair: both are "torturers" (640). In *To the Republic of Benevento*, we are asked to quell the inner "anarchy / Of hopes and fears" (13–14). In an 1821 translation from Brunetto Latini, love, hope, desire, and fear dominate the heart, a "weak" and "wretched thing" "of little wit" (29, 49, *H*, 648).[2]

Passion in general appears positively in the notebook *Note on Shakespeare*, in which Shelley praises certain images in Shakespeare and Greek tragedy for their "intense poetry & passion."[3] The early

Votary of Reason, however, writes of "the slaves of passion & sickly sensibility" (*L*, 1:120). In *Prometheus Unbound* the passions are purified: the new man is not "Passionless," "yet free from guilt or pain" (3.4.198). But in *The Triumph of Life* all passion seems destructive. To escape its depredations, we must sublimate as drastically as Jesus and Socrates, or die young and innocent; a less extreme possibility is the way of "the great bards of old who inly quelled / The passions which they sung" (274–75). Passion at its most frenzied appears in allusions to the Maenads. In the *Ode to the West Wind*, the Maenads are associated with "Angels" of a storm that will sweep away the past (18–23). In the *Notes on Sculptures*, they are associated with "wild errors" and filicidal mania.[4] In *Prometheus Unbound*, as discussed above, they are associated with the disturbing extremes of a beautiful ecstasy (4.467–75).

Sometimes imagination is the heart's ally and defender, even its secret agent: in *Alastor*, we have seen Shelley expressing dangerous energy while trying to convince us and himself that he is disowning it. Sometimes imagination and the heart, as in the motif of Adam's dream, are working as one. But sometimes imagination appears as a saving and clearly distinct counter to the passions of the heart: in the *Speculations on Morals and Metaphysics* the original wishes of human nature are "to inflict pain and to arrogate dominion," but the imagination, developed later and cultivated by poetry and philosophy, can lead us beyond selfishness (*C*, 187–89).[5] Sometimes in order for the imagination to save us, it must become like the heart; in the preface to *The Cenci*, "Imagination is as the immortal God which should assume flesh for the redemption of mortal passion" (*R*, 143–44). Sometimes the heart cannot bear the responsibility Shelley would like to give it: "Until a heart can love & admire & trust & hope & endure, to what end would you propose principles of moral conduct?" he wrote in a draft of the preface to *Prometheus Unbound* and then changed "a heart" into "the mind."[6] Sometimes imagination is allied with mind, not heart: in the *Speculations on Morals and Metaphysics*, "Imagination or mind" is responsible for "every gradation of [human] progress" (*C*, 189).[7] In Blake, imagination, as the Zoa Los, must repair the damage caused by the struggles between Urizen, the reasoning mind, and Luvah, the heart, and to do that must keep a clear identity apart from either. In Blake, the imagination leads to art and vision while the heart leads to the deadly mother goddesses of a restrictive and delusory nature. Blake found poetic power in the separation of imagination and the heart, while Shelley found it in their intermingling or in their dance of merger and differentiation.

Shelley sought power over the mutiny within. He wrote to Claire that he had bought a new boat rather than a horse, for he had "enough to do in taming his own will, without the additional burthen of regulating that of a horse, & still worse, of a groom" (*L*, 2:288). We often think of Romanticism in terms of letting go, but one theme of this study has been the importance of the effort in Shelley to tame and regulate energies and mutinous ambivalences within the self. This does not mean that restraint is a goal in itself. Shelley does not seek mastery of the heart and its passions through Enlightenment reason, ultimately, nor through neoclassic moderation or compromise. The classical ideal of quelling the passions appealed to him but is finally not quite his way. The same is true of transcendence. In *The Faerie Queene*, Spenser describes an age of innocence, in which "each unto his lust did make a lawe, / From all forbidden things his liking to withdraw" (4.8.30.8–9). Shelley does not withdraw from the disturbing passions of the heart; just the contrary, he seeks their energy; he wants the power embodied by Rousseau or by Beatrice Cenci or even by the Maenads, but he wants it without being overwhelmed by it, as they were. We have seen him attempting to purify that energy, to double it, to mirror it as in the shield of Perseus, to revise it, to contain it poetically, to combine it, as he said the Greeks had in a sculpture of the Maenads that he admired, with "ideal beauty and poetical and abstract enthusiasm" (*C*, 349). We have seen him attempting to organize passions into self-regulating dialectics, to master passions with other passions, imaginings with other imaginings. These are the workings of the ego, solving problems, seeking some resolution of conflicting demands and desires; they are also the workings of the imagination at its most comprehensive, seeking transformation, renovation, the liberation of potentiality. We have seen such work come to radically different conclusions. In *Prometheus Unbound* we do reach a "far goal of Time" (3.3.174), a Romantic state of cure, in which conflicting regressive and progressive desires are integrated in a strong and flexible dialectic and in which our destructive and morbid capacities are exposed, regulated, and transformed. In *The Triumph of Life* the "illness" is battled to a fragile standoff: we can poetically contain the heart's dark impulses and passions, understand their patterns and their all-but-inescapable power, make them tragically beautiful; we can't fully transform them. *Pro-*

metheus Unbound is a little like an analysis that reaches an ideally successful termination and then continues internally into the future: we recall Demogorgon reminding humanity that it now has the power to handle Jupiter by itself. *The Triumph of Life* is a little like an analysis that, while working and productive, is inherently interminable and then, after this becomes clear, is abruptly broken off.

19

Imagination
and Vision

SHELLEY MAY NOT WRITE A POETRY OF COMMON OR EVEN RECOGNIZ-able sights, but he certainly writes one of visual imaginings. His poems are filled with light, shadows, reflections, radiance, and evanescent marvels of color: "the green and golden atmosphere / Which noontide kindles through the woven leaves."[1] His speakers and characters often struggle to describe in detail strange or fleeting sights. As in *Epipsychidion,* in which the speaker spends his life searching for "Youth's vision" (42), their lives are often shaped by an internal image that has the force of an actual sight. As in the case of the dream that Asia pursues to redemption, such a vision may be the source of all good in the world, but as in the stories of the *Alastor* Poet and Rousseau, it can also kill or maim. Shelleyan speakers and characters also seek, like Lucretius, to shine "a clear light . . . into the heart of hidden things."[2] From the forehead of the Spirit of the Earth in *Prometheus Unbound* shoot "sunlike lightenings" that "Make bare the secrets of the Earth's deep heart" (4.276, 279). Also part of the topic of Shelleyan vision is a fascination with eyes and gazing. Nathaniel Brown points out the characteristically radiant eyes of his heroines, the hypnotic eyes of his heroes, and the blasted eyes of Rousseau. "The last words he ever wrote," Brown reminds us, "—to Jane Williams—were 'only . . . for the pleasure of tracing what will meet your eyes.'"[3] But inanimate objects also have eyes. Stars are recurrently like eyes; narcissi recurrently gaze on their own reflections; the moon is "like a joyless eye / That finds no object worth its constancy."[4] Shelley's poetic persona is a seer and lives intensely in a poetic world of seeing and being seen. What is seen in his poetry? What does it mean in his poetic world to be a seer?

276

Shelley's visions are often ecstatic, like the sight of the transfig-
ured Asia in *Prometheus Unbound*. But it is the disturbing visions that I
wish to study in this section. Even the beautiful visions are often dis-
turbing in the extremity of their rapture; but some of his visions are
purely appalling, such as the batlike shadows of *The Triumph of Life* or
the revelations of the Furies, which make Prometheus close his eyes
in agony only to see them inwardly "more clear" (1.636). We may
think too of the hallucinations that afflicted him in the last weeks of
his life, when he saw his double strangling Mary or the bloody figures
of Jane and Edward screaming, "The sea is flooding the house."[5]
Sometimes a beautiful vision leads to destruction, as in his recurrent
allusions to Actaeon; in *Adonais* Shelley represents himself as one
who "Had gazed on Nature's naked loveliness, / Actaeon-like," and
then was hunted down by "his own thoughts," "like raging hounds"
(275–76, 278–79).

Shelley treats another myth of dangerous vision in the unfinished
On the Medusa of Leonardo da Vinci in the Florentine Gallery (*H*, 582).
This is a poem about gazing: it describes a "gazer's" reaction to a
painting in which an eft "Peeps" into the Medusa's eyes and the dead
Medusa herself lies "gazing on the midnight sky" (10, 26, 1). The
gazer's spirit too is turned "into stone," astonished, as it were, by "less
the horror" of the Medusa than her "grace" (10, 9). In addition, the
gazer becomes not only like the Medusa's victim but also like the
Medusa herself, since "the lineaments of that dead face / Are
graven" in his spirit (11–12).

In a poet so consumed as Shelley is with a quasi-divine female
principle, we cannot ignore Freud's analysis of the head of the
Medusa as representing the threat of castration associated with the
forbidden sight of the mother's genitals.[6] The Medusa appears else-
where in Shelley's work. In his translation of the Walpurgisnacht
scene from *Faust*, the hero points out a girl who reminds him of
Margaret. Mephistopheles warns him away from her, for "they /
Who meet [her] ghastly stare are turned to stone, / Like those who
saw Medusa" (387–89, *H*, 761). Faust insists, "That is the breast
which Margaret yielded to me" (392). Mephistopheles responds, "It
is all magic, poor deluded fool" (394). His next line is "Denn jedem
kommt sie wie sein Liebchen vor," or "For she appears to every man
as his love."[7] Shelley's version is "She looks to every one like his first
love" (395). "First" is a Shelleyan addition, which fills out the iambic
pentameter line and makes sense because Margaret is Faust's first
great romantic attachment. But it perhaps also suggests that, for

Shelley, Medusa is the other side of the truly primal and paradigmatic love in a man's life. Jane Harrison calls Medusa "the Erinysside of the Great Mother."[8] In the eft that "peeps" at Shelley's Medusa we see a fatal curiosity, and in a maddened bat that flies into the dreadful glare like a moth into a flame we see a fatal compulsion. In the poem Shelley explores the fascination with the forbidden sight of the mother: the painting shows "the melodious hue of beauty thrown / Athwart the darkness and the glare of pain" (14–15).

Even the Medusa's viper-hairs have a certain "radiance" (22). "Kindled by that inextricable error," the Gordian entanglement of the serpents (35), that radiance makes an

> ever-shifting mirror
> Of all the beauty and the terror there—
> A woman's countenance, with serpent-locks,
> Gazing in death on Heaven from those wet rocks.
>   (37–40)

For Daniel Hughes, that mirror takes the place of the reflecting shield of Perseus in the original myth; through that mirror "Perseus-Shelley is able to both distance and seize . . . to confront and find beautiful the shocking central image" of the woman with serpent-locks.[9] The poem then not only dreams that the terrible sights that might destroy us can be transformed into beauty, but it also dreams that the powerful mother, unlike the original Medusa, may provide the mirror with which the son can master her.

I would suggest that Shelley has an additional motive in the poem. His Medusa gazes in her own death, but her gaze also, in effect, may bring death to Heaven. Freud remarks in his essay that "displaying the genitals is familiar in other connections as an apotropaic act. What arouses horror in oneself will produce the same effect upon the enemy against whom one is seeking to defend oneself" (*SE*, 18:274). Harrison writes, "In her essence Medusa is a head and nothing more," that is, a mask. The purpose of such ritual masks is to "'make an ugly face,' *at* you if you are doing wrong . . . *for* you if you are doing right."[10] The head of the Medusa terrifies opponents with the power of the archaic mother, proclaiming that she not only has the genital organ that is primal in a mother-centered culture, but she also has the phallus; further, with her abundance of serpents, she has the phalluses of all the men. In Shelley's poem that power is turned in the last line against the Heaven of the Olympians, the fathers. Mastering the horror of the Medusa means not only containing it but using it against one's enemies.

I have been considering the poem in the context of the ego, but it can also be considered in the context of the id. William Hildebrand finds in the poem not containment but "a numbed reaction to a spell of dizziness . . . a vertiginous experience of something unreflected, unmediated, ultimate."[11] It is as if the poem experiments with the forbidden experience of actually seeing the Medusa. That is, the drive to see the mother in her full beauty and terror feminizes, or castrates, the viewer, who thereby takes on the mother's power to castrate or feminize. Here is a dark version of the benign identification with the mother in *Queen Mab*.[12]

Another kind of forbidden seeing appears in an 1822 letter in which Shelley speaks of the "astonishing etchings" by Friedrich August Moritz Retzsch of scenes from *Faust*; one in particular "made my brain swim round only to touch the leaf on the opposite side of which I knew that it was figured": "Margaret in the summer house with Faust!—The artist makes one envy his happiness that he can sketch such things with calmness, which I dared only to look upon once . . . the etching certainly excited me here more than the poem it illustrated.—Do you remember the 54th letter of the 1st part of the Nouvelle Heloise? Göthe [*sic*] in a subsequent scene evidently had that letter in his mind, & this etching is an idealism of it" (*L*, 2:407). In Letter 54, St. Preux visits Julie's room, and there, alone amid her things, he builds up an Adam's dream: "All the parts of your scattered dress present to my ardent imagination those of your body that they conceal . . . I see you, I feel you everywhere, I breathe you in with the air that you have breathed."[13] Imagining her "cruel father" approaching, he is thrown into panic, but when the door opens Julie herself walks in. In this episode, St. Preux is a spy as well as a dreaming Adam, and then the spy becomes the partner in the primal scene: the anticipated father does not appear, and the two lovers have sex for the first time. In the Retzsch illustration of Goethe, Faust and Margaret are together and Mephistopheles is spying on them.[14] In Goethe's text Mephistopheles walks in just after the lovers embrace for the first time; three scenes later he again intrudes on the lovers, and this time Faust says, "Have you spied on me again?"[15] Retzsch makes explicit the sexual spying implicit in the earlier scene.

The Triumph of Life is Shelley's great poem of spectatorship. It begins with the narrator in a fantasy of being able to see everything, on a mountainside with the world spread out before him, watching a scene of love in which the Earth is uncovered, the day kisses the flowers, and the things of nature "hold / Sweet talk in music through the enamoured air" (38–39). Overcome by a sense of déjà vu, the narrator plunges into a phantasmagoria that includes obscene shapes engaged in mysterious activities and that fills him with perplexities as if he were a child witnessing the primal scene. Indeed, this poem of endless questions anticipates Freud's concept of curiosity, which begins in the child's "looking impulse."[16] Appearing in adjoining stanzas are two curious researchers: Aristotle, who "kept / The jealous keys of truth's eternal doors" (267–68), and Bacon, who compelled Nature "to unbar the caves that held / The treasure of the secrets of its reign" (272–73). Both of them succeed in their quests, but Rousseau is an obstinate questioner and viewer of strange phenomena who comes to a disastrous end; not only is he erotically and intellectually unsatisfied, but he is also crippled and blinded, or symbolically castrated. Blinded too is the four-faced charioteer of the car of Life, the one who potentially could see everything. In the poem in general the looking impulse is answered not only by retribution but also by the appalling nature of what is seen: a painful excess of light—the chariot's glare "forbade / Shadow to fall" (444–45)—and a vision of horror.

The theme of vision is the issue in one of Shelley's favorite complexes of imagery, the veil.[17] Shelley often uses the veil in a traditional way to represent obscurities and barriers: "Who lifteth the veil of what is to come?" he asks in *On Death* (26, *E*, 1:427). Medwin reports Shelley speaking of translating as "throwing the grey veil of his own words over the perfect and glowing forms of other writers."[18] And between Athanase's heart and mind "was drawn an adamantine veil" (87, *E*, 2:318). But the veil can be an allurement; the bodies of sleeping humans appear to the Witch of Atlas as

> diaphanous
> Veils, in which those sweet ladies oft array
>   Their delicate limbs, who would conceal from us
> Only their scorn of all concealment.
>
> (562–65)[19]

In addition to being an obstacle or an allurement, the veil can be beautiful in itself. *Epipsychidion* describes Emily as "Veiling beneath that radiant form of Woman" her full transcendent being (22); she is a radiance concealing a greater radiance.

Unveiling is frequently a creative act. In *Laon and Cythna*, Cythna's words tear "the veil that hid / Nature, and Truth, and Liberty, and Love" (3523–24, *E*, 2:207). In *Prometheus Unbound*, act 4, "the abyss shouts from her depth laid bare, / 'Heaven, hast thou secrets? Man unveils me, I have none'" (422–23). Shelley scorns his Peter Bell the Third, who "touched the hem of Nature's shift, / Felt faint—and never dared uplift / The closest, all-concealing tunic" (315–17). In the *Defence of Poetry* he associates poetry with the aggressive and erotic act of unveiling: it "strips the veil of familiarity from the world, and lays bare the naked and sleeping beauty" (*R*, 533). Poetry itself is something to be unveiled: "All high poetry is infinite . . . Veil after veil may be undrawn, and the inmost naked beauty of the meaning never exposed" (*R*, 528). But poetry also veils: it "arrests the vanishing apparitions which haunt the interlunations of life, and veiling them or in language or in form sends them forth among mankind" (*R*, 532). Poetry even veils and unveils in the same formulation: "Whether it spreads its own figured curtain or withdraws life's dark veil from before the scene of things, it equally creates for us a being within our being" (*R*, 533). Poetic figuration is a veil but one that we actively make, not one that is imposed on us.

In *Prometheus*, life as we thought it had to be is a "painted veil" that is torn aside like a "loathsome mask" (3.4.190, 193). But a sonnet tells us, just the opposite, "Lift not the painted veil," for "behind, lurk Fear / And Hope, twin Destinies, who ever weave / Their shadows o'er the chasm, sightless and drear" (1, 3–5, *R*, 327–28). Elsewhere too unveiling can be dangerous. In her kindness the Witch of Atlas weaves "a subtle veil" to screen her beauty (151); otherwise we would all become *Alastor* Poets: "If you unveil my Witch, no Priest or Primate / Can shrive you of that sin, if sin there be / In love, when it becomes idolatry" (46–48). In *Una Favola* unveiling is purely sinister: the young visionary, seeking his love, is abandoned amid veiled maidens, each of whom, when unveiled, he finds "more hideous and terrible than the other."[20] In *The Cenci*, Orsino falls into evil when "Beatrice unveiled me to myself," exposing to him his own dark motives (2.2.115). In *Prometheus Unbound* the Furies tear a veil to reveal the extremes of human misery (1.539).

Blake tells us to tear through the veil, for all natural existence is a veil woven by the enchantress Vala to seduce and entrap us. "Art can never exist without Naked Beauty displayed," he writes; "No Secresy in Art."[21] In Keats the veil is not a symbol of evil, but there is no ambivalence about the desire to remove it. In *Sleep and Poetry* life is "The light uplifting of a maiden's veil" (92). In *The Fall of Hyperion* the divine muse Moneta unveils her face as part of a process that humanizes the imagination. In contrast to Blake and Keats, Shelley treats the veil with intricate ambivalence. He is possessed by the desire to see the hidden or the unbearably beautiful, to see face-to-face, as Job wanted to do, to see realities rather than shadows, as Plato said we could never do with our eyes. His Gothic hero-villain Ginotti says that "a desire of unveiling the latent mysteries of nature was the passion by which all the other emotions of my mind were intellectually organized."[22] But I cannot agree with Rogers's purely positive formulation that beyond the veil for Shelley lives the "the virtue and power of . . . *that best worship Love*,"[23] for he is also haunted by myths of dangerous seeing: Actaeon, Medusa, Semele, Narcissus. As in *Prometheus Unbound*, he dreams that the veil may be taken off with impunity and to our bliss. But most often he prefers to keep it on, although entrancingly transparent, or to have it in a never-ending process of coming off, as in the infinite unveiling of "high poetry" or the endless unmasking of *The Triumph of Life*. As in the prelude to *The Triumph*, in which the narrator sees the landscape through a transparent trance like a veil of light, the veil is a stimulus to imagination or a beginning phase of it. Shelley's sources of energy are characteristically so by virtue of remaining at least partly hidden. They are evermore about to be seen.

ॐ ॐ ॐ

Some of the most striking sights in Shelley's poetry occur in dreams, and one of his most disturbing dream-descriptions appears in an essay he tried to write about his own dreams. Fascinated by dreams throughout his career, he set out to study them systematically in 1815, the year of *Alastor*, in a *Catalogue of the Phenomena of Dreams, as Connecting Sleeping and Waking* (*C*, 193).[24] "Let us reflect on our infancy, and give as faithfully as possible a relation of the events of sleep," he begins. His goal is to figure out what these events have to do with conscious reality, and he proceeds by discussing experiences of his own in which dreams and waking life seemed to intermingle:

> The most remarkable event of this nature which ever occurred to me happened five years ago at Oxford. I was walking with a friend in the

neighborhood of that city engaged in earnest and interesting conversation. We suddenly turned the corner of a lane, and the view which its high banks and hedges had concealed presented itself. The view consisted of a windmill, standing in one among many plashy meadows, inclosed with stone walls; the irregular and broken ground between the wall and the road on which we stood; a long low hill behind the windmill, and a grey covering of uniform cloud spread over the evening sky. It was that season when the last leaf had just fallen from the scant and stunted ash. The scene surely was a common scene; the scene and the hour little calculated to kindle lawless thought; it was a tame uninteresting assemblage of objects, such as would drive the imagination for refuge in serious and sober talk, to the evening fireside and the dessert of winter fruits and wine. The effect which it produced on me was not such as could have been expected. I suddenly remembered to have seen that exact scene in some dream of long— (C, 194)

Mary Shelley added the following note:

Here I was obliged to leave off, overcome by thrilling horror. This remark closes this fragment, which was written in 1815. I remember well his coming to me from writing it, pale and agitated, to seek refuge in conversation from the fearful emotions it excited. (C, 194)

So ends Shelley's attempt to study his dreams, in "thrilling horror" and writer's block. Here is a sudden disclosure, a dangerous vision that is not an act of spying but an accidental sight or a sight of something that is unexpectedly frightening. Shelley anticipates Freud's understanding of the feeling of déjà vu, which derives from "the recollection of an unconscious phantasy" or a dream, even "*a forgotten (repressed) portion of a dream of the preceding night.*"[25] The imagery of the passage too could hardly be more Freudian. The windmill standing in the enclosed meadow suggests a penis in a vagina, and the stunted ash from which the last leaf has fallen suggests castration. Shelley turns a corner and comes face-to-face with something he once saw before in a dream or a fantasy, a scene of oedipal origins. At the outset of *The Triumph of Life* a sense of déjà vu is followed by an appalling vision, while here it is followed by thrilling horror, and in both cases the scene that prompts the déjà vu is symbolically a sexual one. One of Shelley's great themes is the quest for the lost origin, but in this passage the sudden feeling of a connection with an origin, the sudden sense that behind our common scenes lie prior scenes, or even primal scenes, is unbearable. Discontinuity is what he wants, and so he breaks off.[26]

In some ways this is as Wordsworthian a passage as any Shelley ever wrote. In it, the familiar becomes the strange, and the present is infused by the past. Indeed, this is a Shelleyan Spot of Time, right down to the "visionary dreariness" that characterizes the great Spot of Time in *The Prelude* (12.256). In Wordsworth "feeling comes in aid / Of feeling" until we once again are strong (269–70). Shelley's Spot of Time, however, contains a power not to renovate but to paralyze. In the fragment on dreams Shelley sets out to show that our dreams and our actual experiences intermingle; at the end it is not so pleasant to consider that dreams may change waking reality, that we may all be dreaming Adams.

Another instance of terrifying sight in Shelley's experience appears in a hallucination. Byron's friend Polidori records a scene in 1816 in which Byron "repeated some verses of Coleridge's 'Christabel,' of the witch's breast; when silence ensued, and Shelley suddenly shrieking and putting his hands to his head, ran out of the room."[27] The lines in question describe the undressing of the beautiful Geraldine, revealing her "Hideous, deformed" bosom, traditional mark of supernatural evil.[28] Shelley later explained his reaction to Polidori: "He was looking at Mrs. S[helley], and suddenly thought of a woman he had heard of who had eyes instead of nipples, which taking hold of his mind, horrified him."[29]

This is a fantasy of being looked at not only suddenly and terrifyingly but also from a completely unexpected place, and indeed from a place, a woman's naked breasts, that one might look at in pleasure or, even, that one might spy on. In this fantasy, the object of the voyeur suddenly returns his gaze. Phyllis Greenacre reads the Wolf Man's dream of being stared at by wolves as a reversal of his own staring at his parents in an animal act.[30] After the hallucination, a distraught Shelley told Polidori of Hogg's interest in Mary and his own encouragement of Mary "to love him in turn."[31] Together, that comment and the hallucination suggest that Mary played a disturbing role in Shelley's mind as voyeuristic object.

The hallucination also suggests a nightmarish version of a common association of the oral and the visual. We devour with our eyes not only in metaphor but also, as Anton Ehrenzweig writes, in "primitive wish" (232). For the infant, staring at the mother's eyes while nursing, there would be no clear distinction between eyes and nipples. In early narcissism, Heinz Kohut writes, the self wants to be gazed at by the loving mother, to feel itself, in Barbara Schapiro's paraphrase, " 'reflected' by that first love-object."[32] We recall the *Alastor* Poet dying as the sinking crescent moon becomes two points of light above the horizon and then vanishes. The self can be destroyed by the absence of the mother's nourishing gaze or by its transformation into a hostile force, like the "glare" of the chariot of Life or the gaze of the Medusa. In the hallucination we see a terrible inversion of the dyadic situation; the good woman, Mary, turns into the witch, Geraldine.

In the character of the Witch of Atlas the linked orality and visuality of the dyad have an all-transforming beneficence: "The magic circle of her voice and eyes / All savage natures did imparadise" (103–4). And the savage natures are specifically figures from the realm of the archaic mother: Pan, the satyr Silenus, the nymphs, and monsters, "Dog-headed, bosom-eyed," that "haunt / Wet clefts," the female places (136, 134–35). Shelley in his poetry tries not only to master the anxiety expressed in the hallucination but also to make use of it, identifying, for example, with the dangerous gaze: in the *Ode to Naples* he exhorts the oppressed, "Be thou like the imperial Basilisk / Killing thy foe with unapparent wounds! / Gaze on Oppression" (83–85, *H*, 618). In *The Mask of Anarchy* too the oppressed are told to stare down their oppressors (319–22, 344–47). The victim becomes the aggressor; Shelley appropriates for his own use the terrible power of the mother that threatens him. More generally, sudden reversal, which appears as a catastrophe in the hallucination and also in the allusions to Actaeon, can appear as a saving poetic strategy. In *Adonais*, "he is not dead," but "*We* decay" (343, 348). In *The Sensitive-Plant*, " 'Tis we, 'tis ours, are changed—not they" ("Conclusion," 20). We recall the fondness for reversing terms, as in his calling tyrants slaves, or in Prometheus's repeatedly pitying those who pity him. In such moments, reversal, which is dreadful when passively experienced, becomes when actively employed heroic and redemptive. We see again in Shelley the process that underlies his treatment of the Medusa. Traumatic material, mastered, turned from passive to active, becomes poetic imagination. But the process works both ways: as the hallucination indicates, the passive, devastating form of reversal may return to undo the poetic visionary. Anxious fantasy and saving imagination continue in interaction.

Commenting on the story of Tiresias, whose blindness and prophetic powers both originated in his witnessing of two snakes copulating, Géza Róheim suggests that in a deep sense Tiresias's punishment is "for having witnessed the primal scene, and the reward in 'seeing' is the sublimation of the primal scene."[33] The visionary quality of Shelley's poetry also seems rooted in forbidden or disturbing sight. Characteristic of his poetic style are several ways of responding to disturbing sights or to the visual in general. One is the curtailment of sight: the veiling of the unbearable; the reduction of visible beings to vague forms, shapes, or shadows; the darkening of the visual field. In *To Night*, the Spirit of Night is asked to "Blind with thine hair the eyes of Day" (10, *H*, 636), or in drafts to "Charm to sleep the Argus eye" or "envious eyes."[34] Such curtailment, like the checking of the aggressive impulse in the opening speech of *Prometheus Unbound*, is a negative poetic movement that creates something desirable: here, the gift of a rich and sublime "belovèd Night" (33). Another response to a disturbing sight is to block it out with another sight, as in the recurrent eclipses of *The Triumph of Life*. In still another defense against sight, Shelley moves from common sight to dazzling radiance. Visionary splendor, in which clear visible form is dissolved, can itself be a kind of veil. Cyprian in Shelley's translation of Calderón's *Magico Prodigioso* speaks of "heavens for ever pure, / At once intensely radiant and obscure!" (2.23–24, *H*, 739).

Another response is to transfer the object from the visual field to the realm of feeling, making it thus unbeheld but not unfelt. Another is to transfer it from the visual field to the auditory field, transforming the visible into sound, especially music. The emphasis on the oral and the aural in Shelley is an expression of an impulse toward an idealized pregenitality and primal narcissism. The eye is the chief perceptual organ of the father's world, the mouth of the mother's world: Prometheus and Jupiter behold the universe with their "sleepless eyes" (1.4), while the transfigured Asia loses clear visual outline in a dizzying "Ocean" of song (2.5.83–84).[35] But the move toward orality is defensive as well as wishful; it takes us away from a world of disturbing sights.

Out of physical necessity and also out of allegiance to the higher light of divine inspiration, Milton moved from outer sight to inner sight. Out of dissatisfaction, Wordsworth moved, ambivalently, from outer sight to remembered splendor. Out of anxiety, as well as desire, Shelley moved from outer sight to music, dazzle, feeling. For him, plain seeing, even plain seeing of what one is really looking for, is blinding. Light is something we lose ourselves in, sometimes pleasurably yet terribly as in the burning fountain to which the poet returns at the end of *Adonais*, sometimes horribly as in the cold glare of *The Triumph of Life*. Yet poetic vision is still for him a form of seeing. Even in *To Night*—in contrast, say, to Novalis, who in the *Hymns to the Night* yearns for an "eternal slumber"[36]—he is careful to distinguish Night from Sleep and Death: "Of neither would I ask the boon / I ask of thee, belovèd Night" (32–33, *H*, 637). His Night is a seen darkness; it has "a mantle gray, / Star-inwrought" (8–9). But most often his imagination seeks not darkness but light. In the passage on the sinking sun in *Queen Mab*, examined in chapter 1 above, the viewer watches from the seashore as the sun rests on the water, attended by "intolerable radiancy" (2.10). Just as its "highest point / Peeps like a star o'er ocean's western edge," the viewer's "fancy soar[s]" to "the Faery's fane" (14–15, 19, 21). Shelley describes that "etherial palace" in an imagery of "flashing light," "golden islands / Floating on a silver sea," and "mingling beamings" of "suns" (29, 32, 34–36). When the paternal sun is about to vanish in the maternal ocean, light is preserved by being moved into a new realm, one that includes "suns." So while seeing becomes intolerable, Shelley still wants to see rather than to plunge into the dark, even the maternal dark. In this passage, imagination comes into being as a means of shaping the disturbing visible, first refining it down to that transitional point of light between the dark sea and the darkening sky, and then transforming it into the bright palace. Imagination here involves the wish to recover primal narcissism and orality without giving up visuality and its object world of differentiated forms.

20

Imagination
and Negativity

WITH ITS UNANSWERED QUESTIONS, ITS EPISODES OF ECLIPSE, ITS themes of oblivion and blindness, its narrative beginning in "untold" thoughts (21), its attendant biographical mysteries, and its unfinished status, *The Triumph of Life* brings to a culmination one of the tendencies of Shelley's poetry that I have been following. Its last, empty hemistich can serve as a fit symbol for all the diverse forms of negativity we have observed: the conspicuously absent, the unspoken, the "intense inane," the unknowable, the inexpressible. Negativity is as apparent in his diction as in his themes; observing his fondness for "negative epithets," P. M. S. Dawson lists dozens of examples from *Prometheus Unbound*, including such novelties as "unsandalled," "unerasing," "moveless," "printless," "unpastured," and "unupbraiding."[1] Timothy Webb writes that Shelley's use of negative words leads us "to the very centre of his thinking," and he shows that negativity can have many senses; in *Prometheus Unbound*, the world of Jupiter, Prometheus's resistance to it, and the new world after his liberation are all expressed in negatives.[2]

Psychologically, Shelleyan negativity or absence can express a massive and melancholic feeling of loss, whether of an external love object or of internal supplies, as in images of exhaustion and emptiness. That something is missing or unfinished or present only as a shadow can express a feeling of failure, weakness, fragmentation, lack of nourishment, crippling, castration. In such negativity we can see the child abandoned by the preoedipal mother, the child vanquished by the father, the child betrayed by the oedipal mother.

Shelley is, however, not only the victim but also the perpetrator of negativity. We see this when he speaks agnostically or atheistically,

288

when he sends Jupiter "down the void Abysm," when he calls upon the voice of Mont Blanc "to repeal / Large codes of fraud and woe," and when he speaks of "the dark abyss of—how little we know."[3] What has been studied philosophically as Shelley's skepticism can be understood psychologically as a manifestation of aggression. That aggression includes a wish for a prior greatness to be overcome or not to exist. When Demogorgon says, "the deep truth is imageless,"[4] Shelley is, in effect, attacking the images of his precursors; he is breaking down the icons of even the iconoclasts like Milton, erasing the words of the father, leaving the slate clean. In *The Triumph of Life* he turns extremes of human greatness, as in Plato, Napoleon, and Rousseau, into illusion, corruption, and failure. But in this poem, as we have seen, the aggression is aimed ultimately at the greatness of the mother.

Often negativity seems part of the creative process. Prometheus advances by retracting something he has said. In *Adonais* Shelley moves beyond lamentation for the dead hero and into the transcendence of a dark, terrible voyage to glory by denying the value of life: "Peace, peace! he is not dead, he doth not sleep— / He hath awakened from the dream of life" (343–44). For Daniel Hughes, a frequent pattern in which images or poetic myths are built up and then "collapse" actually has the advantage of returning the poet to a state of potentiality and thus keeps the creative process something evermore about to be.[5] In this sense that last, unfinished line is poetry still to be written. Here vacancy is reserve. To leave something out can foster the sense that supplies have not been exhausted. Then too Shelley cultivates negativity as a way of approaching a marvelous presence. "Bird thou never wert"; "What thou art we know not": negation is a path to the sublime.[6] In the *Defence of Poetry*, poetry "arrests the vanishing apparitions which haunt the interlunations of life" (*R*, 532); Shelley cleaves to the barest traces existing on the very margins of absence and even slipping into it. And those who love what is absent, who "pine for what is not," are, as he said of Peacock's Shelley-caricature, Scythrop, "the salt of the earth."[7]

Negativity or absence can also be something desired for its own sake. In *To Night*, all through the day the poet longs for darkness with its "opiate wand" (13, H637). In *Adonais*, he goes further, yearning for an annihilating oblivion that is also a source and a presence, an emptiness that is also an ideal fullness, somewhat similar to what the Gnostics called the pleroma, the primal being/nonbeing. Negativity thus can be associated with regression, as well as aggression.

Negativity can also appear as a desirable fiction, a wish for nothing to exist where something dreadful to Shelley does exist. It is in that sense comforting to believe that the causes of things can never be known, that the notion of causality itself is philosophically suspect. At times it seems that the deep truth is something Shelley would very much like to keep imageless. But what does Shelley wish to keep imageless? What does he wish not to know? What do his poems speak of in spite of themselves? In this study I have suggested a number of possibilities. He wishes not to know the true identity of his masked figures. He wishes not to know the strength of "self" in him, of unaltruistic ambitious and sexual impulses. He wishes not to know the strength of his positive feelings toward paternal figures— his wishes to be guided and saved, his impulses to imitate—and his negative feelings toward maternal figures—his anger and fear and his anxiety of self-loss. He wishes not to know that his idealization of the female is accompanied by an antipathy toward the maternal or that his idealization of liberty is accompanied by an impulse toward passivity. He wishes not to know the strength of aggressive, competitive, destructive impulses in himself. He wishes not to know, then, how overpowering both his passive and his active impulses are, his impulse toward merger and his impulse toward individuation. He wishes not to know how close to each other the ideal and the morbid are; how good and evil for him often seem to come from the same source; or, as much as he may be willing to acknowledge this abstractly, how deeply they are often involved in a Gordian entanglement. And he wishes not to know specific things or experiences, unknowable to us, that he does know. But he also wishes not to know that not knowing is itself filled with peril: he would like to think of the mind as a beach that can be washed by erasing maternal waters, but those same waters, for him, have the power to drown.

"Things cannot be created out of nothing," says Lucretius, "nor, once born, be summoned back to nothing."[8] But in Shelley's visionary universe things often seem to be flowing out of and back into nothingness. His poems are intriguing for their amnesias. His images and formulations seem to draw aesthetic power from their closeness to dissolution. In various ways, his poems call nothingness into themselves; they tell us that they are not telling us something; they do not finish what they are saying; they make us look for something that we cannot find, a definite position on a provocative and

ambiguous topic, for example, or an explanatory biographical se-
cret. Milton Wilson writes, "His poems are not whole poems, be-
cause oneness must necessarily be outside them" (39). I would say
that his poems try very hard to create the sense of some outside di-
mension. They tell us that there is an answer to the riddle but that
we cannot know it; they make us curious about the poet's life beyond
the poem; they place the deep truth outside themselves. As Wilson
suggests, his poems "have better things to do than assert their aes-
thetic wholeness" (39). That they present themselves as parts of an
as-yet-unknown whole is germane to those "better things." Conceiv-
ing of a poetry that could transform the world, an Adam's dream
that could become reality, Shelley wrote poems that draw the outer
world into their own total text. Conversely, placing truth and whole-
ness beyond themselves is another way in which his poems create a
sense of something evermore about to be. In this perspective, the
nothingness beyond imagination, the blank hemistich, draws us ever
higher. His poems cultivate the hidden or the unspoken as a source
of power, as Prometheus's secret is. But if the nothingness beyond
imagination stimulates imagination, it can also itself be something
imagined. In effect, the empty hemistich is something made up by
the poet. Shelley asks Mont Blanc, "And what were thou, and earth,
and stars, and sea, / If to the human mind's imaginings / Silence
and solitude were vacancy?" (142–44). But vacancy too can be one of
the human mind's imaginings. The "dark abyss of—how little we
know" can itself be another construct of romance. And in still an-
other sense, perhaps making blankness part of a total text is a way of
trying to master or tame or enclose absence. Imagination in Shelley
is a power that reveals and cancels, builds and, to use his word in *The
Cloud*, "unbuilds" (84), makes nothing into something and some-
thing into nothing.

In Shelley's work, J. Hillis Miller writes, metaphysics and nihilism
inhere in each other (230). We should be careful not to confuse
Shelley with contemporary analysts or celebrants of absence.[9] Shelley
does not deny that there is such a thing as meaning or presence; just
the contrary, he affirms meaning and presence and places them out
of reach. With that caution in mind, we can work with Miller's for-
mulation. For metaphysics and nihilism, I would substitute romance
and skepticism, and I would treat the pairing psychologically, seeing
a conflict of a regressive, oceanic impulse and an aggressive, individ-
uating impulse.[10] Each impulse, in addition to expressing a positive

desire, works in defense, or negation, against the dangers inherent in the other. Furthermore, the void abysm can appear on either side of the conflict, either as the consequence of the oceanic feeling or as a protection against a threatening presence. The blankness of that last hemistich was an integral part of Shelley's poetry all along.

21

Imagination and
Self-Knowledge

WHAT MAKES SHELLEY'S WISHES NOT TO SEE AND NOT TO KNOW especially interesting is that they exist together with his intense desire for knowledge, particularly secret or ultimate knowledge. "Let us see the truth whatever that may be," Shelley wrote nine days before he died (*L*, 2:442). He was speaking specifically about the "delusions" of Christianity, but he was also expressing one general impulse of his sensibility. Like Lucretius, he wished to "gaze into the heart of hidden things."[1] The Maniac in *Julian and Maddalo* is destroyed in part because he took on "a blot / Of falshood on his mind which flourished not / But in the light of all-beholding truth" (529–31). And for Shelley the quest for truth was aimed inward, as well as outward. "We do not attend sufficiently to what passes within ourselves," he wrote in the *Speculations on Morals and Metaphysics*, "Let us in the great study of ourselves resolutely compel the mind to a rigid consideration of itself" (*C*, 184). He continued, in a passage I referred to at the outset of this study, that if "a person should give a faithful history of his being from the earliest epochs of his recollection . . . [a] mirror would be held up to all men in which they might behold their own recollections and, in dim perspective, their shadowy hopes and fears—all that they dare not, or that daring and desiring, they could not expose to the open [light] of day" (*C*, 185–86).[2] Of the wise and the great in *The Triumph of Life*, Rousseau says, "their lore / Taught them not this—to know themselves" (211–12). Prometheus, on the other hand, liberates himself through an increase in his knowledge of his own motives and actions. "The unlearned man," wrote Bacon, "knows not what it is to descend into himself or to call himself to ac

293

count" and thereby to improve his life.[3] But self-knowledge in Shelley is not only corrective; it also promises the realization of hidden power: in a fragment he addresses an "immortal deity / Whose throne is in the depth of human thought" (*H*, 661). In the notebook *Note on Shakespeare* the mind is a world that we search for some guiding knowledge as we "would search the external universe for some valued thing which was hidden."[4]

"There is no vexation or anxiety of mind which resulteth from knowledge otherwise than merely by accident," wrote Bacon, "for all knowledge . . . is an impression of pleasure in itself."[5] For Shelley, however, self-knowledge does have a dark side. As noted in the last section, we can infer many specific things that he did not wish to know about himself. Sometimes, as well, he suggests a general anxiety of self-knowledge. In the *Speculations on Morals and Metaphysics*, he writes that thought flows forward "like one in dread who speeds through the recesses of some haunted pile and dares not look behind" and that "the passage from sensation to reflection" is "dizzying" and "tumultuous" (*C*, 186). Thinking about oneself is like a dizzying voyage; the tendency of thought is not to look at the mind from which it comes but to flee from it in dread. The anxiety of looking backward appears elsewhere. In the early *The Retrospect*, he speaks of "The gloomiest retrospects that bind / With crowns of thorn the bleeding mind" (163–64). In Claire Clairmont's journal, he writes lines in which "The thoughts of my past life / Rise like the ghosts of an unquiet dream / Blackening the cheerful morn" (62). In a letter, he writes, "The curse of this life is that whatever is once known can never be unknown" (*L*, 2:6). As I noted above, he found *Faust* "an unfit study for any person who is a prey to the reproaches of memory" (*L*, 2:406). Conversely, he often idealizes forgetfulness. For the newly triumphant revolutionaries in *Laon and Cythna*, "To hear, to see, to live, was on that morn / Lethean joy!" (2089–90, *E*, 2:149); and in *Prometheus Unbound*, love is "nepenthe" (3.4.163).

In other passages, the dangers of self-knowledge go beyond the pains of memory. We recall the "Lionel" notebook entry in which the mind is described as a labyrinth with a monster in its center.[6] In the preface to *The Cenci* Shelley sees in Protestantism "a gloomy passion for penetrating the impenetrable mysteries of our being, which terrifies its possessor at the darkness of the abyss to the brink of which it has conducted him" (*R*, 143). Wasserman distinguishes in *The Cenci* between self-knowledge, which leads to virtue and self-respect, and self-anatomy, which leads to a sense of one's own evil.[7] Self-knowledge is what the play gives spectators, while self-anatomy is what the characters do to their own minds. Wasserman calls self-anatomy a "verbalizing of our subconscious, [which] may make us viciously aware of what should remain suppressed" (114). Insofar as verbalization of the forbidden may lead to evil action in Shelley, it is because of the magic power he attributes to verbalization. The central issue in our present discussion, however, is that self-knowledge has both a saving and a fearsome side, that the mind may have a secret treasure or a monster at its center.

In 1812 Shelley wrote a sonnet expressing his faith in the benign power of the truth. The poem, better than its title, *To a Balloon, Laden with Knowledge*, is based on an unusual method of stirring up political change that Shelley had conceived; he had attached copies of a broadside to fire balloons, which he then released over the Bristol Channel. In the poem, the "Bright ball of flame" will soon "Fade like a meteor in surrounding gloom," but the greater intellectual flame it bears will be "unquenchable," "A Sun which o'er the renovated scene / Shall dart like Truth where Falshood yet has been" (1, 6–7, 13–14). In 1818 he wrote a sonnet *To the Nile* that portrays knowledge more ambivalently. Rains gather in "secret Ethiopian dells," and snow melts on the desert mountains as "Frost and Heat in strange embraces blend," until "Nile's aëreal urn" overflows (2, 4, 7, *E*, 2:350):

> O'er Egypt's land of Memory floods are level
> And they are thine, O Nile—and well thou knowest
> That soul-sustaining airs and blasts of evil
> And fruits and poisons spring where'er thou flowest.
> Beware, O Man—for knowledge must to thee,
> Like the great flood to Egypt, ever be.
>
> (9–14)

The land of memory is flooded with a knowledge, both fructifying and poisoning, that originates in an embrace of contraries, Frost and Heat, and in a coital raining into secret dells, originates, that is, in the primal scene. As in this poem, the quest for knowledge in Shelley may result in more knowledge than bargained for. "Let no man, upon a weak conceit of sobriety or an ill-applied moderation, think or maintain that a man can search too far," wrote Bacon.[8] It was no such moderation that made Shelley stop writing about his dreams or that made him leave the reasons for Athanase's grief "untold" (124, *E*, 2:319): "The Author was pursuing a fuller development of the ideal character of Athanase, when it struck him that in an attempt at extreme refinement and analysis, his conceptions might be betrayed into the assuming a morbid character" (*E*, 2:319).

For a skeptic like Shelley, C. E. Pulos writes, Plato is "a poet of the unknown and unknowable" (88). But Shelley is a poet who all at once celebrated the unknowable, sought to know, and sought not to know. "Shelley's sceptical theory of knowledge," says Pulos, "led him to conceive of Beauty as the unknown cause of a fleeting sense of ecstasy" (88). Yet, as we have seen, while maintaining that causes are inexplicable, Shelley gravitated toward origins. He was a Bacon and a Hume rolled into one. The unknowable nature of cause, however, is more than an article of skeptical rationalism for him. In *The New Organon* Bacon quotes Proverbs 25:2: "The glory of God is to conceal a thing; the glory of the king to search it out."[9] Shelley sought glory both through searching things out and through concealing them. "The reason why all mortals are so gripped by fear is that they see all sorts of things happening on the earth and in the sky with no discernible cause," writes Lucretius (31). "Ignorance of causes," said Vico, is "the mother of wonder" (74). We see in Shelley the Lucretian, Apollonian tendency to liberate the mind from mystery by exposing causes. We also see in him the Dionysian cultivation of wonder. The sense of the unknowable in Shelley is supported both by an anxiety of what may be known and by a love of the enchanted and the numinous. Ovid's Tiresias said of Narcissus that he would live only until he came to know himself.[10] In Shelley we find an interplay of the Delphic, Socratic, and Freudian injunction to know oneself and the narcissistic, oceanic impulse, which, as Ovid suggests, may include an anxiety of self-knowledge and is also associated with self-love. Both tendencies are invested with fantasies: on the one side, the purifying Apollonian liberation from darkness; on the other, a regressive immersion in an ideal origin. These are also fantasies of expression and repression. The fantasy of bringing to light, of expression, is the Adamic, oedipal dream of realizing internal ideals; the fantasy of repression is the Lethean, preoedipal dream of a blissful oblivion. Both tendencies are also attended by anxiety. Knowing is a "dizzying" passage (*C*, 186). Not knowing is a dizzying abyss: "We grow dizzy to look down the dark abyss of—how little we know" (*R*, 508).

Several years before *The Triumph of Life*, Shelley wrote the follow-
ing fragment:

> One sung of thee who left the tale untold—
> Like the false dawns which perish in the bursting,
> Like empty cups of wrought and daedal gold
> Which mock the lips with air when they [are thirsting.][11]

In *The Triumph of Life* the cup is drunk; the tale is told. But its telling
is also an untelling, an obscuring. And if the empty cup torments us
with thirst, the full cup floods and overwhelms us, like the Nile. Tire-
sias and Narcissus, prophecy and oblivion, function together in a di-
alectic of defense, each embodying a contrary wish, each protecting
against the dangers of the other. The dialectic is nowhere more in-
tricate than in *The Triumph of Life:* insistent questions are answered by
full and visionary responses, which provoke the same questions,
which in turn intensify bafflement, provoking the same questions
once again; both the search for knowledge and the tendency to
block or erase are heightened to the state almost of blind mecha-
nisms or compulsions; and the distinction between knowing and not
knowing loses stability, as stripping away masks reveals nothing, as
Rousseau finds both oblivion and vision in the same cup. In this
poem both knowing and unknowing seem equally impossible ideals.
Patricia Parker characterizes romance "primarily as a form which si-
multaneously quests for and postpones a particular end, objective, or
object" (4). In Shelley the pursuit of self-knowledge takes such a
form; the repressed becomes the unattainable in a romantic quest.
"The hiding-places of man's power / Open," Wordsworth writes in
The Prelude; "I would approach them, but they close" (12.279–80).

The charge of self-deception has been made against Shelley many
times. Arnold wrote of his "superhuman power of self-deception"
(323); Stephen Spender called him a "self-deceiver" (19). Arnold
and Spender are concerned with Shelley's personal ethics. But in
terms of the workings of his imagination, self-deception or lack of
self-knowledge can be understood as psychic defense. Such defen-
sive work made a vital contribution to the strengths and beauties of
his poetry. Freud wrote that Goethe "was not only, as a poet, a great
self-revealer, but also, in spite of the abundance of autobiographical
records, a careful concealer."[12] As a poet, Shelley was both a self-re-
vealer and a concealer, and the revealing and the concealing func-
tioned together to help give his work its special character.

When we study the influence of defensive work in Shelley, when we study his ambivalences, when we apply psychoanalytic forms of criticism to his writing, we do not necessarily undermine his ideas or his vision. His self-portrayal as a Sensitive-Plant, a weak and helpless sufferer, a beautiful and ethereal Ariel, an "*ineffectual* angel, beating in the void his luminous wings in vain,"[13] is a reaction to intense inward aggression. This does not make the myth of Ariel or any of his ideals a mere screen or a sham. His unique imagery, his moral fervor, his belief in poetry, love, and passive resistance are no less valid and affecting for being placed in a complex human context. Where there is greatness, as Erik Erikson said, there is great conflict (245). I have studied Shelley's conflict with his own deep sources of energy, his impulses toward aggression and regression, and I have also discussed the ambivalence beneath his idealization of women and his disparagement of fathers. As Heinz Hartmann has said, a psychic defense against an instinctual drive can also function as an adaptation to the external world.[14] We can understand "adaptation" to include adding something of value to the world.

I would like to return to three particular elements of Shelley's vision that are involved in great psychic struggle and that also seem to me adaptive in this sense. One is the attempt he makes at a purification of vision. Shelley speaks strongly for our primal desires, but he also speaks for reflection and correction. So in *Laon and Cythna* he tries to purify the French Revolution of what impeded it from being fully creative. So too in *Alastor* and *The Triumph of Life*, in ambivalent and embattled ways, he tries by means of a self-reflective doubleness to submit his own vision to a purifying fire. And so in the stories of both Prometheus and Asia he tries to show corrective self-knowledge remaking and liberating blocked imaginings.

A second element is his attempt, often through a dialectic of defense, to satisfy both Dionysian impulses toward enchantment and the oceanic and Apollonian impulses toward the ego and its capacities for mastery. A full reading of Shelley will appreciate both tendencies and the varying interplay in his work of the active and the passive, continuity and autonomy, progression and regression. The extremity of the Dionysian impulse in Shelley is clear to most of his readers—and in much of today's literary criticism in general the ego is no hero—but I have also tried to show Shelley's high valuation of the ego as an organizing, directing, actively creating and mastering function, and I have tried to show in his writings a drama of the ego

responding to and wrestling with psychic impulses and ambiva-
lences.

A third element is his attempt to make creative use of regression.
Barbara Schapiro attacks Shelley for a failure to let go of "the glow-
ing dream of the lost harmony and oneness with the mother";
Wordsworth, on the other hand, "is able to confront the loss and in-
tegrate it into a larger, more mature vision of experience" (30). "The
most successful Romantic poems," she writes, "display the effort in-
volved in resisting a regressive tendency toward narcissistic idealiza-
tion, fusion, and dissolution" (32). The strength of regressive fantasy
is as controversial for a modern audience as any element in Shelley. I
have argued that Shelley does, in part, resist it, that the interaction
between regression and resistance to it is a central characteristic of
his imagination. Here, however, I would like to stress the importance
and value of regressive energy in his work. We can value the warmth
and depth of Wordsworth, his consoling power and his wisdom; like
Freud, he teaches us how to live with loss. We can also value the ex-
hilaration and high imaginings of Shelley, and much of what is exhil-
arating in Shelley is owing to regressive energy. "I am one of those
whom nothing will fully satisfy," he wrote to Leigh Hunt, "but who
am ready to be partially satisfied by all that is practicable" (*L*, 2:153).
Here is a refusal to give up the dream of lost harmony; here too is re-
gression in the service of the ego. Without such regression there
would be no aspiration. Without regressive fantasy, this concluding
passage from the *Lines written among the Euganean Hills* with its chas-
tened, bittersweet vision of renovation, or rejuvenation, and of a har-
mony anterior to conflict and jealousy would not have been possible:
Shelley imagines "In the sea of Life and agony," a "calm and bloom-
ing cove" (336, 342),

> Where for me, and those I love,
> May a windless bower be built,
> Far from passion, pain, and guilt,
> In a dell 'mid lawny hills,
> Which the wild sea-murmur fills.
> (343–47)

In this maternal enclosure,

> We may live so happy there,
> That the Spirits of the Air,

> Envying us, may even entice
> To our healing Paradise
> The polluting multitude;
> But their rage would be subdued
> By that clime divine and calm,
> And the winds whose wings rain balm.
>
> (352–59)

Anger is finally overcome, and so is separation, as the air is filled with the primal love

> which heals all strife
> Circling, like the breath of life,
> All things in that sweet abode
> With its own mild brotherhood.
>
> (366–69)

To the "whisperings musical" in nature, the "inspired soul" adds "its own deep melodies" (363–65),

> and soon
> Every sprite beneath the moon
> Would repent its envy vain,
> And the earth grow young again.
>
> (370–73)

Notes

1. Keats, Letter to Benjamin Bailey, November 22, 1817, *Letters of Keats*, 1:185.

2. Blake, "Proverbs of Hell," *The Marriage of Heaven and Hell*, pl. 8, line 33.

3. Arnold, "Shelley," 327; Schapiro, *The Romantic Mother*, 1–32.

4. Pottle, "The Case of Shelley," 291; Arnold, "Shelley," 327.

5. Among other Shelley studies that use a psychological approach and are sympathetic to his idealism are the following: Herbert Read, "In Defence of Shelley" (236–64); Leon Waldoff, "The Father-Son Conflict in *Prometheus Unbound*"; Christine Gallant, *Shelley's Ambivalence*; and Stuart Sperry, *Shelley's Major Verse*. James Bieri's *Percy Bysshe Shelley: A Biography*, too, makes use of numerous psychological concepts within a context of respect for Shelley's idealism. Bieri sets that idealism within a "unique, complex personality" (1:290) and a labyrinthine daily experience consumed with financial and publishing dealings, evasions of creditors, illnesses and drugs, panic attacks, tension-filled personal and sexual relationships, and nearly constant moves from place to place.

6. Sperry, *Shelley's Major Verse*, 106.

7. Rolland, Letter to Freud, December 5, 1927, *Selected Letters of Romain Rolland*, 86–88. See Freud, *Civilization and its Discontents*, SE, 21:64–73, and, for uterine regression, Sandor Ferenczi, *Thalassa*, 44–59, 81–95. Freud wrote that he could not find the oceanic feeling in himself but that it persisted in many people throughout their lives and appeared in religious feeling, "the height of being in love" (66), and pathology. Several authors have treated in detail the intriguing Freud-Rolland correspondence, their intellectual and personal relationship, and their debate on mysticism and the oceanic feeling: David James Fisher, "Sigmund Freud and Romain Rolland: The Terrestrial Animal and his Great Oceanic Friend"; Martin Wangh, "The Genetic Sources of Freud's Difference with Romain Rolland on the Matter of Religious Feelings"; Henri and Madeleine Vermorel, *Sigmund Freud et Romain Rolland: Correspondance, 1923–1936*; and William B. Parsons, "The Oceanic Feeling Revisited." The Vermorels call the first chapter of *Civilization and its Discontents* a dialogue with Rolland (335) and write that Rolland is Freud's "interlocuteur imaginaire" in his analysis of the "malaise dans la culture" (345). Wangh finds that Freud's resistance to Rolland's concept of the oceanic feeling—he said it "left

me no peace" (July 14, 1929, *Letters of Freud*, 388)—is rooted in his own deep sense of "a mystifying, destructive mother-figure, the inexorable representative of an evil Fate"; hence, his elevation of and strong identification with a rationality identified as masculine and paternal (Wangh, 282–83). Parsons makes an interesting distinction between transient mystical states and what Rolland meant by the oceanic feeling proper, a prolonged state, a feeling that he was never without; Parsons also calls that state not a regression but a mature achievement. We might think in this context of Wordsworth, who associates "the first / Poetic spirit of our human life" with the early mother-child bond, a spirit "In most abated or suppressed," but in some "Pre-eminent till death" (*The Prelude*, 2.260–61, 263, 265). In *Hymn to Intellectual Beauty*, Shelley describes a state of elation and connectedness, much like the oceanic feeling, as an increasingly infrequent visitation in his life. Whether it manifests itself intermittently or continuously, as a survival of the archaic or an achievement of maturity, however, the oceanic feeling is rooted in the relationship with the early mother and subject to any ambivalence about that relationship.

8. Róheim, *The Gates of the Dream*, 545. Freud did claim to Rolland that he was using the term *regression* purely descriptively (January 19, 1930, *Letters of Freud*, 393).

9. Rolland, *Selected Letters*, 88; "riche et bienfaisante énergie," H. and M. Vermorel, *Sigmund Freud et Romain Rolland*, 304.

10. It was that need for a father that Freud posed against Rolland's oceanic sensation of eternity as the true source of religious feeling and the deepest need of childhood (*SE*, 21:72).

11. Sperry offers a brief account of the "tortured" relationship that Shelley had in adolescence with both his parents in *Shelley's Major Verse*, 6–12; more details can be found in Bieri, vol. 1, passim.

12. See, for example, Kris, *Psychoanalytic Explorations in Art*, 60–63, 167–69, 177, 312–13; Róheim, *The Gates of the Dream*, 1–4, 101, 116–21, 545–46; Mahler and McDevitt, "The Separation-Individuation Process and Identity Formation," 31–33; Chasseguet-Smirgel, 283–84; Hartmann, "Notes on the Theory of Sublimation," in *Essays on Ego Psychology*, 226–27. Hartmann speaks of "*progressive* and *regressive* adaptations" in *Ego Psychology and the Problem of Adaptation*, 36. See Gallant (73–74) for her thoughts, based on Kris and also Jung, about the positive possibilities of regression.

13. *Catalogue of the Phenomena of Dreams, As Connecting Sleeping and Waking*, which does not appear in the Bodleian Manuscripts but was published by Mary Shelley in P. B. Shelley, *Essays, Letters from Abroad, Translations, and Fragments* (1840), 1:248–51.

14. The quotation follows Clark, *Shelley's Prose*, 185–86, except in the title and one instance of wording. Clark uses the title *A Treatise on Morals*, while Ingpen and Peck follow Mary Shelley (*Essays, Letters from Abroad*, vol. 1) in dividing this and related fragments into two groups, *Speculations on Metaphysics* and *Speculations on Morals* (Ingpen and Peck, vol. 7). Throughout this study, I follow the title used by E. B. Murray, who considers the fragments "parts of a single work-in-progress," "Shelley's potential *magnum opus*" (*Bod. Shelley*, 4, pt. 1:xvii). Also, for "open eyes of day," which Clark follows previous editors in printing, I substitute "open light of day," from Bod. MS. c. 4, f. 184r, in *Bod. Shelley*, 4, pt. 1:192–93; also 13:164–65.

15. Blake, "The Book of Urizen," pl. 22, line 46. Blake developed the motif of Urizen's exploration of his dens in *The Four Zoas*, "Night the Sixth."

16. Heinrich Heine, quoted and translated in "On Narcissism," *SE*, 14:85. The original is "Erschaffend wurde ich gesund," from *Schöpfungslieder*, 7.8, in Heine, *Neue Gedichte*, ed. Elisabeth Genton (1983), vol. 2 of *Historisch-kritische Gesamtausgabe der Werke*, ed. Manfred Windfuhr (Hamburg: Hoffman und Campe, 1973–97), 63.

17. Wordsworth, *Prospectus to the Recluse*, lines 47–58, in *Poetical Works of Wordsworth*, 590; Blake, *A Vision of the Last Judgment*, in *Complete Poetry and Prose of Blake*, 555.

18. Katerina Clark and Michael Holquist, *Mikhail Bakhtin*, 206.

19. Meissner, 163. For the concept of unconscious fantasy, see Jacob Arlow, "Unconscious Fantasy and Disturbances of Conscious Experience."

20. Southey, *The Correspondence of Robert Southey with Caroline Bowles*, ed. Edward Dowden (Dublin, 1881), 52; quoted in M. H. Abrams, "English Romanticism: The Spirit of the Age," 31.

21. Hazlitt, *The Spirit of the Age*, in *Works*, 11:87; quoted in Abrams, "The Spirit of the Age," 27.

22. Peacock, *Nightmare Abbey*, 11, 13.

23. Frye, *The Secular Scripture*, 35–39.

24. McGann, *The Romantic Ideology*, 134, 133.

25. Yeats, *"Prometheus Unbound,"* in *Essays and Introductions*, 419.

INTRODUCTION: ADAM'S DREAM

1. Wordsworth, *Prospectus to the Recluse*, lines 47–48, 50–51, in *Poetical Works of Wordsworth*, 590.

2. Wordsworth, *The Ruined Cottage*, MS. D, lines 374–75.

3. Wordsworth, *Ecclesiastical Sonnets*, pt. 3, sonnet 1, lines 1, 5, 9, in *Poetical Works*, 346.

4. Freud, "On Narcissism," *SE*, 14:98.

5. Christine Froula writes that "Through the dream of the rib Adam both enacts a parody of birth and gains possession of the womb by claiming credit for woman herself," and that Milton in his general portrayal of creativity, both God's and his own, in the poem shows the same appropriation of female power (332, 338). Using Froula, Margaret Homans discusses the ramifications of Adam's dream in *Frankenstein* and *Alastor* (104–19).

6. Harrison, *Prolegomena*, 648.

7. *Milton: Complete Poetry*, 1044.

8. For some analogues to this episode, see *The Works of Edmund Spenser: A Variorum Edition*, 1:267.

9. The phrase is Gayatri Chakravorty Spivak's in her preface to Derrida, *Of Grammatology*, xix.

10. Wordsworth, the 1850 *Prelude*, 6.595.

11. Blake, *The Marriage of Heaven and Hell*, pl. 3.

CHAPTER 1. MAGICIAN OF THE ENLIGHTENMENT

1. Shelley, *Letters*, 1:266, 99, 101; see also 303.

2. Bieri, calling the romances "among [Shelley's] most important self-revelatory writings" (1:112), comments on the impact on Shelley of his father's older, illegitimate child (1:27, 54, 117, 126, 151, 207, 393; see also Bieri, "Shelley's Older Brother").

3. Pp. 123, 133, 198. Quotations from the two romances are taken from the Arno Press edition, *Zastrozzi* and *St. Irvyne*. The romances are also available in vol. 5 of *The Complete Works of Percy Bysshe Shelley*, ed. Ingpen and Peck. The two works were published in 1810, although *St. Irvyne* is dated 1811; see *R*, xvii.

4. *Zastrozzi*, 94–95.

5. While quotations from the poetry of *Queen Mab* are taken from Reiman and Fraistat, quotations from Shelley's notes are taken from Everest and Matthews, vol. 1, where they are given completely.

6. Shelley gives the original from book 4 of *De rerum naturae*: "Et arctis / Religionum animos nodis exsolvere pergo" (*R*, 16).

7. "To accept Necessity," Basil Willey writes, "meant to accept the scientific view of the universe; it meant the acceptance of those unalterable laws which preserve the stars from wrong, and the rejection of superstition and the supernatural." *The Eighteenth Century Background*, 178.

8. Pope, *An Essay on Man*, Epistle 1.155–56.

9. Letter to Shelley, December 10, 1812, in *Letters of Shelley*, 1:341.

10. Milton, *Paradise Lost*, 3.1–55; Plato, *Euthyphro . . . Phaedrus*, trans. Fowler, 485.

11. Wordsworth, *Ode: Intimations of Immortality from Recollections of Early Childhood*, 84.

12. "The notes will be long philosophical, & Anti Christian," he wrote, "—this will be unnoticed in a Note" (*L*, 1:361).

13. See Richard Holmes, 201. Kenneth Neill Cameron writes that Shelley uses the style of "a typical Southey narrative—complete with the magic element of a fairy queen, a spirit, and a trip through the stars in a celestial chariot . . . to ease his readers by degrees into the radical propaganda which forms the core of the poem." *The Young Shelley*, 245.

14. See the rejection in the *Queen Mab* notes of inspiration, enthusiasm, divine revelation, and any mode of knowledge other than "reason and common sense" (*E*, 1:403).

15. David Duff writes that Southey's romantic "Thalaba style" had originally been associated in hostile criticism with that author's then-left-wing politics, and that Shelley was recovering the politics of that style "by linking it with revolutionary subject-matter" (76).

16. Hartman, "False Themes and Gentle Minds," in *Beyond Formalism*, 283–97; Parker, *Inescapable Romance*, 159–67.

17. Keats, *The Eve of St. Agnes*, 41. Hartman, "Romantic Poetry and the Genius Loci," in *Beyond Formalism*, 319. Hartman describes a "romantic struggle with Romance" and writes that, like Milton, some of the Romantics "assured the survival of Romance by the very quality of [their] resistance to it" ("False Themes and Gentle Minds," in *Beyond Formalism*, 285, 297).

18. Quoting Frye (*The Secular Scripture*, 163), Duff writes that "In its 'polarizing between two worlds, one desirable and one hateful,' Shelley's entire political vision

in *Queen Mab* is structured as a romance, being dialectical, teleological, and concerned with the fulfilment of desires" (112).

19. Wordsworth, *Expostulation and Reply*, 24.

20. Rolland, *Selected Letters*, 86–88.

CHAPTER 2. PROTEUS AND MUTABILITY

1. Mary Quinn contrasts the theme of "solitary idealism and death" in the title poem with the "confident public prophecy" of *The Daemon*, in "The Daemon of the World," 763–64.

2. Mary Shelley, "Note on the Early Poems," *H*, 527.

3. Huntington MS. HM 2177, f. *27v reverso, in *Manuscripts of the Younger Romantics: Shelley*, 4:298–99; also in Forman, *Note Books*, 2:113.

4. See Yvonne Carothers, "*Alastor*: Shelley Corrects Wordsworth" (22), and Bloom, *The Visionary Company* (285–87), for discussions of the theme of a struggle with the first generation of the Romantics in the *Alastor* volume.

5. John Frosch summarizes the psychoanalytic concept of the family romance in "Transference Derivatives of the Family Romance," 503–6. See Freud, "Family Romances," *SE*, 9:235–41, and, for the rescue fantasy, "A Special Type of Choice of Object Made by Men," *SE*, 11:172–73; and Rank, *The Myth of the Birth of the Hero*, 65–69, 72.

6. Thomas Medwin, *Medwin's Conversations of Lord Byron*, 194.

7. Shelley, *Letters*, 2:195. In "On Genius and Common Sense," Hazlitt described Shakespeare positively as a chameleon and a Proteus. He contrasts ordinary genius, which "just the reverse of the cameleon . . . does not borrow, but lend its colour to all about it," to the genius of Shakespeare, "the Proteus of human intellect." *Essay 5, Table Talk*, in *Works*, 8: 42–43.

8. See Kim Blank, *Wordsworth's Influence on Shelley*, for an extended discussion of Shelley's poetic relationship with Wordsworth in the context of his disappointment with his own father and his search for other fathers, as well as his disillusionment with authority figures in general (e.g., 30, 144). See also Bieri's description of Shelley's personal relationship with Southey, developing from idealization to a struggle "to maintain [that] idealized image" and finally to "inevitable disillusionment" (1:219). Discussing the family romance, John Frosch writes of adults who project family-romance fantasies on others "by overidealizing them, only to become disillusioned and turn on these with resentment and anger." *Psychodynamic Psychiatry*, 1:175.

CHAPTER 3. THE QUEST FOR THE VEILED MAID

1. Quoted in Ulmer (48), from *The Eclectic Review* (October 1816), reprinted in *The Unextinguished Hearth: Shelley and His Contemporary Critics*, ed. Newman Ivey White (Durham, NC: Duke University Press, 1938), 107.

2. Keats, *Dear Reynolds, as last night I lay in bed*, 67, 96–97.

3. For Jay Macpherson, for example, "His pursuit of the maiden through the external world is delusive and life-devouring" (84). For Andrew Cooper, his ideal-

ism is "suicidal" (166). For Margaret Homans, his beloved is "constructed out of [his] own visionary narcissism" (106). For Diane Hoeveler, he suffers from "fear and loathing of women" (56). For William Veeder, he expresses Shelley's own misogynistic wish to escape from women and the female body (56, 97–98, 107–8, 240).

4. Sperry, *Shelley's Major Verse*, 40.

5. Wordsworth's original text reads "they whose hearts" and ends with a period, not an exclamation point. *The Excursion*, 1.500–502; also *The Ruined Cottage*, MS. D, lines 96–98.

6. Wordsworth, *The Ruined Cottage*, 487.

7. Richard Cronin (92) and Bryan Cooper (65), among others, notice the absence of fire. The Poet's life is later figured as a "decaying flame" (247), and Cooper portrays the Poet as a flame consuming itself.

8. *Shelley*, 3–41, esp. 11, 19–21. Readers have discussed the presence of Wordsworth in the poem in various ways. Keach, who focuses in "Obstinate Questionings" on Shelley's use of the *Immortality Ode*, stresses not Shelley's opposition to Wordsworth but his intensifying of Wordsworth's position as "an elegist of the questing narcissistic imagination" (42). Mueschke and Griggs identify the Poet with Wordsworth, and Blank associates the Poet with one of Wordsworth's characters, the Solitary in *The Excursion*. Blank notes that "The figure who for Wordsworth was an antagonist becomes for Shelley more of a protagonist" (90), and that in *Alastor* Shelley is "figuratively 'killing' his Wordsworthian hero in order to perhaps establish his own poetic identity" (54).

9. See Tilottama Rajan (76) for various similarities between Poet and Narrator.

10. Rousseau, *Confessions*, 142.

11. Wordsworth, "Whither is fled the visionary gleam?" in *Immortality Ode*, 56.

12. Wasserman discusses Romantic wandering in the context of *Sehnsucht* in *Shelley*, 28.

13. Eliade, *Patterns in Comparative Religion*, 100–101, 231–33, 374–79.

14. Mary Frosch develops that comparison in detail in *Narcissus: The Negative Double*, 124–41.

15. Hartman, *Wordsworth's Poetry*, 33–69.

16. Mary Frosch argues that in the description of the forest through which the Poet travels "Shelley's use of ivy, a Bacchic emblem of fertility, recalls Ovid's peculiar placement of the Narcissus myth between myths about Bacchus, implying that Narcissus's sterility is a negation or reversal of Bacchus's fertility" (160).

17. Wordsworth, *The Ruined Cottage*, MS. D, 70. See 362–75 on the strength of Margaret's imagination and its effect on Armytage and 502–6 on the narrator's new powers of imagination in his sense of Margaret's presence still surviving in the ruins of her home and garden.

18. Ulmer writes that in the poem "the imagination inherently resists socialization" (27).

19. See Peacock's discussion of his suggestion in his *Memoirs of Shelley*, in *Works of Thomas Love Peacock*, 8:100. *Alastor* in Greek means both "the Avenging Deity" and "one who suffers from divine vengeance, a sinner, evil-doer, accursed and polluted man" (*Liddell and Scott's Greek-English Lexicon*, abridged ed. [Oxford: Clarendon Press, 1963], 31). Stuart Curran discusses the doubleness of the word in *Annus*

Mirabilis, 21. In his *Memoirs*, Peacock corrected the assumption that *Alastor* was the name of the hero, but according to the meaning of the word, it would not be wrong to call him by that name.

20. "Obstinate questionings," Wordsworth, *Immortality Ode*, 145.

21. See Hartman, "False Themes and Gentle Minds," in *Beyond Formalism*, esp. 297; Bloom, "The Internalization of Quest Romance," in *The Ringers in the Tower*, esp. 15.

CHAPTER 4. DOUBLES AND SIMILITUDES

1. This piece, which Hutchinson follows Garnett (40) in printing as an original poem, is actually a translation from the *Tesoretto* by Brunetto Latini; see Bod. MS. e. 7, back pastedown and 155–59, in *Bod. Shelley*, 16:250–51, 158–63, with editorial comments of Reiman and Neth, p. 159.

2. Shelley, *Letters*, 1:208.

3. Gallant (64) and Kelvin Everest, in "Shelley's Doubles: An Approach to *Julian and Maddalo*," have drawn on Freud and Rank to discuss Shelleyan doubles as products of guilt.

4. See Rank, *The Double*, 85: "The thought of death is rendered supportable by assuring oneself of a second life, after this one, as a double." In "The Uncanny," Freud calls the "invention of doubling . . . a preservation against extinction." *SE*, 17:235.

5. Blake, Letter to Cumberland, April 12, 1827, *Complete Poetry and Prose of Blake*, 783.

6. On the negativism of skepticism, see Wasserman, *Shelley*, 284. Shelley himself writes in the *Defence*, "Whilst the sceptic destroys gross superstitions, let him spare to deface, as some of the French writers have defaced, the eternal truths charactered upon the imaginations of men" (*R*, 529).

7. Thomas Weiskel writes of this passage that "The 'I' can 'love' not merely in spite of the illusion but because of it" (155).

8. Plato, *Euthyphro . . . Phaedrus*, 266 B–C, 535.

9. I discuss another example of the dialectic of defense in a separate article, "Psychological Dialectic in Shelley's 'Song of Apollo' and 'Song of Pan.'"

10. See, for example, Mahler, "On the Significance of the Normal Separation-Individuation Phase," esp. 165–67; Mahler and McDevitt, "The Separation-Individuation Process and Identity Formation" and "Object Constancy, Individuality, and Internalization"; and Mahler, Pine, and Bergman, *The Psychological Birth of the Human Infant*, 95–108.

11. Milton Miller, in his biographical essay "Manic-Depressive Cycles of the Poet Shelley," observes in Shelley a wish to merge with the mother and, at the same time, a dread of such merger. See especially 90–92.

12. Kohut, *The Analysis of the Self*, 116–18. Gallant (19) quotes D. W. Winnicott: "The precursor of the mirror is the mother's face" ("Mirroring-role of Mother and Family in Child Development," in *Playing and Reality*, 111). For another view of mirroring, see Anthony Wilden's exposition of Lacan's famous mirror stage in the commentary accompanying his translation of Lacan's *Speech and Language in Psychoanalysis*, 159–77; the mother is rarely mentioned explicitly in those eighteen

pages. That is also so in Lacan's "The Mirror Stage as Formative of the Function of the I." Lacan is interested in the beginnings of the ego in the child's "jubilant assumption of his specular image" while he is "still sunk in his motor incapacity and nursling dependence" (2). Peter Sacks, in *The English Elegy*, has a fine discussion of the Lacanian mirror stage, stressing the dyadic character of the child's relation to its image (9–10), and he applies the concept usefully throughout his book. Among those who have discussed mirroring in *Alastor*, William Crisman is particularly thorough; he writes, "In the poem's imagery, apparent mirrors go bad and good mirrors appear where they are least expected" (140). Blank calls mirroring "the central image in *Alastor*" (105).

13. In *Keats and the Sublime*, Stuart Ende uses Freud's concept of narcissism to study a conflict between "two incompatible desires" in Keats: "to be sublimed in the ecstasy that is poetic fire, and to retain one's sentient being" (xiv). This conflict is psychologically similar to the one I discuss between impulses toward differentiation and merger. Particularly suggestive on the need to defend against the seemingly omnipotent mother of early childhood—and not only to retain one's sentient being but to develop the sense of a separate being in the first place—is Janine Chasseguet-Smirgel in "Freud and Female Sexuality." A central issue in Richard Onorato's classic of Freudian literary criticism, *The Character of the Poet: Wordsworth in "The Prelude,"* is the interplay between Wordsworth's quest for autonomy and his desire to recover the early relationship with his mother, who died before he was eight; see, for example, 84, 119.

14. See Irvine Schiffer on the "active recreative repetition compulsion" (38–45).

15. Blake, "Golgonooza is named Art & Manufacture by mortal men." *Milton*, pl. 24, line 50. For the making of the semblances and the saving of the "spectres," see *The Four Zoas*, book 7, p. 98, lines 8–24, in *Complete Poetry and Prose of Blake*, 370.

16. Wordsworth, *I wandered lonely as a cloud*, 17–18.

17. Coleridge, *Biographia Literaria*, ch. 13, in *Works*, 7, pt. 1:304.

Chapter 5. The Sole Self

1. While Clark "deliberately adopted the more accurate Latin form, *Colosseum*" (224), I follow the manuscript spelling in Bod. MS. c. 5, f. 12r; for this passage, see c. 5, f. 16v; *Bod. Shelley*, 22, pt. 2:106–7, 124–25.

2. Hartmann, "Contribution to the Metapsychology of Schizophrenia," in *Essays on Ego Psychology*, 192. As Hartmann and others have pointed out, when Freud spoke of the ego in "On Narcissism," he still meant the self or person and not yet one of the three systems—ego, id, and superego—of the structural point of view.

3. Kohut, "Forms and Transformations of Narcissism," 450.

4. Ibid., 451.

5. Ibid., 456.

6. See Kohut, *The Analysis of the Self*, 297–98.

7. Blake, *A Vision of the Last Judgment*, in *Complete Poetry and Prose*, 560.

8. Keats's famous term for the Wordsworthian imagination. Letter to Richard Woodhouse, October 27, 1818, *Letters of Keats*, 1:387.

9. Mahler, *The Psychological Birth of the Human Infant,* 101.

10. Shelley's written words, according to Mary's note, *C,* 194.

CHAPTER 6. THE VOYAGE TO THE SOURCE

1. Hutchinson follows Richard Garnett's reading of these lines (Shelley, *Relics,* 12). In their transcription of lines with many canceled and unclear words, Reiman and Neth read, "Return into the quiver of the Sun / Or could" and "without a strain." Since Shelley canceled "unstained" and "unspotted" and, at least in the facsimile, the "r" in "strain" is not evident, Garnett's "without a stain" makes sense. In the colon at the end of the penultimate line, I follow Reiman and Neth; Hutchinson has a period, and Garnett has a comma. See Bod. MS. e. 7, p. 261 reverso, in *Bod. Shelley,* 16:244–45.

2. For the sacred mountain as the body of the mother in early religion and myth, see Erich Neumann, 44–46 and 273, and Anne Baring and Jules Cashford, 184.

3. See Schapiro, who quotes lines 602–6 to illustrate the association of the moon and the breast (21).

4. Bryan Cooper discusses the imagery of waste as "squandering" (66–67).

5. Wordsworth, *The Prelude,* 6.608; Blake, *The Marriage of Heaven and Hell,* pl. 16.

6. Freud, "On Narcissism," *SE,* 14:100, 89.

7. Huntington MS. HM 2177, f. *19r reverso–*20r reverso, in *Manuscripts of the Younger Romantics: Shelley,* 4:392–97; also in Forman, *Note Books,* 2:101–2. See also Mary Shelley's transcription of the full note, with some differences from the Huntington notebook entry, in Bod. MS. d. 6, pp. 109–10, in *Bod. Shelley,* 22, pt. 1:256–59, with Alan Weinberg's textual discussion, 37–38. The line occurs in Oedipus's second speech in *Oedipus Rex.*

8. Mary Shelley's transcription has "roam," instead of "wander"; *Bod. Shelley,* 22, pt. 1:258–59.

9. Huntington 2177, f. *20r reverso, in *Manuscripts of the Younger Romantics: Shelley,* 4:392–93; also in Forman, *Note Books,* 2:102. Mary Shelley does not include "The dim ghost . . . born" in her transcription; see *Bod. Shelley,* 22, pt. 1: 38, 258–59.

10. Róheim, *The Gates of the Dream,* 543–44. Sandor Ferenczi writes that "the impetuous curiosity to know everything" is one expression of our desire to sustain the illusion of omnipotence, "which at some time or other—even if only in the womb —[we] really partook of." "Stages in the Development of the Sense of Reality," 202, 197.

11. R. E. Latham, introduction to Lucretius, *The Nature of the Universe,* 14. See Virgil, *Georgics,* 2.490; *Bucolica et Georgica,* intro. and notes T. E. Page (London: Macmillan, 1965), 56, 284.

12. Bacon, preface to *The New Organon,* in *Works,* 8:64; *New Atlantis,* in *Works,* 5:398.

13. The poem has also been called *Ye hasten to the dead,* as in Harvard MS. Eng. 258.2: Quire 7: f. 6v = p. 151, in *Manuscripts of the Younger Romantics: Shelley,* 5:148. "Dead" and "grave" are both canceled in the Pierpont Morgan Library fair copy, M.A., f. 3223, f. 2v, in *Manuscripts of the Younger Romantics: Shelley,* 8:314–15.

14. Bod. MS. e. 8, p. 70, in *Bod. Shelley,* 6:226–27. See Rogers, 16–18.

15. *Wilt thou forget the happy hours* was published by Mary Shelley as *The Past* (1824); Hutchinson uses her title (553).

16. Hughes, "Blake and Shelley: Beyond the Uroboros," 82.

CHAPTER 7. PSYCHOSEXUAL PATTERNS IN *Alastor*

1. See Ernst Robert Curtius on the *puer senex* (98–101).

2. The dash appears in Mary Shelley's 1824 and 1839 editions, but the manuscript has a comma. See Shelley, *Posthumous Poems, 1824* (175), *The Poetical Works of Percy Bysshe Shelley* (4:158), and Bod. MS. e. 17, p. 197 reverso, in *Bod. Shelley*, 19:348–49.

3. Jones, *On the Nightmare*, 97.

4. Brisman, *Romantic Origins*, 142–43.

5. Ibid., 144.

6. Alan Richardson writes that, with some exceptions, sibling incest is characteristic of Romanticism, while parent-child incest is characteristic of Gothic literature (738). Bieri discusses Shelley's intense relationship with his sisters, 1:54–56.

7. See Bieri's discussion of Lady Mount Cashell (Mrs. Mason) (2:183–84). He cites Shelley's comment about her to Hunt: "You will think it my fate either to find or to imagine some lady of 45, very unprejudiced and philosophical, who has entered deeply into the best and selectest spirit of the age, with enchanting manners, and a disposition to like me, in every town I inhabit" (*L*, 2:180).

8. Blank relates the wind to the breath of the Veiled Maid and both to the power of poetic inspiration (196–97).

9. See Holmes, 305–6.

10. Freud, *Three Essays on the Theory of Sexuality*, *SE*, 7:226.

11. Freud, *Three Essays on the Theory of Sexuality*, *SE*, 7:194–95.

12. George M. A. Hanfmann, "Sphinx," in *Oxford Classical Dictionary*, 856.

13. See Jung, *Symbols of Transformation*, in *Works*, 5:182. See 179–83 for the sphinx as the Terrible Mother.

14. See Róheim, *The Riddle of the Sphinx*, 1–9, and *The Gates of the Dream*, 529–44.

15. See Baker (73) for a list of Shelleyan studies of sources and analogues of the serpent-eagle figure, which we will also encounter in *Laon and Cythna* and *Prometheus Unbound*.

16. Harrison, *Themis*, 527–28.

17. See chapter 3, note 19, above; H. J. Rose, "*Alastor*," in *Oxford Classical Dictionary*, 27: *Eumenides*, line 236, and *Agamemnon*, line 1501 (lines in the Greek original).

18. Brisman (*Milton's Poetry of Choice*, 140), discussing Shelley's relationship to Milton in *Prometheus Unbound*, quotes Peter Blos: "Nothing can be accomplished without one's coming to terms with the father, or rather, with his image or object representation." *On Adolescence: A Psychoanalytic Interpretation* (1962; New York: Free Press, 1966), 156–57.

19. See Holmes, 69–70, 111, 255.

20. Freud, "A Special Type of Choice of Object Made by Men," *SE*, 11:172–73.

21. Euripides, *Hippolytus*, trans. David Grene, lines 1147–50.

22. Róheim, *The Riddle of the Sphinx*, 8.

23. Wordsworth, *Ode: Intimations of Immortality from Recollections of Early Childhood*, 190, 204, 207.

CHAPTER 8. THE GLORY OF PASSIVITY
AND THE GLORY OF ACTION

1. Wordsworth, *Expostulation and Reply*, 24.

CHAPTER 9. REVOLUTION OF THE GOLDEN CITY

1. My discussion is based on the original version, *Laon and Cythna*, as edited in Everest and Matthews by Jack Donovan (2:30–260). At his publisher's insistence, Shelley toned down *Laon and Cythna*, altering sixty-three explicit references to incest and atheism. In the revised version, these topics merely become implicit, as when the heroine, no longer the hero's sister, becomes an orphan growing up with him in his father's house. But originally Shelley was interested in being defiant, not suggestive. To compare the original and revised versions, see Donovan's footnotes or Hutchinson, 886–93.

2. Shelley, *Letters*, 1:508. The letter is dated September 29, 1816. Shelley began writing *Laon and Cythna* about seven months later. Both Christine Gallant and Charles Robinson discuss Shelley's feelings of competitiveness with Byron throughout their books; see, for example, Robinson, 139–41, and Gallant, 49–50.

3. This quote from an anonymous reviewer appears in Shelley, *Letters*, 2:127, footnote 4. See the letter to his publisher, Ollier, on the same page for Shelley's complaint about the accusation that he has imitated Wordsworth. Blank discusses Shelley's anxieties of influence in both this preface and the preface to *Prometheus Unbound* (10–18). J. Andrew Hubbell studies Shelley's attempt to undo Wordsworth's oedipal priority on the particular theme of the French Revolution, which Wordsworth had dealt with three years earlier in *The Excursion*; Hubbell writes that Shelley in *Laon and Cythna* develops a symbolic conflict of youth and age to try to show that "revolution is intuitively understood by youth, and forgotten under the influence of corrupting maturity" (176).

4. In different ways, Douglas Thorpe and Deborah Gutschera find doubleness at the heart of the poem. Thorpe, pointing out several instances of retelling in the poem, writes of the work's retelling of history as poetry in an "imaginative transformation" (217). Gutschera sees in the poem's structure a principle of "reenactment," in which, like the battle of eagle and snake in the narrative, "the drama is replayed again and again by different speakers" and will continue "until the battle has been won" (125).

5. In *The Solitary Reaper*, Wordsworth's character also sings in a strange language, and, although she is not on a shore, oceanic imagery is present: "the Vale profound / Is overflowing with the sound" (7–8). See Baker (72), for other possible sources of the woman on the shore.

6. Rogers, 110–11. "Demon Lover" appears above lines 307–8: "Then she arose, and smiled on me with eyes / Serene yet sorrowing, like that planet fair." Bod. MS. e. 19, p. 31, in *Bod. Shelley*, 13:66–67.

7. See Jane Harrison, *Themis*, 260–303, 394. She writes of the "association of mother, snake, child, and the wealth of harvest fruits" (286).

8. Rogers's translation, *Shelley at Work*, 100.

9. As David Duff writes, the epigraph calls attention to the poem's primary theme, the problem of how to reach paradise (210).

10. See Sperry, *Shelley's Major Verse*, 56.

11. Bloom, *A Map of Misreading*, 19.

12. On the character and biographical background of the hermit, see Holmes, 25–28; Sperry, *Shelley's Major Verse*, 53–55, and "The Sexual Theme in Shelley's *The Revolt of Islam*," 43–45; and Bieri, 1:93–97. The presumed original of both the hermit and Zonoras in *Athanase* is Dr. James Lind, whom Shelley knew while at Eton. Bieri sees Lind as "both psychotherapist and medical healer of [the] venereal disease" that Bieri, like Nora Crook and Derek Guiton in *Shelley's Venomed Melody*, believes was an important factor in Shelley's life (97).

13. On the French festivals, see Emmet Kennedy, *A Cultural History of the French Revolution*, 330–38, 343–44. Gerald McNiece discusses Shelley's knowledge and poetic use of the festivals, 113–25, 204–5. See also Duff, 158.

14. On the phallic implications of magic horses, see Ernest Jones, *On the Nightmare*, 260, 269–71, 297–300.

15. John Donovan (86) notes the defiant parody of St. Paul: "Unto the pure all things are pure" (Titus 1:15).

16. As Ulmer writes, "Carrying a baby in her womb, Cythna is herself carried in a kind of womb" (67).

17. "I had no human fears," in *A slumber did my spirit seal*, 2.

18. Harrison, *Prolegomena*, 645–47.

19. See, for example, Baker, 65–66.

20. Henry H. Saylor, *Dictionary of Architecture* (New York: John Wiley, 1963), 52.

21. See Ulmer, 51, 57, 60, 72, 74, 75.

22. Sperry interprets Laon's hallucinatory devouring of Cythna as an act of introjection or identification; he understands it as embodying Laon's turbulent ambivalence toward her at this traumatic stage of his psychosexual development. *Shelley's Major Verse*, 52, 211.

23. Alan Richardson writes that Romantic treatments of sibling incest inevitably end in death, and that the death of *Laon and Cythna* is "uncomfortably reminiscent of the ritual deaths [for incest] described by Frazer in *Totemism and Exogamy*" ("The Dangers of Sympathy," 740, 750). John Donovan sees the lovers as "sacrificial victims" in a more positive sense: "Their incest has been the first half of a ritual that will ensure continuation of their essential being; the second . . . is their death" (85).

24. Holmes, 517. Nathaniel Brown is more specific and elaborate, seeing in Shelley generally an ideal of androgyny. Calling *The Revolt of Islam* "the most powerful feminist poem in the language" (181), he regards incest in the original version purely as a metaphor for the true kinship of the sexes (216).

25. John Donovan writes of the "violent and anarchic aspect of [Laon's] desire for Cythna" (58).

26. Bieri's discussion of Shelley's illegitimate older brother is suggestive in this context, although that brother would have shared the father, not the mother, with Shelley. See chapter 1, note 2, above.

27. Aeschylus, *The Libation Bearers*, trans. Lattimore, lines 527–33.

28. *The Libation Bearers*, lines 246–49.

29. "The Delphians were called Hyperboreans," writes Joseph Fontenrose, 431; see also 460–61 for the alternation of Apollo and Dionysos at Delphi.

30. Dawson, *The Unacknowledged Legislator*, 7–8; Nozick, *Anarchy, State, and Utopia* (New York: Basic Books, 1974), 308.

CHAPTER 10. *PROMETHEUS UNBOUND:* THE PROMETHEUS MYTH

1. Harrison, *Themis*, 456.

2. C. Kerényi, *Prometheus*, 27–28, and *The Gods of the Greeks*, 207.

3. Harrison, *Themis*, 454.

4. For Adalbert Kuhn, these energies are symbolically sexual (see Zillman, *Shelley's Prometheus Unbound: A Variorum Edition*, 723–24), as they are for Karl Abraham (197–99) and for Freud, in "The Acquisition and Control of Fire" (*SE*, 22:189–90). For Róheim, they are specifically oedipal; see *The Riddle of the Sphinx*, 253–54, 261.

5. Bachelard, *The Psychoanalysis of Fire*, 12.

6. Hesiod, *Theogony*, 145.

7. Kerényi, *Prometheus*, 50.

8. Ibid., 36–37.

9. Michael Grant, *Myths of the Greeks and Romans*, 186.

10. See Kerényi, *Prometheus*, 4–18, on Goethe's works on Prometheus.

11. Rousseau, *Discourse on the Sciences and Arts*, in *The First and Second Discourses*, trans. Gourevich, 14.

12. Kerényi, *Prometheus*, 100–101.

13. Harrison, *Themis*, 485.

14. Ibid., 453.

15. Kerényi, *Prometheus*, 101.

16. Graves, *The Greek Myths*, 148; Hesiod, *Theogony*, trans. Evelyn-White, 123. Graves points out that "Pandora" or "all-giving" was a title of the earth goddess Rhea.

17. I am following the famous reading of Bachofen in his discussion of "mother right" (158–61).

18. Kerényi, *Prometheus*, 90.

19. Barbara Gelpi writes of the "Father Gods functioning through a power first given and later withdrawn through the greater power of Mother Goddesses" (139).

20. Gelpi, 142–43; see Harrison, *Themis*, 393.

21. Wormhoudt, *The Demon Lover*, 89–90, 97.

22. See Gallant, who studies Shelley's ambivalence toward the mother from a Jungian and Kleinian point of view (13–14, passim).

23. See Janine Chasseguet-Smirgel's discussion of the "powerful maternal imago" that in the early childhood of both sexes is "envied and terrifying" (283). Using Bachofen's reading of *The Eumenides*, she writes that both "Athene, a woman, and Apollo, a man, band together to deny the maternal prerogatives" (284–85).

24. See Shelley, *Prometheus Unbound: A Lyrical Drama in Four Acts, with Other Poems* (1820); repr. in Shelley, *Poems Published in 1820*, ed. Hughes, 1. For the epigraph alone, see *R*, 206.

25. Kerényi, *The Heroes of the Greeks*, 300.

26. For an introduction to the chthonioi, see W. K. C. Guthrie, *The Greeks and their Gods*, 217–53.

27. Bloom, *Shelley's Mythmaking*, 46–48.

28. Bod. MS. e. 11, p. 115, in *Bod. Shelley*, 15:118–19. See Rogers, 66.

29. Wordsworth, *A slumber did my spirit seal*, 7–8; *The Ruined Cottage*, MS. D, 512.

30. Muller, quoted in Bachelard, *The Psychoanalysis of Fire*, 4.

31. Kerényi, *Prometheus*, 51.

Chapter 11. *Prometheus Unbound:* Act 1

1. I first outlined some of the ideas in the following four chapters on *Prometheus Unbound* in an article, "Aggression and Regression in *Prometheus Unbound*," in *Approaches to Teaching Shelley's Poetry*, ed. Spencer Hall.

2. Written in Mary Shelley's *Journal*, dated March 26, 1818, 1:200. Shelley began *Prometheus Unbound* in September 1818. Edward Dowden noted the resemblance of the journal description of the Alps to the setting of act 1, in *The Life of Percy Bysshe Shelley*, 2:189–90; see Zillman, 336. When I cite criticism or draft material that also appears in the widely available Zillman variorum, I give both the original location and the Zillman page.

3. Frye, *Anatomy of Criticism*, 148.

4. See Waldoff on Prometheus's masochism (88–90), and the "unconscious guilt and castration anxiety" (94) that keep him under Jupiter's tyranny.

5. Kerényi, *Prometheus*, 100–101. See also Hesiod, *Theogony*, 145, for the Horae.

6. See Frazer, *The New Golden Bough*, 3–4, 349.

7. Pottle, "The Role of Asia in the Dramatic Action of Shelley's *Prometheus Unbound*," 137.

8. In "Passive Resistance in Shelley," I study this pattern in *The Mask of Anarchy* and elsewhere in Shelley. See Andrew Stauffer, "Celestial Temper," for a general study, with illustrations of Shelleyan anger throughout the poetry, of Shelley's characteristic way of "staging anger's expression and then dispelling it" (154).

9. Rousseau, quoted by Derrida, 173; *Discourse on Inequality*, in *The First and Second Discourses*, 162.

10. Blake, *The Human Abstract* (*Songs of Experience*), 1–2; *The Book of Urizen*, pl. 25, lines 1, 3.

11. Adams, "The Four Elements in the *Prometheus Vinctus*," 100.

12. Bald, quoted in Zillman, 313; "Shelley's Mental Progress," in *Essays and Studies by Members of the English Association*, 13 (Oxford: Clarendon Press, 1928): 115.

13. Holland, quoted in Zillman, 44; "The Soul of Shelley," *The Western* 2 (1876): 157.

14. Scudder, p. L; see Zillman, 55.

15. Hughes, "Prometheus Made Capable Poet," 4.

16. In *The Secular Scripture*, Frye reminds us that the quest for the forgotten is a traditional romance motif: "A romance often begins with a break in consciousness or loss of memory" and ends with "the restoring of the broken current of memory," as in the sudden recognition of a character's true identity. "In the nineteenth

century," he continues, "theories about an unconscious mind that never really forgets anything were starting to be developed, and such a mind supplies a possible setting for the recovery of a lost memory" (145).

17. Harrison, *Themis*, 461–66.

18. Bush, *Mythology and the Romantic Tradition in English Poetry*, 146. More analytically, Bieri notes Shelley's "quest to replace [the] Field Place sisterhood" of his childhood, 1:132.

19. Bailey, quoted in Zillman, 405; "Prometheus in Poetry," in *The Continuity of Letters* (Oxford: Clarendon Press, 1923), 113.

20. Douglas Bush points out the Medea allusion in "Notes on Shelley," 299; cited by Zillman, 370.

21. See Milton, *Paradise Lost*, 6.853–66 and 1.215–19.

22. Blake, *Jerusalem*, pl. 43, lines 41, 46, 37.

23. Curran observes that the curse is both "revengeful and masochistic," *Annus Mirabilis*, 58.

24. Waldoff writes that Prometheus sublimates his aggression into the assertion of moral superiority (94). Waldoff, however, sees as one expression of that moral superiority the pity expressed in Prometheus's opening speech, a pity that I have found psychologically ambiguous. On the sublimation of aggression in general, see Heinz Hartmann, "Notes on the Theory of Sublimation," in *Essays on Ego Psychology*, 226–27, 232.

25. Kerényi, *Prometheus*, 53–54.

26. Medwin, *Life of Shelley*, 213–14; see Zillman, 334.

27. Kerényi, *The Gods of the Greeks*, 48.

28. Aeschylus, *The Eumenides*, 745 ("Darkness of night, our mother"); *Prometheus Unbound*, 1.472.

29. Freud writes on the phallic mother in *Leonardo da Vinci and a Memory of His Childhood*, *SE*, 11:82, 93–96, and "Fetishism," *SE*, 21:152–53.

30. Gelpi uses Melanie Klein to explicate the Furies as mirroring "the infant aggression, anger, and violence against the mother" (153).

31. Harrison writes that Homer's Erinyes were "terrors unseen" but that Aeschylus, who had to put them on the stage, was the first to visualize them (*Prolegomena*, 223). Shelley, in the poetry that accompanies their stage appearance in *Prometheus Unbound*, returns them to what Harrison calls "the Homeric horror of formlessness" (224).

32. Ulmer, in his discussion (99–100), refers to Dawson, *Unacknowledged Legislator* (88–94, 113–21), as well as Cronin (13, 159) and Scrivener (175–80), both of whom also believe that Shelley's rhetoric subverts his political ideals.

33. Mandela writes, for example, that the "freedom struggle" required him to accept "discipline" (228–29) and that it was important, upon his release from prison, to emphasize that he continued to be "a loyal and disciplined member" of his organization, the African National Congress (567). Mandela's autobiography is filled with thoughts that Shelley would have deeply understood. For example, "I knew as well as I knew anything that the oppressor must be liberated just as surely as the oppressed. A man who takes away another man's freedom is a prisoner of hatred" (624).

34. Blake, *The Marriage of Heaven and Hell*, pl. 14.

35. Ingpen and Peck, eds., *Complete Works of Shelley*, 7:189; also in Notopoulos, 455.

36. Lattimore translates Até as not Calamity but Delusion.

37. Shelley, dedication to Leigh Hunt, in *The Cenci*, *R*, 140.

38. See Bloom on limitation and representation in *A Map of Misreading*, 96–98.

CHAPTER 12. *PROMETHEUS UNBOUND:* ACT 2

1. Milton, *Samson Agonistes*, 374–75, 379, 1053–55.

2. Todhunter, *A Study of Shelley*, 141; quoted in Zillman, 110. From a Jungian perspective, we might read act 1 as a confrontation with the shadow, or dark side of Prometheus, and act 2 as a confrontation with the anima, or his female side; Jung writes that when the anima is integrated, it becomes the "Eros of consciousness." *Aion*, in *Works*, 9, pt. 2:16.

3. For Asia and reverie, see Gelpi, 171–72 and 246.

4. For Reiman the shape is the Spirit of the Hour (*R*, 238); for Gelpi, Demogorgon (189); for Cronin, "the poet in his bardic, prophetic role," calling Asia "to 'follow'" (145).

5. Ulmer writes, "The final dream is a single shared dream. Reconstructing it together, the sisters discover the resemblance of their emotional lives" (89).

6. For Wasserman, she is "compelled to follow the old order of things as it shrinks out of existence, not the new birth. . . . For the retreat of the old order into its remote, inactive source is the release of the new order from its ultimate springhead into the sensible world" (317). In my reading, what Asia follows is something much older than Jupiter's old order.

7. Hyacinth's blood also marked the flowers with words ("alas, alas"). See H. J. Rose, "Hyacinthus," in *Oxford Classical Dictionary*, 443.

8. See Gelpi (193, 201–2) on Hyacinth and Adonis and on the story of Venus and Adonis in the background of act 2.

9. Hughes, *Shelley Poems Published in 1820*, 193; cited in Zillman, 433–34. See *Oedipus at Colonus*, trans. Fitzgerald, 122. See also Gelpi on the nightingales of Colonus (203).

10. Bod. MS. e. 2, f. 37r, in *Bod. Shelley*, 9:306–7; see Zillman, 198.

11. See Zillman, 433–34.

12. Wasserman, 310–16.

13. Virgil, *The Pastoral Poems*, trans. Rieu, 77, lines 74–75. Erich Neumann uses Scylla, with her hounds' fangs beneath the waist, as an example of a particularly vivid and disturbing manifestation of the "Terrible Mother": the *vagina dentata* (168–69).

14. Daniel Hughes, "Potentiality in *Prometheus Unbound*," 119.

15. Bod. MS. e. 8, p. 70, in *Bod. Shelley*, 6:226–27. See Rogers, 17.

16. Hungerford (179), summarizing Boccaccio, *Genealogie Deorum Gentilium*, 1:13ff. Zillman gives detailed background and interpretation of Demogorgon, 313–20.

17. Lucan, *The Civil War*, trans. Duff, 341; quoted in Zillman, 314.

18. Lucan, 359; see Zillman, 314.

19. Peacock, quoted in Zillman, 313; for the full text of Peacock's note to his *Rhododaphne,* written in 1817 and accepted as one source of Shelley's knowledge of Demogorgon, see A. M. D. Hughes, 175.

20. H. N. Brailsford, *Shelley, Godwin, and Their Circle* (New York: Henry Holt, 1913), 228; Highet, *The Classical Tradition* (New York: Oxford University Press, 1949), 678; both quoted in Zillman, 313.

21. Boccaccio, *The Genealogy of the Gentile Gods,* Proem, book 14, in *Boccaccio on Poetry,* trans. Osgood, 15.

22. Harrison, *Prolegomena,* 209.

23. Gelpi discusses the association of Demogorgon's cave and Delphi (215). Rieger writes extensively of Demogorgon and snake worship (129–62). See Fontenrose for snakes and the omphalos of Delphi (374–78). William Hildebrand calls Demogorgon the dragon that guards the treasure ("Naming-Day in Asia's Vale," 195).

24. See Gimbutas, 93–95, 101, 112–50, and Baring and Cashford, 21–22, 64–65, 207, 332–33, 497–99.

25. See Fontenrose, 373. For Delphi as womb, see also Kerényi, "The Primordial Child," 50–51.

26. Harrison, *Themis,* 483.

27. Frye, *The Secular Scripture,* 119.

28. Spenser, *The Faerie Queene,* 1590 edition, 3.12.46.1–2, in Hamilton, 421.

29. Fontenrose, *Python,* 13–15, 218–19, 262–63.

30. Wasserman, *Shelley,* 310–15, 333–34.

31. Virgil, *The Pastoral Poems,* 6.45–60.

32. Virgil, *The Aeneid,* trans. Lewis, 6.24, 447.

33. Bod. MS. e. 8, p. 70, in *Bod. Shelley,* 6:226–27.

34. Lucan, 359; quoted in Zillman, 314.

35. Yeats, "*Prometheus Unbound,*" in *Essays and Introductions,* 420.

36. Rousseau, *Essay on the Origin of Languages,* trans. Gourevitch, 266.

37. Seeing Jupiter as a son figure, not a father figure, Ulmer says that Jupiter "does the real dirty work by deposing Saturn, the Titanic patriarch" (82).

38. Irvine Schiffer writes that "For some, both God and the father are personified substitutes for Time—the original unpersonified cosmic intruder between the infant and its mother" (137).

39. Milton, *Comus,* 636–40, 675–77; see Zillman, 469.

40. Pottle, "The Role of Asia," 138.

41. Dante, *Inferno,* trans. Ciardi, 34.111.

42. See Zillman, 488–89; *Paradiso,* trans. Ciardi, 21.4–5. See also *Purgatorio,* 31.136–46.

43. Bush, *Mythology and the Romantic Tradition,* 147.

44. Tennyson, cited in Barnard, 148–49; Zillman, 491.

45. Spender, 32; quoted in Zillman, 491.

46. Bachelard, discussing Shelley's imagery of flight and aeriality, speaks of "la synthèse de la lumière, de la sonorité et de la légèreté." *L'Air et les Songes,* 65. The work has been translated as *Air and Dreams: An Essay on the Imagination of Movement,* trans. Edith R. Farrell and C. Frederick Farrell (Dallas: Dallas Institute of Humanities and Culture, 1988): "a synthesis of light, sound, and lightness," 52. The "risen

body" is a motif in Romantic poetry in general; I discuss it in "The New Body of English Romanticism."

47. Greenacre, "A Study on the Nature of Inspiration," 237.

48. Daniel Hughes sees Asia returning to a realm of potentiality ("Potentiality in *Prometheus Unbound*," 121–22), while Gelpi adds to his concept of potentiality "the significance of human infancy" (193), and Sperry writes of "the pure potential of the unborn child" (105).

49. "The Virgin started from her seat, & with a shriek. / Fled back unhinderd till she came into the vales of Har." Blake, *The Book of Thel*, pl. 6, lines 21–22.

50. Ferber puts it that Asia "attains wisdom through love while Prometheus attains love through wisdom; their reunion ratifies the union each has achieved alone" (87). Cronin writes, "Prometheus moves towards an acceptance of the inner workings of his own mind; Asia moves outwards to a confrontation with external reality. This *rapprochement* is completed in Act 3 in their wedding, the emblem of a new psychological and social wholeness" (154).

CHAPTER 13. *PROMETHEUS UNBOUND:* ACT 3

1. Virgil, *The Pastoral Poems*, trans. Rieu, 4.7, 49.

2. In *The Aeneid*, Virgil pictures Ganymede seized by the claws of Jupiter's eagle as "His aged guardians . . . [raise] their impotent hands to heaven." Trans. Lewis, 5.256. On Laius as homosexual rapist, see George Devereux, "Why Oedipus Killed Laius."

3. Harrison, *Mythology*, 97.

4. As Wasserman writes, the rape is a "gruesome parody" of the union of Asia and Prometheus (290).

5. See Hans Loewald on "the threat of the engulfing, overpowering womb" and the "dread of sinking back into the unstructured state of identity" with the mother (15–16). Working with Loewald's ideas, Herbert Marcuse asks whether "the Narcissistic-maternal attitude toward reality cannot 'return' in less primordial, less devouring forms under the power of the mature ego and in a mature civilization" (211). An affirmative answer to that question is part of the vision of *Prometheus Unbound.* See Gelpi's discussion of Marcuse (162–65).

6. What Michael O'Neill says of Ocean's lines in this scene, that they "[create] a credible vision of a redeemed world" (114), can be applied to Shelley's poetic purpose in act 3 as a whole.

7. Locock, 1:618; cited in Zillman, 521. For "unpastured" in *The Mask of Anarchy* drafts, see Forman, *Note Books*, 2:75; the word is difficult to decipher, and Mary A. Quinn, the editor of the Huntington manuscript, does not offer a guess for it; see Huntington MS. HM 2177, f. 19v, in *Manuscripts of the Younger Romantics: Shelley*, 4:92–93.

8. Bloom, *Shelley's Mythmaking*, 134.

9. Locock, 1:618; cited in Zillman, 521.

10. Bloom, *Shelley's Mythmaking*, 134.

11. Michael Ferber writes that Hercules' "cameo appearance" suggests "the negligible role of violence in a true revolution" (174).

12. Harrison, *Themis*, 467.

13. Spitz, *The First Year of Life*, 61–65.

14. Boccaccio, *Genealogie Deorum Gentilium*, 1:14; see Curran, *Annus Mirabilis*, 79; see also Fontenrose on the Corycian Cave, 406–35.

15. Prometheus's cave contains a fountain, as do Typhon's (see Fontenrose, 408), and Cythna's, as well (*Laon and Cythna*, 2929, E, 2:184). For a discussion of the Shelleyan cave and fountain, see Yeats, "The Philosophy of Shelley's Poetry," 80–87. On this and other caves in Shelley, see Rogers, 147–68; Hogle, 202–3; and Gelpi, 201.

16. Bloom, *Shelley's Mythmaking*, 135.

17. Commenting on this episode, Peter Butter calls attention to Wordsworth's use of the seashell (181, 198). In *The Excursion*, book 4, a child, listening to a shell, hears "Murmurings, whereby the monitor expressed / Mysterious union with its native sea" (1139–40). In *The Excursion* Wordsworth's Wanderer tames the oceanic power of the shell by calling its sound "Authentic tidings of invisible things" as heard by "the ear of Faith" (1144, 1142). There is no taming in book 5 of *The Prelude*, however, in which Wordsworth hears the floodwaters of the abyss in a shell identified with poetry and is then impelled, in effect, to save poetry from the apocalypse promised by poetry. (See Hartman's reading of this episode in *Wordsworth's Poetry*, 225–33.) Butter finds Shelley's use of the shell bland compared with Wordsworth's (198), but I think the relationship between the two poets at this point is more revealing. Asia's shell was given to her by Proteus (3.3.65–66). We recall that Shelley taunted the Lake Poets, the mutable, failed fathers, by calling them Proteus. In the present passage too we can understand Proteus, the original possessor of the shell, as Wordsworth, a prophet of nature, who was sensitive to an oceanic glory beyond common nature but who feared those apocalyptic floodwaters and their political expression, revolution. Shelley never read book 5 of *The Prelude*, but in effect he is taking Wordsworth's shell, approving of those floodwaters, and releasing them. But first—and here is the key point—he gives the shell to Asia. He too tames the oceanic feeling but with Love, not Faith.

18. Freud, "The Acquisition and Control of Fire," *SE*, 22:187–93.

19. Todhunter, *A Study of Shelley*, 175; quoted in Zillman, 326.

20. Kerényi, *Essays on a Science of Mythology*, 51.

21. Ibid., 55. Kerényi sees in this symbol a liminal condition, "not yet separated from non-being, yet still being" (69).

22. Bloom, *Shelley's Mythmaking*, 136.

23. Zillman, 552, cites William Michael Rossetti and others on the vegetarian halcyons and the harmless nightshade.

24. William N. Guthrie, 184–85; cited in Zillman, 552.

25. See Wasserman's discussion of the amphisbaena (362), which appears in Lucan's *The Civil War*, 9.718–19, 723, together with the seps and the dipsas, the serpent of unquenchable thirst, which is used to characterize the Spirit of the Earth's early need for Asia (3.4.18–19).

26. Wordsworth, *Tintern Abbey*, 109.

27. Karen Weisman recognizes this when she writes that the negatives "move toward the nothingness of the inane, until the final qualifications pull the reader . . . back down to earth. The heaven on earth to which Shelley now yearns is one in which humanity is actualized in time, not obliterated in an all-consuming unity. To

give up temporal confinement, that is, to ascend heaven and enter an 'intense inane,' would be to relinquish finite consciousness, which is the ground of individuality" (105).

CHAPTER 14. *PROMETHEUS UNBOUND:* ACT 4

1. Edward Dowden, *The Life of Percy Bysshe Shelley,* 2:298; quoted in Zillman, 567.

2. Jack, *Shelley: An Essay* (London: Constable, 1904), 106; quoted in Zillman, 567.

3. As Ferber writes, the theme of music, building up to the sound of the shell, has been central in the play, and "The culmination and triumph of music is one of the subjects of the final act, and it is no less the form of the act itself" (91).

4. Grabo, *Prometheus Unbound,* 127; quoted in Zillman, 575.

5. See Wasserman (364) on the dance of the Horae. Northrop Frye writes that in the ideal states depicted in literature, "Time becomes less an image of fatality and destruction, and becomes rather an expression of energy, exuberance, and the kind of genuine freedom which is the same thing as discipline. The traditional symbol for this experience of time is the dance." *The Secular Scripture,* 153.

6. Harrison, *Themis,* 185.

7. Ibid., 515.

8. Wasserman, *Shelley,* 369. Wasserman quotes Shelley's argument in the notes to *Queen Mab* that our sense of time depends upon the character of our consciousness: "Perhaps the perishing ephemeron enjoys a longer life than the tortoise" (367–68; *Queen Mab, E,* 1:406).

9. Hughes, "Potentiality in *Prometheus Unbound,*" 112.

10. In Melanie Klein's description of the origins of curiosity, the infant, in the frustrations of weaning, fantasizes about exploring the inside of the mother's body and possessing its secret contents. See, for example, "Early Stages of the Oedipus Conflict," in *Love, Grief, and Reparation,* 187–88.

11. In Melanie Klein, the child fantasizes committing mayhem within the mother's body; the frustrations of weaning overlap with the frustrations of the anal stage, and in these fantasies, "The child desires to get possession of the mother's faeces, by penetrating into her body, cutting it to pieces, devouring and destroying it." *Love, Grief, and Reparation,* 189.

12. Bloom, *Shelley's Mythmaking,* 142.

13. Draft of line 388; Huntington MS. HM 2176, f. *25r reverso, in *Manuscripts of the Younger Romantics: Shelley,* 6:282–83; quoted in Zillman, 667.

14. Wasserman, 273. See Wasserman's discussion of the passage and of Shelley's way of using myths, 271–75, 279–82.

15. Bod. MS.e. 7, p. 70, in *Bod. Shelley,* 6:226–27.

16. Noted by Forman, *Note Books,* 1:74.

17. Freud, *Beyond the Pleasure Principle, SE,* 18:50.

18. In Clark, indeed, the expressions of the Maenads have "a strange inanity" (*Shelley's Prose,* 349). In that wording he is following Ingpen and Peck (*Complete Works of Shelley,* 6:323), who are following Forman (*The Works of Percy Bysshe Shelley,* 7:63). But "inanity" is "delirium" in Thomas Medwin's 1833 transcription in *Shelley Papers* (144) and Mary Shelley's 1840 transcription in *Essays, Letters from Abroad*

(2:268). The wording of the *Notes* is open to question since we do not have Shelley's original manuscript, which Forman claimed as his authority. For a discussion of the problem, see E. B. Murray, "Shelley's *Notes on Sculptures*" (where the suggestion is made that Forman may have been working from not Shelley's manuscript but a transcription made by Claire Clairmont), and Alan Weinberg's remarks in *Bod. Shelley*, 22, pt. 1:18–20.

19. Ehrenzweig, *The Hidden Order of Art*, 104–5, 222, 275–76.

20. Draft of line 501; Huntington MS. HM 2176, f. *17r reverso, in *Manuscripts of the Younger Romantics: Shelley*, 6:314–15; see Zillman, 674.

21. Harrison, *Themis*, 470.

22. See Harrison, *Themis*, 483–85.

23. Kerényi, *The Gods of the Greeks*, 102.

24. Notopoulos (356) and Rieger (154) point to this passage, which was first printed by André H. Koszul in *Shelley's Prose in the Bodleian Manuscripts*, 122. The passage appears twice in manuscript drafts: Bod. MS. d. 1, f. 43r reverso and f. 42v reverso, in *Bod. Shelley*, 4:2:266–69. For other interpretations of the serpent in the closing speech of Demogorgon, see Zillman, 626.

25. Bod. MS. e. 6, p. 137r, in *Bod. Shelley*, 5:286–87. See Rogers, 18–19.

26. Piccoli, cited in Zillman, 630; *Percy Bysshe Shelley: Prometeo Liberato* (Florence: Sansoni, 1924); Byron, *Prometheus*, 20–22.

27. Plato, *Phaedrus*, in *Euthyphro . . . Phaedrus*, 535.

Chapter 15. "The Right Road to Paradise"

1. McGann, "The Secrets of an Elder Day," 29–30.

2. Shelley wrote the passage in the original Greek. Bod. MS. e. 18, back pastedown, in *Bod. Shelley*, 19:312–13. The translation is by Paul Shorey, *The Republic*, 476 D, p. 519.

3. See Shelley, *Posthumous Poems, 1824*, ed. Mary Shelley, 178. Nora Crook specifies late December or early January, in *Bod. Shelley*, 12:liii–liv. For variations in the punctuation of *The Zucca*, see chapter 7, note 2, above.

4. I discuss the Jane Williams sequence in detail in " 'More than ever can be spoken': Unconscious Fantasy in Shelley's Jane Williams Poems."

5. I follow the text of Judith Chernaik in *The Lyrics of Shelley* (259). Mary Shelley puts the comma in line 44 after "Awhile" in her 1839 edition (4:162), as does Hutchinson (667).

6. Rousseau, *Reveries of the Solitary Walker*, trans. France, 88.

Chapter 16. A Dream of Life

1. See the discarded openings transcribed by Reiman in *Shelley's "The Triumph of Life,"* 235 (line 27) and 236 (lines 6–7, 19–21); Bod. MS. c. 4, f. 57v, in *Bod. Shelley*, 1:296–97. Reiman is also the editor of the Bodleian volume. For draft material, I will continue to cite both the Bodleian and the earlier *Shelley's "The Triumph of Life,"* since the latter is more widely available.

2. As Matthews points out, these lines are nearly a translation from *Faust*, whose hero, watching the sunset, dreams of having wings and following the sun:

"before me lies the day, behind the night, / the sky above me and the seas beneath." Salm, trans., p. 69, lines 1087–88; Matthews, "On Shelley's '*The Triumph of Life*,'" 115. Charles Robinson (222–23) and Edward Duffy (127) point out that Shelley turns his narrator around, making him face the night, not the day. This was a second thought, for in a draft he keeps Faust's orientation; see Reiman, *Shelley's "Triumph,"* 236 (lines 29–30); Pforzheimer fragment, recto, in *Bod. Shelley,* 1:278–79.

3. Reiman, *Shelley's "Triumph,"* 234–35 (lines 3–4); Bod. MS. c. 4, f. 56v reverso, in *Bod. Shelley,* 1:292–93. Sperry notes the change in the sun from young man to father (*Shelley's Major Verse,* 186).

4. Reiman, *Shelley's "Triumph,"* 139; Bod. MS. c. 4, f. 20r, in *Bod. Shelley,* 1:140–41.

5. Bloom, *Poetry and Repression,* 109. In a draft of *The Triumph,* Shelley took a jab at Wordsworth, as the narrator refers to those who "tell our sons in prose or rhyme / the manhood of the child." Bod. MS. c. 4, f. 34r, in *Bod. Shelley,* 1:196–97; Reiman, *Shelley's "Triumph,"* 241.

6. Reiman, *Shelley's "Triumph,"* 147; Bod. MS. c. 4, f. 23r, in *Bod. Shelley,* 1:152–53.

7. Reiman, *Shelley's "Triumph,"* 29; *Paradise Lost,* 2.672.

8. David Quint cites Marshall McLuhan's portrayal of Christ and Socrates as representatives of oral, rather than written, culture; see Quint, 653, and McLuhan, 97–99. In the context of *The Triumph,* they can also be regarded as symbolic representatives of the oral culture of infancy.

9. Reiman, *Shelley's "Triumph,"* 159; Bod. MS. c. 4, f. 27r, in *Bod. Shelley,* 1:168–69.

10. Reiman, *Shelley's "Triumph,"* 159; Bod. MS. c. 4, f. 27v, in *Bod. Shelley,* 1:170–71.

11. Duffy, 107–8, 132, 137, 139, 147, 153–55.

12. Small signs of the good mother—melodious fountains, forest breezes, "violet banks where sweet dreams brood" (72)—do appear in the landscape through which the chariot passes but are ignored by its maddened followers.

13. Reiman, *Shelley's "Triumph,"* 241 (lines 12–15); Bod. MS. c. 4., f. 34r, in *Bod. Shelley,* 1:196–97.

14. The reference to Aster, Plato's "star," was first noted by A. C. Bradley, "Notes on Shelley's 'Triumph of Life,'" 449–50. The passage is interestingly ambiguous about Plato's relationship to his teacher. On the one hand, Socrates, not knowing "the joy and woe" of his pupil, may appear to be one who never got beyond innocence. On the other hand, Plato appears as a latecomer who couldn't measure up to his precursor.

15. Bloom, *Shelley's Mythmaking,* 260.

16. Reiman, *Shelley's "Triumph,"* 54.

17. Bacon, *The New Organon,* in *Works,* 8:67–68.

18. Reiman, *Shelley's "Triumph,"* 173; Bod. MS. c. 4, f. 33r, in *Bod. Shelley,* 1:192–93.

19. The difference is like that in the *Defence* between a story, "a catalogue of detached facts, which . . . applies only to a definite period of time, and a certain combination of events which can never again recur," and a poem, "the very image of life expressed in its eternal truth" (*R,* 515).

20. Reiman, *Shelley's "Triumph,"* 183; Bod. MS. c. 4, f. 40v, in *Bod. Shelley,* 1:222–23.

21. In *The Witch of Atlas*, 55–80, the sun dissolves a nymph in a cave containing a fountain, and ten months later a "dewy Splendour" takes "shape" (78–79). In *The Faerie Queene*, the sun "pierst into [Chrysogonee's] womb" after she has been bathing in a fountain (3.6.7.7).

22. In *Shelley's Major Poetry* (266), Baker noted in the image of Iris an allusion to the marriage masque in *The Tempest*, in which Ceres calls Iris's rainbow a "Rich scarf to my proud earth" (4.1.82); Iris has descended to earth as Juno's herald to celebrate the union of Ferdinand and Miranda. *The Tempest* was on Shelley's mind during this period: he wrote *With a Guitar. To Jane* in the persona of Ariel, and Miranda, Ferdinand, and Prospero appear in its lines.

23. Reiman, *Shelley's "Triumph,"* 177. Reiman interprets the letters as an allusion to Sir Humphrey Davy and also notes that "Srumfredevi" appears together with "Sir Humphrey Davy" and "Davi" near the reference to Aristotle and Alexander in line 260 (171). "Devi" may appear still again below line 357 (185). See Bod. MS. c. 4, f. 41r, f. 38r, f. 32v, in *Bod. Shelley*, 1:224–25, 212–13, 190–91.

24. Devi appears in *The Origin of Pagan Mythology*, by George Stanley Faber (1:170), cited by Curran as a major sourcebook of mythology in Shelley's time (*Annus Mirabilis*, xvii–xviii). Curran mentions the goddess Asa-Devi in his discussion of Asia (46). Shelley knew Faber personally, in an odd fashion; Faber was a friend of Hogg's family, and Shelley wrote prank letters to him, baiting him about Christianity; see Bieri, 1:152–53, 163–64. Another possible source for Devi is Edward Moor, *The Hindu Pantheon*, which contains a discussion of Devi (157–68) and numerous visual representations of her (plates 28–33, 36–43); Shelley ordered a copy of this book in 1812; see *L*, 1:342. Perhaps Shelley's marginal wordplay combines associations to both the Shape and the manner of her creation, for Humphrey Davy had written about radiation and its relation to matter (see Grabo, *A Newton among Poets*, 110–13, 154–55). That Shelley was interested in Davy is clear; he left copious reading notes to Davy's *Agricultural Chemistry*; see Bod. MS. e. 6, pp. 172 reverso–155 reverso, in *Bod. Shelley*, 5:322–57. Carlene Adamson writes that Davy's description of the water cycle in *Agricultural Chemistry*, although not part of Shelley's notes, may have contributed to *The Cloud*, written in the same notebook as the Davy notes; see her introduction, *Bod. Shelley*, 5:xlvii. Reiman suggests that Shelley may have thought of Davy as, like Aristotle in the pairing with Alexander, too closely involved with power (*Shelley's "Triumph,"* 171); but, given the placement of "Sir Humphrey Davy" in the manuscript, he may rather have thought of him as a new Bacon, an explorer of nature's secrets.

25. Róheim, *The Gates of the Dream*, 545, and Ferenczi, *Thalassa*, 63–64.

26. Reiman, *Shelley's "Triumph,"* 64; Milton, *Comus*, 65.

27. Ulmer (166) and Quint (649) see in the passage an allusion to Love in *The Symposium* and Delusion in *The Iliad*. See my discussion of Shelley's use of this double allusion in *Prometheus Unbound*, act 1, in chapter 11 above.

28. For a contrary portrayal of this passage as a purely "nightmare version" of an evanescence that Shelley elsewhere treats positively, see Keach, *Shelley's Style*, 151–52. See Keach for many examples of "melting, dissolving, erasing" in Shelley's work, 118–53.

29. See Isakower, "A Contribution to the Patho-Psychology of Phenomena Associated with Falling Asleep," esp. 333, 342.

30. Schapiro sees in the scene "the experience of desolation at the breast" (30).

31. Reiman, *Shelley's "Triumph,"* 193; Bod. MS. c. 4, f. 44r., in *Bod. Shelley,* 1:234–35.

32. Yeats, "The Philosophy of Shelley's Poetry," *Essays and Introductions,* 90.

33. Ibid., 94; see Duffy, 130.

34. Reiman, *Shelley's "Triumph,"* 69.

35. In Shelley's triumphal arch we can see an anxious version of the female symbolism of the ancient roofed megaliths built for goddess worship; on such megaliths, see Baring and Cashford, *The Myth of the Goddess,* 93–101.

36. Reiman, *Shelley's "Triumph,"* 73.

37. Reiman suggests that Shelley's rainbow-triumphal arch combines Milton's rainbow in *Paradise Lost,* 11.864–67, with his bridge "Archt" between Earth and Hell in 10.298–305 (*Shelley's "Triumph,"* 73). This bridge, I would add, is also mentioned in 2.1028, in the same sentence as Satan's track.

38. The end of the *Paradiso,* 33.146, trans. Ciardi.

39. Reiman, *Shelley's "Triumph,"* 207; Bod. MS. c. 4, f. 51v, in *Bod. Shelley,* 1:264–65.

40. Reiman, *Shelley's "Triumph,"* 209; Bod. MS. c. 4, f. 52r, in *Bod. Shelley,* 1:266–67.

41. *The Prelude* and Rousseau's *La Nouvelle Héloïse* both contain crowd scenes that bear comparison to the scene of phantoms around the chariot. Rousseau's St. Preux, when he visits Paris in his exile from Julie, writes of the "crowded . . . wasteland" of false appearances, of "spectres and phantoms": "Until now I have seen a great many masks; when shall I see the faces of men?" (197). Wordsworth describes London as a haunted den of shifting "shapes" "Like spectres" (8.570, 572) and compares the city to a fair, with "phantasma" and "blank confusion" and a "perpetual whirl / Of trivial objects, melted and reduced / To one identity" (7.687, 722, 725–28). For both, the teeming city is an alienated and spectral realm, which Wordsworth and St. Preux enter when they leave the realm of a female-centered or maternal ideal, Wordsworth's nature and St. Preux's Julie. But in *The Triumph of Life* it is, just the contrary, a regressive quest for the mother that leads the character Rousseau into the chaotic realm of shadows and unreality.

42. See, e.g., Klein, "Early Stages of the Oedipus Conflict" in *Love, Guilt and Reparation* (186–98), and "Some Theoretical Conclusions Regarding the Emotional Life of the Infant," in *Envy and Gratitude* (61–93).

43. See Paul Turner, "Shelley and Lucretius," *RES,* N. S., 10 (August 1959), 269–82, cited by Reiman, *Shelley's "Triumph,"* 79; see Lucretius, 131–33.

44. Reiman, *Shelley's "Triumph,"* 83.

45. Ibid.

46. Ibid.

47. Ibid., 211; Bod. MS. c. 4, f. 53v, in *Bod. Shelley,* 1:272–73.

Chapter 17. Shelley's Rousseau and Shelley's Dante

1. Wollstonecraft, 129, 133. See Duffy, 46–48; *Quarterly Review* 11 (April 1814): 174–76, and *Monthly Review* 75 (December 1786): 565.

2. Duffy (73) is commenting on *Childe Harold*, 3, stanzas 76–84.

3. Duffy, 73; *Childe Harold*, 3.76.4, 81.3–4.

4. Frye, "The Drunken Boat," 10.

5. Rousseau, *Emile*, trans. Foxley, 296.

6. Rousseau, *Discourse on Inequality*, in *First and Second Discourses*, trans. Gourevitch, 145.

7. Rousseau, *Discourse on the Arts and Sciences*, in *First and Second Discourses*, 14.

8. Ibid. For Rousseau, art and science are actually founded in our vices: "Astronomy was born of superstition; Eloquence of ambition, hatred, flattery, lying; Geometry of avarice; Physics of a vain curiosity; all of them, even Ethics, of human pride" (14–15).

9. Rousseau, *Discourse on Inequality*, 177.

10. Rousseau, *Confessions*, trans. Cohen, 589.

11. Ibid., 594.

12. Ibid., 104; *Discourse on Inequality*, 213.

13. Rousseau, *Essay on the Origin of Languages*, trans. Gourevitch, 261.

14. Rousseau, *Emile*, 45; see Derrida, 186.

15. Hazlitt, *Conversations of James Northcote*, in *Works*, 2:278; see Duffy, 77.

16. Hazlitt, "On the Character of Rousseau," in *Works*, 4:92; "the principle of Self . . . the Mammon of the world" (*A Defence of Poetry*, *R*, 531).

17. Bieri mentions that Shelley had a prankish and occasionally ribald sense of humor in his adolescence, even as he idealized sex and women and could be offended by vulgarity. Bieri, 1:127–28, 178–80, 263.

18. Derrida, 152; *Emile*, 14.

19. Reiman, "Shelley's 'Triumph of Life': The Biographical Problem," 545–48.

20. See *The Faerie Queene*, 1.9.9–15. Rousseau also dealt with the theme of the bringing to life of an ideal love in a play, *Pygmalion*, which Duffy suggests Shelley must have known since a translation appeared in Hunt's *Indicator* in 1820. Duffy (133) quotes from Hunt's introduction that Rousseau "was a kind of Pygmalion himself . . . perpetually yet hopelessly endeavoring to realize the dreams of his imagination."

21. Reiman, "Shelley's 'Triumph of Life,'" 247.

22. McGann, "Secrets of an Elder Day," 39.

23. Bloom, *Shelley's Mythmaking*, 253.

24. Ibid.

25. Hertz, *The End of the Line*, 217–39.

26. Newman Ivey White writes that Shelley read this *Triumph* aloud to Mary (2:631).

27. Petrarch, *The Tryumphe of Death*, 2.120, in *Tryumphes of Fraunces Petrarcke*, trans. Lord Morley, 126.

28. Petrarch, *The Tryumphe of Divinitie*, lines 192–94, p. 158.

29. Bloom, "Keats and the Embarrassments of Poetic Tradition," in *The Ringers in the Tower*, 132.

30. Kohut, "Forms and Transformations of Narcissism," in *The Search for the Self*, 1:435, 434.

31. Reiman, *Shelley's "Triumph,"* 87–88. See also Cronin's discussion of Shelley's differences from Dante and Petrarch in handling the terza rima (207).

32. Shelley translated the Matilda sequence of the *Purgatorio* separately; see Timothy Webb's text in *The Violet in the Crucible*, 313–17, and Bod. MS. e. 6, pp. 39–42, in *Bod. Shelley*, 5:82–89. See Bloom's discussion of the Shape as a natural parody of Matilda (*Shelley's Mythmaking*, 271).

33. *Purgatorio*, 33.142–46, trans. Ciardi.

34. Ehrenzweig, 104–5.

CHAPTER 18. IMAGINATION AND THE HEART

1. *One word is too often profaned*, line 13, *R*, 475.

2. Hutchinson did not realize that the poem is a translation; see chapter 4, note 1, above. See Bod. MS. e. 7, pp. 156, 158, in *Bod. Shelley*, 16:160–63.

3. Huntington Shelley Notebook HM 2177, f. *19 reverso, in *Manuscripts of the Younger Romantics: Shelley*, 4:396–97; also in Forman, *Note Books*, 2:100. The note also exists in Mary Shelley's transcription, which leaves out an immediately following reference to Aeschylus; see Bod. MS. d. 6, p. 109, in *Bod. Shelley*, 22, pt. 1:256–57.

4. Clark, *Shelley's Prose*, 349. For textual information on the *Notes on Sculptures*, see chapter 14, note 18, above.

5. Called *A Treatise on Morals* in Clark; see preface, note 13, above. See Bod. MS. c. 4. f. 191r, in *Bod. Shelley*, 21:206–7.

6. Huntington 2177, f. *24v reverso, in *Manuscripts of the Younger Romantics: Shelley*, 4:374–75; also in Forman, *Note Books*, 1:11.

7. See Bod. MS. c. 4, f. 193r, in *Bod. Shelley*, 21:214–15. On the same manuscript page, Shelley wrote, "The imagination acquires by exercise a habit as it were of perc[ei]ving and abhorring evil," and then replaced "imagination" with "mind."

CHAPTER 19. IMAGINATION AND VISION

1. *Prometheus Unbound*, 2.2.75–76.

2. Lucretius, *The Nature of Things*, trans. Latham, 31.

3. Brown, *Sexuality and Feminism in Shelley*, 15; Shelley, *Letters*, 2:445.

4. *Art thou pale for weariness*, *H*, 621. Among those who have noted Shelleyan conjunctions of eyes and stars are Rogers (115) and J. Hillis Miller (235).

5. *Letters of Mary W. Shelley*, 1:245. See Holmes (727) on Shelley's hallucinations.

6. Freud, "Medusa's Head," *SE*, 18: 273–74.

7. See Salm's dual-language edition, line 4200, pp. 286–87. Salm translates as follows: "Whoever looks will swear he sees his love."

8. Harrison, *Prolegomena*, 194.

9. Hughes, "Shelley, Leonardo," 205.

10. Harrison, *Prolegomena*, 187–88.

11. Hildebrand, "Self, Beauty and Horror," 159.

12. According to Carol Jacobs, the poem plays dizzyingly with an "endless mirroring" of the beholder, the beheld, and the producer or artist (179, 175). Hildebrand sees in the poem a "demonic mirror-image" of the *Hymn to Intellectual Beauty* with its wish to become one with the inspiring—and, I would add, maternal—Spirit; see "Self, Beauty and Horror," 152.

13. Rousseau, *La Nouvelle Héloïse*, trans. McDowell, 122–23.

14. See Timothy Webb's discussion, *The Violet in the Crucible*, 154.

15. Goethe, *Faust*, trans. Salm, 241.

16. See Freud, *Three Essays on the Theory of Sexuality*, *SE*, 7:194; but I quote "looking impulse" from A. A. Brill's version in *The Basic Writings of Sigmund Freud* (New York: Random House Modern Library, 1938), 594, whereas the *Standard Edition* uses "scopophilia."

17. Shelley's treatment of the veil has received extensive commentary. See, for example, McGann, "Shelley's Veils."

18. Medwin, *Life of Percy Bysshe Shelley*, 249.

19. Barbara Gelpi discusses how such erotic veil imagery is influenced by women's fashions in Shelley's day, which sought simultaneously to conceal and expose the breasts. See *Shelley's Goddess*, 43–60.

20. Written in Italian, trans. Richard Garnett (*C*, 360).

21. Blake, *The Laocoön*, in *Poetry and Prose of Blake*, 275.

22. *St. Irvyne* (Arno Press), 198.

23. Rogers (144) is quoting *Prometheus Unbound*, 3.3.59

24. See preface, note 12, above, for the source of this text.

25. Freud, *The Psychopathology of Everyday Life*, *SE*, 6:266, 268; in the italicized passage Freud is quoting a letter from Ferenczi.

26. See Holmes (295–96) for an extensive interpretation of the episode, which he connects with a recurrent dream that Shelley reports in the same essay about a boy he knew at school. Holmes sees in the episode homoerotic feelings, once involving the boy and now directed toward Hogg, his companion on the Oxford walk.

27. *The Diary of Dr. John William Polidori*, 128; quoted by Holmes, 328–29.

28. "Hideous, deformed," from the original version of *Christabel*, quoted by Polidori, 129, and Holmes, 329.

29. Polidori, 128; quoted by Holmes, 329.

30. Greenacre, "The Primal Scene," 28.

31. Polidori, 128; quoted by Holmes, 329.

32. Schapiro, 27; see Kohut, *The Analysis of the Self*, 116–17.

33. Róheim, *Gates of the Dream*, 531. The story of Tiresias appears in Ovid, *Metamorphoses*, book 3. Callimachus, in his hymn "The Bath of Pallas," tells another version, in which Athene blinded Tiresias when he saw her naked in her bath and then, because of her friendship with his mother, gave him prophetic powers. That he had seen his mother naked at the same time seems, in Callimachus's telling, incidental—an instance of displacement. See Callimachus, 117–23.

34. Huntington Shelley Notebook HM 2176, f. 2v, in *Manuscripts of the Younger Romantics: Shelley*, 6:12–13; also in Forman, *Note Books*, 1:116.

35. Otto Isakower has studied the organic connection between the sense of equilibrium and the sense of hearing in "On the Exceptional Position of the Auditory Sphere," 341–42.

36. Novalis, *Hymns to the Night*, trans. Passage, 13. The original is "Ewge Schlummer," *Hymnen an die Nacht*, line 715, in Novalis (Friedrich von Hardenberg), *Schriften: Die Werke Friedrich von Hardenbergs, Erster Band: Das dichterische Werk*, ed. Paul Kluckhohn and Richard Samuel (Stuttgart: W. Kohlhammer, 1960), 152.

CHAPTER 20. IMAGINATION AND NEGATIVITY

1. Dawson, 119; see also Webb, "The Unascended Heaven: Negatives in '*Prometheus Unbound,*'" 38–39.

2. Webb, "The Unascended Heaven," 40, 48–49.

3. *Prometheus Unbound,* 4.554; *Mont Blanc,* lines 80–81; *On Life, R,* 508.

4. *Prometheus Unbound,* 2.4.116.

5. See Hughes, "Coherence and Collapse in Shelley" and "Kindling and Dwindling: The Poetic Process in Shelley," as well as "Potentiality in *Prometheus Unbound.*"

6. *To a Sky-Lark,* 2, 31. Webb discusses Shelley's use of negatives in terms of the traditional *via negativa* to transcendence in Christian mysticism; see "The Unascended Heaven," 57. See also Keach's chapter on "Evanescence: Melting, Dissolving, Erasing," in *Shelley's Style,* 118–53.

7. *To a Sky-Lark,* 87; Letter to Peacock, *L,* 2:98.

8. Lucretius, *The Nature of Things,* trans. Latham, 35.

9. Ferber writes that "the nihilistic readings of the present age . . . turn [*The Triumph of Life*] into an example of a scepticism far beyond anything Shelley had advocated" (148).

10. For a different approach to such doubleness, see Tilottama Rajan's analysis of Shelley's "pattern of alternation between idealism and . . . skepticism" (83) in *Dark Interpreter,* 58–96.

CHAPTER 21. IMAGINATION AND SELF-KNOWLEDGE

1. Lucretius, *The Nature of Things,* trans. Latham, 31.

2. See preface, note 14, above, for a textual discussion of this passage.

3. Bacon, *The Advancement of Learning,* in *Works,* 6:164–65.

4. Huntington Shelley Notebook HM 2177, f. *20r reverso, in *Manuscripts of the Younger Romantics: Shelley,* 4:392–93; Bod. MS. d. 6, p. 110 (in Mary Shelley's handwriting, with a comma before "which was hidden"), in *Bod. Shelley,* 22, pt. 1:258–59; also in Forman, *Note Books,* 2:102.

5. Bacon, *Advancement of Learning,* in *Works,* 6:95.

6. Bod. MS. e. 8, p. 70, in *Bod. Shelley,* 6:226–27; see Rogers, 17.

7. Wasserman, *Shelley,* 110–15.

8. Bacon, *Advancement of Learning,* in *Works,* 6:97.

9. Bacon, *Works,* 8:161.

10. Ovid, *The Metamorphoses,* book 3, trans. Gregory, 95.

11. *E,* 2:417–18. Hutchinson dates the lines 1819 (*H,* 581), but the time of composition is unknown, and Everest proposes July 1818.

12. Freud, "Address Delivered in the Goethe House in Frankfurt," *SE,* 21:212.

13. Arnold, "Shelley," 327.

14. Hartmann, *Ego Psychology and the Problem of Adaptation,* 14.

Works Cited

This list includes works mentioned more than once in the text and notes or, if mentioned only once, works pertinent to Shelley studies or to the general perspective of this study.

Abraham, Karl. "Dreams and Myths: A Study in Folk Psychology." In *Clinical Papers and Essays on Psycho-Analysis*, vol. 2 of *Selected Papers of Karl Abraham*, 2 vols., 153–209. Trans. Hilda Abraham et al. New York: Basic Books, 1955.

Abrams, M. H. "English Romanticism: The Spirit of the Age." In *Romanticism Reconsidered: Selected Papers from the English Institute*, ed. Northrop Frye, 26–32. 1963; New York: Columbia University Press, 1968.

Adams, S. M. "The Four Elements in the *Prometheus Vinctus.*" *Classical Philology* 28, no. 2 (April 1933): 97–103.

Aeschylus. *Aeschylus I: Agamemnon, The Libation Bearers, and The Eumenides*, trans. Richmond Lattimore; *Prometheus Bound*, trans. David Grene. ed. Grene and Lattimore. Vol. 1 of *The Complete Greek Tragedies*. New York: Random House Modern Library, 1942.

Arlow, Jacob A. "Unconscious Fantasy and Disturbances of Conscious Experience." *Psychoanalytic Quarterly* 38, no. 1 (January 1969): 1–25.

Arnold, Matthew. *Poetry and Criticism of Matthew Arnold*. Ed. A. Dwight Culler. Boston: Houghton Mifflin, 1961.

———. "Shelley." In *The Last Word*, vol 11 of *The Complete Works of Matthew Arnold*, ed. R. H. Super, 305–27. Ann Arbor: University of Michigan Press, 1977.

Augustine, Saint. *Confessions*. Trans. R. S. Pine-Coffin. Baltimore: Penguin, 1961.

Bachelard, Gaston. *L'Air et les Songes: Essai sur l'imagination du mouvement*. 1943; Paris: Librairie José Corti, 1950.

———. *The Psychoanalysis of Fire*. Trans. Alan C. M. Ross. 1964; Boston: Beacon Press, 1968.

Bachofen, J. J. *Myth, Religion, and Mother Right: Selected Writings of J. J. Bachofen*. Trans. Ralph Manheim. Princeton: Princeton University Press, 1973.

Bacon, Francis. *The Works of Francis Bacon*. Ed. James Spedding et al. 15 vols. 1860–64; St. Clair Shores, MI: Scholarly Press, 1976.

Baker, Carlos. *Shelley's Major Poetry: The Fabric of a Vision*. Princeton: Princeton University Press, 1948.

Baring, Anne, and Jules Cashford. *The Myth of the Goddess: Evolution of an Image.* 1991; London: Penguin, 1993.

Barnard, Ellsworth. *Shelley: Selected Poems, Essays, and Letters.* New York: Odyssey Press, 1944.

Bergin, Thomas. *Petrarch.* New York: Twayne, 1970.

Bieri, James. *Percy Bysshe Shelley: A Biography.* 2 vols. Vol. 1, *Youth's Unextinguished Fire, 1792–1816.* Vol. 2, *Exile of Unfulfilled Reknown, 1816–1822.* Newark: University of Delaware Press, 2004–5.

———. "Shelley's Older Brother." *Keats-Shelley Journal* 39 (1990): 29–33.

Blake, William. *The Complete Poetry and Prose of William Blake.* Ed. David V. Erdman, with a commentary by Harold Bloom. New York: Anchor, 1988.

Blank, G. Kim. *Wordsworth's Influence on Shelley: A Study of Poetic Authority.* New York: St. Martin's Press, 1988.

Bloom, Harold. *A Map of Misreading.* New York: Oxford University Press, 1975.

———. *Poetry and Repression: Revisionism from Blake to Stevens.* New Haven: Yale University Press, 1976.

———. *The Ringers in the Tower: Studies in Romantic Tradition.* Chicago: University of Chicago Press, 1971.

———. *Shelley's Mythmaking.* 1959; Ithaca: Cornell University Press, 1969.

———. *The Visionary Company: A Reading of English Romantic Poetry.* 1961; rev., Ithaca: Cornell University Press, 1971.

Boccaccio, Giovanni. *Boccaccio on Poetry: Being the Preface and the Fourteenth and Fifteenth Books of Boccaccio's Genealogia Deorum Gentilium.* Trans. Charles G. Osgood. 1930; New York: Liberal Arts Press, 1956.

———. *Genealogie Deorum Gentilium.* 2 vols. Bari, Italy: Laterza, 1951.

Bradley, A. C. "Notes on Shelley's 'Triumph of Life.'" *Modern Language Review* 9, no. 4 (October 1914): 441–56.

Brisman, Leslie. *Milton's Poetry of Choice and Its Romantic Heirs.* Ithaca: Cornell University Press, 1973.

———. *Romantic Origins.* Ithaca: Cornell University Press, 1978.

Brisman, Susan Hawk. " 'Unsaying His High Language': The Problem of Voice in *Prometheus Unbound.*" *Studies in Romanticism* 16, no. 1 (Winter 1977): 51–86.

Brown, Nathaniel. *Sexuality and Feminism in Shelley.* Cambridge, MA: Harvard University Press, 1979.

Brown, Norman O. *Hermes the Thief: The Evolution of a Myth.* 1947; New York: Vintage, 1969.

Bush, Douglas. *Mythology and the Romantic Tradition in English Poetry.* 1937; Cambridge, MA: Harvard University Press, 1969.

———. "Notes on Shelley." *Philological Quarterly* 13, no. 3 (July 1934): 299–302.

Butter, Peter H. *Shelley's Idols of the Cave.* 1954; New York: Haskell House, 1969.

Byron, George Gordon, Lord. *The Poetical Works of Lord Byron.* 1904; London: Oxford University Press, 1960.

Callimachus. *Hymns and Epigrams.* Trans. A. W. Mair. Loeb Classical Library. 1921; Cambridge, MA: Harvard University Press, 1989.

Cameron, Kenneth Neill. *The Young Shelley: Genesis of a Radical.* New York: Macmillan, 1950.

Campbell, Joseph. *The Hero with a Thousand Faces.* 2nd ed. 1968; Princeton: Princeton University Press, 1973.

Carothers, Yvonne M. "*Alastor:* Shelley Corrects Wordsworth." *Modern Language Quarterly* 42, no. 1 (March 1981): 21–47.

Chasseguet-Smirgel, Janine. "Freud and Female Sexuality." *International Journal of Psycho-Analysis* 57, part 3 (1976): 275–86.

Chaucer, Geoffrey. *The Works of Geoffrey Chaucer.* Ed. F. N. Robinson. 2nd ed. Cambridge, MA: Riverside Press, 1961.

Chernaik, Judith. *The Lyrics of Shelley.* Cleveland, OH: Case Western Reserve Press, 1972.

Clairmont, Claire. *The Journals of Claire Clairmont.* Ed. Marion Kingston Stocking, with the assistance of David Mackenzie Stocking. Cambridge, MA: Harvard University Press, 1968.

Clark, David Lee, ed. *Shelley's Prose, or The Trumpet of a Prophecy.* Corrected ed. Albuquerque: University of New Mexico Press, 1966. Cited as *C.*

Clark, Katerina, and Michael Holquist. *Mikhail Bakhtin.* Cambridge, MA: Harvard University Press, 1984.

Coleridge, Samuel Taylor. *Biographia Literaria.* Ed. James Engell and Walter Jackson Bate. Vol. 7, parts 1–2 of *The Collected Works of Samuel Taylor Coleridge.* Gen. ed. Kathleen Coburn. Princeton: Princeton University Press, 1983.

———. *The Poems of Samuel Taylor Coleridge.* Ed. E. H. Coleridge. 1912; London: Oxford University Press, 1964.

Cooper, Andrew. M. *Doubt and Identity in Romantic Poetry.* New Haven: Yale University Press, 1988.

Cooper, Bryan. "Shelley's *Alastor:* The Quest for a Vision." *Keats-Shelley Journal* 19 (1970): 63–76.

Crisman, William. "Psychological Realism and Narrative Manner in Shelley's 'Alastor' and 'The Witch of Atlas.'" *Keats-Shelley Journal* 35 (1986): 126–48.

Cronin, Richard. *Shelley's Poetic Thoughts.* New York: St. Martin's Press, 1981.

Crook, Nora, and Derek Guiton. *Shelley's Venomed Melody.* London: Cambridge University Press, 1986.

Cross, Tom Pete. "The Celtic Elements in the Lays of 'Lanval' and 'Graelent.'" *Modern Philology* 12, no. 10 (April 1915): 585–644.

Curran, Stuart. *Shelley's Annus Mirabilis: The Maturing of an Epic Vision.* San Marino, CA: Huntington Library, 1975.

Curtius, Ernst Robert. *European Literature and the Latin Middle Ages.* Trans. Willard R. Trask. 1953; New York: Harper & Row, 1963.

Dante. *The Inferno.* Trans. John Ciardi. 1954; New York: New American Library, 1964.

———. *The Paradiso.* Trans. John Ciardi. New York: New American Library, 1970.

———. *The Purgatorio.* Trans. John Ciardi. New York: New American Library, 1961.

Dawson, P. M. S. *The Unacknowledged Legislator: Shelley and Politics.* Oxford: Clarendon Press, 1980.

De Man, Paul. "Shelley Disfigured." In *Deconstruction and Criticism,* ed. Harold Bloom et al., 39–73. New York: Seabury Press, 1979.

Derrida, Jacques. *Of Grammatology.* Trans. and preface by Gayatri Chakravorty Spivak. Baltimore: Johns Hopkins University Press, 1976.

Devereux, George. "Why Oedipus Killed Laius: A Note on the Complementary Oedipus Complex in Greek Drama." *International Journal of Psycho-Analysis* 34, part 2 (1953): 132–41; repr. in *The Oedipus Papers,* ed. George H. Pollock and John Munder Ross, 97–116. Madison, CT: International Universities Press, 1988.

Dodds, E. R. *The Greeks and the Irrational.* 1951; Boston: Beacon Press, 1957.

Donovan, John. "Incest in *Laon and Cythna*: Nature, Custom, Desire." *Keats-Shelley Review* 2 (1987): 49–90.

Dowden, Edward. *The Life of Percy Bysshe Shelley.* 2 vols. London: Kegan Paul, Trench, 1886.

Duff, David. *Romance and Revolution: Shelley and the Politics of a Genre.* Cambridge: Cambridge University Press, 1994.

Duffy, Edward. *Rousseau in England: The Context for Shelley's Critique of the Enlightenment.* Berkeley and Los Angeles: University of California Press, 1979.

Ehrenzweig, Anton. *The Hidden Order of Art: A Study in the Psychology of Artistic Imagination.* Berkeley and Los Angeles: University of California Press, 1969.

Eliade, Mircia. *Patterns in Comparative Religion: A Study of the Element of the Sacred in the History of Religious Phenomena.* Trans. Rosemary Sheed. Cleveland, OH: Meridian, 1963.

Ende, Stuart A. *Keats and the Sublime.* New Haven: Yale University Press, 1976.

Erikson, Erik H. *Young Man Luther: A Study in Psychoanalysis and History.* New York: Norton, 1958.

Euripides. *Hippolytus.* Trans. David Grene. In *Euripides 1,* ed. David Grene and Richmond Lattimore, vol. 5 of *The Complete Greek Tragedies,* 173–240. New York: Random House Modern Library, 1942–56.

Everest, Kelvin. "Shelley's Doubles: An Approach to 'Julian and Maddalo.'" In *Shelley Revalued: Essays from the Gregynog Conference,* ed. Everest, 63–88. Totowa, NJ: Barnes and Noble, 1983.

Everest, Kelvin, and Geoffrey Matthews, eds. *The Poems of Shelley.* 2 vols. to date. Longman Annotated English Poets. Vol. 1, *1804–1817.* London: Longman, 1989. Vol. 2, *1817–1819.* Harlow, UK: Pearson, 2000. Cited as *E.*

Faber, George Stanley. *The Origin of Pagan Idolatry.* 3 vols. London: F. & C. Rivingtons, 1816.

Ferber, Michael. *The Poetry of Shelley.* Penguin Critical Studies. London: Penguin, 1993.

Ferenczi, Sandor. "Stages in the Development of the Sense of Reality." Trans. Ernest Jones. In *Sex and Psycho-Analysis (Contributions to Psycho-Analysis),* and (with Otto Rank) *The Development of Psycho-Analysis,* 181–203. New York: Dover, 1956.

———. *Thalassa: A Theory of Genitality.* Trans. Henry Alden Bunker. New York: Psychoanalytic Quarterly, 1938.

Firkins, Oscar W. *Power and Elusiveness in Shelley.* 1937; New York: Octagon Press, 1970.

Fisher, David James. "Sigmund Freud and Romain Rolland: The Terrestrial Animal and His Great Oceanic Friend." *American Imago* 33, no. 1 (Spring 1976): 1–59.

Fogle, Richard Harter. *The Imagery of Keats and Shelley: A Comparative Study.* 1949; New Haven: Archon Press, 1962.

Fontenrose, Joseph. *Python: A Study of Delphic Myth and Its Origins.* 1959; Berkeley and Los Angeles: University of California Press, 1980.

Forman, Harry Buxton. *Note Books of Percy Bysshe Shelley from the Originals in the Library of W. K. Bixby.* 3 vols. 1911; New York: Phaeton Press, 1968.

Foucault, Michel. "What is an Author?" In *Language, Counter-Memory, Practice: Selected Essays and Interviews,* ed. Donald F. Bouchard, trans. Bouchard and Sherry Simon, 113–38. Ithaca: Cornell University Press, 1977.

Frazer, Sir James George. *The New Golden Bough.* Ed. Theodor H. Gaster. Garden City, NY: Doubleday Anchor, 1961.

Freud, Sigmund. *Letters of Sigmund Freud.* Ed. Ernst L. Freud. Trans. Tania and James Stern. New York: Basic Books, 1960.

———. *The Standard Edition of the Complete Psychological Works of Sigmund Freud.* Trans. under the general editorship of James Strachey. 24 vols. London: Hogarth Press, 1953–74. Cited as *SE.*

Frosch, John. *Psychodynamic Psychiatry: Theory and Practice.* 2 vols. Madison, CT: International Universities Press, 1990.

———. "Transference Derivatives of the Family Romance." *Journal of the American Psychoanalytic Association* 7, no. 3 (July 1959): 503–22.

Frosch, Mary A. *Narcissus: The Negative Double.* Dissertation. City University of New York (CUNY), 1976.

Frosch, Thomas R. "Aggression and Regression in *Prometheus Unbound.*" In *Approaches to Teaching Shelley's Poetry,* ed. Spencer Hall, 70–75. New York: MLA, 1990.

———. " 'More than ever can be spoken': Unconscious Fantasy in Shelley's Jane Williams Poems." *Studies in Philology* 102, no. 3 (Summer 2005): 378–413.

———. "The New Body of English Romanticism." *Soundings: An Interdisciplinary Journal* 54, no. 4 (Winter 1971): 372–87.

———. "Passive Resistance in Shelley: A Psychological View." *JEGP: Journal of English and Germanic Philology* 98, no. 3 (July 1999): 373–95.

———. "Psychological Dialectic in Shelley's 'Song of Apollo' and 'Song of Pan.' " *Keats-Shelley Journal* 45 (1996): 102–17.

Froula, Christine. "When Eve Reads Milton: Undoing the Canonical Economy." *Critical Inquiry* 10, no. 2 (December 1983): 321–47.

Frye, Northrop. *Anatomy of Criticism: Four Essays.* Princeton: Princeton University Press, 1957.

———. "The Drunken Boat: The Revolutionary Element in Romanticism." In *Romanticism Reconsidered: Selected Papers from the English Institute,* ed. Frye, 1–25. 1963; New York: Columbia University Press, 1968.

———. *The Secular Scripture: A Study of the Structure of Romance.* Cambridge, MA: Harvard University Press, 1976.

Gallant, Christine. *Shelley's Ambivalence.* Houndmills, UK: Macmillan, 1989.

Gelpi, Barbara Charlesworth. *Shelley's Goddess: Maternity, Language, Subjectivity.* New York: Oxford University Press, 1992.

Gimbutas, Marija. *The Goddesses and Gods of Old Europe: Myths and Cult Images.* New edition. 1982; Berkeley and Los Angeles: University of California Press, 1990.

Girard, René. *Deceit, Desire, and the Novel: Self and Other in Literary Structure.* Trans. Yvonne Freccero. Baltimore: Johns Hopkins University Press, 1965.

Godwin, William. *Enquiry Concerning Political Justice and its Influence on Modern Morals and Happiness.* Ed. Isaac Kramnick. Harmondsworth, UK: Penguin, 1976.

Goethe, Johann Wolfgang von. *Faust, First Part.* Trans. Peter Salm. A Bantam Dual-Language Book. New York: Bantam, 1962.

Grabo, Carl. *A Newton among Poets: Shelley's Use of Science in "Prometheus Unbound."* 1930; New York: Gordian Press, 1968.

———. *Prometheus Unbound: An Interpretation.* 1935; New York: Gordian Press, 1968.

Grant, Michael. *Myths of the Greeks and Romans.* New York: New American Library, 1962.

Graves, Robert. *The Greek Myths.* Combined rev. ed. London: Penguin, 1992.

Greenacre, Phyllis. "The Primal Scene and the Sense of Reality." *Psychoanalytic Quarterly* 42, no. 1 (January 1973): 10–41.

———. "A Study on the Nature of Inspiration: Some Special Considerations Regarding the Phallic Phase." In *Emotional Growth: Psychoanalytic Studies of the Gifted and a Great Variety of Other Individuals,* 2 vols., 1:225–48. New York: International Universities Press, 1971.

Guthrie, W. K. C. *The Greeks and Their Gods.* Rev., 1954; Boston: Beacon Press, 1967.

Guthrie, William N. *Modern Poet Prophets.* Cincinnati, OH: Robert Clarke, 1897.

Gutschera, Deborah. "The Drama of Reenactment in Shelley's *The Revolt of Islam.*" *Keats-Shelley Journal* 35 (1986): 111–25.

Hall, Jean. *The Transforming Image: A Study of Shelley's Major Poetry.* Urbana: University of Illinois Press, 1980.

Hamilton, A. C., ed. and notes. *Edmund Spenser: The Faerie Queene.* London: Longman, 1977.

Harrison, Jane Ellen. *Mythology.* 1924; New York: Harcourt, Brace & World, 1963.

———. *Prolegomena to the Study of Greek Religion.* 3rd edition. 1922; New York: Meridian, 1959.

———. *Themis: A Study of the Social Origins of Greek Religion.* In *Epilogomena to the Study of Greek Religion* and *Themis.* 1921, 1912; New Hyde Park, NY: University Books [1962].

Hartman, Geoffrey H. *Beyond Formalism: Literary Essays, 1958–1970.* 1970; New Haven: Yale University Press, 1975.

———. *Wordsworth's Poetry, 1787–1814.* New Haven: Yale University Press, 1964.

Hartmann, Heinz. *Ego Psychology and the Problem of Adaptation.* Trans. David Rapaport. 1958; New York: International Universities Press, 1977.

———. *Essays on Ego Psychology: Selected Problems in Psychoanalytic Theory.* 1964; New York: International Universities Press, 1981.

Hazlitt, William. *The Complete Works of William Hazlitt.* Ed. P. P. Howe. 21 vols. London: Dent, 1932.

Hertz, Neil. *The End of the Line: Essays on Psychoanalysis and the Sublime.* New York: Columbia University Press, 1985.

Hesiod. *Hesiod, Homeric Hymns, Epic Cycle, Homerica.* Trans. Hugh G. Evelyn-White. Loeb Classical Library. 1914; Cambridge, MA: Harvard University Press, 1998. Cited as *Theogony.*

Hildebrand, William. "Naming-Day in Asia's Vale." *Keats-Shelley Journal* 32 (1983): 190–203.

———. "Self, Beauty and Horror: Shelley's Medusa Moment." In *The New Shelley: Later Twentieth-Century Views,* ed. G. Kim Blank, 150–65. New York: St. Martin's Press, 1991.

Hoeveler, Diane Long. *Romantic Androgyny: The Women Within.* University Park: Pennsylvania State University Press, 1990.

Hogle, Jerrold E. *Shelley's Process: Radical Transference and the Development of His Major Works.* New York: Oxford University Press, 1988.

Holmes, Richard. *Shelley: The Pursuit.* New York: Dutton, 1975.

Homans, Margaret. *Bearing the Word: Language and Female Experience in Nineteenth-Century Women's Writing.* Chicago: University of Chicago Press, 1986.

Homer. *The Iliad of Homer.* Trans. Richmond Lattimore. 1951; Chicago: University of Chicago Press, 1967.

Hubbell, J. Andrew. "*Laon and Cythna*: A Vision of Regency Romanticism." *Keats-Shelley Journal* 51 (2002): 174–97.

Hughes, A. M. D., ed. *Shelley Poems Published in 1820.* 1910; Oxford: Clarendon Press, 1953.

Hughes, Daniel J. "Blake and Shelley: Beyond the Uroboros." In *William Blake: Essays for S. Foster Damon,* ed. Alvin H. Rosenfeld, 69–83. Providence: Brown University Press, 1969.

———. "Coherence and Collapse in Shelley, with Particular Reference to *Epipsychidion.*" *ELH: English Literary History* 28, no. 3 (September 1961): 260–83.

———. "Kindling and Dwindling: The Poetic Process in Shelley." *Keats-Shelley Journal* 13 (1964): 13–28.

———. "Potentiality in *Prometheus Unbound.*" *Studies in Romanticism* 2, no. 2 (Winter 1963): 107–26.

———. "Prometheus Made Capable Poet in Act One of *Prometheus Unbound.*" *Studies in Romanticism* 17, no. 1 (Winter 1978): 3–11.

———. "Shelley, Leonardo, and the Monsters of Thought." *Criticism* 12, no. 3 (Summer 1970): 195–212.

Hungerford, Edward B. *Shores of Darkness.* New York: Columbia University Press, 1941.

Hutchinson, Thomas, ed. *Shelley: Poetical Works.* 2nd ed., corrected by G. M. Matthews. 1970; London: Oxford University Press, 1971. Cited as *H.*

Isakower, Otto. "A Contribution to the Patho-Psychology of Phenomena Associated with Falling Asleep." *International Journal of Psycho-Analysis* 19, part 3 (1938): 331–45.

———. "On the Exceptional Position of the Auditory Sphere." *International Journal of Psycho-Analysis* 20, parts 3–4 (July–October 1939): 340–48.

Jacobs, Carol. "On Looking at Shelley's Medusa." *Yale French Studies*, no. 69 (1985): 163–79.

Johnson, Samuel. *Rasselas and Other Tales*. Ed. Gwin J. Kolb. Vol. 16 of the Yale Edition of the Works of Samuel Johnson. New Haven: Yale University Press, 1990.

Jones, Ernest. *On the Nightmare*. 2nd ed. 1951; New York: Grove Press, 1959.

Jones, Steven E. *Shelley's Satire: Violence, Exhortation, and Authority*. DeKalb: Northern Illinois University Press, 1994.

Jung, C. G. *Aion*. Trans. R. F. C. Hull. Vol. 9, part 2 of *The Collected Works of C. G. Jung*. 2nd ed. 1967; Princeton: Princeton University Press, 1990.

———. *Symbols of Transformation: An Analysis of the Prelude to a Case of Schizophrenia*. Trans. R. F. C. Hull. Vol. 5 of *The Collected Works of C. G. Jung*. 2nd ed. 1967; Princeton: Princeton University Press, 1990.

Keach, William. "Obstinate Questionings: *The Immortality Ode* and *Alastor*." *The Wordsworth Circle* 12, no. 1 (Winter 1981): 36–44.

———. *Shelley's Style*. New York: Methuen, 1984.

Keats, John. *John Keats: Complete Poems*. Ed. Jack Stillinger. Cambridge, MA: Harvard University Press, 1978.

———. *The Letters of John Keats*. 2 vols. Ed. Hyder Edward Rollins. Cambridge, MA: Harvard University Press, 1958.

Kennedy, Emmet. *A Cultural History of the French Revolution*. New Haven: Yale University Press, 1989.

Kerényi, C. *The Gods of the Greeks*. Trans. Norman Cameron. 1951; New York: Thames and Hudson, 1982.

———. *The Heroes of the Greeks*. Trans. H. J. Rose. 1959; New York: Thames and Hudson, 1981.

———. "The Primordial Child in Primordial Times." In *Essays on a Science of Mythology: The Myths of the Divine Child and the Divine Maiden*, by Kerényi and C. G. Jung, trans.R. F. C. Hull, 25–69. Rev. ed. New York: Harper & Row, 1963.

———. *Prometheus: Archetypal Image of Human Existence*. Trans. Ralph Manheim. New York: Pantheon, 1963.

Klein, Melanie. *Envy and Gratitude and Other Works, 1946–1963*. New York: Delta, 1977.

———. *Love, Guilt and Reparation and Other Works, 1921–1945*. New York: Delta, 1977.

Kohut, Heinz. *The Analysis of the Self: A Systematic Approach to the Psychoanalytic Treatment of Narcissistic Personality Disorders*. New York: International Universities Press, 1971.

———. "Forms and Transformations of Narcissism." In *The Search for the Self: Selected Writings of Heinz Kohut: 1950–1978*, ed. Paul H. Ornstein, 4 vols., 1:427–60. New York: International Universities Press, 1978.

Koszul, André Henri, ed. *Shelley's Prose in the Bodleian Manuscripts*. London: H. Frowde, 1910.

Kris, Ernst. *Psychoanalytic Explorations in Art*. New York: International Universities Press, 1952.

Lacan, Jacques. "Some Reflections on the Ego." *International Journal of Psycho-Analysis* 34, part 1 (1953): 11–17.

———. "The Mirror Stage as Formative of the Function of the I as Revealed in Psychoanalytic Experience." In *Écrits: A Selection*, trans. Alan Sheridan, 1–7. New York: Norton, 1977.

Laing, R. D. *The Divided Self: An Existential Study in Sanity and Madness*. 1960; Baltimore: Penguin, 1966.

Lattimore, Richmond, trans. *The Iliad of Homer*. 1951; Chicago: University of Chicago Press, 1967.

Lawrence, D. H. *Sex, Literature, and Censorship*. Ed. Harry T. Moore. 1959; New York: Viking, 1968.

Locock, Charles D., ed. *The Poems of Percy Bysshe Shelley*. 2 vols. London: Methuen, 1911.

Loewald, Hans. "Ego and Reality," *International Journal of Psycho-Analysis* 32, part 1 (1951): 10–18.

Lucan. *The Civil War (Pharsalia)*. Trans. J. D. Duff. Loeb Classical Library. 1928; Cambridge, MA: Harvard University Press, 1969.

Lucretius. *The Nature of Things*. Trans. and intro. R. E. Latham. 1951; Baltimore: Penguin, 1967.

Macpherson, Jay. *The Spirit of Solitude: Conventions and Continuities in Late Romance*. New Haven: Yale University Press, 1982.

Mahler, Margaret S. "On the Significance of the Normal Symbiosis-Individuation Phase: With Reference to Research in Symbiotic Child Psychosis." In vol. 2 of *Drives, Affects, Behavior: Essays in Memory of Marie Bonaparte*, ed. Max Schur, 2 vols., 161–69. New York: International Universities Press, 1965.

Mahler, Margaret S., and John McDevitt. "Object Constancy, Individuality, and Internalization"; "The Separation-Individuation Process and Identity Formation." In *The Course of Life: Psychoanalytic Contributions toward Understanding Personality Development*, ed. Stanley I. Greenspan and George H. Pollack, vol. 2, *Infancy and Early Childhood*, 19–60. Madison, CT: International Universities Press, 1989.

Mahler, Margaret S., with Fred Pine and Anni Bergman. *The Psychological Birth of the Human Infant: Separation and Individuation*. 1975; New York: Basic Books, 2000.

Mandela, Nelson. *Long Walk to Freedom: The Autobiography of Nelson Mandela*. Boston: Little, Brown, 1994.

Marcuse, Herbert. *Eros and Civilization: A Philosophical Inquiry into Freud*. 1955; New York: Vintage, 1966.

Matthews, Geoffrey M. "On Shelley's 'The Triumph of Life.'" *Studia Neophilologica* 34, no. 1 (1962): 104–34.

McGann, Jerome J. *The Romantic Ideology: A Critical Investigation*. Chicago: University of Chicago Press, 1985.

———. "The Secrets of an Elder Day: Shelley after *Hellas*." *Keats-Shelley Journal* 15 (1966): 25–41.

———. "Shelley's Veils: A Thousand Images of Loveliness." In *Romantic and Victorian: Studies in Memory of William H. Marshall*, ed. W. Paul Elledge and Richard L. Hoffman, 198–218. Rutherford, NJ: Fairleigh Dickinson University Press, 1971.

McLuhan, Marshall. *The Gutenberg Galaxy: The Making of Typographic Man*. Toronto: University of Toronto Press, 1965.

McNiece, Gerald. *Shelley and the Revolutionary Idea*. Cambridge, MA: Harvard University Press, 1969.

Medwin, Thomas. *Conversations of Lord Byron*. Ed. Ernest J. Lovell, Jr. Princeton: Princeton University Press, 1966.

———. *The Life of Percy Bysshe Shelley*. Ed. H. Buxton Forman. London: Oxford University Press, 1913.

———. *Shelley Papers: Memoirs of Percy Bysshe Shelley by Thomas Medwin and Original Poems and Papers by Percy Bysshe Shelley*. London: Whittaker, Treacher, 1833.

Meissner, W. W. *Freud and Psychoanalysis*. Notre Dame, IN: University of Notre Dame Press, 2000.

Mellor, Anne K. *Romanticism and Gender*. New York: Routledge, 1993.

Miller, J. Hillis. "The Critic as Host." In *Deconstruction and Criticism*, ed. Harold Bloom et al., 217–53. New York: Seabury Press, 1979.

Miller, Milton. "Manic Depressive Cycles of the Poet Shelley." *Psychoanalytic Forum* 1 (1966): 188–95.

Milton, John. *John Milton: Complete Poems and Major Prose*. Ed. Merritt Y. Hughes. New York: Odyssey Press, 1957.

Moor, Edward. *The Hindu Pantheon*. London: J. Johnson, 1810.

Mueschke, Paul, and Earl L. Griggs. "Wordsworth as the Prototype of the Poet in Shelley's *Alastor*." *PMLA* 49, no. 1 (March 1934): 229–45.

Murray, E. B. "Annotated Manuscript Corrections of Shelley's Prose Essays." *Keats-Shelley Journal* 26 (1977): 10–21.

———. "Shelley's *Notes on Sculptures*: The Provenance and Authority of the Text." *Keats-Shelley Journal* 32 (1983): 150–71.

Neumann, Erich. *The Great Mother: An Analysis of the Archetype*. Trans. Ralph Manheim. 2nd ed. 1963; Princeton: Princeton University Press, 1983.

Nietzsche, Friedrich. *The Birth of Tragedy* and *The Genealogy of Morals*. Trans. Francis Golffing. New York: Doubleday, 1956.

Notopoulos, James A. *The Platonism of Shelley: A Study of Platonism and the Poetic Mind*. 1949; New York: Octagon Press, 1969.

Novalis. *Hymns to the Night and Other Selected Writings*. Trans. Charles E. Passage. New York: Liberal Arts Press, 1960.

O'Neill, Michael. *The Human Mind's Imaginings: Conflict and Achievement in Shelley's Poetry*. Oxford: Clarendon Press, 1989.

Onorato, Richard J. *The Character of the Poet: Wordsworth in "The Prelude."* Princeton: Princeton University Press, 1971.

Ovid. *The Metamorphoses*. Trans. Horace Gregory. 1958; New York: New American Library, 1960.

The Oxford Classical Dictionary. Ed. M. Cary et al. 1949; Oxford: Clarendon Press, 1961.

Parker, Patricia A. *Inescapable Romance: Studies in the Poetics of a Mode.* Princeton: Princeton University Press, 1979.

Parsons, William B. "The Oceanic Feeling Revisited." *Journal of Religion* 78, no. 4 (October 1998): 501–23.

Peacock, Thomas Love. *Nightmare Abbey* and *Crotchet Castle.* New York: Capricorn, 1964.

———. *The Works of Thomas Love Peacock.* 10 vols. Ed. H. F. Brett-Smith and C. E. Jones. Halliford Edition. London: Constable, 1924–34.

Petrarch (Petrarca), Francesco. "The Ascent of Mont Ventoux." Trans. Hans Nachod. In *The Renaissance Philosophy of Man,* ed. Ernst Cassirer et al., 36–46. 1948; Chicago: University of Chicago Press, 1959.

———. *Lord Morley's Tryumphes of Fraunces Petrarcke: The First English Translation of the "Trionfi."* Ed. D. D. Carnicelli. Cambridge, MA: Harvard University Press, 1971.

Plato. *Euthyphro, Apology, Crito, Phaedo, Phaedrus.* Trans. Harold North Fowler. Loeb Classical Library. 1914; Cambridge, MA: Harvard University Press, 1999.

———. *The Republic, Books 1–5.* Trans. Paul Shorey. Loeb Classical Library. 1930; Cambridge, MA: Harvard University Press, 1994.

Polidori, John William. *The Diary of Dr. John William Polidori, 1816, Relating to Byron, Shelley, etc.* Ed. William Michael Rossetti. London: Elkin Matthews, 1911.

Pope, Alexander. *The Poems of Alexander Pope.* Ed. John Butt. New Haven: Yale University Press, 1963.

Pottle, Frederick A. "The Case of Shelley." In *English Romantic Poets: Modern Essays in Criticism,* ed. M. H. Abrams, 289–306. New York: Oxford University Press, 1960.

———. "The Role of Asia in the Dramatic Action of *Prometheus Unbound.*" In *Shelley: A Collection of Critical Essays,* ed. George M. Ridenour, 133–43. Twentieth Century Views. Englewood Cliffs, NJ: Prentice-Hall, 1965.

Pulos, C. E. *The Deep Truth: A Study of Shelley's Scepticism.* 1954; Lincoln: University of Nebraska Press, 1962.

Quinn, Mary A. "*The Daemon of the World:* Shelley's Antidote to the Skepticism of *Alastor.*" *Studies in English Literature* 25, no. 4 (Autumn 1985): 755–74.

Quint, David. "Representation and Ideology in *The Triumph of Life.*" *Studies in English Literature* 18, no. 4 (Autumn 1978): 639–57.

Rajan, Tilottama. *Dark Interpreter: The Discourse of Romanticism.* Ithaca: Cornell University Press, 1980.

Rank, Otto. *The Double: A Psychoanalytic Study.* Trans. Harry Tucker, Jr. Chapel Hill: University of North Carolina Press, 1971.

———. *The Myth of the Birth of the Hero: A Psychological Interpretation of Mythology.* Trans. F. Robbins and Smith Ely Jelliffe. New York: Robert Brunner, 1952.

Read, Herbert. "In Defence of Shelley." In *The True Voice of Feeling,* 212–87. New York: Pantheon, 1953.

Reiman, Donald H. "Shelley's 'The Triumph of Life': The Biographical Problem." *PMLA* 78, no. 5 (December 1963): 536–50.

————. *Shelley's "The Triumph of Life": A Critical Study.* Urbana: University of Illinois, 1965.

Reiman, Donald H., and Neil Fraistat, eds. *Shelley's Poetry and Prose.* Norton Critical Edition. 2nd ed. New York: Norton, 2002. Cited as *R.*

Richardson, Alan. "The Dangers of Sympathy: Sibling Incest in English Romantic Poetry." *Studies in English Literature* 25, no. 4 (Autumn 1985): 737–54.

Rieger, James. *The Mutiny Within: The Heresies of Percy Bysshe Shelley.* New York: George Braziller, 1967.

Robinson, Charles E. *Shelley and Byron: The Snake and Eagle Wreathed in Fight.* Baltimore: Johns Hopkins University Press, 1976.

Rogers, Neville. *Shelley at Work: A Critical Inquiry.* Oxford: Clarendon Press, 1967.

Róheim, Géza. *The Gates of the Dream.* New York: International Universities Press, 1952.

————. *The Riddle of the Sphinx, or Human Origins.* Trans. R. Money-Kyrle. 1934; New York: Harper and Row, 1974.

Rolland, Romain. *Selected Letters of Romain Rolland.* Ed. Francis Doré and Marie-Laure Prévost. Delhi: Oxford University Press, 1990.

Ross, John Munder. "Oedipus Revisited: Laius and the 'Laius Complex.'" In *The Psychoanalytic Study of the Child* 37 (1982): 167–200. Repr. in *The Oedipus Papers,* ed. George H. Pollock and Ross, 285–316. Madison, CT: International University Press, 1988.

Rousseau, Jean-Jacques. *The Confessions of Jean-Jacques Rousseau.* Trans. J. M. Cohen. 1954; Harmondsworth, UK: Penguin, 1965.

————. *Emile.* Trans. Barbara Foxley. 1911; London: Dent, 1974.

————. *The First and Second Discourses* and *Essay on the Origin of Languages.* Trans. Victor Gourevitch. New York: Harper and Row, 1986.

————. *La Nouvelle Héloïse: Julie, or The New Eloise. Letters of Two Lovers, Inhabitants of a Small Town at the Foot of the Alps.* Trans. and abridged by Judith H. McDowell. University Park: Pennsylvania State University Press, 1968.

————. *Reveries of the Solitary Walker.* Trans. Peter France. 1979; Harmondsworth, UK: Penguin, 1984.

Sacks, Peter M. *The English Elegy: Studies in the Genre from Spenser to Yeats.* Baltimore: Johns Hopkins University Press, 1985.

Scales, Luther L., Jr. "The Poet as Miltonic Adam in *Alastor.*" *Keats-Shelley Journal* 21–22 (1972–73): 126–44.

Schapiro, Barbara A. *The Romantic Mother: Narcissistic Patterns in Romantic Poetry.* Baltimore: Johns Hopkins University Press, 1983.

Schiffer, Irvine. *The Trauma of Time: A Psychoanalytic Investigation.* New York: International Universities Press, 1978.

Scrivener, Michael. *Radical Shelley: The Philosophical Anarchism and Utopian Thought of Percy Bysshe Shelley.* Princeton: Princeton University Press, 1982.

Scudder, Vida D., ed. *Prometheus Unbound: A Lyrical Drama.* Boston: Heath, 1909.

Shakespeare, William. *The Tempest.* Ed. Virginia Mason Vaughan and Alden T. Vaughan. The Arden Shakespeare, third series. 1999; London: Thomson Learning, 2005.

Shelley, Mary. *Frankenstein, or The Modern Prometheus.* New York: New American Library, 1965.

———. *The Journals of Mary Shelley.* Ed. Paula R. Friedman and Diane Scott-Kilvert. 2 vols. Oxford: Clarendon Press, 1987.

———. *The Letters of Mary Wollstonecraft Shelley.* Ed. Betty T. Bennett. 3 vols. Baltimore: Johns Hopkins University Press, 1980.

Shelley, Percy Bysshe. *The Bodleian Shelley Manuscripts: A Facsimile Edition, with Full Transcriptions and Scholarly Apparatus.* Gen. ed. Donald H. Reiman. 23 vols. New York: Garland, 1986–2002. Cited as *Bod. Shelley.*

    Vol. 1, *Peter Bell the Third . . . and The Triumph of Life: Bodleian MS. Shelley adds. c. 4, folios 18–58.* Ed. Donald H. Reiman (1986).

    Vol. 4, parts 1–2, *MS. Shelley d. 1 . . . Drafts of Speculations on Morals and Metaphysics, A Defence of Poetry . . .* Ed. E. B. Murray (1988).

    Vol. 5, *The Witch of Atlas Notebook . . . Shelley adds. e. 6.* Ed. Carlene A. Adamson (1997).

    Vol. 6, *Shelley's Pisan Winter Notebook (1820–1821) . . . e. 8.* Ed. Carlene A. Adamson (1992).

    Vol. 9, *The Prometheus Unbound Notebooks . . . e. 1, e. 2, and e. 3.* Ed. Neil Fraistat (1991).

    Vol. 12, *The "Charles the First" Draft Notebook . . . e. 17.* Ed. Nora Crook (1991).

    Vol. 13, *Drafts for Laon and Cythna . . . e. 14 and e. 19.* Ed. Tatsuo Tokoo (1992).

    Vol. 15, *The Julian and Maddalo Draft Notebook . . . e. 11.* Ed. Steven E. Jones (1994).

    Vol. 16, *The Hellas Notebook . . . e. 7.* Ed. Donald H. Reiman and Michael J. Neth (1994).

    Vol. 19, *The Faust Draft Notebook . . . e. 18.* Ed. Nora Crook and Timothy Webb (1997).

    Vol. 21, *Miscellaneous Poetry, Prose and Translations from Bodleian MS. Shelley adds. c. 4.* Ed. E. B. Murray (1995).

    Vol. 22, part 1: *Bodleian MS. Shelley adds. d. 6.* Part 2: *Shelley adds. c. 5.* Ed. Alan Weinberg (1997).

———. *The Complete Poetry of Percy Bysshe Shelley.* 2 vols. to date. Ed. Donald H. Reiman and Neil Fraistat. Baltimore: Johns Hopkins University Press, 2000–2004.

———. *The Complete Works of Percy Bysshe Shelley.* Ed. Roger Ingpen and Walter E. Peck. 10 vols. New York: Scribner's, 1926–30.

———. *Essays, Letters from Abroad, Translations and Fragments.* Ed. Mary Shelley. 2 vols. Philadelphia: Lea and Blanchard, 1840.

———. *The Letters of Percy Bysshe Shelley.* Ed. Frederick L. Jones. 2 vols. Oxford: Clarendon Press, 1964. Cited as *L.*

———. *The Manuscripts of the Younger Romantics: Shelley.* Gen. ed. Donald H. Reiman. 9 vols. New York: Garland, 1985–1997.

    Vol. 4, *The Mask of Anarchy Draft Notebook: A Facsimile of Huntington MS. HM 2177.* Ed. Mary A. Quinn (1990).

Vol. 5, *The Harvard Shelley Poetic Manuscripts*. Ed. Donald H. Reiman (1991).

Vol. 6, *Shelley's 1819–1821 Huntington Notebook: A Facsimile of Huntington MS. HM 2176*. Ed. Mary A. Quinn (1994).

Vol. 8, *Fair-Copy Manuscripts of Shelley's Poems in European and American Libraries*. Ed. Donald H. Reiman and Michael O'Neill (1997).

———. *The Poems of Shelley*. Ed. Kelvin Everest and Geoffrey Matthews. Longman Annotated English Poets. 2 vols. to date. Vol. 1, *1804–1817*. London: Longman, 1989. Vol. 2, *1817–1819*. Harlow, UK: Pearson, 2000. Cited as *E*.

———. *The Poetical Works of Percy Bysshe Shelley*. 4 vols. Ed. Mary Shelley. London: Edward Moxon, 1839.

———. *Posthumous Poems, 1824*. [Ed. Mary Shelley.] Oxford: Woodstock, 1991.

———. *Prometheus Unbound: A Lyrical Drama in Four Acts, with Other Poems*. London: C. and J. Ollier, 1820.

———. *The Prose Work of Percy Bysshe Shelley*. Ed. E. B. Murray. Vol 1. 1993; Oxford: Clarendon Press, 2001. Cited as *M*.

———. *Relics of Shelley*. Ed. Richard Garnett. London: Edward Moxon, 1862.

———. *Shelley: Poetical Works*. Ed. Thomas Hutchinson. 2nd ed., corrected by G. M. Matthews. 1970; London: Oxford University Press, 1971. Cited as *H*.

———. *Shelley's Poetry and Prose*. Ed. Donald H. Reiman and Neil Fraistat. 2nd ed. New York: Norton, 2002. Cited as *R*.

———. *Shelley's Prose, or The Trumpet of a Prophecy*. Ed. David Lee Clark. Corrected ed. Albuquerque: University of New Mexico Press, 1966. Cited as *C*.

———. *The Works of Percy Bysshe Shelley in Verse and Prose*. Ed. Harry Buxton Forman. 8 vols. London: Reeves and Turner, 1880.

———. *Zastrozzi* and *St. Irvyne, or The Rosicrucian*. New York: Arno Press, 1977.

Sophocles. *Oedipus at Colonus*. Trans. Robert Fitzgerald. In *The Oedipus Cycle*. San Diego: Harcourt Brace, 1977.

Spender, Stephen. *Shelley*. 1952; London: Longmans, Green, 1968.

Spenser, Edmund. *The Complete Poetical Works of Spenser*. Ed. R. E. Neil Dodge. The Cambridge Poets. Boston: Houghton Mifflin, 1936.

———. *The Works of Edmund Spenser. A Variorum Edition*. Ed. E. A. Greenlaw et al. 11 vols. 1932–57; Baltimore: Johns Hopkins University Press, 1966.

Sperry, Stuart M. "The Sexual Theme in Shelley's *The Revolt of Islam*." *JEGP: Journal of English and Germanic Philology* 82, no. 1 (January 1983): 32–49.

———. *Shelley's Major Verse: The Narrative and Dramatic Poetry*. Cambridge, MA: Harvard University Press, 1988.

Spitz, René, with W. Godfrey Cobliner. *The First Year of Life: A Psychoanalytic Study of Normal and Deviant Development of Object Relations*. 1965; New York: International Universities Press, 1977.

Stauffer, Andrew M. "Celestial Temper: Shelley and the Masks of Anger." *Keats-Shelley Journal* 49 (2000): 138–61.

Stevens, Wallace. *The Necessary Angel: Essays on Reality and the Imagination*. New York: Vintage, 1965.

Swift, Jonathan. *Gulliver's Travels.* Ed. John F. Ross. New York: Holt, Rinehart and Winston, 1963.

Thorpe, Douglas. "Shelley's Golden Verbal City." *JEGP: Journal of English and Germanic Philology* 86, 2 (1987): 215–27.

Thurston, Norman. "Author, Narrator, and Hero in Shelley's *Alastor.*" *Studies in Romanticism* 14, no. 2 (Spring 1975): 119–31.

Todhunter, John. *A Study of Shelley.* 1880; Norwood, PA: Norwood Editions, 1976.

Ulmer, William A. *Shelleyan Eros: The Rhetoric of Romantic Love.* Princeton: Princeton University Press, 1990.

Veeder, William. *Mary Shelley and Frankenstein: The Fate of Androgyny.* Chicago: University of Chicago Press, 1986.

Vermorel, Henri, and Madeleine Vermorel. *Sigmund Freud et Romain Rolland: Correspondance, 1923–1936.* Paris: Presses Universitaires de France, 1993.

Vico, Giambattista. *The New Science of Giambattista Vico.* Trans. Thomas G. Bergin and Max H. Fisch. 1948; rev. and abridged, 1961; Ithaca: Cornell University Press, 1970.

Virgil. *The Aeneid of Virgil.* Trans. C. Day Lewis. 1952; Garden City, NY: Doubleday, 1953.

———. *The Pastoral Poems (The Eclogues).* Trans. E. V. Rieu. 1949; repr. with Latin text, Harmondsworth, UK: Penguin, 1954.

Waldoff, Leon. "The Father-Son Conflict in *Prometheus Unbound:* The Psychology of a Vision." *Psychoanalytic Review* 62, no. 1 (Spring 1975): 79–96.

Wangh, Martin. "The Genetic Sources of Freud's Difference with Romain Rolland on the Matter of Religious Feeling." In *Fantasy, Myth, and Reality: Essays in Honor of Jacob A. Arlow,* ed. Harold P. Blum et al., 159–85. Madison, CT: International Universities Press, 1988.

Wasserman, Earl. *Shelley: A Critical Reading.* Baltimore: Johns Hopkins University Press, 1971.

Webb, Timothy. "The Unascended Heaven: Negatives in 'Prometheus Unbound.'" In *Shelley Revalued: Essays from the Gregynog Conference,* ed. Kelvin Everest, 37–62. Totowa, NJ: Barnes and Noble, 1983.

———. *The Violet in the Crucible: Shelley and Translation.* Oxford: Clarendon Press, 1976.

Weiskel, Thomas. *The Romantic Sublime: Studies in the Structure and Psychology of Transcendence.* Baltimore: Johns Hopkins University Press, 1976.

Weisman, Karen A. *Imageless Truths: Shelley's Poetic Fictions.* Philadelphia: University of Pennsylvania Press, 1994.

White, Newman Ivey. *Shelley.* 2 vols. New York: Knopf, 1940.

Wilden, Anthony. Notes and Commentary to Jacques Lacan, *Speech and Language in Psychoanalysis.* 1968; Baltimore: Johns Hopkins University Press, 1981.

Wilkie, Brian. *Romantic Poets and Epic Tradition.* Madison: University of Wisconsin Press, 1965.

Willey, Basil. *The Eighteenth Century Background: Studies on the the Idea of Nature in the Thought of the Period.* 1940; Boston: Beacon Press, 1968.

Wilson, Milton. *Shelley's Later Poetry: A Study of His Prophetic Imagination.* New York: Columbia University Press, 1959.

Wind, Edgar. *Pagan Mysteries in the Renaissance: An Exploration of Philosophical and Mystical Sources of Iconography in Renaissance Art.* Rev. ed. New York: Norton, 1968.

Winnicott, D. W. *Playing and Reality.* New York: Basic Books, 1971.

Wollstonecraft, Mary. *A Vindication of the Rights of Men* and *A Vindication of the Rights of Woman.* Ed. D. L. Macdonald and Kathleen Scherf. Peterborough, Ontario: Broadview Press, 1997.

Woodman, Ross Greig. *The Apocalyptic Vision in the Poetry of Shelley.* 1964; Toronto: University of Toronto Press, 1966.

Woodring, Carl. *Politics in English Romantic Poetry.* Cambridge, MA: Harvard University Press, 1970.

Wordsworth, William. *The Poetical Works of Wordsworth.* Ed. Thomas Hutchinson, rev. Ernest de Selincourt. 1936; London: Oxford University Press, 1964.

———. "The Ruined Cottage, MS. D." In *The Ruined Cottage* and *The Pedlar,* ed. James Butler. Cornell Wordsworth. Gen. ed. Stephen M. Parrish. Ithaca: Cornell University Press, 1979.

Wormhoudt, Arthur. *The Demon Lover: A Psychoanalytic Approach to Literature.* New York: Exposition Press, 1949.

Yeats, William Butler. *Essays and Introductions.* New York: Macmillan, 1961.

———. *The Collected Works of W. B. Yeats.* Vol. 1, *The Poems.* Ed. Richard J. Finneran. Rev. 2nd ed. New York: Scribner, 1997.

Zillman, Lawrence John, ed. *Shelley's "Prometheus Unbound": A Variorum Edition.* Seattle: University of Washington Press, 1959.

Index